The Arapaho

The Arapaho

Alfred L. Kroeber

Foreword by Fred Eggan

University of Nebraska Press
Lincoln and London

The Arapaho was first published in three parts in the *Bulletin of the American Museum of Natural History* in 1902, 1904, and 1907.

Foreword copyright 1983 by the University of Nebraska Press

Manufactured in the United States of America

First Bison Book printing: August 1983

Most recent printing indicated by the first digit below:
      3   4   5   6   7   8   9   10

Library of Congress Cataloging in Publication Data

Kroeber, A. L. (Alfred Louis), 1876–1960.
  The Arapaho.

  "First published in three parts in the Bulletin of
the American Museum of Natural History in 1902, 1904,
and 1907"—T.p. verso.
  Includes bibliographical references and index.
  1. Arapaho Indians. I. Title.
E99.A7K76 1983   978'.00497   83-5749
ISBN 0-8032-2708-6
ISBN 0-8032-7754-7 (pbk.)

Foreword
by Fred Eggan

Originally published as a *Bulletin of the American Museum of Natural History* (1902, 1904, 1907), Alfred L. Kroeber's *The Arapaho* was the first comprehensive account of this important Plains Indian tribe, and its reappearance as a Bison Book paperback is a welcome event.[1] The young Kroeber was Franz Boas's first doctoral candidate in the newly founded Columbia University department of anthropology when Boas sent him out to western Indian Territory (present Oklahoma) at the turn of the century to study the decorative art of the Arapaho for his dissertation. At that time Boas was the foremost anthropologist in the United States; he formulated a program of research and publication that was to dominate American anthropology for the next several decades. Kroeber, one of his most productive students, not only implemented that program but added to it in important ways.

Boas had studied the decorative art of the Northwest Coast in the preceding decade, but the examples of Plains Indian art in the museum collections (the American Museum of Natural History was just beginning its concentration on Plains Indians) were different enough to intrigue him. Morris K. Jesup (president of the board of trustees of the American Museum) had supported Boas's research on the Northwest Coast, and his wife provided the funds for Kroeber's three field trips in 1899, 1900, and 1901. Kroeber had grown up in New York and had come to anthropology with a background in the humanities, but he took the West in his stride. He spent his first season among the Southern Arapaho in Indian Territory, the second among the Northern Arapaho of Wyoming, and the third among the linguistically related Gros Ventre, or Atsina, in Montana.

Kroeber initially concentrated on decorative art and symbolism, while making a collection of material culture for the museum. Soon, however, he extended his studies to other aspects of Arapaho life, particularly to ceremonial organization and religion, and he collaborated on a collection of myths and tales with George A. Dorsey, who had also made a detailed study of the Southern Arapaho sun dance under the auspices of the Field Museum of Natural History.[2]

In the introductory section of the present study, Kroeber provides a brief but perceptive account of Arapaho linguistic and cultural relations, describes the earlier five subtribes and band organization, and discusses the kinship system and life cycle. He then turns to ceremonial organization, which centered on the tribal sun dance, held in early summer, and a series of dances performed by the age-graded societies. (The sun dance is described here for the Northern Arapaho, with comparisons to the Southern Arapaho version previously described by Dorsey.) Throughout Kroeber pays a great deal of attention to decoration—of wearing apparel, tipis, tools and utensils, and a wide range of other paraphernalia—and to the symbolism of the ornamentation.

Kroeber's excellent account of the Arapaho not only remains unequaled, but has provided a solid base for further study. His presentation of Arapaho material culture, both descriptively and in terms of illustrations, is outstanding, and the data have been used for comparative studies of Plains Indian tribes as well as in his own later comparison of Gros Ventre with Arapaho decorative art.[3] Although it was not known in Kroeber's time that the Arapaho were very likely a sedentary horticultural group from the Red River Valley of present northern Minnesota who moved onto the Central Plains in the seventeenth century, adopting the horse and becoming bison-hunting nomads,[4] Kroeber discusses the linguistic affiliations of the Arapaho with other Algonkian-speaking groups. His collection of Arapaho and Gros Ventre kinship terms has led to the further hypothesis that the Arapaho once practiced cross-cousin marriage on the Ojibway model.[5]

Kroeber's account of the age-graded societies of the Arapaho and Gros Ventre—which have also been shown to be characteristic of the Blackfeet and some of the Missouri River village tribes and to have interesting parallels in West African tribes[6]—undergirds more recent work, such as that by Loretta Fowler. Although the age-graded societies as such did not survive into the twentieth century among the Arapaho, she has shown that the age structure survives in modified form in Arapaho society and that its values still determine social and political behavior.[7]

For all these reasons—for its description of the religious and social life of the tribe, and for the illustrations it offers of the tools, utensils, toys, and clothing in use at the turn of the century—Kroeber's work remains an essential book on the Arapaho, as valuable to anthropologists everywhere engaged in comparative studies as to students coming fresh to the Indians of the Great Plains.

Notes

1. Volume XVIII of the *Bulletin* had four parts—Parts I and II (pp. 1–229) and Part IV (pp. 279–454) being Kroeber's study of the Arapaho, and Part III (pp. 231–77) being "Decorative Art of the Sioux Indians" by Clark Wissler. Wissler's study has been omitted from the volume as it is reprinted here, and with it the accompanying plates XXXVIII–LVI and Text Figures 71–102. For the convenience of scholars citing the study, however, the original numbering of pages, plates, and text figures in Kroeber's study has been retained in this reprint.

2. George A. Dorsey and Alfred L. Kroeber, *Traditions of the Arapaho,* Field Columbian Museum Publications no. 75, Anthropological Series no. 5 (Chicago, 1903); George A. Dorsey, *The Arapaho Sun Dance: The Ceremony of the Offerings Lodge,* Field Columbian Museum Publications no. 75, Anthropological Series no. 4 (Chicago, 1903).

3. Alfred L. Kroeber, *Ethnology of the Gros Ventre,* Anthropological Papers of the American Museum of Natural History, vol. 1, pt. 4 (New York, 1908).

4. W. Raymond Wood and Margo Liberty, eds., *Anthropology on the Great Plains* (Lincoln: University of Nebraska Press, 1980).

5. Fred Eggan, "The Cheyenne and Arapaho Kinship System," in *Social Anthropology of North American Tribes,* edited by Fred Eggan (Chicago: University of Chicago Press, 1955), pp. 33–95.

6. Frank H. Stewart, *Fundamentals of Age-Group Systems* (New York: Academic Press, 1977).

7. Loretta Fowler, *Arapahoe Politics, 1851–1978: Symbols in Crises of Authority* (Lincoln: University of Nebraska Press, 1982).

Publisher's Note

This volume is a photographic reprint of *The Arapaho* as it originally appeared in the *Bulletin of the American Museum of Natural History,* volume 18 (1902, 1904, and 1907). Between these parts the *Bulletin* included Clark Wissler's "Decorative Art of the Sioux Indians." Wissler's pages in volume 18, pp. 231–77, are omitted here. The pagination of this reprint of *The Arapaho* text accords with the original pagination in the *Bulletin.*

CONTENTS.

                                                                PAGE

Part   I.— The Arapaho (Plates I–XXXI). By ALFRED L.
          KROEBER.
          Introductory....   1
          Explanations....................................   2
          I.   General Description......................   3
          II. Decorative Art...........................   36
          List of Symbols with Reference to Plates XXVI–
               XXXI.....................................   138
          Conclusion......................................   143
Part II.— The Arapaho (Plates XXXII–XXXVII). By
          ALFRED L. KROEBER.
          III. Ceremonial Organization..................   151
                Second Dance (Biitaha^{n}wu).............   158
                     Highest Degree......................   169
                     Lower Degrees.......................   171
                     Second Degree.......................   175
                     Third Degree........................   178
                     Fourth Degree.......................   178
                     Fifth Degree........................   179
                     Lowest Degree.......................   180
                Kit-fox Men (Nouhinena^n)..............   181
                Stars (Haçaahouha^n)...................   181
                First Dance (Hiitceäoxa^{n}wu)...........   182
                     First Degree........................   184
                     Second Degree.......................   185
                     Lowest Degree.......................   186
                Third Dance (Haha^{n}ka^{n}wu)...........   188
                     First Degree........................   193
                     Lowest Degree.......................   196
                Fourth Dance (Heçawa^{n}wu).............   196
                     First Degree........................   201
                     Second Degree.......................   201
                     Third Degree........................   205
                     Lowest Degree.......................   205
                Fifth Dance (Hinanaha^{n}wu)............   206
                Sixth Dance (Tciinetcei Bähäeiiha^n)...   207
                Women's Sacred Bags......................   209

PAGE

Women's Dance (Bänuxta^{n}wu).......... 210
   First Degree....................... 216
   Second Degree...................... 218
   Third Degree....................... 220
   Fourth Degree...................... 221
   Fifth Degree....................... 222
   Lowest Degree..................... 223
   Place of the Women's Dance........... 224
  Summary............................ 225
System of the Bäyaa^{n}wu................ 227
System of Degrees of the Bäyaa^{n}wu.............. 228
List of Degrees and Illustrated Regalia........... 229

Part III. — Decorative Art of the Sioux Indians, by Clark Wissler, which
      appeared on pp. 231–77, has been omitted from this
      edition.

Part IV. — The Arapaho (Plates LVII–LXXVIII). By AL-
    FRED L. KROEBER.

IV. Religion................................ 279
   Introduction......................... 279
   The Sun-dance....................... 279
     Opening Day...................... 280
     First Preliminary Day............... 282
     Second Preliminary Day............. 283
     Third Preliminary Day............... 285
     First Day of the Dance.............. 290
     Second Day of the Dance............ 292
     Third Day of the Dance.............. 297
     Supplementary Day................. 300
   Comparison of the Sun-dance of the North-
     ern and Southern Arapaho............ 301
   Tribal Religious Customs............... 308
     Sacred Pipe...................... 308
     Sacred Wheel..................... 309
     Sacred Bag....................... 310
     Sacred Pictograph................. 311
     Prayers.......................... 313
     Speeches......................... 315
     Sweating Customs.................. 316
   Modern Ceremonies................... 319
     Ghost-dance Head-dresses............ 321
     Feather Necklaces and Belts.......... 336
     Crow Belts....................... 339
     Women's Dresses.................. 346
     Tent............................ 348

	PAGE
Drums and Accessories	349
Whistles	351
Objects carried in the Hand	352
Model of Sacred Pipe	359
The Crow-dance	363
The Guessing-game	368
The Hoop Game	382
The Wheel Game	386
Dice	387
Balls	394
Other Games	396
The Peyote Worship	398
Character of Ceremonial Objects	410
Number and Color Symbolism	410
Personal Supernatural Powers	418
Characteristics of Individual Supernatural Power	450
Index	455

LIST OF ILLUSTRATIONS.

PLATES.

I. — Designs on Moccasins. Fig. 1 ($\frac{1}{5709}$), length 26 cm.; Fig. 2 ($\frac{50}{583}$), length 27 cm.; Fig. 3 ($\frac{50}{1021}$), length 26 cm.; Fig. 4 ($\frac{50}{585}$), length 25 cm.; Fig. 5 ($\frac{50}{410}$), length 28 cm.; Fig. 6 ($\frac{1}{5707}$), length 28 cm.; Fig. 7 ($\frac{50}{583}$), length 25 cm.; Fig. 8 ($\frac{50}{584}$), length 24 cm.

II. — Moccasins. Fig. 1 ($\frac{50}{1092}$), length 25 cm.; Fig. 2 ($\frac{50}{1063}$), length 22 cm.; Fig. 3 ($\frac{50}{951}$), length 24 cm.; Fig. 4 ($\frac{50}{657}$), length 27 cm.; Fig. 5 ($\frac{50}{381}$), length 28 cm.

III. — Moccasins. Fig. 1 ($\frac{50}{1032}$), length 13 cm.; Fig. 2 ($\frac{50}{1031}$), length 15 cm.; Fig. 3 ($\frac{50}{345}$), length 13 cm.; Fig. 4 ($\frac{50}{1075}$), length 27 cm.; Fig. 5 ($\frac{50}{643}$), length 26 cm.

IV. — Moccasin and Pouch. Fig. 1 ($\frac{50}{305}$), length 24 cm.; Fig. 2 ($\frac{50}{941}$), length 14 cm.

V. — Parts of Girls' and Women's Leggings. Fig. 1 ($\frac{50}{1027}$), length 19 cm.; Fig. 2 ($\frac{50}{325}$), length 13 cm.; Fig. 3 ($\frac{50}{935}$), length 28 cm.; Fig. 4 ($\frac{50}{1054}$), length 55 cm.; Fig. 5 ($\frac{50}{1055}$), length 28 cm.

VI. — Armlets and Head-Dress. Fig. 1 ($\frac{50}{321}$), length 35 cm.; Fig. 2 ($\frac{50}{315}$), length 35 cm.; Fig. 3 ($\frac{50}{995}$), length 34 cm.

VII. — Head-Dresses. Fig. 1 ($\frac{50}{973}$), length 66 cm.; Fig. 2 ($\frac{50}{972}$), length 86 cm.; Fig. 3 ($\frac{50}{996}$), length 58 cm.

VIII. — Navel-Amulets. Fig. 1 ($\frac{50}{1088}$), length 20 cm.; Fig. 2 ($\frac{50}{1078}$), length 27 cm.; Fig. 3 ($\frac{50}{988}$), length 29 cm.; Fig. 4 ($\frac{50}{1026}$), length 25 cm.; Figs. 5 and 6 ($\frac{50}{969}$), length 21 cm.

IX. — Tent-Ornaments. Fig. 1 ($\frac{50}{306}$b), length 24 cm.; Fig. 2 ($\frac{50}{306}$ a), length 59 cm.; Fig. 3 ($\frac{50}{306}$ h), length 24 cm.

X. — Pouches for holding Porcupine-Quills. Fig. 1 ($\frac{50}{1087}$), length 28 cm.; Fig. 2 ($\frac{50}{1086}$), length 35 cm.

XI. — Paint-Pouches. Fig. 1 ($\frac{50}{960}$), length 26 cm.; Figs. 2 and 3 ($\frac{50}{596}$), length 22 cm.; Fig. 4 ($\frac{50}{377}$), length 22 cm.; Fig. 5 ($\frac{50}{1113}$), length 21 cm.; Fig. 6 ($\frac{50}{1029}$), length 17 cm.

XII. — Paint-Pouches. Figs. 1 and 2 ($\frac{50}{929}$), length 24 cm.; Figs. 3 and 4 ($\frac{50}{1022}$), length 21 cm.; Figs. 5 and 6 ($\frac{50}{928}$), length 28 cm.

XIII. — Knife and Awl Cases. Fig. 1 ($\frac{50}{979}$), length 39 cm.; Fig. 2 ($\frac{50}{1020}$), length 16 cm.; Fig. 3 ($\frac{50}{1049}$), length 16 cm.; Fig. 4 ($\frac{50}{1111}$), length 25 cm.; Fig. 5 ($\frac{50}{971}$), length 26 cm.; Fig. 6 ($\frac{50}{1025}$), length 15 cm.

XIV. — Pouches. Fig 1 ($\frac{50}{1062}$), length 12 cm.; Fig. 2 ($\frac{50}{1090}$), length 11 cm.; Figs. 3 and 4 ($\frac{50}{1037}$), length 11 cm.; Fig. 5 ($\frac{50}{1077}$), length 11 cm.; Fig. 6 ($\frac{50}{1036}$), length 11 cm.; Fig. 7 ($\frac{50}{1033}$), length 11 cm.; Fig. 8 ($\frac{50}{968}$), length 13 cm.

XV. — Women's Work-Bags. Fig. 1 ($\frac{50}{1006}$), length 24 cm.; Fig. 2 ($\frac{50}{1002}$), length 32 cm.

XVI. — Soft Bag, Front and Side Views, ($\frac{50}{322}$), length 53 cm.

XVII. — Beaded Bag ($\frac{50}{1042}$), length 59 cm.

XVIII. — Designs on Parfleches. Fig. 1 ($\frac{50}{956}$), length 66 cm.; Fig. 2 ($\frac{50}{1116}$), length 66 cm.; Fig. 3 ($\frac{50}{959}$), length 69 cm.; Fig. 4 ($\frac{50}{918}$), length 59 cm.; Fig. 5 ($\frac{50}{398}$), length 67 cm.

XIX. — Designs on Parfleches. Fig. 1 ($\frac{50}{1120}$), length 74 cm.; Fig. 2 ($\frac{50}{924}$), length 71 cm.; Fig. 3 ($\frac{50}{966}$), length 68 cm.; Fig. 4 ($\frac{50}{947}$), length 56 cm.; Fig. 5 ($\frac{50}{1030}$), length 75 cm.; Fig. 6 ($\frac{50}{952}$), length 63 cm.

XX. — Designs on Rawhide Bags. Fig. 1 ($\frac{50}{1017}$), length 47 cm.; Fig. 2 ($\frac{50}{1045}$), length 62 cm.; Fig. 3 ($\frac{50}{965}$), length 36 cm.; Fig. 4 ($\frac{50}{370}$), length 38 cm.; Fig. 5 ($\frac{50}{1040}$), length 72 cm.; Fig. 6 ($\frac{50}{957}$), length 38 cm.

XXI. — Designs on Rawhide Bags. Fig. 1 ($\frac{50}{945}$), length 26 cm.; Fig. 2 ($\frac{50}{1024}$), length 23 cm.; Fig. 3 ($\frac{50}{925}$), length 63 cm.; Fig. 4 ($\frac{50}{922}$), length 26 cm.; Fig. 5 ($\frac{50}{998}$), length 14 cm.

XXII. — Painted Bags. Fig. 1 ($\frac{50}{1103}$), length 36 cm.; Fig. 2 ($\frac{50}{1085}$), length 42 cm.; Fig. 3 ($\frac{50}{982}$), length 35 cm.; Fig. 4 ($\frac{50}{396}$), length 58 cm.

XXIII. — Designs on Rawhide Bags. Fig. 1 ($\frac{50}{1039}$), length 50 cm.; Fig. 2 ($\frac{50}{1009}$), length 40 cm.; Fig. 3 ($\frac{50}{987}$), length 45 cm.; Fig. 4 ($\frac{50}{994}$), length 36 cm.

XXIV. — Designs on Rawhide Bags. Fig. 1 ($\frac{50}{954}$), length 26 cm.; Fig. 2 ($\frac{50}{981}$), length 35 cm.; Fig. 3 ($\frac{50}{1005}$), length 39 cm.; Fig. 4 ($\frac{50}{1001}$), length 22 cm.

XXV. — Designs on Medicine-Cases. Fig. 1 ($\frac{50}{688}$), length 47 cm.; Fig. 2 ($\frac{50}{659}$); Fig. 3 ($\frac{50}{401}$), length 44 cm.

XXVI. — Arapaho Symbolism. Figs. 1–77.

XXVII. — Arapaho Symbolism. Figs. 78–154.

XXVIII. — Arapaho Symbolism. Figs. 155–231.

XXIX. — Arapaho Symbolism. Figs. 232–308.

XXX. — Arapaho Symbolism. Figs. 309–385.

XXXI. — Arapaho Symbolism. Figs. 386–458.

XXXII. — Dancer of Second Degree, Second Dance.

XXXIII. — Regalia of Dancer of Fourth Degree, Second Dance ($\frac{50}{1108}$).

XXXIV. — Regalia of the White-Fool ($\frac{50}{668-75}$, $\frac{50}{677-8}$, $\frac{50}{680-1}$).

XXXV. — Crazy-Dancer of the Lowest Degree.

XXXVI. — Dog-Dancer of Second Degree.

XXXVII. — Regalia of Dog-Dancer of Third Degree ($\frac{50}{388}$ a–e, $\frac{50}{701}$ b, $\frac{50}{698}$ b).

XXXVIII–LVI. — These plates, illustrating Decorative Art of the Sioux Indians, by Clark Wissler, have been omitted from this editon.

LVII. — Tent for the Keeper of the Sacred Pipe.

LVIII. — The Ceremony with the Buffalo-Skin.

LIX. — First View of the Procession from the Rabbit-Tent.

LX. — Second View of the Procession from the Rabbit-Tent.

LXI. — Raising the Centre Pole.

LXII. — Dance-Lodge of the Preceding Year.

LXIII. — Contents of a Sacred Bag.

LXIV. — Designs referring to Myths of Creation.

LXV. — Feather Attachments. Figs. 1–4.

LXVI. — Feather Head-Dresses. Fig. 1 ($\frac{50}{53}$), length 37 cm.; Fig. 2 ($\frac{50}{397}$ b), length 32 cm.; Fig. 3 ($\frac{50}{393}$), length 29 cm.

LXVII. — Feather Head-Dresses. Fig. 1 ($\frac{50}{115}$), length 31 cm.; Fig. 2 ($\frac{50}{119}$), length 41 cm.; Fig. 3 ($\frac{50}{3901}$), length 29 cm.

LXVIII. — Detail of One Form of Head-Dress. Fig. 1 ($\frac{50}{393}$ g); Figs. 2 and 3 ($\frac{50}{111}$ d).

LXIX. — Feather Head-Dress. Fig. 1 ($\frac{50}{122}$ a), length 34 cm.; Fig. 2 ($\frac{50}{393}$ g), length 38 cm.

LXX. — Cross Head-Dress ($\frac{50}{630}$), length 33 cm.

LXXI. — Cross Head-Dresses. Fig. 1 ($\frac{50}{393}$ f), length 24 cm.; Fig. 2 ($\frac{50}{1114}$ a), length 42 cm.

LXXII. — Head-Dress of Crow-Skin ($\frac{50}{589}$ a), length 28 cm.

LXXIII. — Necklace of Feathers ($\frac{50}{121}$ a), length 90 cm.

LXXIV. — Crow Belt ($\frac{50}{301}$), length 111 cm.

LXXV. — Girl's Ceremonial Dress ($\frac{50}{60}$).

LXXVI. — Girl's Ceremonial Dress ($\frac{50}{27}$).

LXXVII. — Girl's Ceremonial Dress ($\frac{50}{27}$).

LXXVIII. — Ceremonial Whips. Fig. 1 ($\frac{50}{624}$), length 170 cm.; Fig. 2 ($\frac{50}{625}$), length 170 cm.

LXXIX. — Feathered Staff ($\frac{50}{311}$), length 75 cm.

LXXX. — Carved Sticks belonging to the Sacred-Pipe Model. Fig. 1 ($\frac{50}{397}$ c), length 47 cm.; Fig. 2 ($\frac{50}{397}$ d), length 47 cm.

LXXXI. — Carved Sticks belonging to the Sacred-Pipe Model. Fig. 1 ($\frac{50}{397}$ g), length 43 cm.; Fig. 2 ($\frac{50}{397}$ f), length 43 cm.

LXXXII. — Netted Game-Hoop ($\frac{50}{406}$ f), diameter 29 cm.

LXXXIII. — A Peyote Fan ($\frac{50}{1107}$), length 88 cm.

LXXXIV. — A Peyote Amulet ($\frac{50}{123}$ a), length 48 cm.

LXXXV. — Bracelet used as an Amulet ($\frac{50}{300}$ b), length 35 cm.

LXXXVI. — Head-Dress ($\frac{50}{1015}$), length 54 cm.

LXXXVII. — Amulets and Medicine ($\frac{50}{629}$), length 87 cm.

LXXXVIII. — War Charm ($\frac{50}{364}$), length 80 cm.

Text Figures.

		PAGE
1.	Tubular Pipe	21
2.	Pipe-stoker	21
3.	Skin-scraper	27
4.	Quill-flattener	29
5.	Designs on Moccasins	39
6.	Girl's Leggings	47

PAGE

7. Armlets.. 51
8. Front of Beaded Waistcoat............................. 59
9. Tent-ornaments... 61
10. Tent-ornament.. 64
11. Tent-ornament.. 64
12. Quill-embroidered Line................................. 65
13. Buffalo-skin Ornament................................. 66
14. Cradles... 67
15. Beaded Cradle.. 69
16. Cradle-ornament.. 70
17. Beaded Ornament for Ball.............................. 70
18. Diagram illustrating Ceremonial....................... 75
19. Diagram showing Ceremonial Circuit around Tent........ 76
20. Paint-pouches.. 79
21. Paint-pouches.. 84
22. Beaded Knife-scabbard.................................. 88
23. Women's Small Belt-pouches............................ 89
24. Women's Small Belt-pouches............................ 90
25. Toilet-bag... 94
26. Toilet-pouch... 95
27. Toilet-pouch... 96
28. Toilet-bag... 97
29. Bag of Buffalo-skin.................................... 100
30. Hide Bag... 101
31. Beadwork on End of Bag................................ 102
32. Design on Rawhide Bag.................................. 114
33. Design on Rawhide Bag.................................. 115
34. Designs on Rawhide Bags................................ 116
35. Design on Rawhide Bag.................................. 120
36. Design on Bag.. 122
37. Design on Rawhide Bag.................................. 124
38. Design on Rawhide Bag.................................. 124
39. Design on Rawhide Bag.................................. 128
40. Design on Rawhide Bag.................................. 128
41. Design on Rawhide Bag.................................. 129
42. Design on Rawhide Bag.................................. 129
43. Design on a Medicine-case.............................. 134
44. Cover of a Shield...................................... 135
45. Design on a Crupper.................................... 135
46. Rawhide Hats... 136
47. Grandfather's Tent..................................... 161
48. Dancing-lodge.. 163
49. Club of Dancer of Highest Degree, Second Dance....... 170
50. Belts, Second Dance.................................... 171
51. Head-dress, Second Dance............................... 174
52. Arm-ring, Second Dance................................. 175

53. Belt and Lance of Dancer of Fifth Degree, Second Dance... 179
54. Belt and Lance of Lowest Degree, Second Dance.......... 180
55. Rattles of Star-dancers.................................. 181
56. Model of Sword of Dancer of First Degree, First Dance... 184
57. Sword of Dancer of Second Degree, First Dance.......... 185
58. Stick of Lowest Degree, First Dance.................... 187
59. Legging of Dog-dancer, opened out..................... 203
60. Scarf of Dog-dancer of Third Degree................... 205
61. Head-dress of Dog-dancer of Lowest Degree............. 206
62. Rawhide Bag.. 208
63. Woman's Sacred Bag and Contents..................... 209
64. Head-dress of White-woman........................... 216
65. Regalia of White-woman.............................. 217
66. Regalia of Owner-of-the-tent-poles.................... 218
67. Head-band and Part of Belt of Red-stand.............. 220
68. Regalia of White-stand............................... 222
69. Regalia of Lowest Degree of Women-dancers........... 223
70. Designs from Head-bands and Belts of Women-dancers ... 224

71–102. These text figures, illustrating Decorative Art of the Sioux
         Indians, by Clark Wissler, have been omitted from
         this edition.

103. Switch of Horse-tail................................. 316
104. Feather Attachments................................. 321
105. Feather Attachments................................. 322
106. Combination Feather Attachment...................... 323
107. Ghost-dance Head-dress.............................. 325
108. Upright Feather Head-dress.......................... 327
109. Head-dress representing a Bird....................... 329
110. Head-ornament used in the Ghost-dance............... 330
111. Head-ornament used in the Ghost-dance............... 330
112. Head-ornament used in the Ghost-dance............... 331
113. Head-dress of Small Bow and Arrows................. 331
114. Head-dress with Wheel and Bow...................... 332
115. Simple Head-dress of Feathers....................... 333
116. Feather worn in the Hair............................ 333
117. Head-dress of Crow-feathers......................... 335
118. Head-dress of Unusual Form......................... 335
119. A Piece of Bone from a Head-dress................... 336
120. A Gorget of Shell.................................... 337
121. Head-dress resembling an Arrow...................... 343
122. A Hand Drum.. 349
123. Forked Support for a Large Drum..................... 350
124. A Drumstick... 350
125. A Carved Wooden Whistle............................ 351

                                                                    PAGE
126. A Quirt used in the Ghost-dance...................... 354
127. Wooden Frame for a Mirror........................... 356
128. Pointed Stick used in serving Meat................... 359
129. Hypnotizing Wand..................................... 360
130. Model of the Sacred Tribal Flat Pipe................. 361
131. Counters for a Guessing-game......................... 373
132. Feather used as a Pointer in a Guessing-game......... 374
133. Counting-stick for a Guessing-game................... 375
134. Counting-stick for a Guessing game................... 375
135. Pointer used in a Guessing-game...................... 376
136. Feathered Stick for a Guessing-game.................. 377
137. Hiding-buttons....................................... 378
138. Ornament worn by a Player in the Guessing-game....... 379
139. Model of a Game Hoop................................. 383
140. Pair of Red Darts for the Hoop Game................. 384
141. Pair of Blue Darts for the Hoop Game................ 384
142. Seed Dice.. 388
143. Five Kinds of Bone Dice............................. 389
144. Sample Dice from Three Sets......................... 389
145. Three Forms of Bone Dice marked by Burning.......... 390
146. Dice from Two Different Sets........................ 390
147. Bone Dice with Symbolic Ornamentation............... 391
148. Basket for Tossing Dice............................. 392
149. Stick Dice... 394
150. Ball used by Women.................................. 395
151. Ball with Appendage................................. 395
152. Small Decorated Ball................................ 395
153. Bull-roarer.. 396
154. Cup-and-Ball Game................................... 397
155. Mescal prepared for the Ceremony.................... 399
156. Feather used to brush the Body...................... 407
157. Head-ornament.. 408
158. Bracelet... 409
159. Bracelet made of Twisted Cord....................... 409
160. Figure from a Medicine-bag.......................... 422
161. Stuffed Mole-skin.................................... 423
162. Tail of an Elk used in Doctoring.................... 424
163. Rattle with Symbolic Decorations.................... 425
164. A Turtle-tail used as a War-amulet.................. 426
165. Painted Cloth representing a Dream Experience........ 429
166. Necklace bearing an Image of a Supernatural Helper... 430
167. Carved Stick representing a Supernatural Helper...... 430
168. Painting representing a Dream Experience............. 433
169. Wristlet... 435
170. A Cupping Instrument................................. 439

PAGE

171. Design on a Cupping Instrument...................... 439
172. Necklace bearing Amulets............................ 441
173. Amulets representing Teeth......................... 442
174. Amulets representing a Turtle, Bird, and Skunk.......... 442
175. Translucent Pebbles used as Amulets................... 443
176. Amulet representing a Centipede...................... 443
177. Medicine-bag... 444
178. Rattle representing a Person........................ 446
179. Rattle representing a Face.......................... 448
180. Hoof Rattle... 449

BULLETIN

OF THE

AMERICAN MUSEUM OF NATURAL HISTORY.

VOLUME XVIII, 1902.

THE ARAPAHO.

By ALFRED L. KROEBER.

PLATES I–XXXI.

INTRODUCTORY.

IN 1899 Mrs. Morris K. Jesup generously provided the means for a study of the Arapaho Indians, and the writer was entrusted with the work. He visited that portion of the tribe located in Oklahoma in 1899, the Wyoming branch and a number of neighboring tribes in 1900, and the Gros Ventres and Assiniboines in 1901. The principal results of his studies are contained in the present volume, in which the general culture, decorative art, mythology, and religion of the Arapaho will be described. Two preliminary articles on the decorative symbolism of the Arapaho have been published by the writer, —

Symbolism of the Arapaho Indians (Bulletin of the American Museum of Natural History, Vol. XIII, 1900, pp. 69–86).
Decorative Symbolism of the Arapaho (American Anthropologist, N. S., Vol. III, 1901, pp. 308–336).

The former is a preliminary general account of Arapaho symbolism and art, stress being laid particularly on the symbolism. Both decorative art and the more or less pictographic symbolism connected with religion are included in the scope of this paper. The second paper deals with the question of the origin of symbolic decoration.

A. L. K.

NEW YORK, July, 1901.

EXPLANATIONS.

The following alphabet has been used in rendering Arapaho words: —

a, e, i, o, u	have their continental sounds.
ä	as in *that*.
ā̈	as in *mad*.
â	as in *law*.
ô	nearly as in *hot*.
û	somewhat as in *hut*, but nearer *u*.
ê	between *ä* and *e*.
A, E, I, O, U	obscure vowels.
^{a}, ^{e}, ^{i}, ^{o}, ^{u}	scarcely spoken vowels.
a^n, ä^n	nasalized *a*, *ä*.
b, k, n, t, w, y	as in English.
c, s	English *sh* and *s*, but similar
ç	English *th* as in *think*.
h	as in English, but fainter.
tc	English *ch* as in *church*.
x	aspirate *k*.

Owing to the changed conditions under which the Arapaho now live, and to the comparatively short time that the writer was among them, the information presented in this paper could not be obtained to any extent from direct observation, but only by questioning. Unless the opposite is stated or is obviously the case, all statements in this paper are therefore given on the authority of the Indians, not of the writer. In some cases explanatory remarks by the writer have been distinguished by being enclosed in parentheses.

[2]

I.—GENERAL DESCRIPTION.

The Arapaho Indians first became known at the beginning of the last century. Since that time they have inhabited the country about the head waters of the Arkansas and the Platte Rivers. This territory, which they held together with the Cheyenne, covers approximately the eastern half of Colorado and the southeastern quarter of Wyoming. The language of the Arapaho, as well as that of the Cheyenne, belongs to the widely spread Algonkin family, of which they form the most southwesterly extension. These two tribes were completely separated from the Blackfoot, Ojibway, and other tribes speaking related languages, by the Dakota and other tribes inhabiting the intervening territories. In physical type and in culture, the Arapaho belong to the Plains Indians.

The Arapaho have generally been at peace with the Kiowa and Comanche, and at war with their other neighbors. They had no permanent settlements, nor any fixed dwellings. They lived exclusively in tents made of buffalo-skins. For food they were dependent on the herds of buffalo that roamed through their country; and much of their clothing and many of their implements were derived from the same animal. Agriculture was not practised. They had the sun-dance that existed among most of the Plains Indians, and possessed a ceremonial organization of warrior companies similar to that of several other tribes.

The Arapaho men have generally been described as more reserved, treacherous, and fierce, and the women as more unchaste, than those of other tribes. Those acquainted with their psychic nature have characterized them as tractable, sensuous, and imaginative.

The fullest and most accurate account of the Arapaho has been given by James Mooney.[1] On several points, however, Mr. Mooney's information does not agree with that obtained

---

[1] Ghost-Dance Religion (Fourteenth Annual Report, Bureau of Ethnology, pp. 653 et seq.)

by the present writer. Other accounts of the Arapaho, as by Hayden and Clark, are brief and sometimes vague.

One portion of the Arapaho is now settled in Oklahoma; the other part, on a reservation in Wyoming. The Gros Ventres, who form an independent tribal community, but are so closely akin in language and customs that they may be regarded as a subtribe of the Arapaho, are in northern Montana.

Nothing is known of the origin, history, or migrations of the Arapaho. A little light is thrown on their past by their linguistic relations.

Apart from the Cree, the western Algonkin languages belong to four groups,— the Ojibway, Cheyenne, Arapaho, and Blackfoot.

Of these, the Blackfoot is the most isolated, and the most differentiated from the typical Algonkin. Grammatically it is normal: the methods of inflection and the forms of pronominal affixes resemble those of Ojibway, Cree, and more eastern dialects; but etymologically it seems to differ considerably more from all other Algonkin languages than these vary from each other.

Cheyenne and Arapaho are quite distinct, in spite of the identity of habitation of the two tribes. Cheyenne, Arapaho, and Ojibway are all about equally different one from another. Arapaho and Ojibway seem to differ a little more from each other than each varies from Cheyenne; but Cheyenne is by no means a connecting link between them.

Superficially, Arapaho appears to be very much changed from the average Algonkin, etymologically as well as grammatically; but its words vary from those of Ojibway, Cheyenne, and eastern languages largely on account of regular and consistent phonetic changes. When once the rules governing these changes are known, and the phonetic substitutions are made, the vocabulary of the Arapaho is seen to correspond closely to those of kindred languages. This does not seem to be the case with the Blackfoot, which gives the impression of being corrupted, or irregularly modified lexically.

Grammatically, Arapaho is more specialized. It possesses

three features that are peculiar to it. First, it makes no distinction between animate and inanimate nouns in their plural forms, — a distinction which is made in the other Algonkin languages. It recognizes this category only in the verb. Secondly, all the pronominal particles which are used to conjugate the verb are suffixed. In all other Algonkin languages, when there are two such particles (in the objective conjugation), one is generally prefixed and one suffixed; when there is only one such particle (intransitive conjugation) it is prefixed. Except in one form of the negative, Arapaho suffixes its pronominal elements throughout. This gives a very different appearance to its conjugation. Lastly, its pronominal particle for the second person, which elsewhere in Algonkin is k-, is -n in the verb, and a vowel-sound in the noun. In this last feature Arapaho is approximated by Cheyenne, which uses n- to indicate the second person.

Blackfoot and Arapaho, the two most western Algonkin languages, thus appear to be the most specialized from the common type, — one etymologically, the other grammatically. They have so little in common, however, that they probably differ more from each other than from any other languages of the stock. On the other hand, the Arapaho declare that one of their extinct dialects resembled the Blackfoot. Cheyenne and Arapaho are so different that the recent association of the tribes must have been preceded by a long separation. The Cheyenne appear to have been more lately in connection with the Ojibway or kindred tribes, as is also indicated by several resemblances in culture.

The Arapaho call themselves "Ḥinanaē′inaⁿ," the meaning of which term they cannot give. They declare that they formerly comprised five subtribes. These were —

1. Nāⁿwaçinähā′änaⁿ.
2. Hāⁿanaxawūune′naⁿ.
3. Hinanaē′inaⁿ (Arapaho proper).
4. Bääsaⁿwūune′naⁿ.
5. Hitōune′naⁿ (Gros Ventres).

They extended from south to north in the order given.

The term Nāⁿwaçinähā′änaⁿ has some reference to the south,

the windward direction.   The other elements in the word are not clear.   The sign for this subtribe is said to have been the index-finger placed against the nose.   This may mean "smelling towards the south."   This sign is now the usual one for Arapaho in the sign-language of the Plains.

Hā^{n}anaxawūune′na^n means "rock-men."   It is said to have reference to stone-chipping or the working of flint.   The sign for this subtribe is the sign for rock or rough flint.

Hinanaē′ina^n (the Arapaho proper) were indicated by the sign for "father."

Bāäsa^{n}wūune′na^n means "shelter-men," "brush-hut-men." The sign for this tribe is that indicating a round camp-shelter.

Hitōune′na^n (the Gros Ventres) are indicated by the gesture for a large or swelling belly.   The word means "begging men," or "greedy men," or "gluttons."

These five tribes were separate, though allied.   Occasionally they came together.   Later, most of them grew less in number, and were absorbed by the Hinanaē′ina^n.   There is more Bāäsa^{n}wūune′na^n blood among the present Arapaho than there is of that of the other tribes.   The Hitōune′na^n, however, maintained a separate existence.   Known as Gros Ventres, they are an independent tribe considerably north of the Arapaho.   The Gros Ventres have a mythical story, analogues of which are found among other Western Plains tribes, about their detachment from a previous larger tribe; but there appears to be no reference in their traditions to any common origin with the Arapaho.   The Gros Ventres call themselves "Haā′ninin."

Each of these five tribes had a dialect of its own.   The Bāäsa^{n}wūune′na^n speech is very similar to the Arapaho, and is easily understood.   There are several individuals among both the northern and the southern portions of the Arapaho tribe that still habitually speak this dialect.

Next in degree of similarity is the Gros Ventre.   There are several regular substitutions of sounds between the Arapaho and Gros Ventre dialects, but they are not numerous enough to prevent mutual intelligibility.

The Nā^{n}waçinähā′äna^n is considerably different from the

Arapaho. It alone, of all the dialects, has the sound *m*. In the form of its words, it diverges from Arapaho in the direction of Cheyenne. Grammatically, however, it is clearly Arapaho. This dialect is still remembered by some old people, but it is doubtful whether it is still spoken habitually by any one.

The Hāⁿanaxawūune'naⁿ is said to have differed most from the Arapaho and to have been the most difficult to understand. No one who knew this dialect could be found.

It is said that there was once a fight between two of the tribes. This quarrel was between the Hinanaē'inaⁿ and the Bāäsaⁿwūune'naⁿ, over the sacred tribal pipe and a similar sacred lance, and occurred on account of a woman. The Bāäsaⁿwūune'naⁿ were the first to have the pipe and the lance. The Bāäsaⁿwūune'n keeper of them married an Arapaho woman, and lived with her people. Since then the other tribes have all lived together and helped each other in war. The present condition of alliance, and of possession of the pipe by the Arapaho, has come about through intermarriage.

Both the northern and southern Arapaho recognize these five tribes or dialects as composing their people. There seem to be no historical references to the three absorbed tribes, except that Hayden, in 1862, called the southern half of the Arapaho tribe Nāⁿwaçināhā'änaⁿ (Nawuthinihaⁿ). Mooney gives these five tribes somewhat differently.

The northern Arapaho in Wyoming are called Nāⁿk'hāaⁿseine'naⁿ ("sagebrush men"), Bāaⁿtcīine'naⁿ ("red-willow men"), Bāäkūune'naⁿ ("blood-soup men"), or Nänäbine'naⁿ ("northern men"). They call the southern Arapaho in Oklahoma Naⁿwuine'naⁿ ("southern men"). These two divisions of the Hinanaē'inaⁿ appear to have existed before the tribe was confined to reservations. The two halves of the tribe speak alike, except that the northern people talk more rapidly, according to their own and their tribesmen's account. The author has not been able to perceive any difference between the speech of the two portions of the tribe.

There are also said to have been four bands in the tribe. Three of these were the Wāⁿxuē'içi ("ugly people"), who are now about Cantonment in Oklahoma; the Haxāaⁿçine′naⁿ ("ridiculous men"), on the South Canadian, in Oklahoma; and the Bāaⁿtcīine′naⁿ ("red-willow men"), in Wyoming. The fourth the informant had forgotten. Apparently corresponding to these were the four head chiefs that the Arapaho formerly had. These bands were properly subdivisions of the Hinanaē′inaⁿ subtribe, and appear to have been local divisions. A man belonged to the band in which he was born or with which he lived; sometimes he would change at marriage. When the bands were separate, the people in each camped promiscuously and without order. When the whole tribe was together, it camped in a circle that had an opening to the east. The members of each band then camped in one place in the circle. All dances were held inside the camp-circle.

There are no clans, gentes, or totemic divisions among the Arapaho. The local bands of the Gros Ventres seem, however, to partake also of the nature of gentes.

All informants agree that the tribe against which the Arapaho fought most were the Utes, the bravest (after themselves). An old man said that the Arapaho fought most with the Utes because they were the strongest, and next with the Pawnees because they were the fiercest, and that the Osages and Pawnees were the first Indians that wished to establish friendly ties with the Arapaho. His son has a model of the pipe with which friendship was made with these tribes. A younger man said that his ears had been pierced by visiting Osages, because his father had formerly fought chiefly with them.

The first whites with whom the Arapaho came into contact were Mexicans. The word for "white man" is nih′ā′ⁿçaⁿ, which is also the name of the mythic character that corresponds to the Ojibway Manabozho. This word also means "spider."

The Arapaho had four chiefs, as against five of the Cheyennes. They also had no official principal chief, while the Cheyennes did have one. When one of the four head chiefs died, another was chosen from among the dog-company, — men about fifty years old, who have performed the fourth of the tribal series of six ceremonials. If a chief was unsatisfactory, he was not respected or obeyed, and so gradually lost his position. Another informant stated that chiefs were not formally elected: the bravest and kindest-hearted men became chiefs naturally, but there were no recognized or regular chiefs.

The following are the terms of relationship and affinity in Arapaho and Gros Ventre. All the words given have the prefix denoting "my."

English.	*Arapaho.*	*Gros Ventre.*
father	neisa′naⁿ	niiçinaⁿ
mother	ne′inaⁿ	neinaⁿ
elder brother	nääsä′hää	nääçähää
elder sister	nä′bie	nibye
younger brother or sister	nähäbä′hää	näⁿhäbyⁱ
son	ne′ih′äⁿ	neih′ä
daughter	nata′ne	natan
grandfather	näbä′cibä	näbeseip
grandmother	neibä′häⁿ	niip'
grandchild	neicI′	niisä
father's brother	(?)	niiçinaⁿ
mother's brother	nä′ci	nis'
father's sister	nähe′i	nähei
mother's sister	(?)	neinaⁿ
son of brother of a man ⎱ son of sister of a woman ⎰	(?)	neih′ä
daughter of brother of a man ⎱ daughter of sister of a woman ⎰	(?)	natan
son of sister of a man ⎱ son of brother of a woman ⎰	näçää′çä	nêt'êt
daughter of sister of a man ⎱ daughter of brother of a woman ⎰	nääsä′bie	nääçibyⁱ
father-in-law	näci′çä	nêsit
mother-in-law	nähe′ihäⁿ	näheihä
son-in-law	näçä′Ox	nataos
daughter-in-law	nääsä′bie	nääçibyⁱ
brother-in-law of a man	näyaⁿ′	näyaaⁿ
sister-in-law of a woman	nato′u	natou
brother-in-law of a woman ⎱ sister-in-law of a man ⎰	neiçä′bie	niitibyⁱ
husband	nä′äc	(?)
wife	nätä′ceäⁿ	nätiçää

The terms for "niece" and for "daughter-in-law" seem to be identical.   There is another word for "younger sister" or perhaps "sister,"— nătă′se.

The total number of Arapaho kinship terms is thus twenty-three.   Four of these —"father-in-law," "mother-in-law," "son-in-law," and "daughter-in-law"— are clearly related to four others, —"uncle," "aunt," "nephew," and "niece." Several others appear to have common elements: -äbi^e occurs in the words for "elder sister," "niece," and "sister-in-law of a man."

In this series of terms the distinction between elder and younger is confined to the brother and sister relationships. The terms for the consanguinities of a man and for those of a woman are alike, except in the case of brother-in-law and sister-in-law.   Here the category according to which terms are differentiated is not so much absolute sex as identity or contrariety of sex.   Thus, a man calls his sister-in-law neiçăbie, and she calls him the same; brothers-in-law call each other näya^n; sisters-in-law, natou.

Cousins, even of remote degrees of kinship, are called "brothers and sisters."   Among the Gros Ventres, the father's brother is called "father;" the mother's sister, "mother;" so that the terms for "uncle" and "aunt" are used only for mother's brother and father's sister.   The same is true of "nephew" and "niece;" a man calls his brother's children "son and daughter," but his sister's children "nephew and niece;" conversely with a woman.   Even a cousin's or a second cousin's children are called "son and daughter" instead of "nephew and niece," if the cousin is of the same sex as the speaker.   The same may be true among the Arapaho.

The restrictions as to intercourse between certain relations, which are so widespread in North America, exist also among the Arapaho.   A man and his mother-in-law may not look at or speak to each other.   If, however, he gives her a horse, he may speak to her and see her.   The same restrictions exist between father and daughter-in-law as between mother and son-in-law, say the Arapaho (though perhaps they are less rigid).   A brother and sister must not speak to each other more than is necessary.   A sister is supposed to sit at some distance from her brother.   A woman does not speak of child-birth or sexual matters in the presence of her brother, nor he in hers, but in other company no such delicacy is observed. Obscene myths are freely told, even in the presence of children of either sex, except that a man would not relate them before his mother-in-law, daughter-in-law, sister, or female cousin, nor a woman before her corresponding male relatives. Brothers-in-law joke with each other frequently; often they abuse each other good-naturedly; but they may not talk obscenely to each other.   If one does so, he is struck by the other.   A brother-in-law and sister-in-law also often joke each other.   They act toward each other with considerable free-dom: a woman may pour water on her brother-in-law while he is asleep, or tease him otherwise, and he retaliates in similar ways.

When a man died, his brothers took from their sister-in-law as many horses as they pleased.   Sometimes they were gen-erous and allowed a grown-up daughter or son of the dead man to keep some.   Another informant stated that after a man's death, his brothers took all the property they could, especially horses.   The family tried to prevent them.

There are no fixed rules as to inheritance.   When a wealthy man dies, there is generally some jealousy as to who is to take his property and his family.   Those who are not satisfied sometimes kill horses or destroy property of those who took the belongings of the dead man.   Each one tries to get as much as he can.   There is little generosity or charity towards the wife and children.   Adult sons of the deceased may be anxious to secure some of the property; but, as they are in mourning, they cannot resist.   It is generally brothers and sisters of the deceased who go to take his property.

In the absence of any gentile or other organization regulat-ing marriage, the only bar was that of known relationship. Cousins could not marry.   As to distant relations the rule was not so strict.   If relationship was discovered after a marriage, the marriage was not annulled.

The following are statements by the Arapaho on the subject of marriage.

When a young man wants to marry, he sends a female relative to the tent of his desired father-in-law with several horses (from one to ten), which may be his own or his friends'. She ties the horses in front of the tent, enters, and proposes the marriage. The father has nothing to say, and refers the matter to his son. The son decides upon the proposal, unless he wishes to refer it to an uncle or other relative. The woman goes back and reports her success. If the proposal of marriage has been refused, she takes the horses back. If the suitor has been accepted, he waits until called, which is done as soon as the girl's mother and relatives have put up a new tent which is given her, and have got property together. This may be the same day or the same night that the proposal was made. The girl's brothers and father's brothers' sons all give horses and other presents. They bring the things inside the new tent, the horses in front of it. Then the girl's relatives notify the young man's father to come; sometimes they send the bride herself. Then the young man's relatives come over with him to the new tent, and enter it. His entering this tent signifies that he and the girl are married. He sits down at the head of the bed, which is on the left as one enters the tent (the entrance to Arapaho tents is always at the east; the owner's bed, along the southern side, with the head toward the west). The girl sits next to him at the foot of the bed, the other people all around the tent. The girl's father, or, if he is still young, an old man, stands before the door and cries out the names of those invited, calling to them to come and feast. Then they eat and smoke. Sometimes an old person that wants to, prays. Any one of the girl's male relatives makes a speech to her. He says to her that she is a woman now, and tells her to be true to her husband. The visitors leave whenever they please. The friends of the young man each take away as many horses as they gave (to the girl's relatives). Sometimes he gives his friends other presents besides. Now he is married. He pitches his tent by his father-in-law's. The young wife at first does not know how to cook, and goes to her mother's tent for food. The young man, however, does not enter this tent, because he and his mother-in-law may not look at or speak to each other.

Sometimes a young man and a girl run off without the knowledge of their parents. They remain some time in the tent of the young man's father or of some friend. Then his friends contribute horses and other property. The girl mounts a horse and leads the rest. Accompanied by her sister-in-law or mother-in-law, she brings the horses and other gifts to the tent of her parents. Then her parents are not angry any longer, and send her back with horses and presents of property, sometimes with a tent. They also give her food, with which a feast is held in the young man's tent. Then his friends take the horses and goods which he has received. Sometimes a young man, after taking a girl away, abandons her on the prairie.

Relatives know nothing about the courtship of a young man and a girl. This is kept secret by them until she is formally asked for by his relatives.

When a man wishes to run off with another's wife, the two make plans. They go off together a long distance. At first the husband, perhaps, does not know what has happened. When he becomes aware of it, he is angry. He may follow his wife; but he is not allowed to enter the tent where she and her lover are, because he might do them injury. If he finds them and speaks to them, they do not answer him, in order not to enrage him more, because they may not make any resistance to him. The lover tries to find the (ceremonial) grandfather of the husband. He gives him a pipe and two or three horses. The old man takes the pipe, the horses, and the wife to the husband. When the man sees his grandfather, he must do no violence nor may he become angry. The grandfather hands him the pipe. If he takes it, his wife is safe from harm. Sometimes he keeps her, sometimes he sends her back to her lover to keep. Often the husband cuts off the tip of her nose, slashes her cheek, or cuts her hair. Both men and women are jealous. A man will hit his wife for looking at a young man too much.

If a man treats his wife badly, her brothers may take her back to her father, tear his tent down, and take away his household property. Sometimes the man and woman live together again, sometimes she marries some one else. But the man still has a claim on her; and if another takes her, he must pay her first husband one or two horses to relinquish his claim.

Sometimes a husband, to show his love for his wife, gives away several horses to her relatives.

A wife's next younger sister, if of marriageable age, is sometimes given to her husband if his brother-in-law likes him. Sometimes the husband asks and pays for his wife's younger sister. This may be done several times if she has several sisters. If his wife has no sister, a cousin (also called "sister") is sometimes given to him. When a woman dies, her husband marries her sister. When a man dies, his brother sometimes marries his wife. He is expected to do so. Sometimes she marries another man.

In courting women, men cover themselves completely with a blanket except the eyes. Often they exchange blankets, so as not to be known. They wait on sand-hills, or similar places, until the women leave the camp for water or wood. Sometimes at night they turn the upper flaps of the tent, so that the smoke of the fire remains in the tent; when the woman goes outside to open the top of the tent, the man meets her. At night men catch women outdoors and hold them, trying to persuade them to yield to their wishes. (The Arapaho affirm this of the Cheyenne, but have the practice themselves.) Courting is much easier and more open now than formerly. In making advances to a woman, a man often begins by asking for a drink of the water she is carrying.

It is said, that, on account of fear of unchastity, women are married at an earlier age now than formerly. The Omaha, according to Dorsey, make a similar statement. This seems to be an Indian opinion which is not founded on facts.

A man with two wives generally has a tent for each. An Arapaho in Wyoming lived with his two wives, who were sisters, in one tent. His wives' relatives wanted to give him a third sister. The girl objected, and he did not get her.

Once a young man was said to have sat with the women too frequently, and to have teased them too much. A number of them seized him, stripped him, and then buffeted and maltreated him without delicacy. Young men were ashamed to be alone with a number of women too long. There were a few bachelors, who were half-witted, or considered so.

At the sun-dance an old man, crying out to the entire camp-circle, told the young people to amuse themselves; he told the women to consent if they were approached by a young man, for this was their opportunity; and he called to the young men not to beat or anger their wives, or be jealous during the dance: they might make a woman cry, but meanwhile she would surely be thinking of some other young man. At such dances the old women say to the girls: "We are old, and our skin is not smooth; we are of no use. But you are young and plump; therefore find enjoyment. We have to take care of the children, and the time will come when you will do the same."

Women do not spend several days in solitude during menstruation, as is the case among the Sioux, the Utes, and many other neighboring tribes. They sit quietly, keeping away from other people, especially from women and young men. But they eat with other people, and cook for them. They wrap their clothes tightly about the waist. They change their clothes every day, and wash themselves. There is no practice or ceremony connected with a girl's first menstruation. A menstruating woman is not allowed to enter the mescal (peyote) tent; and if a man who has had intercourse with a menstruating woman takes part in this ceremony, he is found out by the smell. Sickly people and menstruating women are not allowed to enter a tent in which there is a sick person. The smell of the discharge would enter the body of the patient and make him worse. A woman just delivered also refrains from going into the tent of a sick person. Medicine-women, after delivery, go into the sweat-house (steam-bath) to cleanse themselves. Menses were called bäätä′äna^n ("medicine," "supernatural," "mysterious"), or näniiçe′hina^n (näniiçext, bäätäät, "she menstruates").

A woman nursing a child does not drink coffee because it burns or cooks the milk. She may not go into the heat of the sun, or work near the fire. She covers her breast and sometimes her back as thickly as she can from the heat. If a mother dies, an old woman takes the infant to another woman who is already nursing a child. This is advantageous to the woman, as it prevents her surplus milk from becoming bad. For this reason pups are sometimes applied to the breast. Early in the morning a man sometimes drains a woman's breast, spitting the milk on the ground; or a child some years weaned drinks from her. This is done that her infant may have the newly formed milk.

If a man is married, his sister may want to make a cradle for his child. She provides food for a number of old people, shows them her materials, and asks how she is to make the cradle. The old people tell her how to make it, and show her the designs with which it is to be decorated. Then they all pray in turn that the child's cradle may be made perfectly, and that it may be for the good of the child. After the woman has finished the cradle, she repeats her invitation to the old people. Then the child is put into the cradle and taken to its father. He receives it, and makes a gift to the maker.

Cradles are embroidered with porcupine-quills or beads. They are used for carrying the child. Some can also be suspended on ropes from two tent-poles, and swung. Several are described on p. 66.

When a person dies, his relatives cry and unbraid their hair. Sometimes they cut their hair. The greater their love for him, the more hair they cut off. Women tear off a sleeve; they gash themselves (lightly) across the lower and upper arm and below the knee. The dead body is allowed to lie so that all the dead person's friends can see it. It is dressed in the best clothing, some perhaps being contributed by friends. Those who thus contribute toward dressing a dead man receive one of his horses or other property. A horse is also given for digging the grave and for similar assistance. The body is buried on the hills, being taken there on horseback.

The grave is made deep enough to prevent coyotes from digging out the corpse; with this object in view, thorny brush is also put on the grave. The relatives go out to the grave for several days. They mourn there, crying while sitting in one place. Hair that has been cut off by friends and relatives is wrapped up with the body and buried. The dead man's best or favorite horse is shot next to his grave, and left lying there. The tail and mane of the horse on which the body was taken to burial are cut off and strewn over the grave. Before the body is taken away to be interred, an old man speaks encouragingly to the relatives. The dead man's family move to another place. They give away the tent in which he died. If he happened to die in a brush shelter, it is burned. Clothing, beds, and other articles that were where he died, are burned, in order that his shadow (spirit) will not come back. Sticks that may have touched him while he was dying are buried with him or laid on the grave. Immediately after the burial the relatives bathe because they have touched the corpse. For several nights they burn cedar-leaves; the smoke or smell of this keeps away the spirit. For some time they wear old clothing and do not paint. They seek no amusements. At first they eat little. As long as they wear old clothes and keep their hair unbound, they are in mourning. This period is not fixed. When they have finished mourning, they provide food and invite in old men and women. An old man paints their entire faces and their hair red. This is called cleaning; it is done in the morning, so that they may be under the care of the sun all day. Now they braid their hair again, and go about as before.

For a murder or accidental killing, horses were given to the relatives of the dead. The murderer had no influence or position, and was shunned. He was not, however, excluded from tribal affairs. He could camp in the camp-circle, and enter dances. Everything that he ate was supposed to taste bad to him.

The name of the dead was apparently as freely mentioned as that of the living. Old men sometimes gave their own name to young men. Red-Wolf (haaxǎbaani) gave his name to his son, and was then called "One-Crow" (houniisi). Names are not infrequently changed.

The giving of presents is a very extensive practice among the Arapaho, as among all the Plains Indians. Horses are given to visitors from other tribes, especially by chiefs, in order to show their position and rank. A horse given to a stranger counts for more in public estimation than one given to an Arapaho. When a party of Utes came on a visit in 1898, the Arapaho decorated their best horses, charged upon the Utes, struck them lightly with switches (symbolically counting coup upon them), and then gave them the horses that they had ridden in the charge. Within the tribe, gifts are also very frequent, especially on ceremonial occasions.

When a woman, especially a young girl, wishes a present, she cooks a puppy and takes it to her brother or some other male relative or friend. If he wishes to distinguish himself before those who are present, he gives her a horse or a tent. Sometimes he gives her less. If he gives a tent, it is left standing when the camp-circle breaks up; then, in the sight of all, the new owners take it down. This custom is practised when the whole tribe is encamped together (the especial time for ceremonials). When no pup is available, the woman makes a gift of other food.

Young men sometimes fill a bucket made of bladder with water, and go about the camp, giving drink to the oldest men and women.

Three semi-ceremonial practices bringing honor and reward to the agent, and supposed to be for the good of the child upon whom they are performed, are piercing the ears (tceita^{n}'hätiit), cutting the hair over the forehead (tawana'axawa^{n}t), and cutting the hair on one side (nakaçä'äciit). Ear-piercing counts for more than the other two. Children's ears are pierced when they are small. It is done during the sundance or some other dance. It makes the children grow up well and become men and women. The more they cry during the operation, the better it is thought to be, for the crying signifies that hardship and pain have already been endured, and that therefore they will grow up. A horse and other presents are given by the father to the man who is summoned, through an old man who cries out in public, to pierce the child's ears. Generally he receives the father's best horse. If the man who is summoned has never killed or scalped any one, he keeps the horse, but gives away his other presents to a man who has thus distinguished himself in war, and who actually does the piercing. If the man who pierces the child's ears belongs to another tribe, the honor is so much the greater. One man, when a child, had his ears pierced by an Osage, because before peace was concluded his father had fought chiefly against the Osages. The piercing is performed with a sewing-awl; but, if the piercer has ever cut or slashed an enemy or cut a scalp, he uses a knife instead of an awl. The awl symbolizes a spear; the hole pierced, a wound; the dripping blood, ear-ornaments; the cutting of the child's hair, scalping. The wound is kept open by means of a little stick.

Berdaches (men living as women) were found among the Arapaho, as among the Cheyenne, Sioux, Omaha, Ute, and many other tribes. They are called haxu'xan, which is thought to mean "rotten bone." The following accounts concerning them were obtained.

The haxuxan^n become so as the result of a (supernatural) gift from animals or birds. Similarly, in the beginning of the world, animals appeared as women (in certain myths, such as that of Elk-Woman and Buffalo-Woman). Nih'a^n'ça^n (the character corresponding to Manabozho and Ictinike) was the first one. This is told in a myth. (He pretended to be a woman, married the Mountain-Lion, and deceived him by giving birth to a false child.) These people had the natural desire to become women, and as they grew up gradually became women. They gave up the desires of men. They were married to men. They had miraculous power and could do (supernatural) things. For instance, it was one of them that first made an intoxicant from rain-water.

Apud Indianos quos Cheyenne vocant, femina vixit cui viri vox genitaliaque fuerunt. Vestibus mulierum usa est, et ut femina cum feminis vixit. Hospitum oculos attraxit moribus magis liberis. Viro connexum petente, consensum præbuit;

dorso recumbens et penem ventri deponens, permisit accessum in anum.

The Arapaho declare that they never had any women that dressed and lived as men, but they have a story of such a woman among the Sioux.

Insanity, when it occurs, seems mostly to be acute and violent delusion. One man became insane from excitement in making a charge in battle. He thought himself a wolf, and ran about like one. He did not, however, attack men or animals; and later he recovered. Another man, who subsequently also recovered, ran about with a knife, and gashed or pierced trees; deinde intromisit penem. A Gros Ventre, an elderly man, recently began to see crowds of spirits close about him; he swung his arms and shouted in order to drive them away. Soon after being taken to an asylum, he was said to be recovering. Among the Oklahoma Arapaho a man named Big-Belly imagined himself a deer, and in consequence of his actions received the name "Deer" (bihii). He had several attacks of his delusion. The following is a translation of an account by an eye-witness.

"*Deer* went hunting. Accidentally he came to a pretty woman. She was completely dressed in deer-skin. Straightway he wanted to court her, when he saw the woman. She motioned to him to approach. 'Well, I will have you for sweetheart,' *Deer* said to her. 'And yourself do so' (please yourself), she said to him. Then he went to her. He was just going to touch her — to his surprise, she gave the cry of a deer, suddenly jumped, and ran off, looking backwards. Then he saw her to be a deer. Then *Deer* was ashamed at being deceived from desire to make love. Then he went back because he was ashamed. Some time afterwards *Deer* became like a deer. In the middle of the camp-circle *Deer* was chased like a deer; like a deer he cried, like a deer he leaped, like a deer he fled on the open prairie; all pursued him. When they caught him, his eyes looked different. *Deer* had his mouth open; all held him. At last he ceased being a deer. For this he is named *Deer*."

Intoxicants seem to have been lacking formerly; but it is

said that when there was a thunderstorm, some people set
out buckets and vessels, and drank the water caught
in them. This water was powerful, and made them
foolish. Of late years the mescal (peyote) worship
has spread among some of the Arapaho. The effects
of this plant are, however, not strictly intoxicating.
It is eaten only in connection with the religious cult,
and occasionally as medicine.

Smoking the pipe plays as large a part in the life
of the Arapaho as among other Prairie tribes. Their
most sacred tribal object is a pipe, that, according
to their cosmology, was one of the first things that
existed in the world. The Gros Ventres had several
such sacred pipes. A man who had eloped
with a woman, and wished to become
reconciled with her husband, sent him
hounaçaniitcaa^n ("a pipe of settlement")
by an old man, together with presents.
When the Arapaho made peace and friendship with the Pawnees and Osages, a pipe
was used in the peace ceremonial.

Pipes are generally of red catlinite and
of the forms usual among the Plains
tribes. Sometimes black stone is used,
especially for small pipes. The wooden
stem is more frequently round than of
the flat shape usual among the Sioux. A
small straight or tubular pipe is shown in
Fig. 1. This is made of the leg-bone of an
antelope. The tobacco is pressed into the
larger end. In one place the bone is
wrapped with a tendon. This was said
to have been put there in order to prevent
the heat from going to the mouth. The
sacred pipe of the tribe is also tubular,
seeming to be made of a piece of black and
a piece of white stone; but it is called
"flat pipe" (säeitcaa^n).

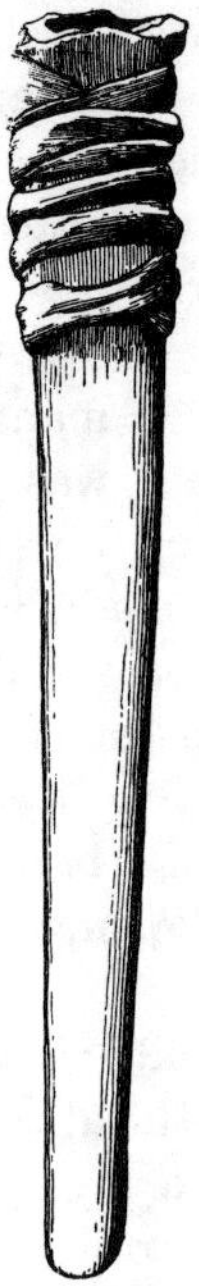

Fig. 1.    Fig. 2.

Fig. 1 ($\frac{50}{1889}$). Tubular Pipe. Length, 19 cm.

Fig. 2 ($\frac{50}{1892}$). Pipe-stoker. Length, 51 cm.

A stick for stoking pipes is shown in Fig. 2. Its end is flat, and is said to represent a duck's bill.

The following is told about the origin of tobacco. Before the fifth (or present) life (generation, or period of the world), cottonwood-bark, buffalo-dung, and dried meat were used as tobacco. Then an old man obtained tobacco supernaturally. He cut it up fine, put it into a pouch, and threw it behind him. Thus he gave it to others.

Fans made of an eagle-wing are used by old men very frequently. Younger men sometimes have fans made of the tail-feathers of hawks or eagles. Such fans are also used in the peyote worship.

Old men use their eagle-wing fans for the good of all (the tribe). They use them as shades for the eyes when they cannot see very well. With them they also drive away flies, brush off dust, fan themselves when sweating, and pat themselves when they have had enough to eat. They have been used since Clotted-Blood (a mythical character) gave one to his father.

Eagles were caught, as among the Blackfoot and other tribes, by a man concealed in a pit covered with brush, on which meat was placed. Only certain men could hunt the eagle. For four days they abstained from food and water. They put medicine on their hands. In four days they might get fifty or a hundred eagles. A stuffed coyote-skin was sometimes set near the bait.

In hunting deer, calls are used. These are made either of wood or of a bone whistle like those used in ceremonials.

The following account of buffalo-hunting was given by an old man.

Bows and arrows were made by the man who was the father of the mythical twins (boyish monster-destroyers, who are the heroes of a myth called "Tangled-Hair"). This was the first bow and arrow. Hā^{n}xäbi′nää (one of the twins), when blown away by the whirlwind, was found in the rushes and called Biaxuyā′n ("found in the grass"). He caused the buffalo to come out of a hole in the ground. When he was about to do this, the people made a strong corral of timber; into this he called the buffalo. The last one of the herd he shot with an arrow just at the opening of the corral, and gave it to his father-in-law. It was the ambition of a young man to make presents of this kind to his father-in-law. The people killed the rest of the buffalo. After they began to butcher them, it was found to be best to slit the belly lengthwise, and then to strip back the flanks without cutting them across. Women now began to make wooden pegs for stretching hides. The best tools and methods of work were discovered only by trial.

When the Arapaho were near the Rocky Mountains, they used snow-shoes for hunting buffalo in winter, when the snow was deep. These snow-shoes were oval and without a point. They were woven of strings of hide, like the netted hoops used to play with. The meat of a buffalo that was killed was packed into the hide, and thus dragged home over the snow.

If old men are smoking together, and a young man by mistake enters the tent, they say, "What are you doing here? You ought to be hunting." Then the young man goes out quickly.

People often went to war because they preferred to be killed in war and leave a good name rather than die old. When a war-party returned victoriously and without losses, they painted themselves black.

When the Sioux introduced the Omaha dance, they brought a bundle of sticks, cloth, etc., called tceăk'ça[n]. This is a sign of friendship. If any tribe refuses it, they will surely be beaten in war by those who offer it. In recounting deeds of war (as is frequently done on ceremonial or social occasions), men told the truth, because if they lied they would surely be killed by the enemy. They even declined coups (blows struck an enemy, a high honor) that were mistakenly ascribed to them by others. Two men once found a (dead) Ute. There was question between them as to who was to strike him first. They pressed each other to take the honor of the first blow. One finally consented. Then they found the body already decomposed, and hence could not lay claim to having counted coup.

Property was formerly transported on dog-travois. Two

poles were harnessed to a dog, the lower ends dragging on the ground.   The two poles were connected by sticks or slats, on which the load was packed.   Later, horse-travois were made. These have now gone out of use among the Arapaho, but are sometimes used by the Gros Ventres, who lash a loosely netted frame to the two poles.   Among the Assiniboine even dog-travois are still used (1901) by old people.   The Arapaho had light cages of willows in which children were transported on travois.   There is still a tradition of the time before there were horses.   Some say that horses were first obtained from the whites, some that wild horses were caught.   Dogs were not used for hunting.

Knives were formerly made of a narrow piece of the shoulder-blade of a buffalo, or of flint.   For handles, the spines of buffalo vertebræ were used.   Large tendons were used to wrap together blade and handle.   As this became dry, it contracted.   Hide-scrapers had their blades fastened in the same way to a handle made of the spine of a buffalo vertebra; or sometimes the blade was inserted in a slit in the handle. When bone knives were worn down, they were used for awls.

Fire was made by striking two stones together.   Subsequently a piece of steel was used with flint.   For tinder, dry, pithy cottonwood was used, which was kept in a horn.   The fire-drill was also known.   It was rubbed by hand.   Sticks of siitcinäwaxu, a plant or shrub growing on the prairie, were used because very hard.   The point had three sides.   Buffalo-dung was used for tinder.

Bows are said sometimes to have been backed with five strips or layers of sinew; when made of cedar, they were covered with sinew on both sides.   Iron for arrows and spear-points was first obtained from the Mexicans.   Native copper was not used.   There were some arrows with detachable fore-shafts or heads made of bone.   Arrow-points, usually of flint, were sometimes made from the last rib of a buffalo.   The bow and arrow are said to have been invented by the man who made the first knives; also by the father of the mythical twin monster-destroyers.

When a young man wants arrows, he secures the materials

for making them, provides food, and invites old men to his tent. These come and remain all day. One makes points, one feathers the shafts, one paints them, and so on. Meanwhile they tell stories of war or of the buffalo-hunt, according to the purpose for which the young man is to use the arrows. They make six or twelve arrows, all painted with the same marks. The old man who does the painting shows the marks to all the others, so that there can be no dispute as to the ownership of the arrows. Were any one else ever to claim this young man's arrow as his own, the old men would recognize the marks, and settle the dispute.

In the time when old men wore their hair drawn in a bunch over the forehead (*i. e.*, in the traditional, not mythic past), baskets of flexible fibre were made. They were used as trays. Some, more finely woven, and covered with pitch inside, were used for drinking. At present small trays of coiled basketry are sometimes used for throwing dice.

Pottery was formerly made of mud (clay?) mixed with a little white sand. Several pieces were made and joined together until a round vessel was formed. This was then baked in the fire. Another informant stated that to make pottery, stone was pounded fine, and mixed with clay. This was worked by hand, just as a swallow builds its nest, until a large vessel was made. This was heated to make it hard. Some vessels were merely dried. The vessels were of various sizes, and were used for cooking. This art must have completely gone out of practice some time ago, as no traces of it remain. One old man denied that the Arapaho ever made pottery.

Meat was boiled in rawhide. A hole was made in the ground, and rawhide pressed down into it, its edges being weighted down with stones. The sack-like rawhide was then filled with water, which was made to boil by means of heated stones. Plates were made of rawhide. Rawhide was used to pound dried meat on. Bowls were made of knots of cottonwood-trees. A spherical knot was cut in halves, and then hollowed out. Spoons, as well as cups, were made of the horns of mountain-sheep.

Several tools are in use for dressing skins.   A chisel-shaped flesher (now generally made of iron, originally of a buffalo leg-bone) is used to clean the inner surface of hides from fat and flesh.   If the hair is to be removed, which is almost always the case unless a blanket is being made, an instrument made of elk-antler is used.   The end of this extends at right angles to the handle, and is provided with a metal blade. This instrument is at times made of wood, but then has exactly the shape of those made of antler.   With this instrument the hair is cut from the skin with little difficulty.   Sometimes a stone hammer is used to pound the hairy side of the skin until the hair comes off.   With the elk-antler scraper the hide is generally thinned down more or less, the surface being flaked or planed off.   All hides used for clothing are thinned to a certain extent.   The scrapings obtained in this process are sometimes eaten.   The elk-horn scrapers are usually marked with a number of parallel scratches or lines, which are a record of the ages of the children of the woman who owns the scraper.   One woman kept count of the number of hides she had dressed with her instrument.   Twenty-six scratches denoted so many buffalo-skins; forty small brass nails driven into the back of the instrument at the bend, signified forty skins of other animals that she had worked.   These scrapers are sometimes used for digging roots.

After the hair has been removed, the skin is stretched on the ground by means of pegs, and dried until stiff, if rawhide is to be made.   If soft hide is desired, as for clothing, the skin is soaked and then scraped or rubbed with a blunt edge until it is dry.   Now, pieces of tin, whose scraping edge is slightly convex, are generally used for this purpose; formerly bone, horn, and perhaps stone, seem to have been used. Another form of scraper for softening or roughening hide consists of a slightly curved stick of wood a foot long; in the middle of the concave side of this is a metal blade.   The whole object somewhat resembles a draw-knife.   This instrument is used more particularly on buckskin, which is hung on an upright post or stick.   A scraper of this kind is shown in Fig. 3.   It has carved upon it in outline the figure of a

deer viewed from the front. On the other side of the handle
is a similarly carved figure of an antelope. The lines representing the flanks of the two animals are run
into each other along the two sides of the
handle. Buffalo-hides are also softened by
being drawn over a rope, twisted of sinew,
about one-third of an inch thick.

The Arapaho say that formerly the men
parted their hair on each side; while in the
middle, over the forehead, they left it standing
upright. Over the temples it was cut into a
zigzag edge. In front of the ears, the hair
fell down; it was either braided or tied together. The hair was worn upright over the
forehead in order to make the wearer look
fierce. When the Arapaho adopted the present style of wearing the hair (braids or
masses tied together over the ears, and the
scalp-lock in the middle of the back of the
head), the Crees, Shoshone, and other tribes
adopted their old style. Some formerly tied
all their hair together in a bunch at the
back of the head. Very old men did not
comb their hair; they rolled it, and, when it
was sticky and matted, gathered it into a
bunch over the forehead. "Our father directed that old men should do this," they
said. Among the Gros Ventres, the keepers
of the sacred pipes were not allowed to comb
or cut their hair.

For women the old way was to wear the
hair loose, with paint upon it. They painted
streaks down their faces, on cheeks, forehead,
and nose. This signified war. Old women
wore their hair loose and generally tangled.
They painted a spot on each cheek-bone, and
one on the forehead. A spot between the
eyes signified a buffalo calf, and a line from the mouth down

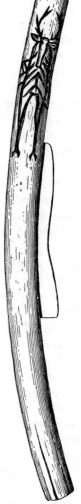

Fig. 3 ($\frac{50}{1177}$). Skin
scraper. Length, 39
cm.

the chin represented a road. This whole painting signified peace. Nowadays women wear two braids of hair from behind their ears, the hair being parted from forehead to nape; old women often wear their hair loose.

The face is painted in ceremonials regularly, almost always when any actions are performed that have any connection with what is supernatural, and often for decoration. Black is the paint to indicate victory. Of other colors, red is far the most frequently used. Old people confine themselves to red exclusively, so that red paint is often symbolic of old age. Paint on the face in general signifies happiness or wish for happiness. Mourners do not paint. Their first painting after the completion of mourning is with red, and is called "washing" or "cleansing." The paint along the part of the hair of both men and women is called "the path of the sun."

The dress of men consisted of a shirt, leggings reaching from the ankles to the hips, breech-cloth, moccasins, and a blanket of buffalo-skin. The women wore an open-sleeved dress not reaching the ankles, moccasins to which leggings were attached that extended to the knee, and a blanket. Small boys often wore nothing or only a shirt. One and the same word denotes the man's shirt and the woman's dress,— biixū'ut. The skin blankets were either painted or embroidered. There is a similarity between the designs on blankets and those on tents, bedding, and cradles.

Sewing was done with needles and awls of bone, and thread of shreds of dried sinew. Needles and awls are now of steel, but sinew is still mostly used for thread. Embroidery formerly consisted chiefly of colored and flattened porcupine-quills sewed firmly on the surface to be decorated. The quills were softened in the mouth and flattened with a bone. A dark fibrous water-plant was used to embroider in black. These materials, while still in use, have been largely replaced by small glass beads of many different colors. The quills are kept in pouches of gut, which they cannot penetrate (Plate x). The women have work-bags (Plate xv) in which they keep awls, sinew, quills, needles, bones for quill-flattening and for painting, incense, paint, medicine, and similar miscellaneous articles. A bone used for flattening porcupine-quills and for painting skins is shown in Fig. 4. It is said to represent a person. The notches cut into the edges denote the age of a previous owner of the instrument.

The following are statements of an old woman. When an inexperienced person tries for the first time to do quill-embroidery, failure ensues. The points of the quills stick out, and the whole embroidery becomes loose. When she was young, she once helped other women to embroider a robe. She had never done this before. The line of embroidery which she was working was spoiled, the quills would not stay fast, and the other women refused to work with her. She arose and prayed that she might be able to work successfully, and said that she would make a whole robe in this style of embroidery. An old woman who was present said that this was good. After this the quills remained fast, and she was able to embroider.

Fig. 4 ($\frac{50}{1717}$).
Quill-flattener.
Length, 22 cm.

A woman, thought to be the oldest woman in the Oklahoma portion of the tribe, kept a small stick with thirty notches. These represented thirty robes that she had made in her lifetime. She said that the usual buffalo-robe had twenty lines of quill-embroidery across it, and was called niisa^{n}ûxt. There were seventeen lines, and then three more close together along the bottom of the robe. The lines were ordinarily yellow. She made one robe with white quill-work, to signify old age. The lines were formerly not made of red quills (as in some modern robes of children). Only certain portions of designs on the lines were red. Sometimes these were green instead of red. Fifty small dew-claws of the buffalo were hung as pendants or rattles along the lower edge of a twenty-lined robe. If the robe had only seventeen lines of quill-embroidery, forty hoof-pendants were attached. She had made a robe for every member of her family but one. Whenever she made and gave away a robe, she received a horse for it. She once began a robe with one hundred lines (bätäätᵃsaⁿûxt), to be given to Left-Hand. She had marked one hundred and worked thirty when her son-in-law died. She buried the robe with him. Later she learned that it was not right to bury this highest kind of robe with any one. It gives her vigor now to think of her past life and what she has accomplished.

There are seven sacred bags owned by old women. These contain incense, paint, and implements for marking and sewing. They are painted red, and kept wrapped. They correspond to seven sacred bags kept by seven old men, and containing rattles, paint, and perhaps other objects. These women's bags are used in ornamenting buffalo-robes and tents, when certain ceremonies are gone through.

The following account was obtained from an old woman who possessed one of the sacred bags.

"Backward, the mother of Little-Raven, was the owner of my bag before it was transferred to me. This bag was owned successively by Night-Killer, Bihiihä ('Female Deer'?), Backward, and myself. When I was about to obtain this bag, I provided food, clothing, and horses (to be given away), and called all the old women who then had bags. There were seven. They were River-Woman, Large-Head, Thread-Woman, Sore-Legs, Flying-Woman, another Thread-Woman, and Backward. A tent was put up. The clothing was laid all around the inside of the tent, the food was set near the fire. I also provided four knives and some fat. The seven old women sat around the tent, each with her bag. I went to each in turn, putting my hand on the top of her head, and prayed. I said that I wished to get a bag in the straight way. Before they opened their bags they spit häçawaanaxu on them (this is a root which is chewed fine, and usually spit on sacred objects before they are handled). Then incense was burned. One of the women took fat and rubbed it with paint; then, holding her hands palm to palm, and turning them from side to side, she painted four spots on my face, and a fifth (in the centre) on the nose; then she painted five spots in similar position (that of a quincunx) on the top of my head.

The food had been placed southwest, northwest, northeast, and southeast of the fire (the tent always faces east, the fire being in the centre). The food towards the southwest was taken up, carried around the tent, and set down in the same place as before, in front of one of the old women. This woman then carried the other food around the tent in the same way, replacing it all. Then she took häçawaanaxu, chewed it, and rubbed it over her body (a very frequent act in rituals). Then she took food from four dishes and placed it on her hand in five spots. Two of these pieces or heaps of food she placed on the ground, southwest and northwest of the fire; two she raised and laid on the ground, northeast and southeast of the fire; and the fifth she put into the fire. Then she took (a dish of) blood-soup or pudding (bääk"). She touched it with a finger, touched this finger on the palm of her hand, and rubbed her hands together. Then she moved her hands downward four times towards the southeast of the tent, representing the planting in the ground of a tent-pole there. Then she touched the pudding in three other places, after each time rubbing her hands, and successively motioning towards the southwest, northwest, and northeast. The fifth time she made a scoop in the middle of the pudding; this she followed by motioning lower down, towards the pegs holding the edge of the tent. While she was doing this, the others looked down, holding their left hand on the top of the head, the right hand on the ground. A small dog had been cooked whole. Backward took the dog by the head, and I took its hind-end, and we walked around the tent. We walked around again, stopping on the southeast side and making a turn there, and then the same successively at the southwest, northwest, and northeast (*i. e.*, going in a circle with the sun). Then we made a turn before the door (inside the tent), and held the dog outside the door, moving its head, and telling it to look about at the people, the clothing, the food, the water, and so on. Then we took pieces of meat from its four paws, its nose, the top of its head, and its tail, and put them on the ground four times, and a fifth time into the fire. Then Backward [1]

---

[1] Possibly it was not Backward, but the narrator herself, who performed this action.

took the dog's tongue, and, holding it at the tip, touched one side of it, and then the other, to the ground at the southeast, southwest, northwest, and northeast successively; and at last, with a downward movement, touched the tongue against the wooden pins fastening the front of the tent above the door. Then the food was eaten. A dish standing southeast from the fire was first taken and passed to each in the tent, travelling in a circle; then the food at the southwest was taken; and so on around the fire until all the food had been passed around. Then friends were called, and the remnants given to them. After the dishes and plates had been taken out of the tent, incense was again burned inside. Then Backward told me to give her the four knives, and a board on which to cut medicine. I took niibaa^{n}tou (hemlock-leaves) and niisêna^{n} (part of a beaver) and cut them fine. Backward took biihtceihina^{n} (a yellow composita) and niäätä^{n} (a greasy carrot-like root) and cut them up together. The rest cut up and mixed niôx^{u} (sweet-grass) with niisêna^{n}, and niäätä^{n} with niisêna^{n}. This made four kinds of incense. Then Backward, with a spoon of mountain-sheep horn, took up the several incenses and put them into the small bags into which they belonged. Again she put incense on the coals. Then they all painted themselves with red paint and tallow. After that they painted their bags: they touched them with their palms in four places, and then in a spot in the middle of these four, and thereupon rubbed the whole bag with paint. They also painted the stones (used for holding coals for incense) and the pieces of bone (used for marking designs on robes) that were in the bags. The latter two incenses are used when a tent is decorated; the former two, with the stones and bones, when a robe is to be made. They replaced all these things in their bags and closed them. Then Backward told me to give her the cloth goods I had provided. I gave them to her. She touched the ground and put her finger to her tongue; then she rubbed me over with medicine from her mouth. She spit medicine on a piece of the goods, and put it under my dress from below, and, passing it under the dress to my other side, took it out there and laid it down. Then she

passed another piece under my dress in the opposite direction.
She repeated this three times more, so that at the end there
were four pieces of goods lying on each side of me (those on
one side having been interchanged with those on the other by
passing them under the dress). Then she pushed two pieces
under my dress on my stomach, and successively placed them
below my shoulder, over the heart, and on my stomach again.
There she left them. The other goods were given away.
Backward told me to leave the pieces of cloth on my stomach
for four days, while I fasted; then to prepare food and invite
all the old women in again. I fasted and cried for four days;
on the fourth, food was prepared, and the old women came
again. After they had eaten, I received the bag, with instructions how to use it. Backward made a motion four
times to give it to me; then, at a fifth motion with it from
her heart, she gave it to me.

"A few days later, Yellow-Woman called me to make a
buffalo-robe. The hide was already dressed and prepared.
I entered the tent. At the back of the tent lay the buffalo-
skin, folded and laid like a buffalo. Its head was toward the
door. By it lay five pieces of goods as payment. I sat down
at the middle of the back of the tent, behind the buffalo-skin.
I told Yellow-Woman to call the other women. After they
came, food was taken around (and sacrificed), as at the time
when I received my bag. Then we ate, and the remainder
was taken out for friends and the children. Then I burned
incense. Then two of the women motioned toward the buffalo-skin with sticks, whipping it as if to make a buffalo rise.
Then I spread the robe (the hair-side to the ground). I put
a burning coal on the ground and placed incense upon it. I
spit medicine on one of the marking-bones five times. I held
the bone successively on four sides of the coal, near the
ground; the fifth time I drew the bone across above the coal,
to signify the marking (which is done by drawing the edge of
the bone along the hide). Then all came close around the
buffalo-robe and held it. Yellow-Woman with the marking-
bone drew lines across it, which were to be embroidered with
porcupine-quills. In her mouth she had häçawaanaxu, and

she wet the end of the bone with saliva. When she had
drawn the lines, she raised her right arm. I took the robe
and four times I made a motion as if to give it to her; the
fifth time I gave it to her, putting it under her arm. Then
Yellow-Woman held out her hands, and I spit medicine on
them four times. Then I laid on her hands four quills tied
together, one each being red, yellow, white, and black; and
with them I gave her sinew (thread) and needles. Yellow-
Woman passed the quills between her lips, and then held them
in her mouth. Then she began to embroider one line, beginning nearest the head of the skin. I watched her and gave
her directions. When she had completely embroidered this
line, she stopped. After this, one line was embroidered a
day. It took a month to complete the robe. A line of embroidery must not be left unfinished over night. When the
robe was completed, Yellow-Woman notified me. She invited me to come the next day to eat. The next day there
was a feast like that given when the robe was begun. The
robe was set up again to resemble a buffalo, and after being
perfumed with incense, was touched as if to make it rise.
Then it was spread out and five feathers laid upon it, — one
at each corner and one in the centre. Then the women sewed
the feathers in those places. Then Yellow-Woman an-
nounced the man for whom she had made the robe, and he
was sent for. He was Bird-in-Tree. He came in, and sat
down in front of me, looking toward the door. Yellow-
Woman spit on the blanket four times, moved it toward him
several times, then gave it to him. Then both he and the
robe were perfumed with incense. Then he gave Yellow-
Woman his best horse; she kissed him for it. Then he went
out with his new robe.''

This robe made by Yellow-Woman had twenty lines of
quill-work. The lowest three, as already described, were
close together and somewhat separate from the rest. The
lines represented buffalo-paths. The greater part of each of
these lines was yellow. On each were three red marks,
each of these red lengths being bordered by a shorter white
portion, and each of these again being bounded on both sides

by still shorter black marks.   There was thus imposed on the
yellow background of the line an ornament composed of the
successive colors black, white, black, red, black, white, black;
the red being longest and the black areas shortest.   This
same arrangement of the four colors is found in other objects
ornamented in conventional quill-embroidery.   Between these
marks on the lines of this robe there were other smaller
marks in red and black, and in several places small tufts of
red feathers (see Plate XVI).   The four colors of this embroidery, taken collectively, signified the four lives since the
beginning of the world (generations or æons).   From the
lower end of the robe hung fifty pendants, at the ends of
which hung small hoofs, and loops covered with quill-work,
this bearing the same design of black, white, black, red, black,
white, black, that was embroidered on the robe.

The use of these sacred bags and the accompanying ceremonies are also referred to in connection with the tent-decora-
tions on pp. 70 *et seq.*

II.—DECORATIVE ART.

The present chapter is a description of the various objects of Arapaho manufacture and use, omitting, however, all objects whose use is ceremonial or religious. This account will deal largely with the ornamentation of the objects and with the significance attached to this decoration. The interpretation of these symbolic decorations was obtained, in every case dealt with, from the Indians. Almost always the information was secured from the possessor or the maker of the article. The specimens described are now in the American Museum of Natural History.

In the illustrations, colors are indicated by the following devices: red, by close vertical shading; yellow, by light dots; green, by horizontal shading. Light blue is indicated by diagonal shading. Black usually represents dark blue, but sometimes brown, very dark green, dark red, or black. Dark dots indicate orange.

Plate I is arranged to show the conventionality of ornamentation in moccasins. All the moccasins illustrated in this series are embroidered with the same fundamental decorative motive, — a longitudinal stripe extending from instep to toe. It will be seen that in this series of eight moccasins only three other decorative elements are used; and these, moreover, are similar to the fundamental element, in that they also are stripes, and bear a definite spatial relation to it, being either parallel or at right angles to it. These three elements are a transverse stripe at the instep, two short bars approximately parallel to the main central stripe, and a transverse stripe bisecting and duplicating this main stripe.

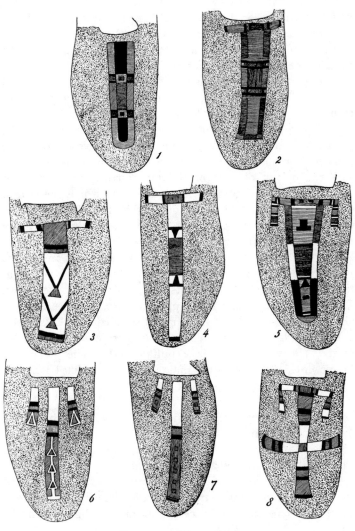

Designs on Moccasins.

The last element occurs only once (Fig. 8).[1] The longitudinal stripe is of two kinds: either it consists of three equal divisions or sections; or it has two parts, the upper one considerably shorter than the lower (Figs. 3, 6, 7).

Fig. 1 of Plate 1 shows a moccasin as to whose symbolic significance there is no information.[2]

In Fig. 2 of Plate 1 all the small stripes of which the beaded design is composed, whether their direction be longitudinal or transverse, represent buffalo-paths.

In Fig. 3 of the same plate the large stripe represents the path that is travelled (by the wearer). The two pieces of the transverse stripe (which, it will be noted, duplicate in miniature the design of part of the main stripe) are insects or worms which are found on the prairie, and which the wearer desired not to be in his path, but beside it. The upper portion of the large stripe is light blue, which signifies (as in many other cases) haze. The red and dark blue bands that edge the white portion of the stripe represent day and night. Red and black, or red and blue, frequently have this signification, both in ceremonial objects and in others not used thus. The winged triangle, which appears twice, signifies sunrise, also the passage over a mountain. It is called bääeikôtaha′ûû.

Fig. 4, Plate 1, shows a moccasin representing a buffalo-hunt. The white stripe is a buffalo-path. The green rectangle in this represents a buffalo. The two black triangular figures are barbed arrows shot into the buffalo. The transverse stripe is a bow.

As to the moccasins shown in Figs. 5 and 6 of this plate, information is wanting.

In Fig. 7, Plate 1, all the stripes represent buffalo-paths. The small blue squares are buffalo-tracks.

In Fig. 8, Plate 1, the two large stripes form a cross, and represent the morning star. The transverse line is the horizon. The two small bars represent rays of light from the star; *i. e.*, its twinkling.

---

[1] Plate 1 is here repeated for the convenience of the reader.
[2] This moccasin, together with those shown in Plate 1, Fig. 6, and in text Fig. 5, *a* and *c*, was secured for the Museum by Rev. Walter C. Roe.

Fig. 5 shows another series of moccasins. The decorative
motive which these all have in common is a border of bead-
work around the edge of the foot. All but one (*a*) also
possess the longitudinal stripe just described. This moccasin

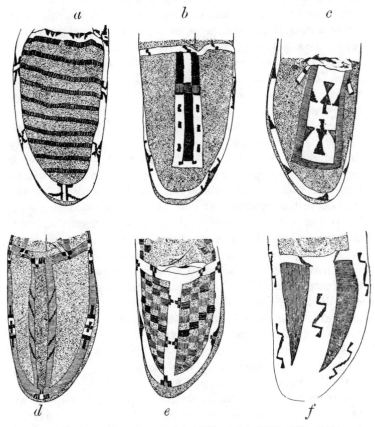

Fig. 5.   Designs on Moccasins.   *a* ($\frac{1}{5708}$), *b* ($\frac{50}{923}$), *c* ($\frac{1}{5730}$), *d* ($\frac{50}{658}$), *e* ($\frac{50}{327}$), *f* ($\frac{50}{1028}$).

has the entire area that is enclosed by the border, traversed
by lines of red porcupine-quill embroidery. Information as
to the meaning of this design is lacking.

On the moccasin shown in Fig. 5, *b*, the longitudinal
stripe signifies häⁿçaeixaaⁿtin (the path to destination).

A small stripe at the heel of the moccasin (not shown in the figure) signifies the opposite idea, häät[i]xa′nin (whence one has come). The variety of colors in the large stripe represents the variety of things (which naturally are of many different colors) that one desires to possess. The small dark-blue rectangles are symbols that are called hiiteni. The white border of this moccasin, on account of its color, represents snow. The figures in it represent hills with upright trees. The stripe over the instep signifies "up hill and down again" (its middle portion being elevated above the ends by the instep of the foot). The dots in this stripe represent places left bare by melting snow.

The writer is unable to give the exact meaning of the word hiiteni, mentioned above. This symbol is said to signify life, abundance, food, prosperity, temporal blessings, desire or hope for food, prayer for abundance, or the things wished for. All these related ideas seem to be identified by the Indians in this symbol. It may be best described as a symbol of happy life, or, since in Arapaho symbolism the representation of an object or condition usually implies a desire for such object or condition, a symbol of the desire for happy life. Briefly, it may be called a life-symbol, and will be thus designated hereafter. It is the abstract symbol most frequently used, and will be often referred to. Its form is generally a trapezoid, rectangle, or square. A variety of forms is shown in Plates XXIX, XXXI, Figs. 237–240, 417–422.

The symbolism in Fig. 5, *c*, is not known. Birds are evidently represented in the wide stripe.

Of the moccasin shown in Fig. 5, *d*, the symbolism is also unknown. In this specimen the longitudinal stripe is extended until it meets the border. The stripe, however, is beaded only at its edges, contrary to the style of embroidery in the other cases, and in its middle portion is merely painted red.

In the moccasin shown in Fig. 5, *e*, there are both the border and the stripe, triangular marks on which represent clouds along the horizon. The open areas are covered by a checker-board design, only every alternate square being beaded. This pattern represents the rough surface of buffalo-intestine. The beads in this pattern are green, blue, and pink; these colors represent respectively grass, sky, and ground.

The moccasin shown in Fig. 5, *f*, is completely beaded. The border and stripe exist in the application of the beads, and show in the coloring, being white. On these white areas are represented pipes. The two large triangular areas are red and green respectively. Together they represent buffalo-horns. The red and green also denote respectively bare ground (soil) and earth covered with grass; it is on these that the buffalo walk and trample. At the heel of the moccasin (not shown in the figure) is a small square, which represents a track. At the instep there is a tongue (also not illustrated), much like the tongue of a shoe, except that when the moccasin is worn, the tongue falls over the front of the foot (a similar tongue is seen in Plate III, Fig. 4). This tongue is beaded in light blue with dark-blue spots, is divided or forked, and has small tin cylinders (rattles) attached to its ends. It represents a rattlesnake. The beading is the spotted skin; the two parts of the tongue, the forked tongue of the snake; and the tin cylinders, its rattle.

Plate II shows several moccasins that are entirely covered with beads. All of these except that shown in Fig. 1, the pattern of which is unusual, are actually embroidered with the border and the longitudinal stripe, though sometimes, as in Figs. 2 and 5, these are not visible in the design because the beads are all of the same color.

In Fig. 1 of Plate II the rows of triangles on the front of the moccasins represent sharp rocks. Two rows of alternating red and blue squares are hills. Three red squares adjacent to each of these rows represent persons sitting on the hills. A light-blue line traversing the middle of the front of the moccasin is a path; small squares adjacent to it are rocks. Two small detached bars, one at each side of the entire design that has thus far been described, represent persons standing. Along the edge of the sole, flat triangles with small upright marks at each end, are hills and pines. Marks

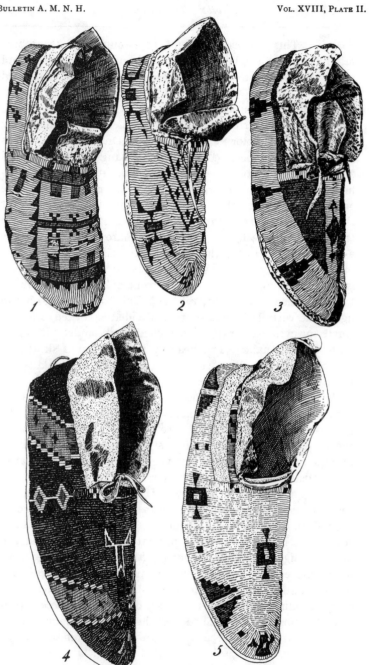

MOCCASINS.

consisting of two triangles touching at their vertices, represent rough places in the path: those that are red denote prominences; those that are blue signify holes. Crosses are the morning star. A horizontal stripe at the heel represents a caterpillar.

On the moccasin shown in Fig. 2 of Plate II the white groundwork of beads represents sand. The parallel angles on the instep of the moccasin are tents. Small rhomboidal marks are stars. At the toe a wide cross is the morning star. At the sides claw-shaped figures represent hakîxta^n (buffalo-hoofs). Between each pair of these figures is a yellow and red rectangle, which represents an eye. Small squares on the transverse stripe at the instep, and at the heel, represent tracks.

On the moccasin shown in Fig. 3 of Plate II the white background represents snow. The dark-blue triangles with squares in them are tents and their doors. The two large, greenish-blue triangular areas on the instep represent lakes. Between them a diamond represents the navel (or perhaps a child's navel-amulet). Triangles at each end of this diamond are arrow-points. A greenish-blue stripe around the ankle represents both smoke and water. Small squares at the instep and at the heel represent tracks.

The moccasin illustrated in Fig. 4 of Plate II is one of the few solidly-beaded Arapaho moccasins of which the ground color is not white. It is a rich blue, and the figures upon it are chiefly pink and red. The blue represents the sky. The large parallelograms are clouds with white edges, piled up one on the other. Red crosses or diamonds in these are stars. Larger, white-edged rhombi in the blue are also stars. A triangle at the toe is a tent. In the middle of the front, a red figure represents a crayfish or scorpion.

Fig. 5 of Plate II shows another solidly-beaded moccasin. Green squares, enclosing a smaller square that is white and red, are life-symbols (hiiteni). Small red triangles in contact with the life-symbols are tents. Small black squares in several places on the white ground are rabbit-tracks in snow. The triangular figures represent seats (çiôku'utaana^n). The stripe around the ankle represents biisä^n, any snake or worm. Separate parts of this stripe have other additional significations. The forward portion is yellow, and denotes sunlight. Black squares are again rabbit-tracks. Five red squares in quincunx on a white ground are a turtle. The posterior portion of the stripe is green, and denotes the earth.

Three children's moccasins are shown in the first three figures of Plate III.

In Fig. 1, Plate III, the two lateral convexly triangular areas on the front of the moccasin are green, and represent horse-ears. It may be noted that analogous areas on other moccasins represent buffalo-horns, lakes, and fish. The figure between these two green areas represents a lizard. The head is supposed to be at the toe. Two blue slanting lines are legs. White and yellow spots on the red body are the markings of the animal. Below the ankle, a red stripe with two blue diagonal lines represents a butterfly.

Fig. 2 of Plate III shows a moccasin which is beaded around the edges, but has its front surface traversed by a number of quilled lines (*cf.* Fig. 5, *a*). The white beadwork represents the ground. Green zigzag lines upon it are snakes. The quilled lines represent sweat-house poles. These lines are red, blue, and yellow, and the colors represent stones of different colors, used for producing steam in the sweat-house. At the heel of the moccasin, which is not shown in the figure, are two small green squares. These represent the blankets with which the sweat-house is covered.

The design of a snake was embroidered on this moccasin in order that the child wearing it might not be bitten by snakes. The symbols referring to the sweat-house were embroidered on the moccasin in order that the child might grow to the age at which the sweat-house is principally used; namely, old age.

The moccasin shown in Fig. 3, Plate III, bears a design similar to several that have been described. All the stripes represent paths.

Fig. 4 of Plate III shows an unusually large moccasin. The two large convex, triangular areas on the front are barred

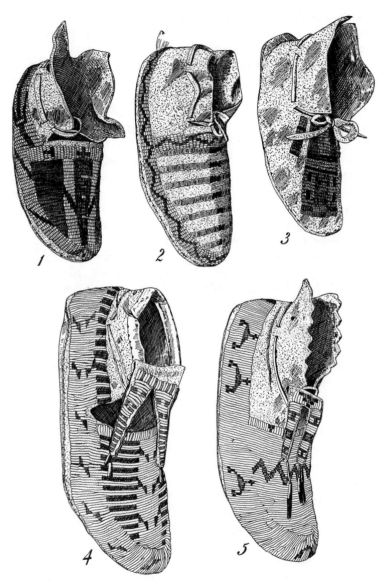

MOCCASINS.

dark blue and white. They represent fish. The similarly barred stripe around the ankle also represents a fish (or the markings on a fish). Small figures, some red, some blue, consisting of a pair of triangles joined at the vertices, represent butterflies. The double tongue over the instep represents a horned toad (*i. e.*, its markings).

On the moccasin shown in Fig. 5 of this plate the zigzag band across the front represents lightning.

What may be considered a typical solidly-beaded moccasin is shown in Plate IV. The white represents snow. The green, both in the triangular areas and in the stripe around the ankle, represents grass-covered earth. The blue and yellow figures consisting of three triangles represent the heart and lungs. The white stripe bisected by two shorter ones, inside the green triangular areas, is a dragon-fly. Groups of three small light-blue squares near the instep were described as halves of stars (five squares in quincunx sometimes represent a star). At the heel, four small green rectangles (invisible in the illustration) represent caterpillars. The design on this moccasin was embroidered as it was previously seen in a dream.

Fig. 6 shows two views of one of the leggings worn by a little girl. The moccasin is attached to the legging. The skin of which the legging is made is painted yellow wherever it is not covered by beads, excepting in the white-bordered stripe running alongside the shin of the leg; in this the skin is painted red. The designs worked on the legging were seen in a dream or vision. This pair of leggings was considered exceptionally handsome by the Arapaho; it always attracted attention at once. The design on each side of the legging, consisting of two connected triangles, represents a mountain with the morning star above it. (The figure of the mountain is symmetrically duplicated, which gives the star, represented by a cross, the appearance of being between two mountains, the upper one inverted.) At the back of the legging the rhombus represents the morning star when it is rising; the two crosses are the morning star when it is high up above the horizon. The contact of the crosses with the

1

2

Moccasin and Pouch.

line signifies that the star appears just before daybreak. The yellow painting of the skin represents daylight. The two white beaded stripes up the front of the legging represent the partly divided milky way. The colored designs in these stripes de-

Fig. 6 ($\frac{50}{6144}$). Girl's Leggings.

note small stars of many colors along the edge of the milky way. On the moccasin the large, green triangular areas represent the earth in spring. The diamond situated between these green areas is a star supposed to be visible directly over-head at noon. The six diamonds connected by a line passing

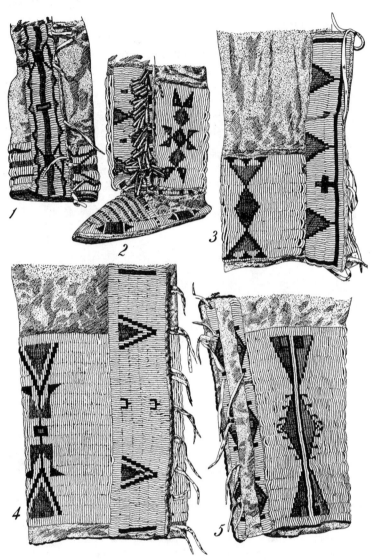

PARTS OF GIRLS' AND WOMEN'S LEGGINGS.

around the edge of the moccasin are a ring of stars, probably the constellation Corona.

Another legging worn by a little girl is shown in Fig. 1 of Plate v. The moccasin has been removed. The design appears twice, once on the vertical band, and again on the horizontal band extending around the ankle. The two rows of small triangles represent ranges of hills. The red stripe along the middle of the white band of beads represents ground. Two green squares in this are springs. Four blue lines issuing from each of these squares are streams flowing from the springs. A small yellow bar bisecting the red stripe is a river; its dark-blue border is timber along its course. A row of green and blue beads along the edges of the legging represents game of various kinds.

Fig. 2 of Plate v shows another girl's legging and moccasin. The three diamonds in the centre of the figure that is on the side of the legging are the life-symbols. Above and below the three diamonds are figures, each consisting of two dark-blue right-angled triangles. These represent deer-tracks. Two similar figures, wider and green in color, touch the middle one of the three diamonds; they represent elk-tracks. This whole design is repeated on the opposite side of the legging. At the back, also invisible in the illustration, is a long red line crossed by nine short lines; this represents a centipede. Along the front of the legging the triangular designs are tents; and the red rectangles, life-symbols. The tin rattles are attached to the legging in order that by their noise they may frighten away insects or snakes that would bite the child wearing the legging. On the lower border of the moccasin are rectangles of red and green beads. These are again life-symbols. This symbol thus has three different forms on one object. Dark-blue triangles, two of which are near each of the life-symbols last mentioned, represent the designs, largely composed of triangles, with which rawhide bags and parfleches are painted. The red lines of quill-work extending across the toe of the moccasin represent the paths of children.

Embroidered portions of girls' and women's leggings are

shown in Figs. 3, 4, 5, of Plate v. In Fig. 3 the triangles represent arrow-points. Those that have three small dark triangles at their base also represent tents. The cross is the morning star. The line with which it is in contact is a path. At the back of the legging, invisible in the illustration, is a figure of a buffalo-leg, symmetrically duplicated; the hoof of this resembles the deer-track design on the legging last described.

In Fig. 4, Plate v, the triangles denote tents. Between the two triangles on the side of the legging, whose points are directed toward each other, are two figures which coalesce in the middle. These figures represent the hä^{n}tcäciihi teihiiha^n, a powerful dwarf cannibal people several times mentioned in Arapaho myths. The tents are supposed to belong to them. The blue bar at the base of the wide vertical stripe of embroidery indicates the range or limit of habitation of the dwarfs. The dark Y-shaped marks are horse-tracks; they imply (in this connection) human beings (as opposed to monstrous or supernatural people). At the back of the legging there is a vertical row of these horse-tracks. The green beads at the edges of this legging represent vegetation.

In Fig. 5 of Plate v the yellow and green right-angled triangles, each with a small square of the opposite color at the base, represent tents. The white stripe dividing them is a path. Between the figures of tents, a green and a yellow isosceles triangle are each a cactus-plant. The projections arising from them represent the cactus-spines. On one of the figures these projections are red, and therefore represent also the red edible fruit of the cactus. This whole design is repeated on the opposite side of the legging. At the back of the legging is a vertical row of seventeen (green and red) isosceles triangles, the base of one resting upon the point of the next lower one. These represent ant-hills. They are not shown in the illustration. Along the front of the legging the flat triangles represent brush-shelters. The small upright marks at the ends of each figure are the tent-pegs at the sides of the shelter.[1] The rows of beads along the edges of the legging represent animals or variety of game.

---

[1] The brush-shelter is often partially covered with canvas. Formerly hides were used for this purpose. This cover may be pegged down like a tent.

Fig. 7, *a*, represents one of a pair of armlets covered with beadwork. Such armlets or sleeve-holders are generally worn chiefly on gala occasions; that is, at dances. The red and green bisected squares represent black beetles with hard *elytræ*. Small loops of beads along the edge represent worms or maggots. The large beads on the two attached strings rep-

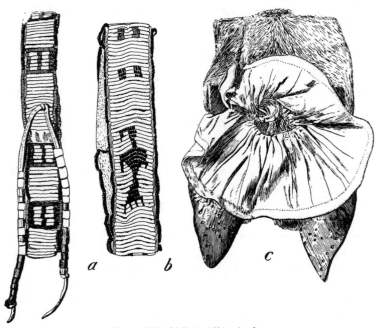

Fig. 7, *a* (⁵⁰⁄₉₉₆), *b* (⁵⁰⁄₁₁₀₀), *c* (⁵⁰⁄₉₇₈). Armlets.

resent ants. These various insects were represented because they are constantly moving and crawling, just as the people travelled and roamed over the earth.

One of another pair of armlets is shown in Fig. 7, *b*. The figure of a bird represents both an eagle (on account of the crooked beak) and a swallow (on account of the forked tail). The squares, both blue and red, are stars. The white ground-work of beads represents haze or smoke; the blue beading at the edge represents clouds or the sky.

Fig. 7, *c*, shows an unembroidered armlet, made of the skin from an elk-foot. A round piece of green cloth attached to the skin represents the sun. The two pieces of hoof represent the long, curving nails of old persons. The small holes in these hoofs represent the various things possessed by the owner of this armlet. These holes also have another signification: those around the edges of the hoofs denote stars; and five holes in quincunx in the middle of each hoof represent (the five fingers of) the hand, which is symbolically equivalent to possession of property.

One of a pair of red quill-embroidered armlets is shown in Fig. 1 of Plate VI. It was worn in the ghost-dance. The black squares represent buffalo. The red quill-wound strings falling from the armlet are kakau'çetcana^n (thoughts, reason, imagination, hope, desires, or anything mental). The ornaments at their ends represent näii'täte'ihi (fulfilment of desire).

Fig. 2 of Plate VI shows a woman's ghost-dance armlet, embroidered with yellow quill-work. The bird embroidered in green quills represents a magpie. The red cross is the morning star. The red rectangle is the symbol of life.

The fringe of green-dyed buckskin represents rays of light, and (on account of its color) the earth. The attached magpie-feathers represent persons (presumably spirits); and small yellow plumes attached to these represent the sun.

Fig. 3 of Plate VI shows a head-dress. It consists of a small hoop wound with yellow quills. Two owl-feathers are attached to it. It is worn on the side of the head. The circular quill-wrapped portion with four black spots on it represents a sun-dog.

A peculiar head-dress, which is found among many of the Plains tribes, consists of a strip of skin, measuring about two inches by eight, which is covered with beads or quills, and has various strings or appendages attached to it. It is worn hanging from the scalp-lock, at the back of the head. Among the Arapaho, a horse-tail is generally attached to the lower end of this head-dress. It is worn by young men on festive occasions and at ceremonials at which uniform regalia are not prescribed. Many of these head-dresses represent animals.

ARMLETS AND HEAD-DRESS.

The specimen shown in Plate VII, Fig. 1, represents a rat. The possessor and maker of this head-dress explained his choice of this animal as an object of representation, by the occurrence of the rat in a number of tales about the mythic personage Nih'a^{n}ça^n. It is a fact, however, that all the objects of Arapaho manufacture which represent animals at all, denote small animals such as the lizard, frog, fish, or rat. The cross on this specimen is the conventional na^{n}kaox, or morning star.

Fig. 2 of the same plate shows one of these head-dresses worked in quills. The horse-tail is dyed golden-yellow. This color was chosen by the wearer of the head-dress because he was desirous of possessing a horse of this color. The horse-hair is also a symbol of good luck, because horses are the usual gifts when presents are made.

The animal symbolism is fairly well worked out in this specimen. The quill-work is the body of a rat; the horse-tail, its tail. The long pendants at the four corners are of course the legs. Two loops at the top of the head-dress are the rat-ears, and two strings of red beads at the top represent the pointed mouth. Down the middle of the red quill-work runs a green stripe, which is a path. Blue, yellow, and green squares at the sides of this stripe represent (the tracks of?) rats running into the path.

Fig. 3 of Plate VII shows a similar head-dress representing a lizard. It is worked in beads, and the tail is twisted and dyed red. The bead-work design is the morning-star cross.

The navel-strings of Arapaho girls are preserved and sewed into small pouches stuffed with grass. These pouches are usually diamond-shaped and covered on both sides with beads. The child wears this amulet, which contains its navel-string, on its belt until it is worn out.

Such amulets are found among many tribes. Among some they are worn by boys as well as girls, or two are worn by one child. Among the Sioux these amulets sometimes have the shape of horned toads. Among the Assiniboine they are generally diamond-shaped, but less elongated than among the Arapaho. Among the Gros Ventres they are often diamond-

3

1

2

HEAD-DRESSES.

shaped; they sometimes represent a person, but more usually a horned toad, and sometimes have the figure of this animal. Among the Utes these navel-amulets are also diamond-shaped, but they are attached to the infant's cradle. Among the Arapaho they usually represent a small animal.

In connection with the usual diamond shape of these amulets, it may be observed that throughout the decorative symbolism of the Arapaho the navel is represented by a diamond-shaped symbol.

Fig. 1 of Plate VIII shows the only example of navel-amulets possessing realistic shape, seen among the Arapaho. It is further unique in not being beaded on the under side. It represents a lizard (säni'wa^n). This word, in Gros Ventre, means "horned toad," but in Arapaho seems to signify "lizard." The Arapaho regard the horned toad, which they call by the same name as a mule (bihiiha^{n}x), as a good animal, and do not kill it.

The more decoratively conventionalized form of navel-amulet is seen in Fig. 2 of Plate VIII. This object represents a fish. The diagonal lines indicate its appearance (*i. e.*, the markings of the fish).

The amulet shown in Fig. 3, Plate VIII, represents a tadpole (hiseinôtä^n, literally " woman's belly "). Two figures upon it in dark-blue beadwork represent stars. These forms appear to be modifications of the cross, which usually denotes the morning star. The red ornament in the middle represents the butterfly, or possibly the dragon-fly; it could not be determined which. The white beaded background represents snow.

Fig. 4 of Plate VIII illustrates another amulet representing a lizard (säni'wa^n). The dark blue and yellow areas signify its markings, while the bisecting lines represent paths.

The previous specimens are alike on both sides. Figs. 5 and 6 of Plate VIII, however, represent the two differing sides of one navel-amulet. The whole object represents the navel itself, also a frog. The two dark-blue trapezoidal ornaments in Fig. 5 represent miniature or toy bags, resembling those ordinarily used, but made for children. Below, a (red and

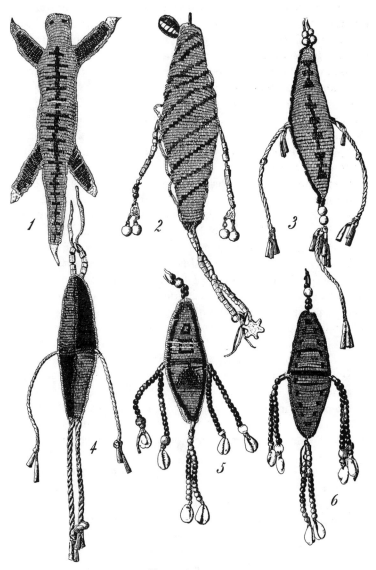

NAVEL-AMULETS.

pale-blue) triangle with a stripe across its point represents a female dress (evidently that of the little girl who wore the amulet). The golden-yellow background and the black stripe around it represent (the color of) the girl's hair respectively as it is now in her youth (her hair being light brown) and as it will be when she has grown older. On the other side (Fig. 6) the stripes or lines represent navel-strings. The green and blue single lines of beads at the seam or edge of the pouch represent sinew. The loose pendants of large beads represent navel-strings; the shells at their ends represent teeth.

In addition to the representation of a frog, there are three lines of symbolism in this object. First, teeth and color of hair are often used in symbolism to denote age, and express a wish for old age; the toy bags, and possibly the dress and navel-strings, also refer to the age of childhood. Secondly, the dress, and perhaps the sinew (which serves as thread, and therefore denotes sewing, woman's occupation), symbolize sex. Thirdly, the navel, and therefore also the navel-strings, symbolize the human being (ini'tä^n).

It will be seen from these figures that the navel-amulet of the conventional diamond form has a pair of strings at the sides, which denote the legs or fins of the animal represented. When a lizard, frog, or fish is represented, these strings aid the slight similarity of the pouch to the animal; but when a tadpole is represented, as in Fig. 3, it is evident that their effect is the opposite, and that their presence is due to the prevalence, in this point, of stylistic convention over accuracy of symbolism. But a specimen like the first one described (Fig. 1) shows the opposite predominance of representative accuracy over decorative convention. From this it would seem that there is always some tendency toward realistic symbolism, and some toward ornamental convention, but that the relative proportion of the two varies considerably in different individuals making decorated objects.

One-half of the front of a bead-covered waistcoat is shown in Fig. 8. This garment is of course modern. The figures that may be described as inverted Y's are sticks or racks set up inside the tent to hang saddles and blankets upon. The designs above them are saddle-blankets. The cross is the morning star. A row of blue squares represents rocks. A blue stripe represents a rope. Below this are ornaments consisting of a line with a hollow square at the bottom. These represent men's stirrups. On the back of the waistcoat, instead of these ornaments, are others consisting of a line with a triangle at the bottom. These represent women's stirrups. The Arapaho at present use saddles of their own manufacture for women. These have triangular stirrups of wood and rawhide. The men ride American saddles, which usually have oval wooden stirrups. Thus, as in many other cases (the sky, the earth, the sacred hoop), the square or rectangle here represents something circular or oval. In symbolism anything four-sided or four-cornered is equivalent to a circle, and anything circular is considered to have four ends.

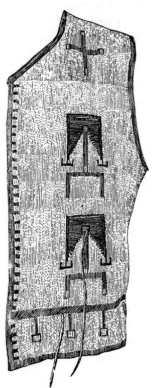

Fig. 8 ($\frac{50}{1000}$). Front of Beaded Waist-coat.

Tents, even now that canvas has replaced buffalo-hides, are still often decorated with a conventional set of ornaments. These ornaments are the following.

1. A circular piece of hide about eight inches in diameter, covered with embroidery of beads or quills (Plate IX, Fig. 2). This is sewed to the back of the tent at its very top, just below the place where it is fastened to the hiinana'kaya[n], — the pole in the middle of the back which is used to raise the tent into position. To the bottom of this ornament are

attached two buffalo (or cattle) tails. This ornament is called kaⁿeibiihi.

2. Four similarly embroidered pieces of skin considerably smaller (Plate IX, Fig. 1). These are attached to the sides of the tent, several feet above the bottom, at the southeast, southwest, northwest, and northeast (the tent always facing east). To the middle of each of these ornaments is attached a buffalo-tail and a pendant consisting of three quill-wrapped strings which have at their ends the small dew-claws of buffalo and a quill-wrapped loop.

3. A series of pendants, each triple, with dew-claws and loops at the ends (Plate IX, Fig. 3). These resemble the pendants just described, except that instead of strings, wider strips of skin are wound with porcupine-quills. When quills are not to be had, corn-husk or plant-fibres are used. These pendants, called xaxanäähihi, are attached in two vertical rows to the front of the tent, where it is fastened together above the door; also to the edge of the two flaps or ears at the top (which give light and ventilation, but can be closed when it rains).

These three sets of objects constitute the regular ornamentation of a tent.

These tent-ornaments are of three different kinds, the patterns in the circular embroidery varying slightly.

Fig. 9, *a*, shows one of the three kinds. The design consists of alternating black and yellow concentric circles and of four black-edged white radii.

Fig. 9, *b*, shows a second style, which contains four colors, whereas the first contains three. This may be described as similar to the preceding, excepting that the two sectors enclosed by the four radii are solidly red instead of continuing the black and yellow circles that cover the main part of the surface. The specimen figured has teeth around its edge. Such teeth may be either present or absent in any of the three styles.

The black and yellow concentric rings represent the whirlwind, or perhaps more exactly the course of Whirlwind-Woman. When the earth was first made (and was still small),

Näyāaⁿxati'sei (Whirlwind-Woman) did not know where to stop (to rest), and went from place to place. As she circled, the earth grew until it reached its present extent. When she stopped, she had gone over the whole earth. It was she who first made this tentornament, which represents what she did.

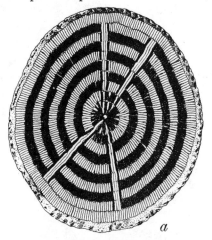

The two preceding styles are both known as "black" on account of their black circles. The third style lacks these, and is therefore called "white." It is also called xanāⁿkū'bää, *i. e.*, "straight-standing-red," on account of its two opposite red sectors. This third style is like the second except that instead of being banded black and yellow, it is solid yellow.

The specimen shown in Fig. 2 of Plate IX is of this third kind. It represents the sun, on account of both its shape and its prevailing yellow color. The two red sectors are tents containing persons (red sometimes signifies man-

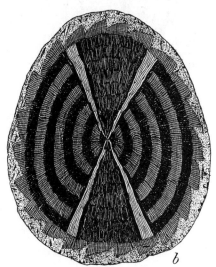

Fig. 9, *a* ($\frac{50}{388}$), *b* ($\frac{50}{298}$a). Tent-ornaments. Longest diameter, 19 cm., 26 cm.

kind in Arapaho color-symbolism). The teeth at the circumference represent persons.

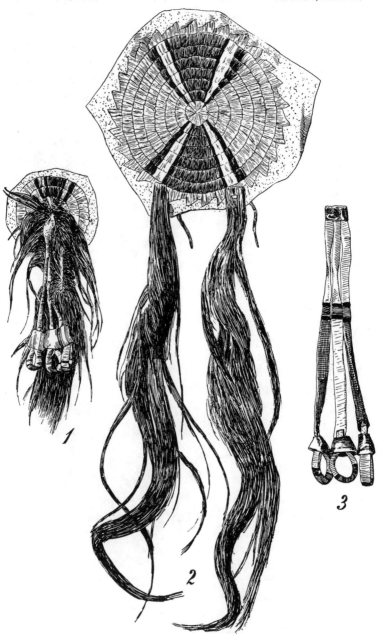

TENT-ORNAMENTS.

Another specimen of this third kind, worked in beads, was said to represent, as a whole, the sun.   The red sectors, at the opposite sides (ends) of the circle, are the red of sunrise and sunset.   The white and black radii bordering these sectors can be regarded as two intersecting diameters, forming a cross. Therefore they are the morning star.

The four small circular ornaments going with each of the large ones that have been described are miniature reproductions of these, except that the small ornaments of the first two styles omit radii and sectors, consisting only of concentric black and yellow circles.

The pendants are more variable than the circular tent-ornaments.   Sometimes they are entirely yellow.   Generally they contain some red.   Very frequently there is a white portion with black edgings.   The one shown in Plate IX, Fig. 3, has green upon it.   The rule seems to be to employ only the four colors red, yellow, black, and white.

One kind of pendant is entirely orange; another (Fig. 10), from the upper part downward, yellow, purple, white, purple, orange.   The purple probably stands for black.   The arrangement of colors in Fig. 10 is similar to that shown in Plate IX, Fig. 3, except that the middle strip is white and of greater width.   Generally the upper part, at which the three pendants hang together, is wrapped with quills of the same color as the upper parts of the pendants.   The rings at the lower ends of the present specimen are red, white, and black.

Instead of the large circular embroidery, a rectangular or trapezoidal figure of beadwork is sometimes attached to the top of the back of the tent.   Fig. 11 shows such an ornament. It is called nīhā^{n}xā$''^n$hayā^n ("yellow-oblong"?).   It is worked in red, yellow, black, and white.[1]

This rectangular form is probably more typical of the Cheyenne than of the Arapaho, though the Cheyenne also have the circular ornaments.   The Gros Ventres formerly possessed circular ornaments similar to those of the Arapaho, but no longer use them; merely a few detached specimens are still

---

[1] By mistake the yellow in this specimen is indicated as green in the illustration.

in existence.   Among the Shoshone, Bannock, and Ute, the writer has not seen any tent-ornaments.   The Blackfeet also did not use them.

A Cheyenne tent-ornament in the American Museum of Natural History exactly resembles the Arapaho one illustrated in Plate IX, Fig. 2, except that blue is substituted for the white.   Another Cheyenne tent-ornament seen by the

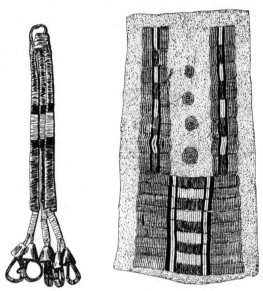

Fig. 10.   Fig. 11.
Figs. 10 ($\frac{50}{1000}$b), 11 ($\frac{50}{896}$).   Tent-ornaments.   Length, 27 cm., 23 cm.

writer was identical with these two, except that it was green where these were respectively white and blue.

It appears that the combination of red, yellow, black, and white, while not confined to the Arapaho, is more characteristic of their tribal ornamentation than of that of their neighbors.   When green is used by the Arapaho in the embroidery of such tribally-decorated objects, it may replace either red or white.

Designs and color combinations very similar to those of tent-ornaments are found on other objects in which a highly conventional style of quill-embroidery formerly prevailed.

These objects are particularly buffalo-robes, buffalo-skin blankets or pillows, and cradles.

Fig. 12 shows one of twenty lines embroidered in quills across a buffalo-robe, previously mentioned on p. 34. The line represents a buffalo-path. The four colors — the conventional red, yellow, black, and white — represent the four lives (generations or periods) since the beginning of the world, one for each color.

If one follows the circumference of one of the circular tent-ornaments (as of Fig. 2, Plate IX), excepting the first style, which lacks red, one meets in the course of this circumference the same succession of colors, and the same relative amount or proportional width of each, as on this straight line on the buffalo-robe. In each case the bulk or body of the line is

Fig. 12. Quill-embroidered Line.

yellow; there are red spaces of considerable size; these are bordered by smaller white spaces; and these, finally, are bordered by still narrower black spaces.

Buffalo-skins, from the head and neck of the animal, were used to hang over the head of the bed. One of these skins seen by the writer was ornamented in the following manner.

1. The horns were not attached to the skin. Where the eye had been there was sewed one of the small circular tent-ornaments consisting of yellow and black concentric rings. 2. The place of the top of the head was covered by a quill-work ornament called the "brain," which was nothing else than one of the large circular tent-ornaments of the style that lacks the black concentric rings. 3. The place of the ear was covered by a figure embroidered in beads and quills. This was trapezoidal, the smaller of the bases being convexly rounded. This ornament is shown in Fig. 13. Most of it is yellow. The middle portion is red; this is bordered by two white stripes, which are edged by black lines. 4. Along the "throat," that is, along one of the sides of the piece of skin, was a fourth ornament. This consisted of two strips of hide extending the length of the skin, parallel to each other at a

distance of about six inches. Connecting these were about thirty short strips of hide, each about half an inch wide. These strips were wound with corn-husk of the four colors,— red, yellow, black, and white. The arrangement and proportion of colors on these strips were identical with those on the ornament representing the ear. In addition, three or four smaller strips, with the same color-pattern, were put on each of the long pieces of hide, extending in the same direction as these; that is, vertically. This entire ornament, in its general character, somewhat resembled the long ornament hanging from the cradle shown in Fig. 14, *b*.

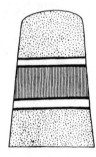

Fig. 13.   Buffalo-skin Ornament.

These buffalo-skin pillows with the tribal ornamentation were decorated, like tents and robes, under the direction of the old women possessing the sacred seven workbags. It is probable that the last specimen of this kind has now perished.

Cradles, or infant-carriers, are also decorated in a style similar to tent-ornaments. The embroidery is altogether in quills. Sometimes, however, only three colors are used on these cradles, instead of four. There are two chief lines of symbolism connected with this ornamentation. According to one interpretation, the various ornaments represent the child that is in the cradle. According to the other interpretation, these ornaments represent parts of the tent. When the child grows up, it will inhabit its own tent as now it inhabits the cradle. Therefore this symbolism serves to express a wish that the child may reach the age of manhood or womanhood.

Fig. 14, *b*, shows such a cradle. The round ornament near the top of the cradle, situated over the top of the child's head, represents the head or skull of the child. The long ornament, consisting of two strips of hide connected by red, black, and white quill-wrapped strips, represents the child's hair. The smooth, slippery quills denote the greasy hair of the child. At the lower part of the cradle the long quill-covered thongs represent ribs. The lowest pair, however, are the legs. Of the three colors in the embroidery, red represents blood; black, the hair (of youth and middle age); white, (the hair of) old age. Of the sticks forming the framework inside the cradle, one is unpeeled, the other peeled. The unpeeled one denotes that the child is as yet helpless and dirty in its cradle;

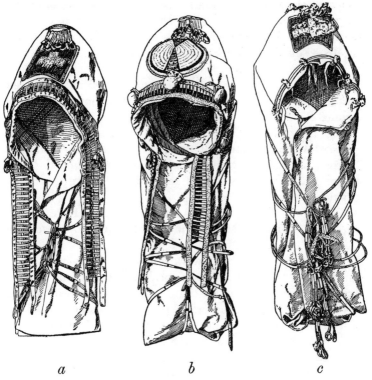

a   b   c

Fig. 14, *a* ($\frac{50}{1075}$), *b* ($\frac{50}{988}$), *c* ($\frac{50}{1060}$).   Cradles.

the peeled stick represents its subsequent more cleanly condition.

The round ornament at the top of this cradle, besides denoting the head of the child, represents also a tent-ornament, which indeed it closely resembles. The tent-ornament signifies that the child, when it has grown up, will have a tent. Above the round ornament are pendants having small hoofs and quill-wrapped loops at their ends. These represent the pendants or rattles above the door of the tent. Still higher up than these on the cradle, are two quill-wound strips lying parallel to each other. These represent man and woman, since a man and a woman own a tent together. On the ornament representing hair are several pairs of pendants having loops at their ends. These loops represent the holes in the bottom of the tent through which the tent-pegs pass. The whole cradle, owing to its shape and the fact of its being stretched on a framework of sticks, resembles a tent-door, and therefore represents it.

Both of these extensive symbolic interpretations were given by one and the same person to the ornamentation of one cradle.

Fig. 14, *a*, shows a cradle like the preceding, except that in place of the round ornament over the head there is a rectangular one of red quill-work on which is a white cross. The shape of this probably has reference to the rectangular tent-ornaments sometimes used.

Very similar to the two cradles just described are two in the Field Columbian Museum in Chicago. One of these contains green in its quill-work.

Fig. 14, *c*, shows a cradle worked in yellow quill-embroidery instead of red. The rectangular ornament containing a white cross is similar to that on the cradle last described, but in several other respects this cradle differs in ornamentation.

The oblong ornament at the top represents the head of the child. Yellow wool embroidered upon it is hair. A stripe of blue beads surrounding this ornament represents face-paint. At the lower part of the cradle are the ribs of the child.

The oblong ornament also represents a tent-ornament. The pendants above it are the rattles at the top of the tent. They signify that it is wished that the child may become old enough to possess a tent. Yellow strips surrounding the opening of the cradle represent the circumference of the base of the tent. Tufts of wool at intervals between these strips represent the places of the tent-pegs. The ornaments that are called ribs are also the pins used for fastening together the front of the tent, just above the door. Rattle-pendants attached to them represent the pendants on the tent alongside of these pins, lower down than those referred to at the top of the tent.

Quill-embroidered cradles have been seen by the writer only among the northern Arapaho. Beaded cradles, which are used among both portions of the tribe, are very different in design and symbolism.

A beaded cradle is shown in Fig. 15. Dark-blue triangles represent tents. Green rectangles, with three projections at each end, represent brush-shelters or sun-shades, with the poles on which they stand. A long red stripe is a path. Around the edge of the cradle are marks that are blue, red, and yellow. These represent piles of stones marking the extent of the camp-circle. At the bottom a border passing completely around the cradle represents the camp-circle of tents. At the very top an attached square with a broad cross in it represents the morning star. In a similar square from the top of a Cheyenne cradle, Ehrenreich[1] found designs that had a highly abstract significance.

A Sioux cradle in the American Museum of Natural History bears a resemblance to this one that is very remarkable. Nothing is known of the symbolism attached to this cradle by the Sioux.

Fig. 15 (₅₀/₈₅). Beaded Cradle. Length, 69 cm.

Fig. 16 shows a figure in the shape of a tent-ornament, which was intended to be attached to the head of a cradle.

---

[1] Ethnologisches Notizblatt, 1899, II, 1, p. 27.

Fig. 17 shows the tent-ornament design slightly altered, and used to cover one side of a ball.

Tent-ornaments are generally attached to the tent with a certain amount of ceremony. This is done by an assemblage of old women, one or more of whom are possessors of one of the seven sacred women's bags that have been referred to. The ceremonies are similar to those that have been described as taking place in connection with the transfer of one of the sacred bags or with the embroidering of a robe (pp. 30 et seq.).

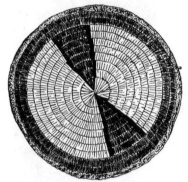 

Fig. 16 (₁₅₈₇). Cradle-ornament. Fig. 17 (₇₈₉). Beaded Ornament for Ball.
Diam., 14.5 cm. Diam., 15 cm.

The following is a description of the ceremonies accompanying the ornamentation of a tent, as witnessed by the writer.

A middle-aged woman who wished her tent decorated had prepared the ornaments. These consisted, when the ceremony began, of a piece of skin on which the large circular ornament had been beaded; of the four smaller ornaments, also of embroidered hide; of cow-tails to be attached to the circular ornaments; of four sets of thin pendants, to be attached, with the tails, to the four small circles; of fourteen quill-wound yellow pendants, bearing small hoofs at the ends; of sixteen similar yellow pendants which were ornamented with the design black, white, black, red, black, white, black, that has been previously described (p. 34); and of red flannel to be cut into pieces to be hung on the pendants next to the hoofs. The canvas tent which was to be ornamented had been taken down, but the poles had been left standing, and all the household property was still in place under them. The ceremonial attachment of the ornaments took place in another tent, perhaps a hundred feet away from the bare framework of poles. The camp broke and moved that morning, and soon these two tents were the only ones left standing. The woman who had been called to preside over the ceremony was the one from whom the account of the use of the sacred bags was obtained by the writer (see p. 30). She was called Cedar-Woman.

The owner of the tent that was to be ornamented sent a wagon to bring Cedar-Woman. She, however, was not ready, and remained in her tent, painting herself and putting on a good dress. Finally she came on foot, followed by another old woman who possessed a sacred bag, and by a third elderly woman. The food, which is a requisite of the ceremony, was already in the tent, set on the ground around the fireplace. There was now a delay in order that more elderly women might be secured. At last enough were found. With the last comers the writer entered the tent, from which men are ordinarily supposed to be excluded. Cedar-Woman, the head of the ceremony, sat at the back of the tent (*i. e.*, opposite the door, which, as always, faced east). At each side of the tent sat four women, the owner of the tent sitting next to the door. The women were cutting the red cloth into strips and attaching it to the ends of the pendants. The entirely yellow pendants were being worked upon on one side of the tent, the four-colored ones by the women on the other side. Cedar-Woman had the piece of hide on which the large circular beaded ornament was embroidered, and was cutting out the ornament from it. Later she fastened the thin pendants to the cow-tails. While at work putting the ornaments together, all the women seemed to speak and laugh freely. The owner of the tent once went out to get an awl.

The owner of the tent now arose from her place by the door and kneeled before Cedar-Woman, who took medicine from her sacred bag and began to chew it. The kneeling woman held out her two palms together. Cedar-Woman touched her

finger to the ground, and then placed it five times on the
other woman's joined palms, in four spots forming a circle. and
then in the middle.   The course of her finger was from right
to left, contrary to the usual ceremonial order.   Then she spit
a minute quantity of medicine on the same places on the
woman's two hands; the latter then rubbed herself all over
with her hands.[1]   Cedar-Woman spit on her two cheeks, and
then on her own hand, which she placed on the kneeling
woman's breast and then on the top of her head.   She also
took some of the medicine from her own mouth and put it
into the other's.   The woman then rose and walked around
past the fire and the dishes (which occupied the centre of the
tent) to the door.   Then she took up a dish of food that stood
towards the southeast (*i. e.*, not far from the door), and, holding it just above the ground, walked around the fireplace
from left to right.   Then she gave it to the woman before
whom it had stood.   Going to the southwest quarter of the
tent, she took up a dish there, and, after having made a complete circuit with it, gave it to the woman nearest whom it
had stood.   Then she did the same at the northwest and
northeast.   The rest of the food, other than these four dishes,
was not moved.   The women all produced plates or kettles,
and the owner of the tent ladled out food to them from one
dish.   The remaining dishes she set before Cedar-Woman.
Cedar-Woman took five crumbs from one of the dishes and
laid them on the tent-owner's palm.   This woman then went
around the tent, laying one crumb on the ground at each of
the four ends or sides (southeast, etc.) of the tent.   The fifth
she placed on the fire in the middle.   Then she came back to
Cedar-Woman, who placed five pieces from another dish on
her palm.   The woman then rubbed her hands together, and,
going around the fire, stood before a tent-pole on the southeast side of the tent.   She moved her hands down in front of
it with a motion as if she held it and were letting her hands
glide down along it.   She went successively to the southwest,
northwest, and northeast of the tent, and made the same mo-

---

[1] This is a common practice in ceremonials; a root called hãçawaanaxu is used for
the purpose.

tion before the tent-poles there. The fifth motion she made in the same way before the door. Then, going to Cedar-Woman a third time, she received five grains of corn on her hand, and placed them on the ground and on the fire, just as she had placed the first food given her by Cedar-Woman. The fourth time, Cedar-Woman put pieces of a soft food on her hands, which she "fed" to the poles as previously. Then she brought Cedar-Woman a pot of food standing northeast of the centre (*i. e.*, to the left of the door, viewed from inside the tent), and, having had a little of the contents placed on her hands, made the same motions in front of the four tent-poles and the door as before. From a dish at the southeast (to the right of the door), she then again "fed" the ground. Occasionally she mistook the place or made a wrong motion, whereupon all the other women laughed at her. After she had sat down, a young woman, apparently her daughter, entered the tent and kneeled before Cedar-Woman. She also had her palms touched by the old woman's finger after it had been placed on the ground, and she also had chewed medicine spit upon her. Then Cedar-Woman fed her with a spoon; she passed her hand lightly down over Cedar-Woman's arm several times, apparently as a sign of thanks. Rising, she carried several dishes of food to the door; then took a dish from Cedar-Woman to the other old woman who possessed a sacred bag. Leaving the tent, the young woman returned with plates on which the food in the dish last mentioned was distributed. She went out for more plates, and all the food was dished out. Then she sat down against the door. All now ate. The second old woman with the sacred bag once held up a piece of food and said a short prayer, and one of the other women did the same. When they had nearly finished eating, the young woman left the tent, taking several dishes with her. Several women were now called in from outside, and food was given to them to carry away. At last all the food had been removed from the tent.

Then the owner of the tent, who had again been sitting near the door, went out and brought in live coals, which she put on the fireplace. (As it was summer, there was no fire in the tent.) Cedar-Woman took out from her bag a root which looked like that called niäätä[n], and sliced pieces from it. The owner of the tent now took two forked sticks and with them picked up two live coals from the heap which she had brought in; she laid them on the bare ground before Cedar-Woman, and kneeled before her. With her arm guided by Cedar-Woman, she slowly took a small amount of the finely-cut root from Cedar-Woman's other, outspread hand. Still guided by Cedar-Woman, she moved her arm up and down four times, then four times made a motion as if dropping the root on the two coals, and with the last of these motions dropped it. Then she returned to her seat by the door. Cedar-Woman put the remainder of the finely-cut root on the two coals, and, as the smoke rose, began to pray. She prayed a long time. All the women in the tent bowed their heads, and some covered their eyes. Most of them wept a little. The owner of the tent, then replaced the two coals in the fireplace.

This done, she brought in the cover of her tent. It was laid on the ground, to the south of the fireplace, folded so that it was about a foot wide and perhaps twelve feet long. The head was next to Cedar-Woman, the other end near the door. Cedar-Woman rose, and, followed closely by the owner of the tent, walked around the fire, touching the canvas with the two forked sticks that had been used to pick up the coals. Again she circled around the fire, followed by the woman owning the tent, who carried the ornaments that were to be attached. This time, in walking around the fire, they stepped over the tent four times (see Fig. 18). Then the top of the tent was spread out. The owner of the tent stood up, motioned four times with the bundle of ornaments, and threw them on the canvas. Cedar-Woman gathered them together, and holding them up, spoke a short prayer. Then she handed the four smaller circular ornaments to four women. All now gathered around the canvas, which was rolled out somewhat, though not fully spread. All the participants were now on the south side of the fire, where the canvas lay, except Cedar-Woman, who kept her place at the middle of the back of the tent, west of the fire, and one woman who remained idle on the other side of the tent, north of the fire. The five circular ornaments were now sewed on the canvas. The large one at the top of the tent was attached under Cedar-Woman's direct supervision, but neither she nor the other old woman possessing a bag sewed. The owner of the tent also did not sew. As one woman remained idle, there thus were five who were sewing on five ornaments. While they worked, they conversed freely. Cedar-Woman never exposed her bag plainly, but kept it covered and wrapped even while taking something from it. This caution may have been due to the presence of the writer.

When the circular ornaments had all been sewed to the canvas, Cedar-Woman took two of the cow-tails, and directed one of the women how to attach them to the large ornament. When this had been done, the part of the canvas that would be at the front of the top of the tent was spread out and held flat on the ground. Then seven of the yellow pendants were laid in a row upon it, and their places

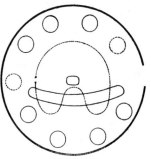

Fig. 18. Diagram illustrating Ceremonial.

marked with a bit of charcoal. In these places holes were then made in the canvas with an awl. The tent had been folded so that it was pierced twice, which made two rows of seven holes. By means of strings of buckskin and small squares of hide, the fourteen yellow pendants were then attached in these places. Then the four-colored pendants were attached in the same manner, below the others, and just above the door; they formed two vertical rows of eight each.

The tent was now bundled together and taken out by the woman who owned it. Together with her daughter, she at once began to put it up on the poles that were already standing. This was done, as usual, by taking out the pole at the middle of the back (called hiinana′kaya[n]), laying it on the ground, and tying the canvas to it near its top, so that by raising the pole the canvas was elevated to the proper height. The other women now all came out from the tent in which they had been. Cedar-Woman took the pole that was lying on the canvas and partially raised it four times. Then the owner of the tent, unassisted, raised it altogether, put it in its place, and spread the canvas around the framework of poles, though without fastening it either in front, over the door, or at the bottom edge; so that it sagged and hung loosely.

Cedar-Woman now took the four tails which had had embroidered pendants attached to them, and which were to be

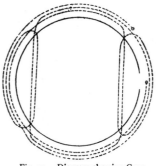

Fig. 19.   Diagram showing Ceremonial Circuit around Tent.

fastened to the four small circular ornaments that were a few feet above the ground on the southeast, southwest, northwest, and northeast sides of the tent. Starting from before the door, and followed by the owner of the tent, she took a complex course that finally brought her before the northeast side of the tent, where one of the tails was to be attached to the beaded ornament. Her course is shown in Fig. 19.

Altogether she walked past every part of the circumference of the tent three times (excepting the distance between the place where she stopped and the door from which she started); crossed the tent four times from north to south or south to north, lifting up the canvas once at each of the places where the ornaments were, going under it, and emerging under the ornament directly to the north or south; and in all her course kept turning from left to right, making five complete revolutions. When the two women had stopped on the northeast of the tent, the owner pierced the ornament with an awl, and Cedar-Woman fastened the tail to it. The remaining participants in the ceremony, together with several other persons who had been watching outside, looked on from a distance, sitting on the ground.   The two women then went to the ornament on the southeast side of the tent, and, having fastened a tail to it in the same manner, did the same at the southwest and then at the northwest.   Then Cedar-Woman sat down with the others; and the owner of the tent, assisted by her daughter, took down the now completely ornamented tent.

Ordinarily this would have ended the ceremony; but the same woman had another tent to be ornamented.   Accordingly the women re-entered the tent in which they had been, and the owner brought in to them a second canvas.   Presumably this was decorated and set up like the first, although without another meal preceding.

This ends the account of the tribal decoration of the Arapaho.

Plate x represents two of the gut cases or pouches used to hold porcupine-quills.   Generally these pouches are not embroidered.   On the larger one (Fig. 2) the blue and yellow triangles in the beadwork at each end represent rocks.   On the other one (Fig. 1) red and blue lines on the white beadwork represent leeches.

The Arapaho keep the dry finely pulverized paint, which they use to put on their persons, in small pouches of soft skin. Old people may have plain little sacks without any decoration.   Generally, however, the pouches are about half covered with beadwork.   They take two main forms.   One has a fringe hanging from the bottom of the pouch.   The other typical form has, in place of the fringe, a pointed triangular flap of skin about as long as the pouch itself.   These paint-bags are usually intended to represent other objects.   Many represent one half of a saddle-bag.   Saddle-bags were made of soft skin, deep, beaded, and with a long fringe.   They were double, so that one end hung on each side of the horse. One half of a saddle-bag had much the shape and appearance of many of the paint-pouches.   Others of these paint-pouches represent small animals.   The pouch itself is the body of the animal, its opening is the mouth, the strings with which the

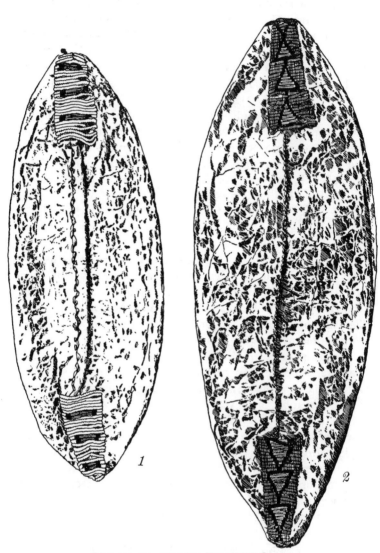

POUCHES FOR HOLDING PORCUPINE-QUILLS.

opening is tied together are limbs, other strings or attachments are hind-limbs or tail, and so on.   The beadwork on
the pouch is generally entirely independent in its symbolism,
but sometimes has reference to the animal symbolism of the
whole pouch.   Thus the beadwork may represent the markings or habitation of the animal, or parts of its body.

Fig. 20 shows four paint-pouches in outline.   The strings
that represent legs, fins, etc., are extended, to make the similarity to an animal as apparent as possible.   *a* represents both
a beaver and a fish.   With the latter signification, the upper
pair of strings are barbels; the lower pair, fins.   *b* is a lizard.
The sound made by the small tin rattles that are attached to

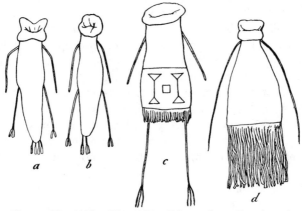

Fig. 20, *a* ($\frac{50}{361}$), *b* ($\frac{50}{362}$), *c* ($\frac{50}{343}$), *d* ($\frac{50}{301}$).   Paint-pouches   About ⅓ nat. size.

flap and strings denotes the cry of the lizard.   *c* and *d* are
pouches with a fringe in place of a flap.   *c* represents a frog;
the fringe is grass in which it is sitting.   The beadwork
design of this pouch is shown in the illustration; the four
triangles represent the four shoulder and hip joints of the
frog; the square is food in its stomach.   *d* represents one-
half of a saddle-bag.

It is evident that the pouches are similar in their general
pattern, however diverse their symbolic significance.

Unless otherwise specified, the paint-bags to be referred to
are ornamented alike on both sides.

The paint-pouch shown in Plate XI, Fig. 1, represents a saddle-bag. The triangular design upon it is a tent. The stripe along the side of the pouch is a snake. The beads at the edge of the opening are variously-colored rocks. The five-pointed mouth of the pouch represents a star.

The pouch shown in Figs. 2 and 3, Plate XI, represents a beaver. The triangular design in beadwork is a tent. It rests upon a green horizontal line, which represents the ground when the grass is green. On the other side of the pouch is another, differently-colored triangular design, which is also a tent. This rests upon a yellow band, which represents the ground in autumn, when the grass is yellow. Light-blue stripes at the two sides of the pouch represent the sky. On the flap, the two converging white stripes are an arrow-head. The small dark-blue triangles are also arrow-heads. The line of beads projecting from the edge of the flap represents the scales on the beaver's tail. It will be seen that one side of this flap is left bare, which is unusual.

In the pouch shown in Fig. 4 of Plate XI the opening is four-pointed, and represents the morning star.

The pouch shown in Fig. 5 of Plate XI represents a saddle-bag. The triangular design is a mountain. The gray-blue area on which it is imposed is hazy atmosphere. The blue-and-yellow border represents mountain-ranges. This pouch is beaded on one side only.

The pouch shown in Fig. 6 of Plate XI represents a greenish lizard. For this reason the ground-color of the beadwork is green. In most pouches it is white. The design represents a mountain: this species of lizard lives mostly on mountains. The whole bag with its opening, besides being the lizard itself, is also the hole in which the animal lives; and the vertical green stripe with two bands across it represents the lizard with the markings of its skin. The opening of the pouch is also the lizard's mouth; and the projections at the opening, its ears.

The bag shown in Figs. 1 and 2 of Plate XII represents a lizard. The rectangular design (Fig. 1) with six projections represents a cricket. Below it, the crosses are stars, and the

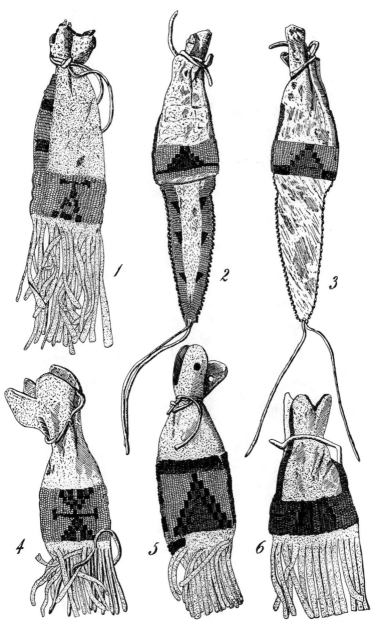

PAINT-POUCHES.

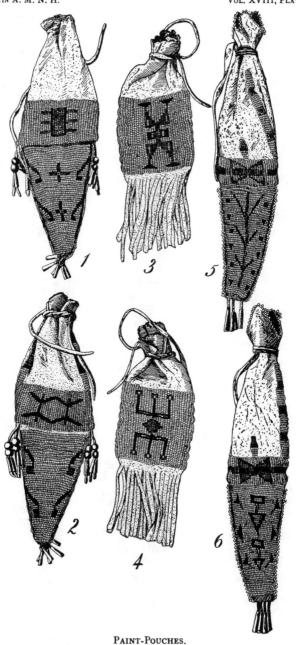

PAINT-POUCHES.

lateral figures pipes.   On the other side (Fig. 2) is a representation of a turtle and of several pipes.   The two narrow
stripes extending to the mouth of the pouch are caterpillars.

The bag shown in Figs. 3 and 4 of Plate XII represents both
a saddle-bag and a prairie-dog.   On one side (Fig. 3), four
right-angled triangles represent mountain-peaks.   Small white
patches on these represent snow.   Dark figures at the points
of these triangles are eagles on the mountains.   The figure
between the mountains represents the crossing of two paths.
On the other side (Fig. 4), the diamond in the middle represents a turtle.   The two three-pronged figures are turtle-
claws.   Small white spots on these are turtle-eggs.

It will be noticed that identical white spots mean on different sides of the bag respectively snow-patches and turtle-eggs.
What signification they have depends in each case on the
symbolic context.   Similarly a three-pronged figure like that
on this bag often signifies the bear's foot, but here, when
adjacent to a turtle-symbol, a turtle's foot.   Such representation of different objects by the same symbol — or such
different interpretation of the same figure, according as one
may wish to state it — is constantly found in the decorative
art of this tribe.

The pouch shown in Figs. 5 and 6, Plate XII, again represents a lizard.   The large ornament about the middle of the
bag (Fig. 5) represents a butterfly.   The two triangles are
its wings, and the rhomboidal figure of beadwork projecting
on the leather surface is its body.   On the flap is represented
the centipede.   The rows of small squares are its tracks.   On
the other side (Fig. 6) there is the butterfly again.   On the
flap is a dragon-fly, or perhaps two.   The detached, somewhat triangular figures, at the sides of the dragon-fly, are its
wings.

The pouch shown in Fig. 21, *a*, represents a saddle-bag.
The design is a tent.   The conventional stripe towards the
opening, only part of which is shown in the illustration, is a
snake.

In the paint-pouch shown in Fig. 21, *b*, each of the triangles
with the two lines at its ends represents a tent.   The space

enclosed by the triangle and the two lines represents the place where the tent is. In the stripe reaching to the opening of the bag are representations of worms, each row or thread of

Fig. 21.   Paint-pouches.   About ⅔ nat. size.

a ($\frac{50}{661}$), b ($\frac{50}{1119}$), c ($\frac{50}{990}$), d ($\frac{50}{1043}$), e ($\frac{50}{542}$), f ($\frac{50}{1114}$), g ($\frac{50}{1071}$), h ($\frac{50}{975}$), i ($\frac{50}{1008}$).

beads being a worm. The beading at the edge also represents worms.

The bag shown in Fig. 21, c, represents a saddle-bag. The large diamond, as well as the crosses on the vertical stripes, are the morning star. Metallic beads in these figures express the lustre of the star.

The pouch shown in Fig. 2i, *d*, represents a horned toad. The design represents caterpillars (*cf.* Plate xvii). The white represents snow.

The pouch shown in Fig. 21, *e*, also represents a horned toad. The triangles are mushrooms.

On the paint-pouch shown in Fig. 21, *f*, the ground-color is yellow, instead of the usual white, and represents ground. The pattern represents rocks. More accurately, dark blue in this design indicates rocks; red and pink, earth; and green, grass among the rocks. The stripe toward the opening symbolizes a narrow range of hills, and dark blue on this stripe is again rock.

The pouch shown in Fig. 21, *g*, represents a rat. Two triangular pink marks just below the mouth are ears. The rest of the design is very dilapidated, most of the beads having been worn off.[1]

The paint-pouch shown in Fig. 21, *h*, represents a saddle-bag. The ornamental design represents a lizard. Stripes along the sides, toward the opening of the pouch, are worms. Red squares on these stripes are the holes of the worms. The beading at the edge of the opening represents light and dark colored maggots.

The paint-pouch shown in Fig. 21, *i*, represents a reddish bivalve mollusk, probably a mussel.

Representation of an animal by an entire object which bears little visual resemblance to the animal, is not confined to paint-pouches or navel-amulets. An awl-case, made of hide wound with black and white beads, was intended to represent a lizard (Plate xiii, Fig. 1). Here, as in other cases, the particular animal represented could not well be recognized even by an Indian; and that this awl-case represents a lizard, and not a snake or fish or rat, is a matter of the individual purpose or interpretation of the maker. Perhaps even a distinct motive or intention for this symbolism was lacking in

---

[1] By mistake the design shown in the figure below the ears is the one on the opposite side of the pouch; that on the same side as the ears is similar but less dilapidated.

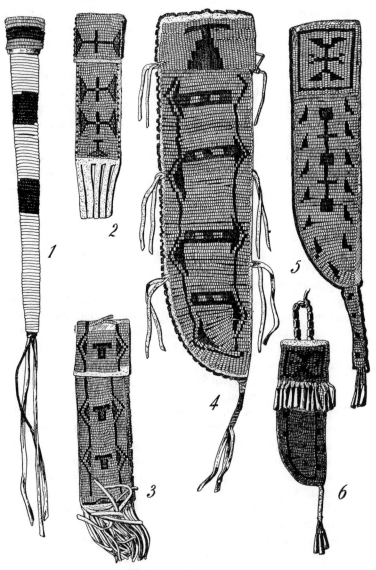

KNIFE AND AWL CASES.

this person's mind, for the lizard is the most common of all animals represented in this way; so that the symbolism of this awl-case may have been as conventional as its form.

A small knife-case is shown in Plate XIII, Fig. 2. The crosses have the usual meaning of the morning star. The triangles are tents. At the bottom end of the case is a small design that looks like half of the double figure occurring above it three times. The triangle in this design again represents a tent, but the T-shaped figure denotes the sun overhead, with its rays shining into the tent. All the figures are repeated in different colors, but with the same signification, on the other side. The white background represents sand or light-colored soil; the separate green beads along the edge are biisääna^n (insects or worms); and a yellow stripe of beadwork at the side of the case, which, however, is invisible in the figure, is a path.

A similar knife-case (Fig. 3 of the same plate) represents, as a whole, a fish. The design upon it represents mountain-ranges. The T-shaped figures are trees. On the other side of the specimen the mountain-ranges are repeated in other colors, while the trees are replaced by crosses, signifying the morning star.

A larger knife-scabbard is shown in Fig. 4 of Plate XIII. At the top is the figure of a tent. A wavy red line enclosing the rest of the design is a path. The green triangles inside are buffalo-wallows, and the stripes connecting them are buffalo-paths. The white background represents snow. The little attachment at the end of the scabbard is called the tail. The other loose thongs represent small streams of water. At the upper edge, around the rim of the opening, are red beads, to signify that the bloody knife used in butchering reddens that part of the scabbard.

On the knife-case shown in Fig. 5 of Plate XIII, the symbolism is so incoherent that it must have been secondary, in the mind of the owner, to the decorative appearance. The green lines forming a square at the top represent rivers. The figure within it is an eagle. The two larger dark portions of this figure are also cattle-tracks. The two rows of triangles on the body of the scabbard represent arrow-points. The squares in the middle are boxes, and the lines between them are the conventional morning-star cross. The small squares on the pendant attached to the point of the scabbard are cattle-tracks.

The signification of the ornamentation on another knife-case (Fig. 6, Plate XIII) is as follows. The yellow background is the ground. The dark blade-shaped line is a mountain, its small projections being rocks. The light-blue squares are lakes. The lines forming the rectangle at the top and the horizontal line within it are rivers, The two triangles are tents.

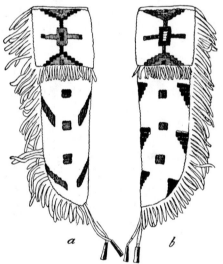

Fig. 22 ($\frac{50}{1170}$). Beaded Knife-scabbard. Length, 12 cm.

Fig. 22 shows two sides of a small beaded knife-scabbard. At the top is the cross, nankaox. In this case it represents a person. Adjacent to it are two triangles, which represent mountains. Below, are three green squares. These are the symbol of life or abundance. Red slanting lines pointing toward the squares are thoughts or wishes (kakauçetcanan), which are directed toward the desired objects, represented by the life-symbols. On the other side the colors are different, but the design is identical, except that instead of the red lines there are blue triangles, which represent knife-scabbards such as this specimen itself.

Small pouches are worn by the women, hanging from their belts. In these they keep matches, money, or other small articles. These bags are generally partly covered with bead-work, and are often further decorated by the attachment of

leather fringes, tin cylinders, or buttons.   A number of these
belt-pouches are illustrated in Fig. 23 and Plate XIV.[1]

In Fig. 23, *a*, the white beadwork represents ground.   The
ornament in the middle represents mountains.   The two
dark-blue rectangles connected with this ornament symbolize
rocks on the mountains.   On the flap that closes the pouch,
red and blue squares denote piles of rock or monuments
(çiayaana^n).

In Fig. 23, *b*, the large triangular figure, the red lines forming a rectangle, and the variously-colored beading along the

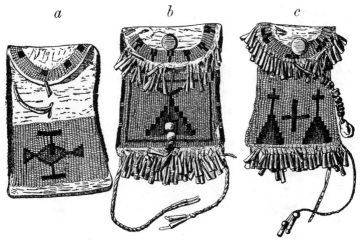

Fig. 23, *a* ($\frac{50}{820}$), *b* ($\frac{50}{893}$), *c* ($\frac{50}{1008}$).   Women's Small Belt-pouches.   ⅓ nat. size.

edge of the pouch, all represent rocks.   Red and blue are
often employed to denote rocks.   On the point of the large
triangular rock is a representation of an eagle.   On the flap
of the pouch is a white stripe which represents rocks, and
blue figures on this are eagles sitting on the high rocks where
they nest.

Similarly, on the pouch shown in Fig. 23, *c*, two triangles
represent tents, while cross-like figures at their ends represent

[1] These pouches, as well as the larger ones shown in Figs. 25–28, are made of
dark leather, while the body of the beadwork is white.   In the illustrations the
leather appears lighter in color than the beadwork.

eagles sitting on the tent-poles.   Between them is the morning-star cross.   Above, covered in the illustration by the
fringe of tin rattles, is a beaded design representing a rack on
which meat is dried.   It consists of a stripe of blue beads,
from which three inverted T-shaped figures descend, the stem
of the T being composed of four beads, while the cross-bar has
three beads.   The figures in the white stripe on the flap
denote stars.

In Fig. 24, *a*, the large design near the lower edge is the
bear's foot, generally conventionally represented by the

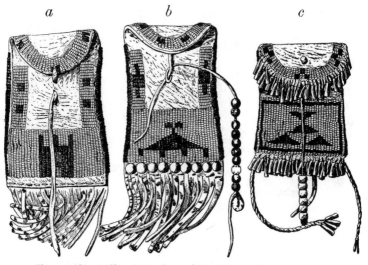

Fig. 24, *a* ($\frac{50}{921}$), *b* ($\frac{50}{937}$), *c* ($\frac{50}{970}$).   Women's Small Belt-pouches.   ⅓ nat. size.

Arapaho with only three claws.   Square pink spots on the
body of the design are the bare skin on the sole of the foot.
The white beadwork is sand or soil.   The curved band on
the flap is a mountain.   The leather fringe at the bottom of
the pouch represents trees.

On another pouch (Fig. 24, *b*) the white is sand.   Green
beading at the edges, on account of its color, denotes timber.
Two designs that may be described as compressed crosses represent the morning star.   Squares on the flap are rocks.   The

large figure near the bottom is a mountain, with a tree on its summit; below it are four small red and blue rectangles which denote little streams flowing from a spring near the foot of the mountain.   This spring is represented by a green square in the large triangle.

In Fig. 24, *c*, the rectangle of beadwork on the front of the pouch represents the earth or the world.[1]   The white denotes snow; and the red and blue triangles, rocks.   The stripe on the flap is continued around the edge of the back of the pouch. It represents an ant-hill.   The small squares on it represent dirt.   The tin cylinders are ants.   Stripes at the two sides of the pouch are ant-paths.

The signification of the design on the belt-pouch shown in Fig. 1 of Plate xiv is the following.   The six triangles all represent tents.   The lines enclosing the trapezoidal area within which these triangles are, represent trails.   In the two stripes immediately above this area, stars are represented both by red rectangles crossed by a green line, and by green crosses on a red field.   The white zigzag line on the flap of the pouch is a snake; the beaded stripes along the seams denote rivers.

Sometimes these small bags are made to hold the cards or tickets which entitle the bearer to the rations issued by the government.   When this is the purpose of the bag, the flap or cover is sometimes left off.   Such a pouch is shown in Fig. 2, Plate xiv.   All the figures are geographical representations.   The pink border is a large river, the triangles are islands in it.   The green area within this represents the earth. Two large red A-shaped marks represent a stream, called by the Arapaho Fox-Tent Creek.   The two rectangles represent mountains, called by the Arapaho House Mountains.   The short yellow stripe connecting these represents Yellow Canyon. All these natural features are said to be situated to the north or northeast of the present location of the tribe in central Wyoming.   Such representation of actual specific mountains, valleys, and rivers, is uncommon, though this case is not unique.   It will be noted that the ornamentation is

---

[1] The same word means "world," "earth," "land," "ground," "soil."

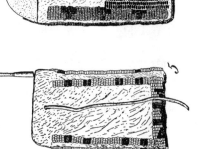

POUCHES.

symmetrically duplicated, in spite of the quasi-map-like nature of the design.

Another of these ration-ticket pouches is that shown in Figs. 3 and 4, Plate xiv. On the front are represented flint arrow-points. On the other side (back and flap) the stripes represent arrow-shafts, the colored portions being the property-marks with which arrow-shafts are painted. Arrows are the means of securing game; game is used as food; so is the beef that is issued by the government, and this is obtained by means of the ration-card kept in the pouch. Such is the reason for representing arrows by the ornament on this little bag. Associations of this sort (arrows, game, meat, beef, ration-card) are not uncommon among the Arapaho, especially among the speculative and the old. They remind one strikingly of the symbolic identification, on account of analogies in single respects, that is so prominent in the religion of the Indians of the Southwest, and which has been treated of extensively by Cushing among the Zuñi, and lately, in more detail, by Lumholtz among the Huichols.

Another pouch is shown in Fig. 5, Plate xiv. The squares along the sides are bee-holes. The figure at the bottom is a bee. The red beads at the lower edge of the pouch are bees. The white edges on the sides are trails, the red spots denoting holes.

Fig. 6, Plate xiv, shows another pouch in which ration-cards were kept. The black beads covering the lower half of the bag represent coffee, which is obtained at the ration-issue. The light-blue bands at the sides, on account of their color, represent the sky. The ornaments upon them are mountains. The single lines of dark-blue beads along the edges represent wolves.

On the tasteful pouch shown in Fig. 7, Plate xiv, the red diamond in the centre of the design represents a person. The four forked ornaments surrounding it are buffalo hoofs or tracks.

In Fig. 8 of Plate xiv the main ornament is a tent. The rectangle above the apex of the triangle represents the spreading upper flaps or ears of the tent, and the two lateral hand-shaped designs are buffalo-tails attached to the top of the tent. The white background denotes ground; its red border, water (evidently streams). On the cover is a design which is continued as a border on the back of the pouch. This is mostly red, and, on account of this color, denotes flame, and therefore, by a series of symbolic equations, matches, which are kept in the pouch. White marks upon this border represent ashes.

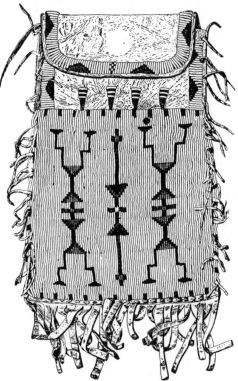

Fig. 2, Plate IV, shows a belt-pouch. The white background represents snow. The blue lines enclosing the design are mountains, while lines of green beads at the very edge of the pouch represent trees. On the face of the pouch, two triangles are tents; a rectangle or stripe between them is a stream of water. On the flap, a blue spot is a rock, and two groups of red squares are two stars.

Bags about a foot in length, made of dark leather, and nearly covered with beads on the front are used to hold

Fig. 25 ($\frac{50}{1004}$).　Toilet-bag.　Height, 38 cm.

combs, paint-bags, and other more modern articles of toilet use.

Fig. 25 shows a typical bag of this kind. The large ornament that is duplicated on each side of the design represents persons. The narrower ornament in the middle represents two dragon-flies. Both the persons and the dragon-flies are to be conceived as having their heads joined. Rectangular red marks all around the edge of the beaded area represent a fence, symbolized by its posts. The four ornaments standing up above this beaded field represent worms. On the flap of the cover, and just below, are white stripes. On these are designs of mountains; in the middle of the stripe on the cover is a small checkered ornament which represents rocks.

In another toilet-pouch (Fig. 26) three crosses represent, as usual, the morning star, and four three-pronged ornaments denote bear-claws. In two square areas, situated between the bear-foot ornaments, pink triangular surfaces represent tents, while the blue and white diagonals separating them are trails. A dark-blue line enclosing all the ornaments that have been mentioned signifies mountain-ranges. Two H-shaped marks near the top of the pouch

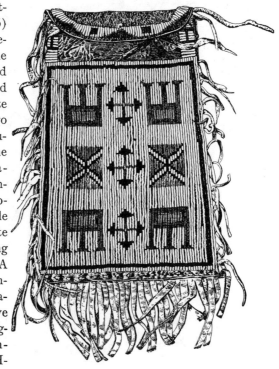

Fig. 26 (⁵⁰⁄₉₄₂). Toilet-pouch. Height, 39 cm.

represent racks for drying meat. On the white stripe upon the cover are mountains (represented by triangles) and lakes (represented by squares).

Fig. 27 illustrates a toilet-pouch[1] somewhat larger than most

---

[1] In the specimen itself there is a pleasing contrast between the brown leather and the white beadwork, which is not indicated in the illustration.

others, and more delicate in ornamentation.   The two ornaments, placed symmetrically, one on each side of the square
white field, are worked chiefly in green; the design between
them is mostly blue.   At the centre of this last design there
is a cross, the Arapaho word for which means also "morning

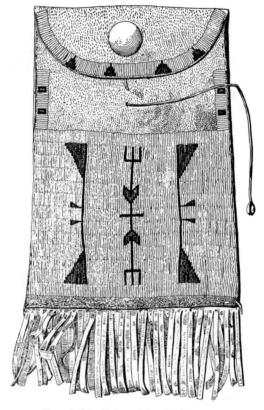

Fig. 27 ($\frac{50}{1038}$).   Toilet-pouch.   Height, 42.5 cm.

star."   The notched marks adjacent to this represent clouds,
also the heart.   A few brass beads within these figures denote
the gleaming of the cloud.   The three-pronged figures at the
ends are bear's claws (wasixta).   The line connecting this with
the cloud-symbol is the bear's leg.   In the lateral figures, the

green triangles and red lines represent respectively the leaves and stems of yellow-weed (niha^{n}naxu^{i}n), a common plant used as medicine.   Within the leaves are small red rectangles which represent face-paint.   Two small blue triangles, just touching the representations of the stems, are eyes.   Brass beads within these denote the gleam of the eye.   Outside of this decorative area, on the two white stripes at the edge above, are small rectangles, also of blue and metallic beads, which also denote eyes. The entire white background of beadwork symbolizes clouds.   On the cover, triangles represent tents;   because they are arranged on the curved white band, they also symbolize the camp-circle. The leather fringe at the bottom of the bag denotes various trails.

Fig. 28 ($\frac{1.8.0}{1.8.1}$).   Toilet-bag.   Height, 43 cm.

The last bag of this series is shown in Fig. 28. In the middle of the white decorative field are three red crosses, representing, as usual, the morning star. The four ornaments on the bordering stripes above are also crosses, or the morning star.   Four large green triangles, each with two projections, represent frogs.   The two squares between these triangles represent floating scum in which the frogs have their heads.   The centre of these squares is red; this symbolizes the face-paint which is kept in the pouch. The white represents clouds. On the cover are hills, rising and falling along the horizon.

It is noteworthy that, with all the diversity of symbolism on these four pouches, their designs should be so similar. On all of them there is a large white decorative field, approximately square. Above this the leather is left bare except for a narrow strip upward along each side. The convex edge of the cover is also bordered by a band of white beadwork. On the main decorative area there are three figures or groups of figures, extending vertically. The outer two of these three figures are alike, which gives symmetry to the whole design. The middle figure is always different from the two others, and narrower. Each of these three figures falls into three parts, which may be connected or separate. The resemblance can be traced still farther, as in the shape of these parts of the three figures. A glance at the illustrations will show this better than a verbal description.[1]

Yet with this general unity of decorative scheme there go hand in hand, first, an astounding diversity of detail; and, secondly, an equally great diversity of symbolism. Ornaments that are analogously placed and somewhat similar in form represent, on different pouches, objects as different as men, bear-feet, leaves, and frogs; or, again, dragon-flies, stars, bear-feet, and clouds and stars. The diversity in ornamental detail is as noticeable as the general decorative similarity. The co-existence of these two apparently contrary traits is due to the fact that the Indians, while strongly impressed with certain conventional styles or patterns of decoration, do not directly copy the ornamentation of one pouch in making another, but always exercise their inventive powers in designing ornamental forms. This constant variability of detail within narrow limits has been shown above to exist in ornamented moccasins, and is perhaps still more striking as regards the painted rawhide bags and the parfleches treated below (see pp. 104 et seq.).

---

[1] These bags are of course not specially selected to show similarity of design, but comprise all the toilet-pouches from the Wyoming Arapaho that the American Museum of Natural History possesses. A pouch from the Oklahoma Arapaho, with a different style of design, was described and illustrated in Symbolism of the Arapaho Indians (Bulletin A. M. N. H., Vol. XIII, 1900, pp. 82, 83).

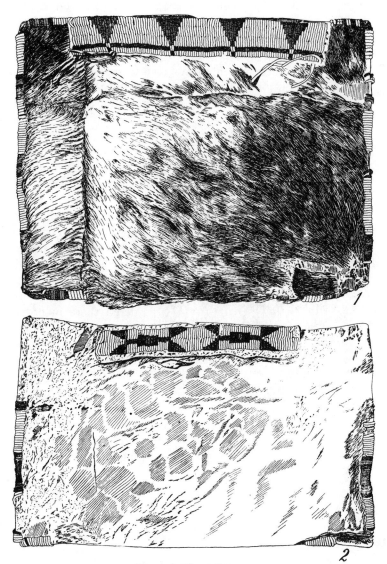

WOMEN'S WORK-BAGS.

Plate XV shows two women's work-bags. These are made of hide on which the hair has been left. The opening extends at the top along the border of beadwork. Both the bags are much worn. The first (Fig. 1) is ornamented with designs of tents and a path, represented by green triangles and a dark-blue line at the top. White beading around the edge represents mountains. Green and yellow marks on this represent

springs. From the second bag (Fig. 2) the hair is almost completely worn off. The white stripe at the top is a trail. The marks on this denote four elk-legs. Just below this stripe are the remnants of a line of quill-work, which was embroidered there in order to symbolize quill-embroidery (perhaps because the bag was used to hold sewing-appliances). The borders at the other edges represent paths.

These ordinary sewing-bags must not be confounded with the women's seven sacred bags that have already been mentioned (see p. 30). The sacred bags are quite different in appearance.

Fig. 29 ($\frac{50}{1085}$). Bag of Buffalo-skin. Height, 32 cm.

Two bags that are made of skin that has the hair left on it are shown in Figs. 29 and 30. The one shown in Fig. 29 is made of woolly buffalo-skin. It represents, in its entirety, a

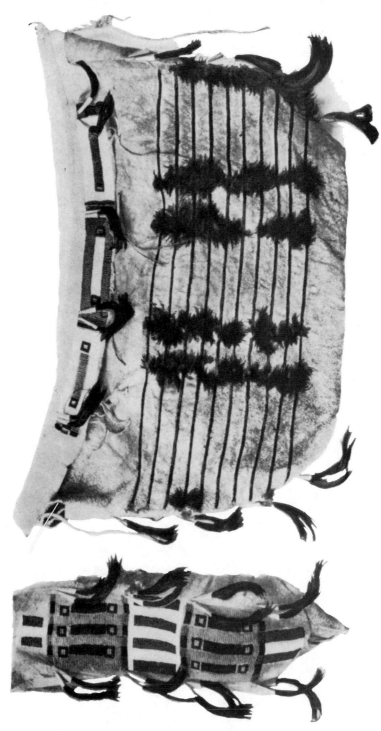

SOFT BAG, FRONT AND SIDE VIEWS.

beaver. That shown in Fig. 30 is made of the skin of a buffalo calf. Around the opening, a band of beadwork, with red
squares in it, represents the camp-circle. Plum-pits attached
to the bag near this beadwork represent burrs sticking in the
hair of buffalo. At the lower end, a small beaded attachment
represents the tail of a buffalo.

Bags of soft pliable hide are used for keeping and transporting clothing and similar arti-
cles. They are beaded along
two edges and on the cover.
Sometimes the front is also
covered with embroidery in
beads or quills. These bags
must be distinguished from
rawhide bags, which are stiff
and hard, and painted instead
of embroidered. Rawhide
bags and parfleches are sometimes used to hold clothing
and household articles, but
seem primarily intended for
food.

Plate XVI shows such a
bag. The five-colored pattern
which extends along each
end of the bag is typical.
In this specimen the longitudinal stripes were said to
represent the marks of tent-
poles on the ground; that is,
camp - trails. The shorter
transverse stripes are ra-

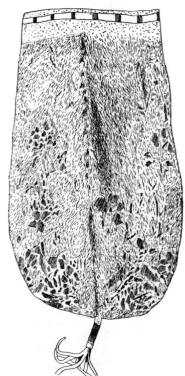

Fig. 30 ($\frac{50}{1081}$). Hide Bag. Height, 69 cm.

vines; that is, camping-places. The squares are life-symbols.
On the flap forming the cover the symbolism is the same.
On the front of the bag the horizontal lines of quill-work,
which resemble the lines on buffalo-robes, are paths.
Bunches of feathers on these lines represent buffalo-meat
hung up to dry. Adjoining the beadwork are small tin

cylinders with tufts of red hair; these represent pendants or rattles on tents.

Fig. 31 shows the beadwork on the end of another soft hide bag. This design, like the last, represents camp-trails and camping-places. Another individual explained the analogous design on another bag as representing buffalo-paths.

Fig. 31 ($\frac{50}{380}$). Beadwork on End of Bag. Length, 46 cm.

Plate XVII shows a bag of soft hide with considerable beadwork.[1] On the front each of the two large figures, with four pairs of projections each, represents a centipede. They are also caterpillars and leaves, the green rectangles with the cleft figures at their ends being the caterpillars ; and the intermediate yellow rectangles, leaves. In the middle of this side of the bag are four figures representing butterflies.

The design at the end of the bag, while resembling those which represent paths in previous specimens, represents worms; each of the stripes, longitudinal or transverse, being one animal. At the centre of this design, a square, green outside, then yellow, then red, and light blue inside, represents an ant-hill.

[1] In the illustration of this specimen, red is represented by horizontal, yellow by diagonal, and green by vertical shading.

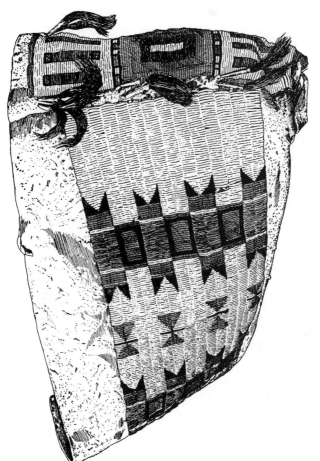

Beaded Bag.

Many bags, pouches, and receptacles of the Arapaho are made of stiff white skin, from which the hair has been scraped. The most typical form is that called "parfleche." This consists of a single piece of rawhide, generally half a buffalo-skin, approximately rectangular. The two long sides are folded inward to meet in the middle. The opening where the two long edges come together is closed by turning over the two short ends of the folded hide so that they also meet in the middle, where they are tied together (see Fig. 3, Plate XVIII). The rawhide is stiff and keeps its folded shape, but is elastic enough to allow of the parfleche being pressed very flat when empty, and widely distended when filled. The two upper covers of the parfleche are painted each with the same design, which is rectangular in shape, and composed chiefly of triangles. The parfleches are used particularly for storing and transporting dried meat. They are also convenient and much used for holding clothing and household articles. They are usually made in pairs. In travelling, one is hung on each side of a horse, the painted side of course being outside.

Bags or pouches, when made of rawhide, are also made of one piece. There is a fold along what constitutes the lower edge of the bag; the edges along the two sides are sewed together. The top is covered by a triangular flap, which is part of the back, and is drawn down over the front of the bag (Plate XXI, Fig. 1).

Sometimes a somewhat larger bag is made without the flap to cover the opening. The fold in the hide is along one of its long sides; the other edge is stitched. Or the bag may be composed of two pieces sewed together along both of their long edges. The two ends are composed of soft hide or cloth. The opening is merely a slit in one of these ends. This kind of bag is more distendible than the simple pouch-like form. It is used chiefly to store food. One is shown in Fig. 3, Plate XXI. The more common form of rawhide bag is used for gathering berries and fruits.

Almost all rawhide bags are painted on the back, though the design is simpler than that on the front. Parfleches, however, are unpainted on the back or bottom.

In the following illustrations, only one of the painted flaps of each parfleche is shown; but of bags, the back and cover, as well as the front, are in most cases represented. The bags are illustrated as if the stitches at their edges had been removed and the piece of hide composing the bag spread out flat.

Fig. 1 of Plate XVIII shows the design on the flap of a parfleche. The red areas along each side of the design represent a red bank along a stream. The adjacent unpainted space represents sand. Adjacent to this, a triangle formed by blue lines is a hill. The upper part of this is green, and represents grass; the basal portion, yellow, and represents earth of that color. On the other half of the symmetrical design, the figures of course have the same significance. Between these two halves is a longitudinal stripe which is red in the middle, but white at the ends. This represents a trail. As a road cannot be alike in all its length, this representation of it also has more colors than one. The entire rectangle of the design is the earth.

While bags of rawhide open along one edge, parfleches, as explained, open in the middle. The two covering flaps of hide are there tied together by strings. These strings pass through holes near the ends of the two covering pieces (*cf.* Fig. 3 of this plate). In this specimen (Fig. 1) there are two such holes near the edge of the design where the symbol of the road ends. Through these holes the fastening-strings are passed. Therefore they control access to the contents of the parfleche. As the parfleche does not open except at this place, it is necessary, in order to obtain its contents, to reach these holes; therefore the road is painted leading to them (see Fig. 3 of this plate). Moreover, the white sections of this road are oblong, which is the shape of the parfleche itself. The two hills and the road between them form a roughly rhombic figure; and very nearly such is the shape of the hide of which this parfleche is made, when it is unfolded and spread out (ordinarily this piece of rawhide is more nearly rectangular than rhombic).

The maker of this parfleche, an old woman, said that it was made to resemble another one. It represents the land as it is, as nearly as it can be represented. People try to paint

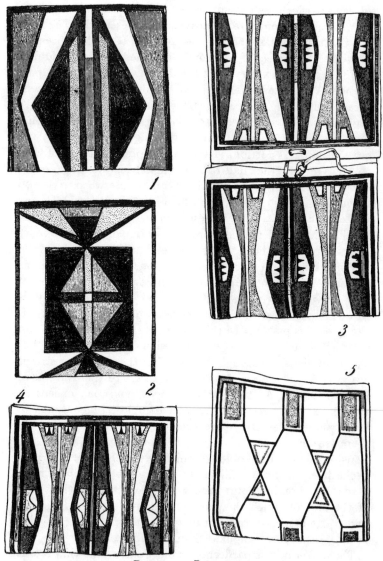

DESIGNS ON PARFLECHES.

their parfleches so as to be as pretty as possible.   Often they dream of the designs.

Fig. 2 of Plate xviii shows the design on another parfleche. In the centre of this design is a green rectangle, which denotes the earth.   A yellow stripe traversing this longitudinally represents a large river; a blue stripe bisected by it, streams of water flowing into the river.   The small white unpainted square at the intersection of these stripes is called the centre.   The red triangles forming a diamond in the green rectangle represent mountains.   At the two ends of the design are two triangular areas, also representing mountains. In each there is an equilateral triangle, which denotes a tent; the lower part of this triangle, which is red, is the door of the tent.   Yellow, outside of this tent-symbol but adjacent to it, denotes day or sunlight.   Four green lines which enclose the whole area represent the camp-circle.

Fig. 3 of Plate xviii shows an entire parfleche with its two flaps painted with the same design.   The long triangular areas, which are blue, represent, of course wholly on account of their color, the sky.   The white areas in them, having rounded tops, are sweat-houses; the black tooth-like marks are people in the sweat-house.   A red stripe at the foot of the sweat-house represents red earth or paint.   Between each pair of the long, blue sky-triangles is a pair of figures stretching the whole length of the design; one of each pair is red, the other yellow.   These figures denote four sticks such as are used in painting parfleche designs like this one.   White trapezoidal areas at the ends of these stick-figures are life-symbols. The longitudinal curved spaces left unpainted between the sky-symbols and the stick-figures represent thongs or ropes of rawhide, such as that used to fasten this parfleche.   The narrow white stripes, of which there are several, are trails.   The green lines enclosing each design represent grass.   On each of the four sides near the edge, as well as in the very middle, of the design, is a yellow stripe; these stripes, on account of their color, represent sunlight and yellow clouds (literally, "yellow day").   These yellow stripes are bounded at their ends by small dark-brown (black) rectangular marks, invisible in the illustration; these represent black water-beetles, called in Arapaho "buffalo-bulls" (the buffalo is at times also represented by a black rectangle).

A parfleche design very similar to the last is shown in Fig. 4 of Plate xviii. The four long flat triangles are again blue, and the figures between them are half yellow and half red. The blue triangles also again enclose a white area with rounded top, within which is a figure with three points. In spite of this similarity to the design last described, the symbolism differs considerably. In the present specimen the flat blue triangles are mountains; the red three-toothed figures are red hills, the white spaces between their projections being basins or valleys; a yellow stripe at the base of this hill-and-valley figure represents a flat or plain; the red-and-yellow figures, which taper toward the middle, are tents; the trapezoidal white areas enclosed at their bases are life-symbols; and the black marks bisecting the life-symbols are tent-pegs, this interpretation being probably suggested by their shape and by their position at the foot of the tents; the straight lines or narrow stripes, whether red, blue, or unpainted, are paths. On account of its four-sided shape, the whole design represents the earth.

A parfleche which, both in the color and the shapes of its design, is unusual, though a pattern somewhat resembling the more common one is recognizable in it, is shown in Fig. 5 of Plate xviii. The six rectangles are yellow; they are exteriorly bordered by red, as are the four triangles interiorly. The rest of the designs consists of black lines. The six rectangles are bear-feet (the claws, sometimes the most prominent feature, being omitted). The triangles are flint arrow-points. The black lines are ropes. The black lines enclosing the entire design are (because forming a rectangle) the earth. At each corner are two short red stripes, forming an angle. These are life-symbols. Evidently each stripe is regarded as an elongated quadrilateral, the square or trapezoid being the regular figure for the life-symbol.

On the parfleche shown in Fig. 1, Plate xix, the triangles represent tents. Strictly, the equilateral triangles and the

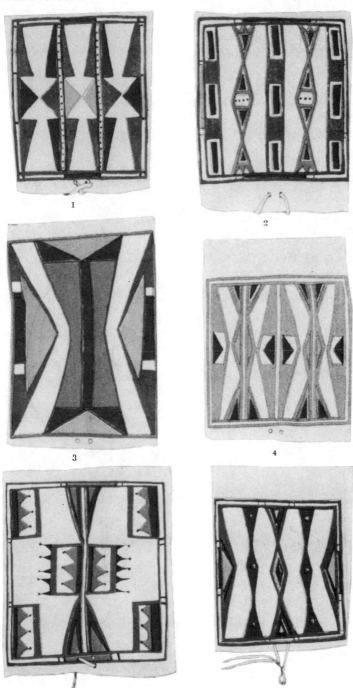

DESIGNS ON PARFLECHES.

pairs of right-angled triangles represent tents; but the four
blue right-angled triangles at the corners of the design, half
of a tent.   Their colors denote the colors (red, yellow, blue, or
green, but not black) with which tents were formerly painted.
The design is longitudinally trisected by two white stripes,
which represent paths.   Black dots in them are coyote-tracks.
These stripes are edged on one side by red, and on the other
by blue; these colors denote night and day, and, because
night and day are opposite, are on opposite sides of the white
stripe.   The blue lines enclosing the whole design represent
tent-pegs.   The white stripes which they enclose are rivers;
the red and yellow stripes which they enclose are camp-sites.
The small squares in the corners of the design are the ends of
the earth (häneisa^n biitaawu).   The white areas within the
design, consisting each of a high narrow trapezoid surmounted
by an equilateral triangle, represent women.   This design
(*i. e.*, style of design), as well as that called wasixta ("bear-
foot"), was first made by the mythic cosmological character,
Whirlwind-Woman.

In the parfleche design shown in Fig. 2, Plate XIX, the three
wide blue stripes represent rivers.   Evidently both form and
color are symbolic.   The red rectangles in them are islands,
and the white border around these is sand.   The triangles are
bear-feet (wasixta).   The red portions of the triangles represent the bare skin of the sole of the foot; the projections at
the base of the triangles are the claws.   The white hexagonal
areas represent the prairie (*i. e.*, land, ground); the black
spots in them are coyotes.   Enclosing the whole design are
the customary lines or stripes.   These signify paths.   Those
of them that are blue represent buffalo-paths; the white,
antelope-paths; the yellow, elk-paths; and the red, deer-paths.

In the parfleche design of Fig. 3, Plate XIX, the large yellow
triangles, one along each long side of the rectangular design,
represent mountains or the earth; the red stripes at their bases
are red banks along rivers; the white squares at the ends
of these red stripes are lakes; the blue areas adjoining the
squares represent smoke, haze, and heavy atmosphere; the large
white areas represent bare ground.   In the middle, the entire

hourglass-shaped figure is a bed. The green portion is grass-covered ground. The red stripe is a path. The red triangles at the end are again red banks. The small yellow triangles at the ends represent a hill on the Wind River Reservation in Wyoming, which is said to be yellow in appearance, and at which a fight once occurred. It is called niha^{n}nŏû′tă^n.

In the parfleche shown in Fig. 4, Plate XIX, color is more important than form, so far as symbolism is concerned. The blue represents mountains; this is presumably both on account of its color and because the blue areas are all obtuse iosoceles triangles, the usual symbol for a mountain. The red represents fruit or berries. The yellow, wherever it occurs on the parfleche, represents wood, especially willow on account of its yellowish-green bark. In addition, the colors used here also represent all objects having those colors. The acute red triangles also represent flame. The red, yellow, and blue acute triangles represent tents. The white and red pentagonal areas within the blue represent the door or opening in the mountain from which the buffalo originally issued on the earth. The long straight lines represent rivers.

Fig. 5, Plate XIX, shows a parfleche design that is not very frequent, but old. It is called wasixta ("bear-foot"). It was said to be the oldest of the parfleche designs, and to have been invented by Whirlwind-Woman, the first woman on earth. All the points or projections represent bear-claws. The lines enclosing the whole design, and forming a square, represent the camp-circle.

In the parfleche design shown in Fig. 6, Plate XIX, the two long isosceles triangles along the sides represent mountains. At each end of the design are three acute triangles, which represent tents. To each belongs one half of the diamond adjoining its vertex, this half-diamond being the projecting tent-poles. At the corners of the middle diamond are two small black triangular marks, which represent the rope passed around the poles near their tops to hold them together. The two middle tents also have their doors shown. In the other triangles, blue circular spots denote the place or situation of the tent. The entire square of the design is the earth. The stripes enclosing the design are rivers, red portions of them denoting river-banks of red soil. Minute black marks crossing these stripes represent paths.

Fig. 1 of Plate xx shows a bag which appears to have been made out of one end of a parfleche. The design is also a typical parfleche design. In the middle are two long flat triangles which are green; these represent grass-covered mountains. In each there is a pentagonal white area, which denotes a cave or hole in the mountain, and black pointed marks, which represent buffalo in the cave, from which they are supposed originally to have come. At the two sides of the pattern, mountains are also represented. The yellow acute triangles represent tents, and three red teeth at the base of each are its pegs. Lines and stripes denote paths, and the white portions of the design signify water.

In the parfleche design shown in Fig. 2, Plate xx, the circles, a very unusual ornamental figure in rawhide painting, represent lakes. They also represent buffalo-eyes. Near them, the triangles with the three-toothed bases are tents with their tent-pegs. A row of black dots just above the base of the tent represents people inside. Two small green triangles just above this row of dots are the dew-claws of buffalo. Along the two sides of the design, right-angled and equilateral triangles represent mountains. The double blue lines surrounding the whole design are rivers; the white and red stripes between the blue ones are paths. In the middle of the design, extending longitudinally, are two tents. The stripe bisecting them is a path, black dots in which signify tracks. The lower part of each of these middle triangles is divided off by a black line, and forms a white quadrilateral area resembling the life-symbol. These areas represent bears' ears, which are used as amulets. Two small black points in each of these figures are also bears' ears.

Fig. 3 of Plate xx shows the design on a very small parfleche. The design is bordered by a pattern in four colors. In this border-design red lines, forming an edging, are paths. The body of the border is green, and represents the earth.

DESIGNS ON RAWHIDE BAGS.

Blue triangles on this are mountains; and small yellow triangles enclosed within the blue are yellowish rocks on the
mountains.   Inside of this border the white unpainted skin
represents earth or ground.   The triangles are all tents, whatever their colors.   Some of them have two small dark-brown
marks at their bases; others, one such mark at the vertex.
These small figures represent respectively tent-pegs and projecting tent-poles.   Straight red lines are again paths, while
white lines with black rectangular spots on them represent a
row of buffalo-tracks.

Fig. 4 of Plate xx shows the design on another unusually
small parfleche.   The green lines enclosing the whole design
are the camp-circle.   The long flat triangles are hills.   The
six acute triangles are all tents: the interior red is the fire
inside; the yellow line, next to the red, is the tent itself,
i. e., the skins of which it consists; and the green outer border
of the triangle is the ground on which the tent stands.   Four
black tooth-figures at the base of some of the triangles are
tent-pegs.   The rhombus in the centre of the design represents both the eye and the navel.   In each of the hills there
is an oblong area, in which a red stripe denotes earth, a yellow
stripe sunlight, and two white trapezoids the symbol of life.
In general, without reference to their location in particular
places in the design, the colors on this parfleche have the following signification: green is the earth, yellow is day or light,
red is humanity, black is the sky.

In the parfleche design shown in Fig. 5 of Plate xx, two
elongated central diamonds, which were originally red, represent lizards.   Green lines in them, forming a cross, are their
bones.   The red diamonds are surrounded by a white area,
which is rhombic-elliptical.   This entire area, white and red,
represents a buffalo-scrotum.   The surface adjacent to it is
blue, which denotes haze and smoke.   At the ends of this blue
area are somewhat irregular white trapezoids; and in them, irregular green triangles.   Both are life-symbols.   All the figures
thus far described are enclosed by yellow and red lines, which
denote paths.   Along the two sides of the whole pattern is a
series of convex yellow and concave green figures.   These

denote yellow water and green water respectively. Each pair of them represents a lake. The white rectangles separating these lake-figures represent bare ground.

Fig. 6 of Plate xx shows the design on a particularly large parfleche. This design represents the appearance of the country where the maker of the parfleche lived. The triangles represent the mountains visible there. The red and yellow coloring represents the appearance of their surface. These mountains were said not to be rocky, else their representations would have been colored blue. The green on these triangles, as well as the unpainted hide, represent grass and vegetation. All the green lines are paths. The red and yellow rectangles within the wide stripes along the sides are

Fig. 32 ($\frac{50}{1981}$). Design on Rawhide Bag. Width of bag, 46 cm.

sticks, pointers, or pins for fastening together the front of the tent. The quadrilateral of green lines enclosing the design represents the ends of the earth (häneisa^n biitaawu).

On the rawhide bag shown in Fig. 32 a diamond in the centre represents a lake. Two short blue lines at its corners are streams of water flowing into the lake. In the centre of this large diamond is a smaller green one, which represents a frog. Black lines radiating from this green rhombus are the frog's legs. Besides the diamond, the central white area, which itself signifies sandy soil, contains two acute triangles. Short black lines in these, corresponding to those denoting frog-legs in the diamond, represent buffalo-tails attached to the ornaments on the tent. The border surrounding this interior ornamental area consists of a pattern of red and blue triangles. The red triangles are tents; the blue, mountains.

The blue lines enclosing this border represent the ocean, or the large body of water which is called by the Arapaho hääⁿtetc without being geographically localized or known.

On the back, the enclosing blue lines have the same signification of the ocean. The longitudinal blue lines form trails. Alternating red and blue marks in them represent tracks.

Fig. 33 shows one of a pair of hide bags that are used for coffee, sugar, berries, or other food that must be kept, especially during travels, in a pouch with a small and close opening. For this reason there is no loose flap serving as cover, as in most other bags; but the ends of the pouch are closed with soft skin (so that the whole bag is much like a bellows), and a slit is cut into one of these ends. The two large triangles at the two ends represent tents. The central diamond represents two tents. Between them a white stripe with black dots in it represents a buffalo-path with buffalo-tracks in it. The four red obtuse triangles along the sides are mountains. Small yellow triangles enclosed by them are

Fig. 33 ($\frac{50}{8044}$ a).   Design on Rawhide Bag.   Width of bag, 44 cm.

tents. The double blue lines surrounding the entire pattern represent mountain-ranges. Small rectangles in this border, colored red and yellow, represent lakes.

On the back, all the stripes of double blue lines are mountain-chains, and the small red and yellow rectangles are again lakes.

Fig. 34, *a*, shows a small square bag. The rectangles with three teeth each are bear's claws (wasixta). The long triangles are mountains. The small acute triangles within these are caves inhabited by bears. As in the last bag described, the blue enclosing lines are mountains seen in the distance. On the back, the blue square with its diagonals represents the bääxôti, or big wheel, one of the Arapaho sacred tribal objects. It is a wooden hoop with two strings tied across it. As has been stated before, the square and the circle are often equivalent in Arapaho symbolism, the circle being generally regarded as something four-sided, so that the symbolism here is not so forced as it might appear. On the

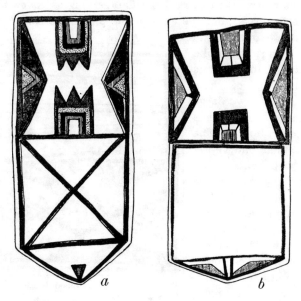

Fig. 34, *a* ($\frac{50}{5178}$), *b* ($\frac{50}{1058}$). Designs on Rawhide Bags. Width of bags, 20 cm., 22 cm.

triangular piece forming the cover-flap, the blue line bordering the edge represents the rainbow, and the small red triangle is the heart.

Fig. 34, *b*, shows a bag of about the same size as the preceding, with much the same pattern and symbolism. The rectangles represent bear-feet. The triangles are the places where the bears live, *i. e.*, the mountains. The small black marks just below the vertices of these triangles are wild cherries, which the bears eat. On the back, the blue lines at the edge are rivers, along which the cherries grow. On the cover-flap the blue lines have the same signification, while the red segments bordering them are the red banks of the rivers.

Fig. 5, Plate xxi, shows the design on the front of a very small hide bag, probably intended for a little girl to use in picking berries. The design is very similar to the two last described, but the symbolism is different. The triangles, it is true, represent in this case also mountains; and the small squares in them, caves in the mountains. But the two rectangles with the three-toothed ends were said to represent, not bear-feet, as their form would lead one to expect, but steep, high mountains, the narrow white space between them being a deep canyon. The yellow area within the rectangles represents earth. The blue lines at the top and bottom of the design represent "the lowest ground." The back of this bag is not shown in the illustration. It resembles exactly the back of the bag shown in Fig. 34, a; but whereas the design in that case represented a ceremonial hoop, in this case it represents the earth, or its four ends or directions (häneisa^n). It should be added, however, that this ceremonial hoop is itself a symbol of the earth.

Three square, rather small bags, with very similar designs, are shown in Figs. 1, 2, and 4 of Plate xxi. In Fig. 1 the two equilateral yellow and red triangles situated at the middle of the sides of the bag represent the heart. Two diamonds in the middle of the design, each consisting of two triangles, represent the morning star. At both ends of these diamonds are trapezoidal figures, one half red and one half green. These represent the body, also the life-symbol, also tents. The straight lines bordering the design, and trisecting it, are rivers. On the cover the small red triangle is again the heart. The line following the edge of the cover is a mountain.

Fig. 2, Plate xxi, shows a medicine-bag. As in most medicine-bags, whether square or cylindrical, the rawhide is not white, but brown. All the triangles, whatever their shape, represent mountains. The uncolored stripes trisecting the design are paths. The dark-green stripes enclosing the design

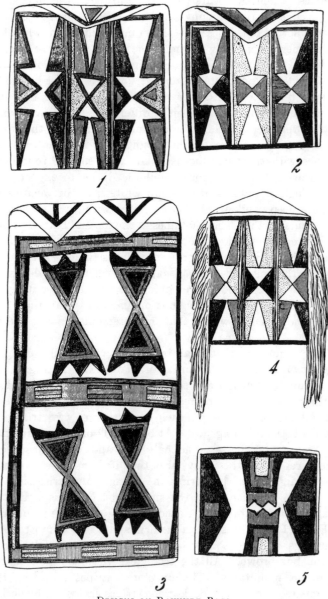

DESIGNS ON RAWHIDE BAGS.

are rivers. The unpainted portion of the pattern represents ground. On the cover, red triangles represent mountains.

Fig. 4, Plate xxi, shows another square medicine-bag made of browned rawhide. All the equilateral triangles are tents; the right-angled ones, mountains. The lines trisecting the design are buffalo-paths. The whole pattern represents the sky. This bag has a fringe along each side, which is not generally found on any objects made of rawhide except cylindrical medicine-cases.

These last three bags are all colored only with red, yellow, and dark green. In pattern they agree closely, without being identical or copied one from another.

A food-bag or bellows-shaped pouch, opening at the end, is shown in Fig. 3, Plate xxi. The familiar three-toothed triangular figures are bear-claws. The wide stripes are all mountain-ranges. The small blue and yellow bars contained in these stripes are dark and yellow rocks on the mountains.

A rawhide bag is shown in Fig. 1 of Plate xxii and Fig. 35. The triangles and segments of circles represent hills. The two large triangles, yellow in the centre, are tents. The rhombus between them represents the interior of a tent. The green, which is outside, represents the beds along the walls of the tent. The red is the ground. The blue is ashes around the fireplace. The yellow in the centre is the fire in the middle of the tent. The red, yellow, and green rectangle between this rhombus and the opening of the bag (Fig. 35) represents a parfleche. The yellow and blue squares at the corners of the bag represent bags of soft hide, used to hold clothing, etc.

On the back of the bag (Fig. 35) the entire rectangular design represents a shelter or brush-hut of branches, the parallel stripes being sun-rays falling through interstices in the foliage. The small white rectangle, containing a red equilateral triangle and enclosed by green lines, is the body, the red triangle being the heart.

On the triangular flap of hide serving as cover, the four low segments of circles, colored yellow and green, represent hills. The rest of the design, which can be described as a red and blue triangle with a white rectangle set up on its point, represents a red hill, with a road going up and down it (*i. e.*, over it).

The bag as a whole represents a turtle, loose strips of green cloth hanging from the corners being legs.

The bag shown in Fig. 2 of Plate XXII is much browned by

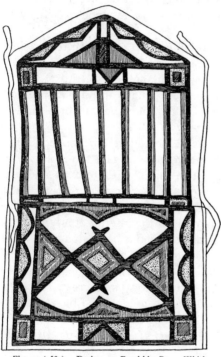

age. The figure in the middle of the bag was said to represent a pattern painted on buffalo-robes and called biinäbĭ't. This robe-design, like all other designs in Arapaho art, is not altogether fixed and constant. One form of it occurs on a buffalo-calf blanket which has been described elsewhere.[1] Other forms of it are more conventionalized. The biinäbĭ't design is considered sacred among the Arapaho. It is said to have come from the Apaches.

Fig. 35 ($\frac{50}{1683}$). Design on Rawhide Bag. Width of bag, 36 cm.

The bag shown in Fig. 3, Plate XXII, has an unusually vari-colored appearance, because the four paints upon it are distributed in small areas. All the isosceles triangles represent tents. The smallest and lowest of the triangles enclosed in each are considered as doors. The three-pronged black figures represent the poles projecting above the tent. The diamond in the middle of the whole design, having at-

---

[1] Bulletin of American Museum of Natural History, 1900, p. 85.

1

3

2

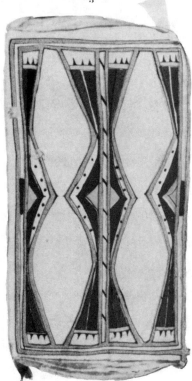

4

PAINTED BAGS.

tached to it two of these figures, is regarded as representing two tents.   Inside this diamond, two red lines represent the crossing of paths ; the yellow represents the sun ; and the green, the sky.   Both at the top and at the bottom of the front surface of the bag is a red rectangle containing a blue one, which in turn encloses a yellow one.   This entire rectangular figure represents a path.   At each end of this figure is a blue right-angled triangle, representing, on account of its color, grass or vegetation.   A similar yellow triangle adjacent to each of these represents wood or sticks.   The red lines separating these blue and yellow triangles represent trails.   The blue lines enclosing the entire design on the front of the bag are also trails.   The white ground-color of the bag represents sand.

It will be noted that on this bag green denotes the sky; and blue, grass.   Such identification of green and blue occurs in other instances, but is not usual when both colors are present on the same object.   Ordinarily the same word is used for " green " and " blue " in Arapaho.

On the back of the bag is a design in blue.   It consists of a rectangle divided into four parts by three lines parallel to the short sides of the bag.   On each of these sections there is a row of from three to four circular black dots placed parallel to the short sides of the bag.   The blue lines all represent water; *i. e.*, streams.   The dots are horse-tracks.   On the serrated cover-flap, low red and yellow triangles are hills or mountains; blue lines bisecting them, trails.

Fig. 4 of Plate XXII shows a bag made to hold food, especially coffee or sugar.   Formerly it would probably have been used for berries.   The design on this bag, like several others mentioned, and like the tent-ornament designs, was said by the owner of the bag to have been first made by the mythical character, Whirlwind-Woman.   All the triangles, whatever their color, represent hills.   The yellow signifies daylight. The small, black, pointed marks represent monuments of stones on hill-tops, such as are often left there by those who have sought the supernatural; they also represent the buffalo-robes of old men, set up to be prayed to; lastly, they represent tent-pegs. The series of six black spots, which is repeated four times, denotes that Whirlwind-Woman successively sat down in six places around the bag that she was painting with this design. In a similar manner, a parfleche is sometimes painted by four women sitting on four sides of it, so that the hide does not have to be turned to be painted at all its ends. The ten black diagonal lines in the white stripe that longitudinally bisects the design were the last marks made in process of painting.[1]

On the back of this bag a rectangle formed or enclosed by

double green lines represents the whole earth. The lines themselves are also rivers. Alternating red and blue transverse lines, which divide the rectangle into eight parts, are buffalo-paths leading to the river. The red denotes meat of the buffalo, the blue (equivalent to black) represents buffalo-hides.

Fig. 36 (₇₈₈⁵⁰). Design on Bag. Width of bag, 47.2 cm.

Fig. 36 shows the two sides of another food-bag. The pattern on the front is longitudinally bisected by a narrow unpainted stripe, which represents a river. Several small black marks in this stripe represent dried meat; *i. e.*, the contents of this bag. The triangles are all mountains. Of the colors, red and yellow signify

---

[1] The black, brown, or dark-blue thin lines with which the colored areas painted on rawhide are usually bordered, are put on after the colored areas, not before. Their purpose seems to be, not to assist the maker in the application of the colors, but to give to the colored areas a sharper outline.

earth; blue, haze or smoke. The decoration on the back consists of two very different halves. One half is painted in blue and yellow; the other seems merely sketched in outline in brown, having an unfinished appearance. It was, however, made thus intentionally. The two halves are also different in design. This lack of symmetry is exceptional. The colored half represents inhabited country; the uncolored, a country that is wild and uninhabited. In the colored half the flat, low, blue triangles are mountains, the pentagonal areas in them being lakes. The six acute triangles are also lakes. The yellow in these triangles represents vegetation in autumn. The blue lines enclosing the design are streams of water.

The uncolored design is enclosed by blue lines representing the sky, and itself represents distant scenery. The triangles are mountains. Small triangles in two of these represent caves; small squares in two of the others are camp-sites. The T-shaped figures on these same triangles represent imaginary figures of persons seen on mountain-tops.

The entire bag also represents a mole. The opening of the bag is the mouth of the mole. Four loose strips of red cloth at the corners of the bag are its legs. Two small painted triangles not shown in the illustration are the ears of the animal.

In the bag illustrated in Fig. 37 the spaces between the figures on the front side are not left white and unpainted, as is generally the case, but are colored yellow. This yellow represents daylight. All the triangles on this side, as well as the diamond in the middle, represent mountains. The interior of the diamond, and the interior of the equilateral triangles touching the diamond, represent caves. Round spots on the four triangles nearest the corners of the bag are rocks.

On the back, blue lines are buffalo-paths, blue diamonds in these are buffalo-wallows. Blue triangles are very high mountains, while yellow triangles were said to be that portion of these mountains which is underground.

A small square bag of hide is shown in Fig. 38. The acute

triangles represent tents. The obtuse triangles are mountains. Of the colors on these latter, the green represents
forests; the red, foot-hills; the blue, rocks; and the white.
sand. The two large white areas represent snow.

On the back, the square formed by the four green lines
along the edges is the whole earth. The two diagonals are
rivers. The crosses are the morning star.

On the triangular flap serving as cover, the two crosses are

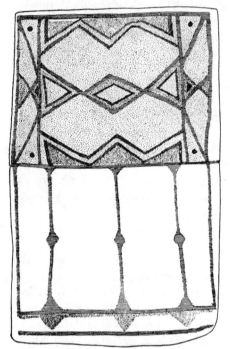

Fig. 37 ($\frac{50}{999}$). Design on Rawhide Bag. Width
of bag, 44 cm.

Fig. 38 ($\frac{50}{717}$). Design on Rawhide Bag. Width of bag, 20 cm.

again the morning star, the two border-lines forming an
angle are the rainbow, a round hole in the hide near the
corner of the cover is the sun, and two vertical lines proceeding from this hole are the rays of the sun.

Fig. 1 of Plate XXIII shows a food-bag. On the front, the
straight lines enclosing the whole design represent roads.

Two low, flat triangles extending along the sides of the bag are mountains; three smaller triangles contained in each represent hills. The unpainted surface of the hide, adjacent to these mountain-designs, represents the open prairie. The diamond in the middle represents the centre of the earth. Red and yellow areas within it represent earth of those colors. At each end of the diamond is a large triangle, which represents a tent. The various colors on this figure of a tent indicate the various colors with which tents are painted or embroidered. The white triangles inside the tent-figure are back-rests or pillows such as are used at the head and foot of beds. The blue in the figure of the tent is smoke. It is said by the Arapaho that when any one in a tent is angry or bad-tempered, the smoke from the fire does not rise, but remains inside; but when all are pleasant and cheerful, the smoke goes straight outside. The blue triangles represent smoke hanging in the tent; the blue line, smoke that is rising to issue from the top of the tent. Underneath these representations of tents are blue and yellow triangles, forming a pattern. The blue here represents ashes that have been taken out of the tent; the yellow is the earth on which the tent stands. A red zigzag line separating the blue and the yellow represents paths.

On the back, the lines or stripes represent sun-rays of various colors. Fine black lines separating stripes of different colors represent the black vegetable fibres sometimes used for embroidery.

The fringe on the bag represents niitcaantetäinani, what we do not know; that is, objects out of our possession, or various things too numerous to mention.

Fig. 2 of Plate XXIII shows a bag used for gathering cherries. It is hung around the neck by a thong attached to it. The design on the front has the following meaning. The rhombus in the middle is the earth as it first appeared after emergence from the original water. The red of the rhombus symbolizes paint; the green, earth; the red bisecting line, the course of the sun. The entire square design is the earth as it is now, after it had been extended, with mountains and soil

DESIGNS ON RAWHIDE BAGS.

and rocks of various colors upon it. These mountains are of course represented by the triangles forming the design. On a small yellow triangle, duplicated for symmetry, are two small black lines; these are the first people.

On the back, a square with its diagonals represents, as in a previous instance, the sacred wheel or hoop. This design also represents a shield, both because the shield resembles the hoop in shape and size, and because the bag is suspended by a string around the neck, like a shield. The line bordering the edge of the cover-flap represents a bow.

The bag shown in Fig. 3 of Plate XXIII has two diamonds in the centre of the design painted on its front. Each of these consists of four smaller diamonds, which represent the navel. Two small triangles adjacent to these diamonds represent small loops of hide wound with porcupine-quills, such as are attached to the ends of pendants on tents, cradles, etc. (touçiikǎ'hääna[n]). Four larger triangles adjacent to the diamonds are tents. Segments of circles below these are brush-shelters. Four long right-angled triangles at the sides of the design are awl-cases.

On the back of this bag the segments represent, as on the front, shelters. The enclosing lines represent the earth. The transverse stripes are paths. On the cover a vertical row of squares represents wooden buckets or bowls.

In the design on the bag shown in Fig. 4 of Plate XXIII, acute and obtuse isosceles triangles represent, as in most cases, tents and mountains. A blue rhombus in the middle is a lake. Yellow and red areas in the figures of mountains represent lakes. Double blue lines enclosing the whole of the design, as also that on the back, are mountain-ranges. Yellow squares on the back of the bag are lakes, black dots denoting their centres (invisible in the figure); and white squares are ravines. The stripes following the notched edge of the cover also represent mountains.

Fig. 39 shows a bag. On the front, a rectangular area contains two triangles and a rhombus, bordered by green lines. These lines represent water. The red and blue backgrounds of the triangles and rhombus represent clouds of those colors.

In each there is a cross, which is the morning star. This rectangular open area is bordered by a four-colored pattern. Along the long sides of this middle space, triangles that are blue, red, and green are tents; small white triangles at their bases are doors. Yellow areas between the triangles are the ground. In the border at the two ends of the rectangular space, similar figures represent tents and their doors; additional small inverted triangles at the vertices are projecting tent-poles. White areas between these tent-figures are the

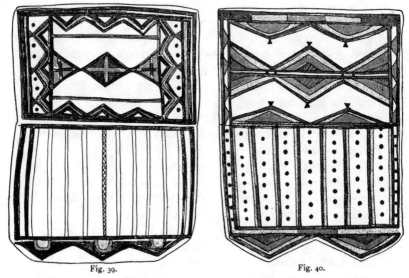

Fig. 39.   Fig. 40.

Figs. 39 ($\frac{50}{868}$), 40 ($\frac{50}{870}$).   Designs on Rawhide Bags.   Width of bags, 39.5 cm., 49.4 cm.

ground; and black dots, horse-tracks. Blue lines enclosing this border represent the earth.

Similar lines bordering the back have the same signification. Except for these, the back of the bag is uncolored. Stripes drawn across it in outline are paths. The central one of these stripes, however, is cross-hatched in black. This represents water. On the flap of the bag are three representations of tents with their doors.

·Fig. 40 shows a bag painted with red, yellow, and blue.

All the triangular figures are mountains. Small brown inverted triangles at their vertices are imaginary figures that are seen on mountain-tops and look like persons. The long white stripe bisecting the design is a path through a valley between the mountains; and four brown squares in this path are camp-sites. At the two ends of the design, small red triangles are tents. Along the two sides of the design, red, yellow, and blue bands in one line are tent-pins. The two central triangles, together forming a diamond, are also the eye.

On the back, stripes are paths, and rows of black dots are strings of buffalo travelling toward the mountains represented by triangles on the flap.

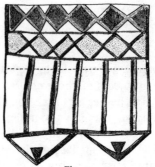

Fig. 41.   Fig. 42.

Figs. 41 ($\frac{50}{1000}$), 42 ($\frac{50}{1018}$).   Designs on Rawhide Bags.   Width of bags, 32.3 cm., 24.5 cm.

A small narrow bag, used to hold feathers, is shown in Fig. 41. The design on the front is cut into halves by a blue-bordered white stripe, with circular spots in it. The stripe represents the trail of a moving camp; the spots, camp-sites. On each side of this central vertical stripe is the same design. Nearest the edge, blue triangles are mountains. Adjacent to this, a yellow border represents low ground with dried or burned grass. The black lines bounding this yellow border represent dark timber. Adjacent to the yellow is a white zigzag stripe, which is a river. Next to this are two yellow triangles (tents) and a yellow diamond (the eye).

On the back, blue lines framing the entire area are the

earth. Transverse stripes and rows of dots are the various trails and sites of camps on the earth. On the cover, obtuse triangles are mountains.

Fig. 42 shows a small narrow bag like the one just described as a feather-bag. This one was used to hold porcupine-quills, which are generally kept in pouches of gut.

On the front, two rows of irregularly drawn rhombi — one row yellow, and one green — represent strings of german-silver plates formerly worn by the men, hanging from their scalp-locks. The white unpainted triangles adjacent to these rhombi are tents.

On the back, transverse lines represent ropes. On the two flaps serving as a cover, the lines forming angles represent mountains. Small green trapezoidal marks represent the bunches of hair often worn by children over the forehead (itceiçaa^n).

Of the colors on this bag, green represents the earth; red, paint; yellow, daylight. The colors also represent all existing objects of those colors.

In the design on the bag shown in Fig. 1 of Plate xxiv the obtuse triangles are hills; the acute triangles, tents. The two diamonds in the middle are the navel of man and woman. The lines enclosing the design are the camp-circle. The same meaning obtains on the back of the bag. Here transverse stripes are also tent-poles. On the cover, angular figures represent the ears or flaps of the top of the tent; small pointed figures are the wooden pins holding together the front of the tent.

Fig. 2 of Plate xxiv shows another bag. On the front, at each end, are four trapezoids. These represent the "hills" or periods of life. Two at each end are green, and two red and blue. These latter represent red and black paint,— a frequent combination in ceremonials. The white spaces between these trapezoids are lakes. All the triangles in the design are hills and mountains. The white unpainted surface is all water, except the white stripes along the edges and through the middle of the design; these stripes are roads.

On the back, black spots are buffalo-dung. Three trans-

DESIGNS ON RAWHIDE BAGS.

verse white stripes with green edges are rivers. Blue squares in them are islands, and red rectangles are red soil or gravel. Four narrow black lines are cracks in the ground. On the flap, triangles represent mountains.

Another bag is shown in Fig. 3 of Plate XXIV. Flat and acute triangles mean, as in so many other cases, mountains and tents. A diamond in the middle is both the navel and a mountain. Dark-green (almost black) lines are creeks; yellow lines, paths.

On the back the unpainted surface represents the earth. Three transverse stripes are paths. Colorèd marks in these stripes are rocks.

Fig. 4 of Plate XXIV shows a small berrying-bag. Small triangles at the edges of the design on the front are hills. Two very acute isosceles triangles are mountain-peaks. A diamond between them is a round hill. Two lines traversing the design longitudinally are streams. The red and yellow of which they are composed represent two kinds of bushes or trees (red and yellow willow ?) growing along the banks. The blue lines enclosing the design are häneā$^{/n}$kaa^n ("as far as the eye can reach," or the horizon, probably equivalent to the earth).

On the back, narrow black lines are paths, and black spots are clouds.

Hide cases that are approximately cylindrical but taper slightly toward the bottom, and are usually somewhat over a foot long, are generally known as "medicine-cases" and "feather-cases," and are used, as their names indicate, to hold small shamanistic and ceremonial objects. They are made of rawhide, which is not, however, white, as it is in ordinary bags and in parfleches, but brown, perhaps from having been smoked. There are in the Arapaho collection of the American Museum of Natural History three flat rectangular rawhide bags that are also brown; but all three of these were used, like the cylindrical cases, to hold medicine or ceremonial objects.

The most frequent painting on the cylindrical medicine-cases is a pattern of inverted tents. There may be either

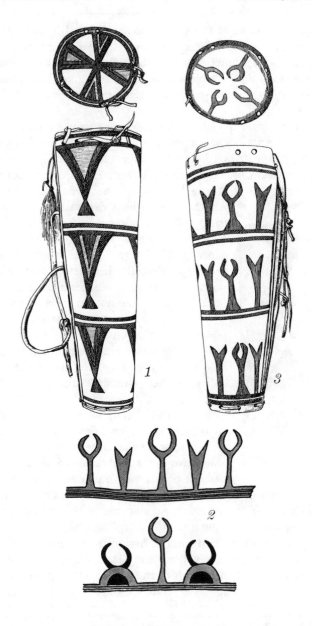

DESIGNS ON MEDICINE-CASES.

two or three rows of tents.   These are painted in red, black, and yellow, — the only colors that appear to be used on medicine-cases; sometimes even the yellow is omitted.   Fig. 1 of Plate xxv shows such a case.   The top cover has a design which may be considered as four tents or as the morning-star cross.

A second kind of design on medicine-cases is shown in Fig. 2 of Plate xxv.   The symbolism of this design is elaborate. It has been described before.[1]   It represents with some detail the acquisition of supernatural power, especially of control of the buffalo, by the owner of the case. Another case, whose design is very similar to the last, is shown in Fig. 3 of Plate xxv.   Nothing is known of the significance of this design.   The Arapaho declare that the symbolic decoration that occurs on this kind of medicine-case was used (this probably does not mean invented) by a medicine-man who was famous for his power over the buffalo, and by his followers.   This medicine-man is said to have died not very long ago.   How far the symbolism of these similarly ornamented cases was alike, is not known.

Fig. 43 ($\frac{60}{955}$).   Design on a Medicine-case.   Length, 50 cm.

In the Field Columbian Museum in Chicago there is a Kiowa medicine-case whose design is somewhat intermediate between these two kinds of Arapaho designs.   This pattern consists of inverted triangles resembling the inverted tents of Fig. 1 of Plate xxv.   At their vertices are wide crescents, causing the entire figures to resemble some of the figures of Fig. 3, Plate xxv.

Fig. 43 shows a third kind of design from a medicine-case. This is painted in red, yellow, and black, on one side or half of the case.   The other half of the case is left unpainted, and the top is missing.   The triangles (eight in all) represent

---

[1] Bulletin of the American Museum of Natural History, 1900, p. 82; and American Anthropologist, 1901, p. 319.

tents.   The two long red areas along the sides of the design
are the red of evening.   The diamond in the centre is called
the navel, and therefore a person.   There are three small red
figures in this diamond.   The one in the very centre represents the person [1] owning the case; the two at the corners of
the diamond represent human beings.   In general pattern,

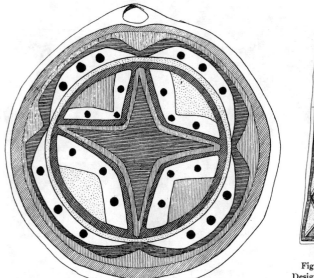

Fig. 44 (⁵⁰⁄₈₃₂).   Cover of a Shield.   Diam., 28 cm.

Fig. 45 (⁵⁰⁄₁₀₀₈).
Design on a Crup-
per. Length of de-
sign, 47 cm.

this cylindrical case resembles the average parfleche more
than it does the average medicine-case.

An Arapaho medicine-case with a fourth kind of design is
in the Field Columbian Museum of Chicago.   The figures on
this resemble bear-foot symbols.

A piece of rawhide used to cover a shield is shown in Fig.
44.   The large cross or star-shaped figure in the middle represents the morning star.   All the triangles on the shield are
tents.   The circles, both inner and outer, represent the sun.
The round black spots represent bullets, evidently those that
the shield is intended to stop.

[1] This may possibly mean the spirit-person that owns or inhabits the medicine-case.

The design painted on the rawhide portion of a crupper is shown in Fig. 45. On each half there is a dark-blue zigzag line in the centre, which represents a range of mountains. The red on the inner side of the zigzag line represents the earth. Light-blue[1] stripes dividing the red area into sections, and surrounding the whole design, are rivers. The

Fig. 46, *a* ($\frac{50}{931}$), *b* ($\frac{50}{984}$). Rawhide Hats. Length, about 35 cm.

light-blue color also represents the prairie covered with a certain blue flower (tcänäätänäeinoûû).

Young men sometimes wear a sun-shade that may be described as the brim of a hat without the crown. It consists of a piece of rawhide somewhat over a foot long. Near the back end of this, a circular area about six inches in diameter has a number of radii slit into it. When this part of the

---

[1] The light-blue is represented by horizontal shading.

rawhide is pressed upon the top of the head, the two dozen
or more sectors yield, and stand up, forming a circle around
the head.   Fig. 46 shows two of these hats or sun-shades as
they appear seen from above, with the points (sectors) standing
nearly upright.

On one such sun-shade, shown in Fig. 46, *a*, a number of
differently-colored zigzags (on the front projection or brim
of the head-dress) represent tents.   Each bend in the zigzag forms a triangle, and these represent tents.   At the
opposite end of the sun-shade a row of smaller triangles also
represents tents.   All the straight lines on the piece of hide
represent paths.   The pointed projections of hide standing
up around the head-opening in a circle represent men dancing.   A blue circular line at the base of these projections
represents a circle worn in the ground from their dancing.

In another such sun-shade (Fig. 46, *b*,) the circular row of
projections was interpreted as signifying the camp-circle of
tents.

A summary of the symbolism of the decorative forms that
have been described is presented in Plates xxvi–xxxi.   The
decorative forms of the same symbolic significance are here
brought together.   Thus all the forms taken by the symbols, for instance, of a man or of a tent, are readily review-
able and comparable.

From this summary have been excluded all symbols whose
significance depends altogether on their position, like the beads
denoting rat's ears in Fig. 21, *g*.   In such cases the shape of
the symbol itself obviously is often of no consequence.   On
the plates are shown all the distinct forms of each symbol.
Whenever a symbol has been found a number of times with
the same form, these occurrences are represented only once in
the illustrations.

Inasmuch as the technique of embroidery and that of
painting are necessarily quite different, it has seemed best to
separate the symbols which are embroidered, whether in
beads or in porcupine-quills or in fibres, from those which are
painted on rawhide.   For the same reason a third separate

summary has been made for those symbols that are neither embroidered nor painted, but consist of attachments such as pendants, fringes, strings, loops, or feathers: in short, all the symbols consisting of decorations which are not flat like bead or paint designs, but three-dimensional.

In the list below is also given the total number of occurrences of each symbolic signification, on all the objects that have been described.

A preliminary list of symbols was illustrated in an earlier paper.[1] On that occasion, however, symbols on objects of a religious nature were included in the series, while in the present case such objects have been left for subsequent separate treatment, and the list has been made up from specimens on which the ornamentation is decorative rather than ceremonial or pictographic.

LIST OF SYMBOLS WITH REFERENCE TO PLATES XXVI–XXXI.

Objects represented.	Embroidered Designs. Fig. No.	Painted Designs. Fig. No.	Three-Dimensional Designs. Fig. No.	Number of Occurrences.
Human Figures.				
Person..........................	1–3	242–246	—	8
Person sitting...................	4	—	—	1
Person standing................	5	—	—	1
Persons dancing in a circle........	—	—	430	1
Persons in tent or sweat-house....	6	247–248	—	3
First human beings..............	—	249	—	1
Mythic dwarfs..................	7	—	—	1
Women.........................	—	250	—	1
Imaginary human figure..	—	251–252	—	2
Body and Parts of the Body.				
Body..........................	—	253–254	—	2
Navel..........................	8	255	—	4
Navel-string....................	9	—	431	2
Heart..........................	—	256	—	4
Heart and lungs.................	10	—	—	1
Head..........................	11	—	—	1
Matted hair....................	—	257	432	2

Objects represented.	Embroidered Designs. Fig. No.	Painted Designs. Fig. No.	Three-Dimensional Designs. Fig. No.	Number of Occurrences.
Eye	12-14	258-260	—	6
Tooth	—	—	433	1
Fingers	—	—	434	1
Legs	—	—	435	1
Ribs	—	—	436	1
Track	15	—	—	2
Animals.				
Buffalo	16	261-263	—	4
Wolves	17	—	—	1
Coyotes	—	264	—	1
Rats	18	—	—	1
Eagle	19-22	—	—	5
Thunder-bird	23	—	—	1
Magpie	24	—	—	1
Swallow	25	—	—	1
Snake	26-27	—	—	4
Lizard	28-30	265	—	4
Turtle	31-34	—	—	4
Frog	35	266	—	2
Fish	36	—	—	1
Bees	37-38	—	—	2
Ants	—	—	437-438	2
Butterfly	39-43	—	—	5
Beetle	44	—	—	1
Water-beetle	—	267	—	1
Dragon-fly	45-47	—	—	3
Cricket	48	—	—	1
Spider	49	—	—	1
Crayfish	50	—	—	1
Centipede	51-53	—	—	3
Leeches	54	—	—	1
Caterpillar	55-59	—	—	5
Worms or maggots	60-64	—	—	9
Game, variety of animals	65	—	—	2
Parts of Animals.				
Bear-foot	66-68	268-272	—	9
Bear-ear	—	273-274	—	2
Bear-den	—	275	—	1
Coyote-tracks	—	276	—	1
Buffalo-eye	—	277	—	1
Buffalo-skull	—	278	—	1
Buffalo-scrotum	—	279	—	1
Buffalo-intestine	69	—	—	1
Buffalo dew-claw	—	280	—	1
Buffalo-hoof	70-71	—	—	3
Buffalo-track	72	281-282	—	3

EXPLANATION OF PLATE XXVI.

ARAPAHO SYMBOLISM IN EMBROIDERED DESIGNS.

∗*∗ Numbers in parentheses, when accompanied by Roman numerals, refer to plate figures, otherwise to text figures. Where the specimen bearing the symbol is not illustrated, reference to its catalogue number is given.

FIG.
1. Person. (XIV, 7)
2. "   (22)
3. "   (25)
4. Person sitting. (II, 1)
5. Person standing. (II, 1)
6. Persons in tent or sweat-house. (Bull. Am. Mus. Nat. Hist., XIII, p 8.3)
7. Mythic dwarf. (V, 4)
8. Navel. (II, 3)
9. Navel-string. (VIII, 6)
10. Heart and lungs. (IV, 1)
11. Head (14, b)
12. Eye. (II, 2)
13. "   (27)
14. "   (27)
15. Track. (II, 2)
16. Buffalo. (I, 4)
17. Wolves. (XIV, 6)
18. Rats. (VII, 2)
19. Eagle. (XIII, 5)
20. "   (XII, 3)
21. "   (23, b)
22. "   (23, c)
23. Thunder-bird. (Bull. Am. Mus. Nat. Hist. XIII, p. 83)
24. Magpie. (VI, 2)
25. Swallow. (7, b)
26. Snake. (III, 2)
27. "   (XI, 1)
28. Lizard. (III, 1)
29. "   (XI, 6)
30. "   (21, h)
31. Turtle. (II, 5)
32. "   (20, c)
33. "   (XII, 4)
34. "   (XII, 2)
35. Frog. (28)
36. Fish. (III, 4)
37. Bee. (XIV, 5)
38. Bees. (XIV, 5)

FIG.
39. Butterfly. (III, 4)
40. "   (XVII)
41. "   (III, 1)
42. "   (VIII, 3)
43. "   (XII, 6)
44. Beetle. (7, a)
45. Dragon-fly. (IV, 1)
46. "   (25)
47. "   (XII, 6)
48. Cricket. (XII, 1)
49. Spider. (Cat. No. $\frac{50}{328}$)
50. Crayfish. (II, 4)
51. Centipede. (V, 2)
52. "   (Cat. No. $\frac{50}{642}$)
53. "   (XII, 5)
54. Leech. (X, 2).
55. Caterpillar. (IV, 1)
56. "   (II, 1)
57. "   (21, d)
58. "   (XVII)
59. "   (XII, 2)
60. Worms or maggots. (Cat. No. $\frac{50}{328}$)
61. Worm. (I, 3)
62. "   (21, h)
63. "   (25)
64. Worms. (21, h)
65. Game, variety of animals. (V, 5)
66. Bear-foot. (24, a)
67. "   (27)
68. "   (26)
69. Buffalo-intestine. (5, e)
70. Buffalo-hoof. (II, 2)
71. "   (XIV, 7)
72. Buffalo-track. (I, 7)
73. Buffalo-path. (31)
74. "   (XIII, 4)
75. Buffalo-wallow (XIII, 4)
76. Buffalo-horns. (5, f)
77. Mythic cave of the buffalo. (Cat. No. $\frac{50}{648}$)

ARAPAHO SYMBOLISM.

EXPLANATION OF PLATE XXVII.

ARAPAHO SYMBOLISM IN EMBROIDERED DESIGNS.

*** Numbers in parentheses, when accompanied by Roman numerals, refer to plate figures, otherwise to text figures. Where the specimen bearing the symbol is not illustrated, reference to its catalogue number is given.

FIG.
78. Cattle-track. (XIII, 5)
79.   "   (XIII, 5)
80. Horse-ears. (III, 1)
81. Horse-track. (V, 4)
82. Elk-leg. (XV, 2)
83. Elk-hoof. (V, 2)
84. Deer-hoof. (V. 2)
85. Rabbit-tracks. (II, 5)
86. Beaver-rib. (20, a)
87. Scales on Beaver-tail. (XI, 2)
88. Beaver dam and huts. (20, a)
89. Turtle-claw. (XII, 4)
90. Turtle-egg. (XII, 4)
91. Snake skin-markings. (5, f)
92. Horned-toad skin-markings. (III, 4)
93. Joints and stomach of frog. (20, c)
94. Markings of lizard. (20, b)
95. Bee-hole. (XIV, 5)
96. Ant-hills. (24, c)
97.   "   (V, 5)
98. Ant-hill. (XVII)
99. Ant-path. (24, c)
100. Dragonfly-wing. (XII, 6)
101. Spider-web. (Cat. No. $\frac{50}{328}$)
102. Centipede-tracks. (XII, 5)
103. Worm-hole. (21, h)
104. Tree. (XIII, 3)
105. Trees on mountain. (24, b)
106. "   "   "   (II, 1)
107. "   "   "   (5, b)
108. Leaf of "Yellow-herb" (27)
109. Willow-leaf. (XVII)
110. Mushrooms. (21, e)
111. Cactus. (V, 5)
112. Mountain. (6)
113.   "   (Bull. Am. Mus. Nat. Hist., XIII, p. 83)
114. Mountain. (25)

FIG.
115. Mountain. (XI, 6)
116.   "   (XIV, 6)
117.   "   (24, a)
118.   "   (XIII, 6)
119. Mountains. (23, a)
120.   "   (II, 1)
121.   "   (XI, 5)
122. Mountain. (XIV, 2)
123. Snow-covered mountain. (Bull. Am. Mus. Nat. Hist., XIII, p. 83)
124. Snow-covered mountain. (XII, 3)
125. Valley or canyon. (XIV, 2)
126. The Earth. (Cat. No. $\frac{50}{642}$)
127.   "   "   (XIII, 5)
128.   "   "   (24, c)
129. Dirt, clay. (24, c)
130. Rocks. (24, b)
131.   "   (II, 1)
132.   "   (25)
133.   "   (8)
134.   "   (II, 1)
135.   "   (24, c)
136.   "   (X, 1)
137.   "   (21, f)
138.   "   (23, b)
139.   "   (23, b)
140. Path. (I, 4)
141.   "   (XV, 2)
142.   "   (XVI)
143. Crossing paths. (XII, 3)
144. Holes in a path. (XIV, 5)
145.   "   "   "   (II, 1)
146. Path going over a hill. (I, 3)
147. River. (V, 1)
148.   "   (24, b)
149.   "   (IV, 1)
150. River with islands. (XIV, 2)
151. River. (XIV, 2)
152. Spring. (24, b)
153. Lake. (Bull. Am. Mus. Nat. Hist., XIII, p 83)
154. Lake. (II, 3)

ARAPAHO SYMBOLISM.

EXPLANATION OF PLATE XXVIII.

ARAPAHO SYMBOLISM IN EMBROIDERED DESIGNS.

₊ Numbers in parentheses, when accompanied by Roman numerals, refer to plate figures, otherwise to text figures. Where the specimen bearing the symbol is not illustrated, reference to its catalogue number is given.

FIG.
155. Lake. (XIII, 6)
156. Scum. (28)
157. Sun. (XIII, 2)
158. Sunrise. (I, 3)
159. Sun-rays. (XIII, 2)
160. Star. (IV, 2)
161.   "   (III, 1)
162.   "   (IV, 1)
163.   "   (Cat. No. $\frac{50}{812}$)
164.   "   (6, a)
165.   "   (7, b)
166.   "   (XII, 1)
167.   "   (VIII, 3)
168. Morning star. (8)
169.   "   "   (V, 3)
170.   "   "   (VII, 1)
171.   "   "   (15)
172.   "   "   (27)
173.   "   "   (XIV, 1)
174.   "   "   (VII, 3)
175.   "   "   (24, b)
176.   "   "   (I, 8)
177.   "   "   (6, a)
178.   "   "   (21, c)
179. Morning star at the horizon. (6, a)
180. Morning star with rays. (I, 8)
181. Constellation. (6, a)
182. Milky way. (6, b)
183. Cloud. (27)
184.   "   (II, 4)
185.   "   (Cat. No. $\frac{50}{812}$)
186. Lightning. (III, 5)
187.   "   (Bull. Am. Mus. Nat. Hist., XIII, p. 83)
188. Rainbow. (20, d)
189. Rain. (Bull. Am. Mus. Nat. Hist., XIII, p. 83)
190. Tent. (IX, 2)
191.   "   (15)
192.   "   (XI, 2)

FIG.
193. Tent. (XIII, 2)
194.   "   (V, 2)
195.   "   (XIII, 4)
196.   "   (21, a)
197.   "   (XIV, 8)
198.   "   (21, b)
199.   "   (V, 3)
200. Camp-circle. (15)
201.   "   (27)
202.   "   (30)
203. Boundary of habitation. (V, 4)
204. Brush-hut. (15)
205.   "   (V, 5)
206. Pole of sweat-house. (III, 2)
207. Covering of sweat-house. (III, 2)
208. House. (XV, 1)
209. Fence. (25)
210. Rock monuments. (23, a)
211.   "   (15)
212. Soft bag. (VIII, 5)
213. Box. (XIII, 5)
214. Knife-case. (22)
215. Sinew. (VIII, 6)
216. Rack for saddlery. (8)
217.   "   "   "   (II, 1)
218. Rack for meat. (23, c)
219. Rope. (8)
220. Saddle-blanket. (8)
221. Man's stirrup. (8)
222. Woman's stirrup. (8)
223. Lance. (Cat. No. $\frac{50}{1069}$)
224. Bow. (I, 4)
225. Arrow. (XIV, 4)
226. Arrow-point. (XVIII, 5)
227.   "   (XI, 2)
228.   "   (XI, 2)
229.   "   (I, 4)
230.   "   (XIV, 3)
231.   "   (II, 3)

ARAPAHO SYMBOLISM.

EXPLANATION OF PLATE XXIX.

ARAPAHO SYMBOLISM IN EMBROIDERED AND PAINTED DESIGNS.

⁎ Numbers in parentheses, when accompanied by Roman numerals, refer to plate figures, otherwise to text figures. Where the specimen bearing the symbol is not illustrated, reference to its catalogue number is given.

FIG.
232. Arrow-point. (XIII, 5)
233. Pipe. (XII, 2)
234. " (5, f)
235. Gambling-counters. (20, d)
236. Female dress. (VIII, 5)
237. Hiiteni (life, prosperity). (Cat. No. $\frac{50}{642}$)
238. Hiiteni (life, prosperity). (V, 2)
239. Hiiteni (life, prosperity). (II, 5)
240. Hiiteni (life, prosperity). (5, b)
241. Thought. (22)
242. Person. (XXV, 2)
243. " (XXV, 2)
244. " (43)
245. " (43)
246. " (43)
247. Persons in tent or sweat-house. (XX, 2)
248. Persons in tent or sweat-house. (XVIII, 3)
249. First human beings. (XXIII, 2)
250. Woman. (XIX, 1)
251. Imaginary human figure (36)
252. Imaginary human figure (40)
253. Body. (XXI, 1)
254. " (35)
255. Navel. (XX, 4)
256. Heart. (35)
257. Matted hair. (42)
258. Eye. (XX, 4)
259. " (41)
260. " (40)
261. Buffalo. (Bull. Am. Mus. Nat. Hist., XIII, p. 85)
262. Buffalo. (XXV, 2)
263. " (40)
264. Coyotes. (XIX, 2)
265. Lizard. (XX, 5)
266. Frog. (32)
267. Water-beetle. (XVIII, 3)
268. Bear-foot. (XVIII, 5)

FIG.
269. Bear-foot. (XIX, 2)
270. " (34, a)
271. " (34, b)
272. " (XIX, 5)
273. Bear-ear. (XX, 2)
274. " (XX, 2)
275. Bear-den. (34, a)
276. Coyote-tracks. (XIX, 1)
277. Buffalo-eye. (XX, 2)
278. Buffalo-skull. (XXV, 2)
279. Buffalo-scrotum. (XX, 5)
280. Buffalo dew-claw. (XX, 2)
281. Buffalo-track. (XX, 3)
282. " (33)
283. Buffalo-path. (XXI, 4)
284. Buffalo-wallow. (37)
285. Buffalo-dung. (XXIV, 2)
286. Mythic cave of the buffalo. (Cat. No. $\frac{50}{642}$)
287. Mythic cave of the buffalo. (XX, 1)
288. Mythic cave of the buffalo. (XIX, 4)
289. Abundance of buffalo. (Bull. Am. Mus. Nat. Hist., XIII, p. 85)
290. Horse-tracks. (39)
291. Wild-cherry. (34, b)
292. Fibrous water-plant. (XXIII, 1)
293. Mountain. (XX, 4)
294. " (38)
295. " (35)
296. " (XVIII, 4)
297. " (XX, 1)
298. " (XXIII, 2)
299. " (XXI, 4)
300. " (XXV, 2)
301. " (XXIV, 3)
302. Mountains. (32)
303. " (33)
304. " (XXIV, 2)
305. " (XX, 2)
306. " (37)
307. " (XXIII, 4)
308. Mountain-peak. (XXIV, 4)

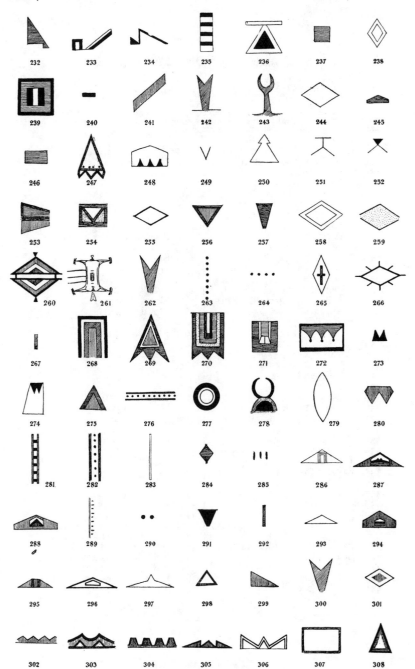

ARAPAHO SYMBOLISM.

EXPLANATION OF PLATE XXX.

ARAPAHO SYMBOLISM IN PAINTED DESIGNS.

_**_* Numbers in parentheses, when accompanied by Roman numerals, refer to plate figures, otherwise to text figures. Where the specimen bearing the symbol is not illustrated, reference to its catalogue number is given.

FIG.

309. Mountain-peak. (xxi, 5)
310. Cave. (36)
311.   "   (xxi, 5)
312. Valley or Canyon. (xviii, 4)
313.   "   "   "   (xxi, 5)
314.   "   "   "   (xxiii, 4)
315. Meadow. (Cat. No. $\frac{50}{925}$)
316. The earth. (xxv, 2)
317.   "   "   (xix, 6)
318.   "   "   (xxii, 4)
319. Ends of the earth. (xix, 1)
320. The earth at its first emergence. (xxiii, 2)
321. Cracks in the ground. (xxiv, 2)
322. Rock. (37)
323.   "   (xxi, 3)
324.   "   (xxiv, 3)
325. Path. (xxiv, 4)
326.   "   (xxii, 3)
327.   "   (xxii, 3)
328.   "   (xxiv, 3)
329.   "   (xxiii, 3)
330. Crossing paths. (xxii, 3)
331. Path with tracks. (xx, 2)
332.   "   "   "   (32)
333. Path going over a hill. (35)
334. Circle worn by dancing. (46, a)
335. River. (xxii, 4)
336.   "   (38)
337.   "   (xxiv, 3)
338.   "   (39)
339.   "   (32)
340. River with islands. (xxiv, 2)
341. River with islands. (xix, 2)
342. Lake. (32)
343.   "   (xx, 2)
344.   "   (xx, 5)
345.   "   (xxiv, 2)

FIG.

346. Lake (xxiii, 4)
347.   "   (xxiii, 4)
348.   "   (36)
349.   "   (36)
350. Ocean. (32)
351. Sun. (44)
352.   "   (xxv, 2)
353. Sun-rays. (xxiii, 1)
354.   "   "   (35)
355. Star. (44)
356. Morning star. (xxi, 1)
357.   "   "   (39)
358.   "   "   (38)
359. Sky. (36)
360. Cloud. (xxiv, 4)
361. Rainbow. (38)
362. Flame. (xix, 4)
363. Smoke. (xxiii, 1)
364. Tent. (xxiv, 1)
365.   "   (42)
366.   "   (43)
367.   "   (43)
368.   "   (xviii, 4)
369.   "   (33)
370.   "   (46, a)
371.   "   (xix, 1)
372.   "   (Cat. No. $\frac{50}{688}$)
373.   "   (xxii, 3)
374.   "   (39)
375.   "   (xix, 6)
376.   "   (xix, 6)
377.   "   (xx, 4)
378.   "   (xx, 1)
379.   "   (xx, 3)
380. Tent-door. (xxiv, 1)
381. Tent-pin. (xx, 6)
382.   "   "   (xix, 1)
383.   "   "   (xxiv, 1)
384.   "   "   (xviii, 4)
385. Loop for tent-pins. (xxiii, 3)

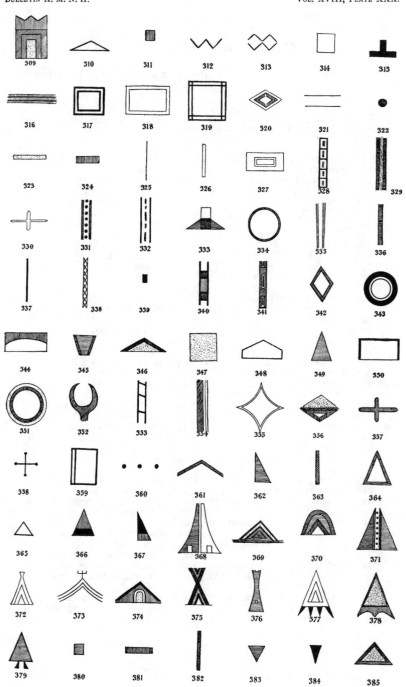

EXPLANATION OF PLATE XXXI.

ARAPAHO SYMBOLISM IN PAINTED AND THREE-DIMENSIONAL DESIGNS.

∗ Numbers in parentheses, when accompanied by Roman numerals, refer to plate figures, otherwise to text figures. Where the specimen bearing the symbol is not illustrated, reference to its catalogue number is given.

FIG.
386. Tent-poles. (XXIV, 1)
387. Tent-flaps. (XXIV, 1)
388. Tent-pendant. (32)
389. Interior of tent. (35)
390. Tent-site. (XIX, 6)
391. Camp-site. (41)
392. " (36)
393. " (XIX, 1)
394. Camp-circle. (XVIII, 2)
395. Brush-hut. (XXIII, 3)
396. " (35)
397. Sweat-house. (XVIII, 3)
398. " (XXV, 2)
399. American tent. (46, b)
400. Rock monument. (XX, 4)
401. Bed. (XIX, 3)
402. " (XXIII, 1)
403. Parfleche. (35)
404. Soft bag. (35)
405. Bucket or vessel. (XXIII, 3)
406. Medicine-case. (XXV, 2)
407. Awl-case. (XXIII, 3)
408. Paint-stick. (XVIII, 3)
409. Rope. (XVIII, 3)
410. " (42)
411. Bow. (XXIII, 2)
412. Bullets. (44)
413. Ceremonial wheel. (34, a)
414. Ceremonially used robe. (XX, 4)
415. Robe design. (XXII, 2)
416. Metal hair-ornaments. (42)
417. Hiiteni (life, prosperity). (XVIII, 3)
418. Hiiteni (life, prosperity). (XX, 5)
419. Hiiteni (life, prosperity). (XXI, 1)
420. Hiiteni (life, prosperity) (Bull. Am. Mus. Nat. Hist., XIII, p. 85)
421. Hiiteni (life, prosperity). (XVIII, 5)

FIG.
422. Hiiteni (life, prosperity). (XX, 4)
423. Contents (of bag). (36)
424. Centre. (XXIII, 1)
425. " (XVIII, 2)
426. " (XXIII, 4)
427. Stops (in a course). (Cat. No. $\frac{50}{925}$)
428. The four hills (periods) of life. (XXIV, 2)
429. Supernatural instruction. (XXV, 2)
430. Persons dancing in a circle. (46, a)
431. Navel-strings. (VIII, 5)
432. Hair. (14, b)
433. Tooth. (VIII, 5)
434. Fingers. (7, c)
435. Legs. (14, b)
436. Ribs. (14, b)
437. Ants. (7, a)
438. " (24, c)
439. Burrs in buffalo-hair. (30)
440. Snake-rattle. (5, f)
441. Snake-tongue. (5, f)
442. Paths. (27)
443. Rivers. (XIII, 4)
444. Sun. (7, c)
445. Sun-dog. (VI, 3)
446. Stars. (7, c)
447. Star. (XI, 1)
448. Tent-pin. (14, b)
449. Loop for tent-pins. (14, b)
450. Tent-pendants. (14, b)
451. " (XVI)
452. Camp-circle. (46, b)
453. Dry meat. (XVI)
454. Ear-pendant. (XIV, 8)
455. Coffee. (XIV, 6)
456. The many things unknown. (XXIII, 1)
457. Property possessed. (7, c)
458. Desire of accomplishment. (VI, 1)

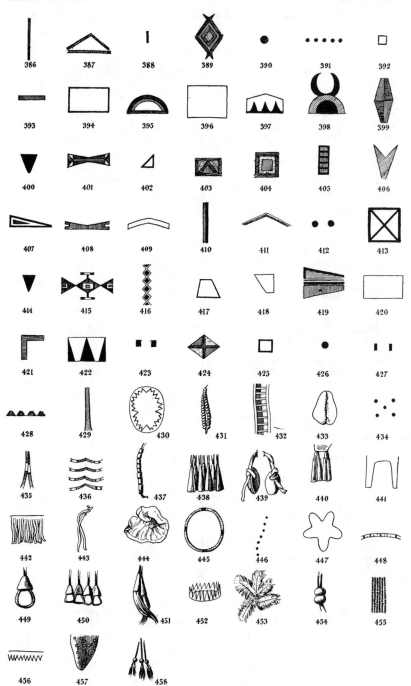

ARAPAHO SYMBOLISM.

Objects represented.	Embroidered Designs. Fig. No.	Painted Designs. Fig. No.	Three-Dimensional Designs. Fig. No.	Number of Occurrences.
Buffalo-path......................	73–74	283	—	5
Buffalo-wallow...................	75	284	—	2
Buffalo-horns....................	76	—	—	1
Burrs in buffalo-hair.............	—	—	439	1
Buffalo-dung....................	—	285	—	1
Mythic cave of the buffalo.........	77	286–288	—	4
Abundance of buffalo............	—	289	—	1
Cattle-track......................	78–79	—	—	2
Horse-ears........	80	—	—	1
Horse-tracks.....................	81	290	—	3
Elk-leg..........................	82	—	—	1
Elk-hoof.........................	83	—	—	1
Deer-hoof.......................	84	—	—	1
Rabbit-tracks....................	85	—	—	1
Beaver-rib.......................	86	—	—	1
Scales on beaver-tail.............	87	—	—	1
Beaver dam and huts............	88	—	—	1
Turtle-claw......................	89	—	—	1
Turtle-eggs......................	90	—	—	1
Snake-rattle....	—	—	440	1
Snake-tongue....................	—	—	441	1
Snake skin-markings.............	91	—	—	1
Horned-toad skin-markings......	92	—	—	1
Joints and stomach of frog........	93	—	—	1
Markings of lizard................	94	—	—	1
Bee-holes.......................	95	—	—	1
Ant-hills........................	96–98	—	—	3
Ant-paths.......................	99	—	—	1
Dragonfly-wing	100	—	—	1
Spider-web......................	101	—	—	1
Centipede-tracks.................	102	—	—	1
Worm-holes......................	103	—	—	1
Plants.				
Tree............................	104	—	—	1
Trees on mountain..............	105–107	—	—	3
Leaf of "Yellow-herb"..........	108	—	—	1
Willow-leaf....	109	—	—	1
Wild-cherry.....................	—	291	—	1
Mushrooms......................	110	—	—	1
Cactus....	111	—	—	1
Fibrous water-plant.............	—	292	—	1
Earth.				
Mountains, hills, and ranges......	112–122	293–307	—	71
Mountain-peak..................	—	308–309	—	3
Snow-covered mountain.........	123–124	—	—	2
Cave............................	—	310–311	—	3

OBJECTS REPRESENTED.	EMBROIDERED DESIGNS. Fig. No.	PAINTED DESIGNS. Fig. No.	THREE-DIMENSIONAL DESIGNS. Fig. No.	NUMBER OF OCCURRENCES.
Valley or canyon................	125	312–314	—	5
Meadow........................	—	315	—	1
The earth......................	126–128	316–318	—	16
Ends of the earth..............	—	319	—	4
Visible world..................	—	—	—	1
The earth at its first emergence...	—	320	—	1
Cracks in the ground...........	—	321	—	1
Dirt, clay......................	129	—	—	1
Rocks.........................	130–139	322–324	—	20
Path..........................	140–142	325–329	442	39
Crossing paths.................	143	330	—	2
Path with tracks...............	—	331–332	—	2
Holes in a path................	144–145	—	—	2
Path going over a hill..........	146	333	—	3
Circle worn by dancing.........	—	334	—	1
Water.				
Rivers or streams...............	147–149, 151	335–339	443	33
River with islands.............	150	340–341	—	3
Spring........................	152	—	—	3
Lake..........................	153–155	342–349	—	14
Scum.........................	156	—	—	1
Ocean........................	—	350	—	1
Heavens, Light, Fire				
Sun...........................	157	351–352	444	5
Sunrise.......................	158	—	—	1
Sun-rays......................	159	353–354	—	4
Course of the sun..............	—	—	—	1
Sun-dog.......................	—	—	445	1
Star..........................	160–167	355	446–447	13
Morning star..................	168–178	356–358	—	25
Morning star at the horizon......	179	—	—	1
Morning star with rays..........	180	—	—	1
Constellation..................	181	—	—	1
Milky way.....................	182	—	—	1
Sky...........................	—	359	—	3
Cloud.........................	183–185	360	—	4
Lightning......................	186–187	—	—	3
Rainbow.......................	188	361	—	3
Rain..........................	189	—	—	1
Flame.........................	—	362	—	1
Smoke........................	—	363	—	1
Manufactured Articles.				
Tents.........................	190–199	364–379	—	55
Tent-door.....................	—	380	—	1
Tent-pins.....................	—	381–384	448	6

Objects represented.	Embroidered Designs. Fig. No.	Painted Designs. Fig. No.	Three-Dimensional Designs. Fig. No.	Number of Occurrences.
Loops for tent-pins.............	—	385	449	2
Tent-poles......................	—	386	—	1
Tent-flaps.....................	—	387	—	1
Tent-pendants of rattles........	—	—	450–451	2
Tent-pendants of buffalo-tails.....	—	388	—	1
Spaces between tent-poles........	—	—	—	1
Interior of tent.................	—	389	—	1
Tent-site......................	—	390	—	1
Camp-site.....................	—	391–393	—	4
Camp-circle...................	200–202	394	452	8
Boundary of habitation..........	203	—	—	1
Brush-hut....................	204–205	395–396	—	5
Sweat-house...................	—	397–398	—	2
Poles of sweat-house............	206	—	—	1
Covering of sweat-house.........	207	—	—	1
House........................	208	—	—	1
American tent.................	—	399	—	1
Fence........................	209	—	—	1
Rock monuments...............	210–211	400	—	4
Bed.........................	—	401–402	—	2
Triangular head-rest............	—	—	—	1
Parfleche....................	—	403	—	1
Soft bag.....................	212	404	—	2
Box........................	213	—	—	1
Bucket or vessel...............	—	405	—	1
Medicine-case.................	—	406	—	1
Knife-case....................	214	—	—	1
Awl-case.....................	—	407	—	1
Sinew.......................	215	—	—	1
Rack for saddlery..............	216–217	—	—	2
Rack for meat.................	218	—	—	1
Paint-stick...................	—	408	—	1
Rope........................	219	409–410	—	4
Saddle-blanket................	220	—	—	1
Man's stirrup.................	221	—	—	1
Woman's stirrup...............	222	—	—	1
Lance.......................	223	—	—	1
Bow........................	224	411	—	2
Arrow......................	225	—	—	1
Arrow-point..................	226–232	—	—	8
Bullets......................	—	412	—	1
Pipe........................	233–234	—	—	2
Ceremonial wheel..............	—	413	—	2
Gambling-counters.............	235	—	—	1
Female dress..................	236	—	—	1
Ceremonially used robe.........	—	414	—	1
Robe design..................	—	415	—	1
Metal hair-ornaments...........	—	416	—	1
Dry meat	—	—	453	1

OBJECTS REPRESENTED.	EMBROI-DERED DESIGNS. Fig. No.	PAINTED DESIGNS. Fig. No.	THREE-DIMEN-SIONAL DESIGNS. Fig. No.	NUMBER OF OCCURRENCES.
Ear-pendant...................	—	—	454	1
Coffee.........................	—	—	455	1
Abstract Ideas.				
Hiiteni (life, prosperity).........	237–240	417–422	—	14
The many things unknown.......	—	—	456	1
Property possessed..............	—	—	457	1
Contents (of bag)..............	—	423	—	1
Centre........................	—	424–426	—	3
Stops (in a course).............	—	427	—	1
Direction whence...............	—	—	—	1
Direction whither..............	—	—	—	1
The four hills (periods) of life.....	—	428	—	1
Desire of accomplishment........	—	—	458	1
Supernatural instruction.........	—	429	—	1
Thought......................	241	—	—	1

Although the technique of embroidering and of painting, and the appearance of the objects made in these two styles, are quite different, yet a comparison of the two series of symbols (Figs. 1–241 with Figs. 242–429) shows that the individual symbols of the same meaning are generally considerably alike, whether they are embroidered or painted. The embroidered symbols, while often very simple, sometimes reach greater elaborateness and realism than any of the painted ones. Painting is of course capable of much further development in these directions than is beadwork, but the decorative painting of the Plains Indians is more conventionalized and less realistic than their embroidery.

It is apparent that there is much individuality in the interpretation given to the decorative designs employed by the Arapaho. One person attaches a certain significance to the ornaments on an article belonging to him; another person may possess an article ornamented in a similar fashion, and interpret the ornamentation entirely differently. Even the identical symbol may have many different significations to the various owners of different objects. For instance, on the objects that have been described in this paper, the rhomboid or diamond-shaped symbol can be found with the following ten significations: the navel, a person, an eye, a lake, a star, life or abundance (hiiteni), a turtle, a buffalo-wallow, a hill, the interior of a tent. All of these meanings, except the first two, are totally unrelated. If the significance of the decoration on a larger number of specimens had been obtained, it is probable that the known number of meanings attached to this symbol would be still larger. What makes the variability of this system of decorative symbolism appear still more plainly is the fact that nearly all of these ten significations have also been found attached to very different symbols. Thus a person is denoted, on other specimens that have been described, by a small rectangle, triangle, square, or cross, by a dot, by a line, as well as by rudely realistic designs. The eye is represented by a rectangle, and again by a nearly triangular figure. A lake is represented on different specimens by a square, a trapezoid, a triangle, a pentagon, a circle, or other figures. A star is often represented by a cross; the life-symbol by a trapezoid, hills by triangles. In fact, of these ten significations, that of the navel is the only one that was found several times and always represented by the same symbol.

It thus appears that there is no fixed system of symbolism in Arapaho decorative art. Any interpretation of a figure is personal. Often the interpretation is arbitrary. Much depends upon what might be called symbolic context. In a decoration which symbolizes buffalo-hunting, a stripe naturally represents a bow; on a parfleche whose decoration represents such parts of the landscape as mountains, rocks, earth, and tents, an identical stripe would naturally have the signification of a river or of a path; but whether a path or a river, would depend on the fancy of the maker of the parfleche. On another man's parfleche such a stripe may represent a rope; on still another, red paint or the blue sky, because the maker of this particular article thought of the color of the stripe before he did of its shape. Naturally one person cannot guess what the decorations on another person's par-

fleche or moccasin or pouch signify. Usually an Indian refuses to interpret the ornamentation on an article belonging
to some one else, on the ground that he does not know; but
he may give a tentative or possible interpretation.

Where such a wide variability exists, and where every individual has a right to his opinion, as it were, it follows that
it is impossible to declare any one interpretation of a given
ornamental design as correct or as incorrect. Even the
maker or possessor of an article can give only his personal
intention or the signification which he individually prefers.
Since the decorative symbolism on his article is not intended
as a means of communication, he is satisfied to follow his own
fancy in private; and if any one else chose to attach a different meaning to his ornamental designs, he would probably
make no objection. He might criticise the other for his pre-
sumption, but he could not well prove him incorrect.

Naturally there is great difference in the degree of interest
shown in the symbolism of decoration by different individuals.
One person thinks about the significance of his designs,
another chiefly of their appearance. The former will probably give a coherent interpretation of his designs if he is
questioned; the symbols of the latter will have their most
common conventional meaning, without much reference to
each other. Young people especially are likely to think and
care little about designs that they make or see. On the other
hand, a person interested in symbolism sometimes has two or
three interpretations for one symbol or for a design. Such
double sets of significations given by one person are generally
not hesitating or doubtful, but apt and happy, as well as
elaborate and coherent; the reason being that the maker of
the design has planned it with more than the usual amount
of attention to its meaning, or has subsequently studied it
with interest. One must not be misled on this point by
analogy with the pictorial, undecorative, unceremonial art of
our civilization. The Indian, in embroidering a moccasin or
painting a parfleche, never dreams of making a picture that
can be recognized by every one at sight.

It is probable that, among the hundred and fifty and more

specimens whose symbolism has been described, there are some whose owners were not their makers, and had never given a thought to the significance of their decorations previous to the occasion on which they explained these decorations at the request of the author. That this should not have happened, can hardly be expected; but in all such cases, these persons undoubtedly fell back upon the common conventional symbolism that is current in the tribe. This is shown by the fact that all the decorative symbolism that was learned runs along certain lines. For instance, tents are very frequently represented; but in only one single case was a house, such as the Indians now largely live in, represented by the decorations. Hence there seems to be a conventional system of symbolism, a fairly distinct and characteristic tribal manner of viewing and thinking about decoration. What this way of thought is among the Arapaho, it has been the purpose of the preceding pages to show by bringing together as large a mass of individual cases of decorative symbolism as possible. That here and there an interpretation may be poor, even from the Indian's standpoint, or another untrustworthy, is of little moment. As has been said, no interpretation of a design can be considered really right or wrong. If the explanations of decorated objects, taken all together, illustrate one method of thinking, and are evidences of one system of symbolism, the purpose of their presentation will have been achieved.

The lack of desire or attempt to represent realistically in art which is in any degree decorative, and the accompanying lack of absolute or fixed meaning of designs, are not new and unparalleled phenomena. On the northwest coast of America, Dr. F. Boas has told the author, an Indian is often unable to state what a carving or painting represents, unless he has made or is using the object. This is really a more remarkable case than among the Arapaho, for the art of the North Pacific coast is far more realistic than that of the Plains Indians. While highly conventionalized and always decorative, it remains sufficiently realistic to enable a white man to see in nearly every case that a representation of something is intended (which in the case of Arapaho art, if he had no knowledge of the subject, he would probably not suspect); and with a little practice the student can often recognize, without the Indian's help, the particular animal or object represented.

In northwestern California the situation is analogous. Here the principal art is basketry. The number of names of basket-patterns is small, and they are known to most of the women. The patterns on many baskets will be given the same names by every member of the tribe. On other baskets, the design will be differently called by two persons. It is then usually to be seen that the design is of a form more or less intermediate between two patterns, and that both persons who gave differing names for it were right: each had as much reason as the other. Moreover, both the names given in such a case are generally taken from the limited list of standard and well-known pattern-names of the tribe. So in this part of the continent, also, there is a conventional system of decorative symbolism; and, though this system is much more narrow and rigid than that of the Arapaho, there is a similar variability of interpretation among individuals.

Corresponding to individual variability of symbolism in Arapaho art, is the almost infinite variation of the decoration. Narrow as are the technique and scope of this art, almost every piece of work is different from all others. There seems to be no attempt at accurate imitation, no absolute copying. An Arapaho woman may make a moccasin resembling one that she has seen and liked, but it is very seldom that she tries to actually duplicate it. Of common objects, the writer does not remember to have seen two that were exactly identical, or intended to be identical. Two classes of articles, however, do not fall under this rule. These are, first, certain ceremonial objects, which naturally are made alike, as far as is possible, for ceremony is the abdication of personal choice and freedom; secondly, objects which are decorated with a more or less fixed tribal decoration. These objects are tents, robes, bedding, and cradles. It has been shown, however, that at times there is some variation even in the decorations of these objects. This distinctly tribal ornamentation forms

a class quite apart from the more personal ordinary ornamentation. For instance, the seven sacred work-bags that
have been mentioned, and the ceremonies connected with
them, are used only in the making of the "tribal" ornaments.

This endless variety and absence of direct copying are common in American Indian art. Dr. Boas has seen only very
few pieces of art of the North Pacific coast that were dupli-
cates. In California the author has found that, unless baskets
are made for sale, a basket is rarely reproduced exactly
by the same woman, and just as rarely by another. The
same seems to be true of the pottery of the Southwest.
Everywhere each piece is made independently, though always
under the influence of the tribal style.

Conventionality of decoration has been referred to repeatedly in descriptions of specimens. It can often be followed
out into minute detail. A glance at Plates I, XX, XXI, and
Figs. 5, 23-28, 32-34, will show to what extent it obtains.

The conventionality of symbolism which has been mentioned appears most clearly in the frequency of certain classes
of objects in the symbolism, and the almost total absence of
others. The scope of this symbolism may be briefly described
as follows.

Plants are very rare in representation; human beings are
not abundant; while animals, in comparison with these two
classes, are numerous. Of plants, trees are most frequently
represented, flowers not at all. Of animals, the larger mammals are rare. Only the buffalo and wolves and coyotes have
been found, and these generally represented in a very simple
manner, as by dots or small rectangles. Deer, elk, horses,
and dogs are not represented. Almost all the animal representations are of small animals,— the reptiles, fish, rats, and
especially insects and invertebrates in considerable variety.
It may be remembered that paint-pouches, navel-amulets,
knife-cases, and other articles which are representative in
their entirety, generally represent small animals. Of parts
of the body, of man, the navel is the most frequent in symbolism; of animals, the foot or track. Of the total number
of symbols, animal representations, however, form only a

minor part. Of natural objects, mountains and hills, singly and in ranges, are very frequent. Rocks, earth, vegetation, ravines, and the world are also found often. Representations of water are less frequent than the preceding; but rivers, creeks, lakes, and springs are all not rare. Of celestial objects, the sun, moon, clouds, sky (except as denoted by color alone), rainbow, and milky way are all represented infrequently. Stars, and especially the morning star, whose name and symbol is the cross, one of the simplest and most obvious geometric figures, are exceedingly abundant. Paths are common symbols. Of objects of human use or manufacture, tents are most frequently represented. Of symbols of abstract ideas, the hiiteni, which seems to signify life and abundance, is the most common.

The symbolism of colors irrespective of forms is generally the following. Red represents most commonly blood, man, paint, earth, sunset, or rocks. Yellow denotes sunlight or day, or earth. Green usually symbolizes vegetation. Blue represents the sky; haze, mist, fog, or smoke; distant mountains; rocks; and night. White is the normal background; when it has any signification, it denotes snow, sand, earth, or water. Black and brown rarely have any color significance; they are practically not used in Arapaho decorative art except to give sharpness of outline to colored areas, and occasionally in very minute figures. Water does not seem to be associated very strongly with any color. Clouds are as rarely symbolized by color as by forms.

The symbolic decoration that has been described is of course far from pictography. A pictograph serves as a means of record or communication, and is normally not decorative; while this art is too decorative to allow of being read. Yet there is considerable similarity in the symbols used in both systems. Moreover, the significance of a piece of decoration is at times as extended and coherent as that of a pictograph.

There is a class of ceremonial objects, used especially in the modern ghost-dance and related ceremonies, whose form and decoration are not fixed and prescribed, but depend upon the taste and desire of their owner. Many of these objects are nearly pictographs, yet are made with a considerable attempt at ornamentation: they may, as a class, be described as decorative — but not geometrically decorative — and highly symbolic. Usually these objects are painted or carved in outline, with free lines. Ceremonial articles of this class are not described in the present chapter, but are mentioned here because they reveal a form of art that is midway between symbolic decoration and picture-writing.

Another variety of symbolism that is found chiefly in connection with ceremonial objects, but which it may be well to refer to here, attaches signification to various parts or appendages of such objects. For instance, feathers sometimes denote spirits, or again clouds, or wind, and hence breath and life. Fur, hoofs, sticks, strings, bells, pendants, fringes, etc., are often symbolic in this way.

In closing this discussion of Arapaho decorative symbolism, it is desired to state that the closeness of connection between this symbolism and the religious life of the Indians cannot well be overestimated by a white man. Apart from the existence of a great amount of decorative symbolism on ceremonial objects not described in this chapter, it should be borne in mind that the making of what have been called tribal ornaments is regularly accompanied by religious ceremonies; that some styles of patterns found on tent-ornaments and parfleches are very old and sacred because originating from mythic beings; that a considerable number of objects are decorated according to dreams or visions; and, finally, that all symbolism, even when decorative and unconnected with any ceremony, tends to be to the Indian a matter of a serious and religious nature.

NOTE.

After p. 9 had been printed, I secured the missing terms of relationship in the Arapaho dialect.

father's brother.....................	neisa′naⁿ
mother's sister.....................	ne′inaⁿ
son of brother of a man } son of sister of a woman }	ne′ih'äⁿ
daughter of brother of a man } daughter of sister of a woman }	nata′ne

It will be seen from these terms that the Arapaho system is identical with that of the Gros Ventres.

III. — CEREMONIAL ORGANIZATION.

Like most other Indian tribes, the Arapaho have numerous
ceremonies, some public or tribal, others individual, either
shamanistic or consisting of observances connected with birth,
death, sex, and food. Of the public ceremonies, some are
accompanied by dancing or singing; others, such as the tribal
ceremony of the unwrapping of the sacred flat pipe, and the
rites attending the use of the women's sacred bags, are without
such accompaniment. Of the ceremonies in which there are
dancing and singing, some are directly connected with war;[1]
others are modern, such as the ghost-dance, the crow-dance,
and the peyote or mescal ceremonies. The remaining dances,
which are to the Arapaho the most important and sacred of
all their ceremonies, are united by them under the name
bäyaä'ⁿwu.

The bäyaaⁿwu ceremonies divide into two groups. One
group consists of a form of the well-known sun-dance of the
Plains tribes. The other class comprises a series of dances
made by men grouped into societies of the same age, and a
single corresponding dance for women. Similar series of ceremonies are found among other Plains tribes,[2] and have been
described as organizations of warrior societies or military and
social associations, while vulgarly they are known as "dog
soldiers."

The Arapaho call their dances "lodges," after the enclosures

---

[1] The tiaxanätiit, tcäätceciinätiit, tceäätiit, niinaⁿtahªwaaⁿt, comprising the seine-
niinahªwaaⁿt, are referred to in Traditions of the Arapaho, by G. A. Dorsey and the
author (Field Columbian Museum, Anthropological Series, Vol. V, p. 49).

[2] The Gros Ventre, Cheyenne, Blackfoot, Kiowa, Crow, Mandan, Arikara, and perhaps
other tribes. Compare Grinnell, Blackfoot Lodge Tales, p. 221; Mooney, The Ghost-
Dance Religion (Fourteenth Annual Report, Bureau of Ethnology, pp. 986, 989);
Schurtz, Altersklassen und Männerbünde, pp. 151–169.

in which they are held; and the name bäyaa^nwu seems to mean "all the lodges." [1]   As the Arapaho themselves use this term, it includes the sun-dance; but this ceremony is quite distinctly of a different character from the ceremonies of the age-fraternities.

The Arapaho sun-dance is similar to that of the Sioux and Blackfoot.[2] It is called haseiha^nwu, which means "sacrifice-lodge" or "offerings-lodge." It is held in summer, according to a pledge made in the course of the preceding year by an individual, the motive of the vow being usually the cure of sickness. The ceremony is held in a circular lodge, open above except for log rafters. These rafters extend from the walls to a forked cottonwood trunk set in the centre, and ceremonially the most important part of the structure. The lodge is open to the east, while at the west end the dancers form an arc of a circle facing the central tree. It is at this side of the lodge that what might be called an altar is arranged on the ground. The dancers, who are mostly young men, refrain from food and water during the ceremony proper, which lasts three days and nights, or, as the Indians count, four days. Towards the end of the ceremony the dancers were formerly fastened to the central tree by thongs attached to skewers passed under the skin of the breast, which they tore out. The erection of the lodge is accompanied by continual ceremonies, almost all of them having some reference to war. The trees of which it is built, especially the central fork, are spied out, felled, and brought home as if they were enemies. The erection of the lodge, and the spectacular ceremony for it, are preceded by a less public observance, lasting about three days, and held in what is called the "rabbit tent." Men of any age or ceremonial affiliations may enter the sun-dance, and not infrequently repeat their participation. The dancers wear no characteristic regalia other than ornaments of sage, and bone whistles; and, excepting to some extent the pledger of the ceremony, they are all of the same degree or rank.

[1] The etymology is not quite certain, though the Indians give the same translation. Bä- is the root of the word for "all," and frequently occurs as a prefix; a^nwu is a suffix meaning "house" or "lodge."
[2] Grinnell, Blackfoot Lodge Tales, p. 264; Bushotter, in A Study of Siouan Cults, by J. O. Dorsey (Eleventh Annual Report, Bureau of Ethnology, p. 450).

The second group of ceremonies in the bäyaaⁿwu form a progressive series. They are held by bodies of men of approximately the same age, who virtually constitute societies, and who can enter each group only after they have passed through all that regularly precede it. These ceremonies cover the entire period of manhood from youth to old age, those of the oldest class being the most sacred. In general character the successive ceremonies are similar, but each has a distinct name and organization. The dances are held in what appears to be an enclosure or open tent, rather than an edifice, and last, like the sun-dance, four days. There is no central tree, and the elaborate ceremonies accompanying the erection of the sun-dance lodge are wanting. As in the sun-dance, there is a preliminary and a public portion of the ceremony; but whereas in the sun-dance the preliminary rabbit-tent ritual is quite different in scope from the subsequent dance, the first three days in each of the age-society ceremonies are strictly days of preparation. The fasting and the self-infliction of torture that give the sun-dance much of its impressiveness are also lacking in these dances. On the other hand, there are fixed and in part elaborate regalia for each of the ceremonies; and these are of several kinds in each dance, indicating degrees of rank or honor.

There is a single women's dance reckoned by the Arapaho as paralleling the series of men's dances, and quite clearly corresponding to it in general character. The age of the participants is not, however, an element in the ceremony, and in many of its details it is naturally somewhat different from the men's dances.

The full series of ceremonies constituting the bäyaaⁿwu is the following: [1]

Sun-dance:
    Haseihaⁿwu ("sacrifice-lodge").

Men's Ceremonies:
    Nouhinenaⁿ ("kit-fox men").
    Haçaahouhaⁿ ("stars").

---

[1] Compare Hayden, Ethnogr. Philol. Missouri Valley (Transactions of the American Philosophical Society, 1863, N. S., Vol. XII, p. 325); and Mooney, Ghost-Dance Religion (Fourteenth Annual Report of the Bureau of Ethnology, p. 986).

Hiitceäoxaⁿwu[1] ("tomahawk-lodge").
Biitahaⁿwu [2] (" [?] lodge").
Hahaⁿkaⁿwu [3] ("crazy-lodge").
Heçawaⁿwu ("dog-lodge").
Hinanahaⁿwu [4] ("[?] lodge").
Tciinetcei bähäeihaⁿ [5] ("water-sprinkling old men").

Women's Ceremony:
Bänuxtaⁿwu [6] ("buffalo [?] lodge").

The participants in any ceremony are called by a name composed of the characteristic element of the term for their ceremony, and h-inen ("man") or h-isei ("woman") in place of -aⁿwu ("lodge"): thus, biitaheinen, bänuxtisei. Bä-n-iinen-aⁿ means the men composing the bäyaaⁿwu; in other words, all the companies.

In this paper the following English terms have been adopted for these ceremonies:

Kit-fox-men (nouhinenaⁿ, "kit-fox men").
Stars (haçaahouhaⁿ, "stars").
First dance (hiitceäoxawu, "tomahawk-lodge").
Second dance (biitahaⁿwu, "[?] lodge").
Third or crazy dance (hahaⁿkaⁿwu, "crazy-lodge")
Fourth or dog dance (heçawaⁿwu, "dog-lodge").
Fifth dance (hinanahaⁿwu, "[?] lodge").
Members of the sixth dance (tciinetcei bähäeihaⁿ, "water-sprinkling old men").
Women's dance (bänuxtaⁿwu, "buffalo [?] lodge").

The terms "lodge" and "ceremony" have been used instead of the rather inadequate term "dance" whenever they seemed more appropriate.

When the societies are enumerated, the kit-fox and star companies are generally included; but when the ceremonies constituting the whole series are reckoned, these two dances

---

[1] Tceäox is a weapon consisting of one or two long points set at right angles into a stick.
[2] Biitahaⁿwu cannot be translated by most of the Arapaho. Some explain it as "earth-lodge," from biitaä'wu ("earth," "land," "world"). This etymology seems very doubtful. A Gros Ventre gave the meaning as "drum-lodge."
[3] Hahaⁿkaⁿwu may be translated either "fool-lodge" or "crazy-lodge."
[4] For hinanahaⁿwu no translation could be obtained. It is not improbable that the word contains the root of the word for "man" (hinen) or "Arapaho" (hinanaei).
[5] Tciinetcei is said to designate the sprinkling or pouring of water in the sweat-house; bähäeihaⁿ means "old men."
[6] Bänuxtaⁿwu is always translated as "buffalo-lodge," but the meaning of the first part of the word is obscure.

are usually omitted.[1] This may occasionally be due to a desire to bring the total within the ceremonial number seven; but more often it is on account of the comparative religious insignificance of these two societies, whose ceremonies lack the accurately prescribed regalia that give character to the older fraternities. At the other end of the series also, the members of the sixth dance stand somewhat apart. They consist of seven old men, each the owner of a sacred bag, who have direction of the conduct of all other dancers; they themselves hold a singing ceremony in a sweat-house, but lack the dancing and the lodge of the other societies. The fifth dance somewhat resembles the sixth—embodying the oldest men—in lacking elaborate, showy features. The four ceremonies from the first to the fourth dance, however, constitute a well-defined group with constant analogies. In all of them the main body of participants are called naçan^i, which is about equivalent to "rank and file." [2] Above these are the honorary degrees, which range in number from one in the third to five in the second dance. The number of dancers is fixed for each degree, but varies, according to the degree and the ceremony, from one to four. The participants in each dance are instructed either singly or in groups, and receive their regalia from older men who have gone through the ceremony and are called the dancers' grandfathers. These men again, and the entire ceremony as a whole, are under the direction of the seven old men constituting the sixth society.

Whether a society can repeat a dance that it has performed, is not certain. Among the Gros Ventres, whose ceremonial organization is in great part the same as that of the Arapaho, such is the case, but no instances were heard of among the Arapaho.[3]

---

[1] Compare Traditions of the Arapaho, op. cit., p. 18.

[2] Naçan^i means "unreal," "not true;" thus naçaninetc is irrigation water as distinguished from natural streams.

[3] As the period covered by the six or eight ceremonies is at least forty years, the interval between succeeding performances of the same ceremony or between the successive performances of the same company, must have averaged from five to eight years, if there were no repetitions. Among the Gros Ventres there are several times as many age-companies as ceremonies; so that each ceremony, even without repetitions of it by the same company, was held several times in the period of from five to eight years. These companies have names that sometimes have a totemic appearance, but for the most part are similar to the class of nick-names customary for bands or clans among the non-totemic Plains tribes. No company participated in another's dances. As

The societies of the bäyaa[n]wu are strictly not associations of men, but classes or divisions to which men belong at certain ages. It appears that normally every man of the tribe is a member of the bäyaa[n]wu (a bäniinen), and that if he lives long enough he will pass in the course of his life, automatically as it were, through the entire series of ceremonies. While there is instruction in each lodge, there is no initiation, and no requirement for entrance into it other than that the preceding ceremonies shall have been gone through. Least of all is there any requirement such as characterizes certain religious societies of, for instance, the Kwakiutl, the Omaha, and the Sioux, that all the members shall possess a common dream or be initiated by the same spirit.[1] Membership is not limited in any way except by age; and the basis of organization is tribal, not supernatural.[2]

Just as the organization into societies is not primarily supernatural, so the degrees within the societies do not indicate anything religious. They do not represent a higher stage in occult knowledge, and therefore have no resemblance to the degrees of the midewiwin of the Ojibwa, or to such leadership as that of the honaaite in the Sia secret societies. The Arapaho degrees or ranks are purely distinctions of respect and tribal confidence, bestowed of course chiefly for bravery. At the beginning of each ceremony certain older men connected with the society, and called the "elder brothers" of the members, meet and select those of the members who seem to them most worthy of the honor. The recipients of the

---

there were always several companies that had gone through the ceremonies of each dance, the number of participants in each performance was several times less than if the number of companies and ceremonies had been the same. In the latter case, among a tribe of two or three thousand, some of the younger companies would number a hundred or more. It is not impossible that something like the Gros Ventre scheme of organization may have existed among the Arapaho, but no traces of it were found.

[1] Alice C. Fletcher (Annual Reports Peabody Museum, III, p. 276); J. O. Dorsey (Third Annual Report, Bureau of Ethnology, p. 348). A similar motive occurs occasionally among the Sia: cf. M. C. Stevenson (Eleventh Annual Report, Bureau of Ethnology, p. 86).

[2] The Kwakiutl ceremonial organization described by Boas (Report U. S. National Museum, 1895, p. 419) in some ways resembles that of the Arapaho. The ordinary basis of social organization of the Kwakiutl is a sort of clan system. In the ceremonial winter season this disappears. In this period all the people are divided into two great divisions, called the Seals and the Quē'qutsa. The Seals comprise a number of the highest dancers and dance-societies. The Quē'qutsa consist of all the others. They are divided into ten groups, — seven for men and three for women, — according to age and sex. The men's societies, beginning with the youngest, are the boys, killer-whales, rock-cods, sea-lions, whales, Koskimos, and eaters. While these seven do not possess any specific ceremonies, the scheme of their grouping is almost identical with that of the Arapaho.

degrees have not had any religious experience different from that of the rest of the society. During the progress of the dance, their ceremonial functions are naturally somewhat differentiated from those of the rank and file of the dancers; and this is especially true of the highest degree, which in all the lodges is held by only one member. Even outside of the ceremony a certain behavior is sometimes imposed on the holders of degrees. Since many of the regalia are also weapons or have reference to war, the dancers of higher degrees formerly used them frequently in war. In the dog-society the members of the highest three degrees were expected not to flee even in the most imminent danger, except after certain conditions had been fulfilled; so that the bestowal of these honors was not only a recognition of past deeds, but an obligation involving future risk.

That the functions of the series of societies are not altogether ceremonial, appears from this imposing of obligations in war. Some of the societies also have certain public regulative and disciplinary powers and duties, as is customary among other Plains tribes. These powers pertain particularly to the hunt, the march, and the camp-circle.[1] In some of the accessory ceremonies of the sun-dance the young men of the tribe participate by societies. The connection with war is apparent in the instances that have been mentioned, as also in the fact that the members of three societies carry respectively tomahawks, lances, and bows as insignia. Such circumstances are, however, natural among a people the only activity of whose men, besides religion, love, the hunt, and gambling, is war, and with whom honor and fame are primarily to be obtained only through war. It must also be remembered, that, in the old life on the Plains, going to war was as much a part of the normal life of an ordinary man as participation in the ceremonies was the natural function of all members of the tribe. It would therefore be surprising if the ceremonials of the bäyaaⁿwu were not filled with references to war; but to regard these Arapaho societies as primarily social bodies with

---

[1] Traditions of the Arapaho, op cit., p. 30.

police functions, or as organizations specifically of warriors, would result in a very inadequate conception of them.

The origin of the bäyaa^{n}wu ceremonies, as given by the Arapaho themselves, has been published.[1] In brief this myth tells that a murderer was expelled from the camp-circle. He tried to shoot a white buffalo that approached him, but was unable to and desisted. The buffalo then spoke to him. He received buffalo to kill, and was given the lodges either by the white buffalo or by the mythic character Nih'ā^{n}ça^n. Most of the versions of this myth include both the sun-dance and the women's dance among the ceremonies that were derived on this occasion and now constitute the bäyaa^{n}wu. Independent accounts of the origin of the women's dance are, however, also given. According to these, the ceremony was derived directly from the buffalo themselves.[2]

None of the bäyaa^{n}wu ceremonies were seen by the author; and the following descriptions are based entirely upon accounts given by the Indians, and upon a series of the regalia that were secured for the Museum. The last of the dances among the northern Arapaho was held about 1898; while the southern Arapaho appear to have discontinued the ceremonies, especially the more sacred ones, some time before that date.[3]

In the following accounts the dances will be treated in order, beginning with the youngest, except that the second one, on which the fullest information was obtained, will be described first, in order to make the briefer accounts of the other ceremonies clearer.

SECOND DANCE (BIITAHA^{N}WU).

The ceremonies of the second dance are performed as the result of a pledge. If a man of the first lodge is sick or in danger, he may vow that he will hold the second dance in case his life is saved. When he is once more well, he an-

---

[1] Traditions of the Arapaho, op. cit., pp. 17, 22, 23.
[2] Ibid., p. 49.
[3] The first ceremony (hiitceãoxa^{n}wu) was to have been held by the Oklahoma Arapaho in October, 1903.

nounces his pledge, and the news of it is spread. When the ceremony is arranged, all the members of his society must join in it, even though it is the result of a single individual's determination. If a member of the company is sick or absent, a substitute must take his place. This substitute may be a younger brother, so that occasionally a man is found who has gone through a dance which is really beyond his years. It is said that formerly every man belonged to a society. The pledger of the dance is called ya′nahūt[i].

When the time for the dance approaches, the "elder brothers" (bääsahaa[n]) of the society select a good place for the dance, and the people gather there. These elder brothers were secured by the company on its first formation. Often they are reluctant to serve. They are then captured by stratagem, and a pipe is forced into their hands. This act constitutes them elder brothers of the company. This pipe can be carried to the man intended for an elder brother only by a member of the society who has been to war.

On what may be regarded as the first evening of the ceremony, the elder brothers assemble and select certain men in the society to be the holders of the degrees in the dance. They are said to choose the bravest men in the company for these honors. There are five such degrees in the second dance above the rank and file. One dancer is of the highest degree, and is called hiitawa[n]hä[n]hit[i]. He carries a club called tawa[n]hä[n]. There are two dancers each of the second, third, and fourth degrees, and four of the fifth. These and the rank and file all carry lances. Each of the two dancers of the second degree carries a lance crooked at one end and wrapped with otter-skin. They are called hiinousäeitciçaniçi. The dancers of the third degree (called hiibiixa[n]uçi) have similar but straight lances. The dancers of the fourth degree are two boys not properly members of the society, who are called biitaheisana[n], which means "biitaha[n]wu children" or "little biitaha[n]wu dancers." They carry small lances painted black, called biitaheisa[n]nau. The men of the fifth degree have similar black lances, on account of which they are called hiiwaotä-na[n]xä[n]yaniçi. The rank and file (naçan[i] biitaheinena[n]) have lances that are wrapped with red cloth. These insignia will be described more fully.

As soon as the men to hold the higher ranks have been selected, the dancers hurry to find older men who shall make their regalia, paint them, and guide them through the ceremony. These men they call "grandfathers." The men who have been chosen to be of a certain rank go to a grandfather who held the same rank when he went through the dance. In some cases the grandfathers appear to give the new dancers the very regalia which they themselves used; in other cases the regalia are made by the grandfather during the first three days of the ceremony. These two methods of furnishing the dancers with their ceremonial implements are regarded as equivalent by the Indians. Even an object which has just been made is spoken of as having been handed down from the past, because it is made in conformity with tradition, and preceding pieces have served as models for it.

Several dancers generally go together to secure a grandfather. Coming to his tent, they say from the outside, "Grandfather, we are coming" (Näbäciwa^n tcanani). He answers, "Well, come in, my grandsons" (Wa^{n}hei, tciitei, neicihahaa^n). One of the young men, having entered, gives him a pipe. If the pledger of the dance is among these young men, it is he who gives the pipe. The grandfather receives the pipe and lays it down. Then he leaves the tent. He goes out for one of the old men who are to be the directors of the entire ceremony. This old man will also be called grandfather by the dancers. The man to whom the dancers have come takes a horse or some other present to this older man, and brings him with him to his tent, carrying another pipe. When they have entered the tent, the old man prays, holding the pipe with its bowl upward. Then he smokes and passes the pipe, and the others smoke. Then, still in the same tent, they eat a meal of food that is sent there by relatives. The same night the women relatives of the dancers prepare food. This is brought to the tent of the grandfather. There it is kept until the next morning, when it is warmed up and eaten. In the tent (Fig. 47), the grandfather (A) sits in the customary place for the owner of the tent, on the south side. The old man (B) has the place of honor at the back. The young men (C) are opposite their grandfather on the north. Such old women (D) as may be present are at the door. The gifts of food by the young men to their grandfather are in front of him (E), and the food given to them by him stands before them (F). Before the old man at the back of the tent lie two pipes; the one nearer to him (1) is the grandfather's, the one farther in the middle of the tent (2) belongs to the leader of the group of young men.

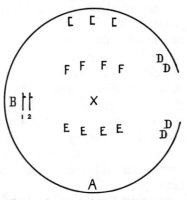

Fig. 47.   Grandfather's Tent (Biitahaⁿwu).
A, grandfather, owner of the tent ; B, old man, instructor of the grandfather ; C, young men, dancers ; D, old men's wives, etc. ; E, food given by the young men to their grandfather ; F, food given by the grandfather to the young men ; X, fireplace ; 1, grandfather's pipe ; 2, pipe of young man.

Such are the events of what may be regarded as the first day of the ceremony. The next three days are given to making the regalia worn in the dance. On the first two evenings of these three days the members of the society dance, but without their implements, as if for practice. On the afternoon of the third day the regalia have all been finished, and the ceremony proper begins with a dance in which they are worn.

On the first morning of these three days of preparation the old man must be given another present by the young men's grandfather for showing him how to paint them. If he thinks the gift insufficient, he says, "Paint them as you like." When the gift is sufficient, he goes to the grandfather's tent and describes to him how to paint the young men. The younger man listens carefully to his instructions. The old man prays again, and he and the young men and their grandfather smoke the pipe that he uses in this prayer. Then they eat the food prepared the night before. After this the grandfather paints the young men. Then they begin to make regalia for the dance.

The grandfather makes only one set of regalia. If more than one young man has come to him, he secures other elderly men, each of whom makes a set of regalia for one of the dancers. Thus each dancer virtually has a grandfather to himself. The work is done in the grandfather's tent. The old man who has been called by the grandfather does not work, but sits still and directs the making. The regalia are finished on the third day. When they are completed, they are hung at the top of a pole set up in front of the grandfather's tent. In case of rain they are taken indoors. Every noon during these three days the grandfather provides food for his grandchildren the dancers, and they bring him food. The old man who directs the making of the regalia and later the conduct of the dance receives food from both. Before these mid-day meals are eaten the old man always prays, though these prayers are no longer accompanied by raising the pipe toward the sky.

The first two evenings of the preliminary period the young men dance to their grandfathers' singing. Before they dance they give their grandfathers pipes, which they smoke. As stated, this dancing takes place without the proper insignia of the dance, but appears to be held in the lodge erected for the dance in the middle of the camp-circle.

On the afternoon of the third of the preliminary days all the participants in the ceremony, both dancers and grandfathers, gather in the lodge. This appears to be round, with the eastern side left open [1] (Fig. 48). Along this eastern end there is, however, a screen. The sides of the lodge are made of tent-skins, but are so low that people can look over them. The top seems to be left uncovered. Between the middle of the lodge and the entrance on the east is a fireplace (F). At the very back or west end of the lodge sit the old men and the grandfathers of the dancers (G). In this place also are the drums. Along the northern and the southern sides of the lodge sit the dancers, divided into two groups. Along the southern side of the lodge sit the "short men" (tcäixi-

[1] According to another statement, the lodge is oval, being longest in the direction from east to west

hinena"), O; on the northern side, the "stout men" (hana"-ka"biihinena"), X. These two divisions of the company are maintained through all its ceremonies. At the eastern end of one of these two rows of dancers, nearest the entrance to the lodge, sits the dancer of the highest rank (A). Next to him is one of the two members of the second degree (B); and in the same place on the opposite side of the lodge, with the other division, the other. Next to these two men, and farther from the entrance, sit the two dancers of the third degree (C), also one on each side of the lodge. To the west of these sit the two boys (D). Next to these are the four men of the fifth degree (E), two on each

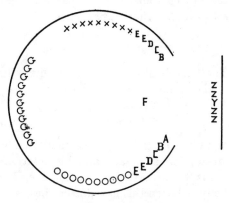

Fig. 48.   Dancing-lodge (Biitaha"wu).
A, dancer of highest degree, with club ; B, dancers of second degree, with crooked otter-skin lances ; C, dancers of third degree, with straight otter-skin lances ; D, dancers of fourth degree, boys with black lances ; E, dancers of fifth degree, men with black lances ; X, naçan¹ hana"-ka"biihinena", rank and file, stout men ; O, naçan¹ tcäixi-hinena", rank and file, short men ; Y, yanahut, pledger ; Z, companions of yanahut ; F, fire ; G, grandfathers and old men.

side of the lodge, facing each other. Then follow the rank and file, extending westward along the north and south sides of the lodge to its back, where are the grandfathers. The pledger of the dance (Y), with a few companions (Z), sits in front of the screen at the eastern end of the lodge, thus being directly opposite but farthest removed from the grandfathers. The elder brothers of the company sit among the dancers. The people are outside the lodge, presumably mostly at its eastern end, as in the sun-dance, looking in. Four young men who are somewhat younger than this company have been selected as servants (haçiana"). Two of them wait on each of the two divisions, bringing them their food and performing other offices.

At the opening of the ceremony in the lodge, the lances

constituting the regalia, each with its accompanying belt and other insignia tied in a bundle near the bottom, are stood up in a line at the back of the tent just in front of the grandfathers. The old men smoke. One of them prays. Then one of the grandfathers arises, and, recounting a coup in the fashion customary in Arapaho ceremonials, gives away the set of regalia that he has made. The usual formula begins, —

"Nānāⁿçi   nāniihiiçanaⁿ   [waotānāhiçi]."
"It is they   I mention   [the Utes]."

The tribe is always mentioned first, then follows the account of the exploit. At the end he says, —

"Neicɪ,   hiiyuu   haⁿxawaⁿ,"
"My grandson,   here is   the lance,"

and gives his grandson his regalia. The young man raises the lance with a shout; and his relatives enter the lodge and thank his grandfather, passing their hands down his face and body. When this grandfather has sat down, another one follows; and thus they do until all the lances have been given to the dancers. If a grandfather should not have distinguished himself in war, he must pay another man to count a coup and give away his regalia for him. After all the dancers have received their regalia, the old man directing the dance smokes the pipe of one of the dancers. When he has finished, he says to the owner of the pipe, who appears to be the pledger of the dance, "Grandson, here is your pipe." The young man arises from his place, goes to the old man, receives the pipe, and, lighting it, gives it to his grandfather. After his grandfather has smoked it out, the young man receives it again, and, going back to his place, lays it in front of himself.

Then the old men in charge of the dance say, "Now get ready." The young men take their implements and go to their grandfathers and pay them for putting the regalia on them. They say, "Grandfather, this is for you. I want to dress." Then they crouch down. The grandfathers take hāçawaanaxu (a root much used in ceremonials), chew it, and then, spitting on their hands, rub the young men all over the body. They also put this medicine on the belt, the lance,

and the other things the young man will wear. Each grandfather motions with the belt three times as if he would put
it on the young man in front of him. On the fourth motion
he puts it around him and ties it on. The same motions are
made with each of the other pieces before they are put on the
young man's body. After having been dressed, the young
men all return to their places and sit down.

After this the wives of the grandfathers bring in food to
the young men, who receive it with the ceremonial word for
"thanks" (hoiii). They set the food in the middle of the
lodge. Here they dance about it in a ring.

The pledger takes a split willow stick, and, using it as
tongs, picks up a live-coal, which he carries to the old men.
These put niox^u (a sweet-scented grass much used for incense)
upon it, and incense the drums that are to be used. These
drums are the ordinary small drums of the Plains tribes, a
foot or a little more across, with skin only on one side, and
held in the hand by the strings where they cross underneath.
In the sun-dance a larger drum suspended from four forked
sticks is used. For the second dance from three to six drums
are said to have been borrowed from people that possessed
them, being returned after the dance. The leader of the
singers is called hää^{n}çinää^{n}hinen. There is also a leader for
the women who sing. She is called hää^{n}çinä^{n}sei. The women
who sing, like the men, appear to be old, and sit at the back
of the lodge with the men. The leaders in the singing do not
enter the lodge and take their places of their own accord: they
must be sent for from their tents, and must receive property.
Large gifts are made to them for coming, and other presents
are added later. They are of course provided with food during the ceremony. They begin the songs, and the remaining singers join in.

The first of the participants in the ceremony to dance are
the pledger and his immediate companions. In dancing they
face their grandfathers, who dance with them. Then the two
boys among the dancers rise and dance, each facing his grandfather. The four men having the curved and straight lances
wrapped with otter-skin, the insignia of the second and third

degrees, dance facing their grandfathers, who dance with them. They are followed by the four dancers with black lances of the fifth degree. The last of the dancers of higher degree to dance is the highest of all, the hiitawa^{n}hä^{n}hit^i. As the young men dance, their relatives come into the lodge and dance with them, standing next to them, or sometimes, if too numerous, forming two rows. The relatives of each grandfather also dance with him. After dancing, the young man's relatives approach the grandfather and thank him in the customary ceremonial manner, saying "hoiii," and passing their hands down in front of his face. When a young man dances, his father and actual grandfather, if alive, will also dance where they stand outside the lodge, accompanying him.

After the young men of higher degree have danced, the rank and file, including the pledger and his companions, if they are not of a higher degree, form a circle and dance, making the circuit from left to right four times, while the dancers of the higher degrees dance outside in a circuit from right to left. They dance to the accompaniment of two songs. The screen at the eastern end of the lodge where the pledger has been sitting has been removed and a stick set up at some distance. At the end of the two songs the dancers dart out of the lodge to this stick and back, racing in a crowd. The two divisions race against each other. The dancers all rush off from the place at which they happen to be when the song ends. The one who returns last is pelted by the others with buffalo-dung.

These ceremonies on the afternoon or evening of the third day bring to a close the preliminary period and mark the beginning of the dance proper. The functions of the old men are now ended. The elder brothers go among the dancers and incite them to activity. For the three following nights the dancers are without restrictions. As it is put, they may do anything they want. They dance at least the first night, and presumably the others also. For the three following mornings they dance before sunrise, racing at the conclusion of the dance. These three mornings' dances, together with the one on the preceding evening, occupy the four days during which the ceremony proper lasts. The dancing at night during this period is carried on in two large tents, — one on the north side of the camp-circle, and one on the south. The society divides into its two halves, the stout men and the short men, and each uses one of the tents.

During the first night the company goes to four tents to sing and dance for gifts. Four chiefs or other good men are selected; and their names are called out by an old man, so that they may be prepared. The four men selected have their tents at four opposite sides of the camp-circle. After the concluding dance and race of the evening, the lodge in the middle is taken down. The members of the society sit about under small shelters. They go first to the one of the four men who is at the northwest of the camp-circle. They stand abreast before his tent. The rank and file of the company are in the middle; the men with degrees, at the ends. The elder brothers of the company, who seem to take the places of the grandfathers as soon as the religious element of the dance has given way to a more social one, stand in a row just behind the dancers, singing and drumming for them. Having reached the tent, the line of dancers curves so as to form a semicircle or three-quarter circle just in front of the tent. At first they sing slowly. The members of the company participate in this singing, as well as the elder brothers. Next they sing faster, and the members of the company dance, moving in a circle, singing, and shaking their lances. Small bunches of hoofs are attached to the lances, so that a rattling in time to the music is produced. The owner of the tent comes out, bringing food or other gifts. He lays the property in a pile. If he gives a horse, he lays a stick across the top of the pile. The four servants of the society take the food and presents, and carry one-half to each of the large tents used by one of the divisions of the company. After having sung at this man's tent, the dancers visit in turn the three others at other sides of the camp-circle. The four tent-owners who give this food to the company are called hita"eeçana".

The next morning before sunrise the members of the

society again dance to two songs, as on the evening before. The body of the dancers circle four times from left to right, while those who wear higher regalia dance in an opposite direction outside of them. At the end of the second song they again all rush off to race. In this race the two divisions, the stout men and the short men, race against each other. The division to which the winner of the race belongs receives the breakfast. The other division has nothing to say, but looks on and eats whatever is left. The next two mornings, before sunrise, they also dance and race in this way. On these two mornings, however, they do not race for their food. After they have raced on the third morning, the members of the company separate and go to their tents. This is the end of the ceremony.

After this the young men give presents to their grandfathers. It is said that until this time the grandfathers have received nothing from them. They themselves, however, have given considerable property to the old men in charge of the lodge. The grandfathers' wives have also supplied the dancers with food. There is no definite regulation for the amount of payment that is made to the grandfathers. The young men give them what they think right and what they wish.

During the dance the relatives of a young man will sometimes call him, lead a horse into the lodge, and give it away for him. This public giving-away, which is practised also in the sun-dance and on other occasions, is called "chief gives away" (nä^{n}tcänahaa^{n}t^i). It is a sign of affection or esteem of the young man's relatives for him. Sometimes one of the dancers, instead of running the race with the rest of the company, will ride on a horse. At the end of the race the horse, with all its accoutrement, is received by the wife of his grandfather.

The second dance has particular symbolic reference to thunder. This is especially clear in the highest degrees. The dormant, fierce temperament of the dancer of the highest degree is supposed to be similar to that of the thunder. The carving on his club (see p. 170) represents the thunder-bird and lightning. The long eagle wing-feather tied at its end symbolizes lightning. The rain which follows the pointing-upward of the club is thought to be caused by the Thunder, who is angered. The crooked lance of the second degree (see Plate XXXII) and its accompanying regalia are also symbolic of the thunder in several respects.

The characteristic paint-design of the members of the second lodge is described as a figure consisting of four parallel lines, which are crossed at each end by four shorter lines (see Plate XXXIII). This figure is painted on the forehead, the cheeks, the chin, the upper arm, the lower arm, the thigh, and the calf. This distribution is very similar to that of the figures painted on the body in the sun-dance. As to the direction of these designs and the colors used in painting, the accounts obtained differ. It is clear, however, that there is a lack of symmetry between the painting of the right and that of the left side of the body. One informant stated that on one side the direction of the figures was lengthwise the limbs, and on the other side across them. Another informant said that the dancers were painted green on one side, and yellow on the other. A third informant stated that the left and right sides were painted alternately, the paint on one side being rubbed off when it was put on the other. Different colors of paint seem to be used. The body is, as in the sun-dance, covered with one color, and the figures are then painted over this in a darker color. One informant stated that the men dancers were painted red over their body; the two boys, yellow.

Highest Degree. — The dancer of highest degree (hiitawa^{n}hä^{n}hit^i) in the second dance sits at the extreme end of one of the rows of dancers in the lodge. Which side he sits on depends upon which of the two divisions of the company, the short men or the stout men, he belongs to. Though of the highest rank, he dances after the other members of the high ranks. He is selected as the bravest man in the company. He is supposed to be slow to anger or to move, but, when aroused, to be exceedingly fierce. He alone of all the dancers carries no lance, but has instead a round club called tawa^{n}hä^n. He oversees the dancers. He makes them assemble early. If they are tardy in coming, he goes to them and strikes them with his club. If they sit down to rest while the dance is going on, he strikes them until they get up and dance again. His club is not stood upright, as are the lances of the other dancers, but must be laid horizontally on the ground with the end pointing away. It is thought that if the club is allowed to point upward, it will soon rain.

This club (Fig. 49) is a cylindrical stick 90 cm. long and 5 cm. in diameter. The end is cut off diagonally. The resulting elliptical surface is painted green, and notched around the edge. An eagle wing-feather is attached to this end of the club. Near the other end the club is thinned somewhat into a sort of handle. This portion is wrapped with a quill-wound thong colored yellow. This quilled thong holds in place a piece of red cloth and sweet-grass. At the handle there is also attached a kit-fox skin. It is said that small bells should be tied to the legs of the skin and to the handle of the club. On the club there is carved in angular outline a figure of the thunder-bird, its head being nearest the feathered end of the club. The head and neck of this bird are represented by two lines meeting at an angle. From near the head two zigzag lines separate and extend along the club toward the handle. They are carved and painted green.

Fig. 49 (₇₀⁵₈). Club of Dancer of Highest Degree, Second Dance.

Lower Degrees. — The regalia of all the dancers excepting the highest consist of the lances that have been mentioned; of belts or waist-pieces of skin about 25 cm. wide; of
head-dresses consisting of several feathers inserted in a small
piece of trapezoidal rawhide, worn upright at the back of the
head; of fur leg-bands worn below the knee; and of armlets
for some of the higher degrees. A set of these regalia is shown

Fig. 50, *a*, *b* ($\frac{50}{332}$, $\frac{50}{304}$ a). Belts, Second Dance.

on Plate XXXIII, p. 177. The waist-pieces are called touktcihi-
tana^n or toutciciit; the head-dresses, naa^ntita^nänähiitana^n,
or wakuu, the generic term for "head-dress;" the armlets,
bääsçenäyana^n; and the leglets, waxuuk. In general, all
the regalia excepting the lance are much alike for all degrees,
including the rank and file, the differences appearing to be
chiefly individual and unintentional.

The waist-pieces (Fig. 50; also Plate XXXIII) are painted
red, and are ornamented with strips of red cloth along the
upper edge, on the two end edges, and down the middle.
Green lines are painted along or under the cloth strips. Four

other vertical lines, and green crosses between them, are painted on the belt. Waist-pieces of the second and fourth degree, both obtained among the northern Arapaho, are yellow instead of red. The former is painted with green lines and crosses, like the ordinary red waist-piece. The latter (Plate XXXIII) is painted with green lines, but not with crosses. A red belt of the fifth degree from the southern Arapaho (Fig. 50, *a*) also lacks the painted crosses. The lower edges of all the belts are cut into notches. These are comparatively small in all the belts, excepting the belt of the fourth degree, that has just been mentioned. This has only six or seven notches, each several inches deep and wide. To the lower corners of the belts, as well as to the middle, where the red cloth strip ends, are attached small bunches of crow-feathers whose ends have been cut off. Only the yellow belt of the second degree has magpie instead of crow feathers. There are usually also either small bells or small cones of tin. Presumably small hoofs were formerly used in these places, having been replaced by metal ornaments on account of the greater effectiveness of the latter in producing a sound when the belt is shaken. The two upper corners of the belt sometimes have a few crow-feathers and bells or rattles attached. Small ornamented loops of the kind much used by the Arapaho for decorative purposes are also attached to the upper corners. In four places on the belt there are usually little strips of thong or rawhide which are wound, like the loops just mentioned, with quills or fibres, and are attached to the belt by their ends. The two ends of these short strips are usually white, sometimes yellow; the middle, red, yellow, or violet bordered by black or dark violet. At each end of the strip hang two or more crow-feathers, sometimes with a few tin cones or small bells. Usually these four attachments are so placed on the belt that they come over the middle of the four green vertical lines. The two yellow belts of the second and fourth degrees alone lack these attachments of ornamented skin strips and feathers. It is not certain whether this is a characteristic distinguishing these waist-pieces of higher degree from those of lower rank, or whether it is due to a slight local difference between the type of waist-piece used by the northern and that used by the southern Arapaho.

The symbolism of these belts appears to vary more than the designs on them. On one specimen the straight lines were said to denote straight paths, signifying good life; the crosses were the morning star. On another belt, which had been worn by the pledger of a dance, the long horizontal green line along the upper edge was also said to denote a straight path; and the crosses, the morning star, which makes life good and is a father of mankind. The red flannel at the edge denoted the first glimpse or shining of the star; the four vertical green lines marked the four days of the dance; the notches along the bottom of the belt were interpreted as clouds. The symbolism of the yellow waist-piece of the second degree (see Plate XXXII, opp. p. 175), as given by one of the old men in charge of the ceremony at which it was worn, is as follows. The vertical green lines are sunbeams, representing the day. The four crosses are the four old men that are mentioned in prayers. The red cloth on the belt represents paint, which symbolizes the people. The yellow on the belt is earth-paint; it is therefore the earth; it is also the yellow day when this was first shown the four old men. In painting the crosses and lines, häça-waanaxu is chewed and spit on the belt four times; then a pipe-stem is moved four times toward the spot where the cross or line is to be made. On the fourth movement the pipe-stem is touched to the skin and a mark made. Then the cross or the line is painted there. A pipe-stem is used for this purpose, because the pipe, containing fire, is the sun, and it is wished that the sun will listen to the dancers and look at them. The feathers attached to the belt symbolize flight, and make the wearer's horse run swiftly. Magpie-feathers are used both on account of their handsome appearance and because the bird flies swiftly. Magpies also come about habitations of men for food and fly off with it, just as warriors attack tents and depart with booty. The notches along the bottom of the belt represent mountains, and thus the earth on which we live.

The head-dresses worn in this dance show more individual

variation than the waist-pieces, but few or none that are indications of difference of degree. To a more or less square but approximately trapezoidal piece of rawhide (Fig. 51; also Plate XXXIII), the outside of which is painted green, are attached upright feathers. The rawhide is sometimes cut from a parfleche or painted rawhide bag. The feathers are most commonly hawk-feathers. Their ends are usually tipped with ornaments of dyed plumes or horse-hair. Each head-dress contains from five to nine feathers; but they so cover each other that the entire width is not more than that of two or three feathers. The shafts of three feathers are each covered with a strip of quill-work or ornamentation in fibres. This embroidery is subject to some variation. The embroidered strips may be white, yellow, or red. The middle portion, which is bounded by black on all three strips, is always of a different color, and bears a design of small squares or spots.

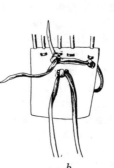

Fig. 51, *a, b* ($\frac{50}{1100}$ d). Head-dress, Second Dance. Height, 32 cm.

The number of these small squares may vary from about four to sixty. In some cases this vari-colored portion is longest on the middle strip, so that the general outline of the spotted parts of the ornament somewhat resembles a broad cross. To the two upper corners of the rawhide, just below where the feathers rise, are attached small loops of hide covered with quill or fibre. From the

DANCER OF SECOND DEGREE, SECOND DANCE.

back of the rawhide (Fig. 51, *b*) come two strings by means of which it is fastened at the back of the head, the strings passing around the forehead.

The leg-bands (Plate XXXIII, below) are usually of badger-skin, but at the present day other fur is sometimes used in place of this. They have cut crow-feathers, small rattles or bells, embroidered loops, and sometimes a fringe of slit fur, attached at the place where they are tied at the back of the calf. Sometimes larger bells are attached at several places on the leg-band.

Fig. 52 ($\frac{50}{663}$). Arm-ring, Second Dance.

The armlets (Fig. 52) worn in some of the higher degrees of this dance are made of rawhide, completely covered on the outside with three rows of embroidery in yellow quills or fibres, with a red design of a wide cross. Sticking out at right angles to the armlet, and attached to it by a wrapping of embroidered thong, is a bunch of buffalo or horse hair. The armlets are worn on the right arm, above the elbow.

It is by means of the lances that the different degrees are chiefly distinguished.

Second Degree.—A crooked lance carried by dancers of the second degree (hiinou-säeitciçaniçi), and the accompanying re-galia, are shown on Plate XXXII. They were obtained among the northern Arapaho. The symbolism of the waist-piece has already been described. The lance is called nousäeitciça^n. This set of regalia was conferred in a session of old men on the dancer thought worthiest. Eight horses were given for it by the recipient to his grandfather. In the race after the dancing, while carrying this lance, he rode a horse which he left for his grandfather. When he was about to receive the lance and regalia from his grandfather, the latter prayed. If the owner should go to battle, he would carry the lance. He would stand it in the ground and hold it. Unless the spear were plucked out by another man and given to the owner, he would not fly, whatever the danger to his life. The lance is made of a stick of willow, one end of which has been steamed and bent. The end of the crook is bound to the shaft by a sinew string to prevent it from straightening. The stick is painted red. It is closely wrapped with strips of otter-skin passing spirally around it. The maker began to put the skin on the stick at the crooked end. When the stick was completely covered with the otter-skin, he tied two eagle-feathers so that they hung from the end of the crook, and spit medicine on them. Then he tied three other pairs of eagle-feathers at three places on the straight portion of the lance, going from the crooked end towards the point. A pair of feathers is now missing from the lance. Where the feathers are attached to the stick, the latter is wrapped with a narrow piece of white fur, which should properly be wolf-skin. As the various parts were attached to the lance, the maker prayed to the father. This lance is a gift from the father to the people. It is not made by men themselves, but is made as the father directed that it should be made. The animals whose fur is used for the lance, such as the wolf and eagle, are also prayed to. Near the lower end of the lance a piece of sweet-grass and a strip of red cloth are bound to the fur by a thong wrapping of quill-work. This is the place at which the lance is usually held.[1] At the bottom of the lance is a knife, serving as a spear-point. There are also tufts of horse-hair at the lower end. The eagle-feathers are tipped with plumes and bunches of yellow hair.

The symbolism of the parts of the lance is as follows. The otter-skin represents the earth, for the otter lives on the earth and in the water; it is soft, and softness prevents injury from blows or violence. The red cloth represents red paint, which, being a common symbol of human life, here expresses a wish that the children who are born in the tribe may live to be

---

[1] An old southern Arapaho, in describing the crooked lances, of the second dance, said that they had a crow's beak attached at the place where they were held.

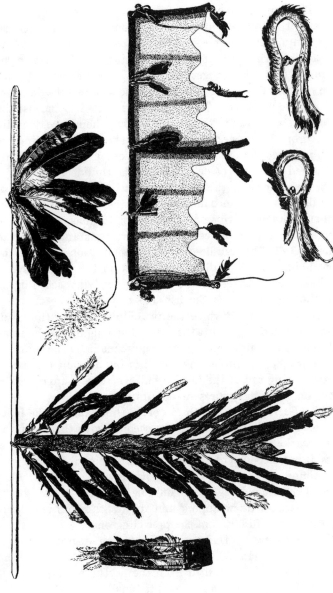

Regalia of Dancer of Fourth Degree, Second Dance. Cat. No. $\frac{50}{1108}$.

old. The hair at the bottom of the lance is from the mane of a horse; it therefore represents the front or advance against the enemy. The yellow tips on the eagle-feathers are the sun-rays entering a tent in the morning through the holes where the tent is held together by pins over the door. At this place — just above the outside of the door — the lance is kept in good weather. The sweet-grass is used to incense the lance if it should fall to the ground through being accidentally dropped or blown over by the wind. The sinews holding the crook in place denote strength. The crook itself represents the curved nose (the eagle's beak) of the thunder.

The head-dress of this set of regalia is much like those of other degrees. Red ornamentation on the middle of the three quill-embroidered strips on the feathers outlines the shape of a broad cross and represents the morning star. Six small white spots in the middle of this ornamentation indicate the star's light. Small quill-covered loops on the lower part of the head-dress represent the rainbow, which, according to Arapaho mythology, is the fish-line or trap of the thunder. The green color with which the rawhide portion of the head-dress is painted represents the sky. The jangling of the small bells on the belt also represents the noise made by the thunder. In the armlet, the projecting bunch of buffalo-hair represents the projecting tail of the buffalo-bull when he is angry. The fringe on the leglet represents sun-rays.

Third Degree. — In the third degree (hiibiixa^{n}uçi) the lance used is said to be like that of the second, with the exception that it lacks the crook. Like the lances of the following degrees, it is sharpened at the butt-end, by which it is stuck into the ground so that the knife points upward. The crooked lance of the second degree can only be set in the ground by its iron point. In its wrapping and its attachments this lance appears not to differ from the preceding one.

Fourth Degree. — Dancers of the fourth degree (biitaheisana^{n}) carry a lance like that shown in Plate xxxiii. This specimen was also obtained from the northern Arapaho. It was carried by a boy, and is quite small. The shaft is not wrapped, but is painted dark green. In other cases the color

is said to be dark blue or black.   At the knife end of the shaft
there is a bunch of hawk-feathers, and, hanging by a string,
a white plume.   From the lower end of the shaft hangs a strip
of skin to which two rows of black magpie and eagle feathers
are attached.   This strip of skin is painted dark green, like the
shaft.   Like all the other lances of the second dance, this
weapon should have a small strip of red cloth and a braid of
sweet-grass bound to the handle by a thong wrapping covered

Fig. 53 ($\frac{50}{332}$, $\frac{50}{333}$).   Belt and Lance of
Dancer of Fifth Degree, Second Dance.

with porcupine-quills.   This, however, is lacking in the specimen.   The belt worn with this lance has been referred to
above as differing in several respects from the ordinary
second-dance belt.   It is painted yellow, is without the usual
green crosses, has a few large notches on the bottom, and
lacks the four attachments of embroidered thong, crow-
feathers, and rattles present on most other belts, but has
such feathers and tin rattles attached to three places along
the upper edge.   The head-dress consists of brown hawk-
feathers instead of the more usual white or light-colored ones,
and its rawhide is painted dark green.

Fifth Degree. — Fig. 53 shows a restoration of a lance of

the fifth degree (hiiwaotăna^{n}xäyaniçi). The Arapaho at the present day generally have destroyed the shafts of their lances used in the second dance, keeping merely the various parts attached to the wooden stick. In general this lance is described as being similar to the smaller one carried by the boys. At the knife end is a bunch of hawk-feathers and a plume; at the lance end, a strip of skin to which crow-feathers

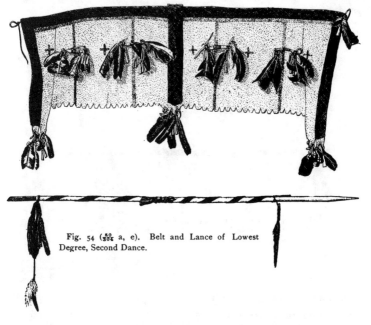

Fig. 54 ($\frac{50}{304}$ a, e). Belt and Lance of Lowest Degree, Second Dance.

are attached. The shaft in this specimen is said to have been painted blue. It was wound with a long, double string of dark-blue beads. The waist-piece worn with the lance is also shown in Fig. 53. The belt is red, but agrees with the yellow belt of the fourth degree in lacking the usual painted green crosses.

Lowest Degree.— A lance of an ordinary dancer (naçan^i) is shown restored, with the accompanying belt, in Fig. 54. Like the preceding lances, this has inserted at one end an iron spear-point. At the present day the point is often a knife-blade. The shaft is wrapped with a strip of red cloth, which does not entirely cover the wood. From the lower end of the shaft hangs a single wing-feather of an eagle; from the other end, just below the iron point, a bunch of hawk-feathers, and a single white plume at the end of a somewhat longer string of white beads. The set of regalia to which this lance and belt belong were worn by the pledger of a dance. The leg-bands of this set were not obtained. The symbolism of the belt has been described.

KIT-FOX MEN (NOUHINENA^{N}).

The first society of all, and the third before the second dance (biitaha^{n}wu), is one of the boys or young men who are called "kit-fox men" (nouhinena^{n}). They are recognized as a society, and have a dance. They regulate their own dance, however, and have no grand-fathers. Consequently they also lack prescribed regalia and degrees. They have elder brothers. In fact, it is while each company forms the kit-fox society that it secures its elder brothers, whom it thenceforth retains through all its successive cere-monies. Being the youngest company, the kit-fox men stand in the slightest honor.

STARS (HAÇAAHOUHA^{N}).

The second company, called "stars" (haçaahouha^{n}), occupies a position similar to that of the kit-fox company, like it lacking grandfathers and definitely fixed regalia or recognized ranks. In

Fig. 55, *a, b* ($\frac{50}{1010}$, $\frac{50}{1007}$). Rattles of Star-dancers.

Fig. 55 are shown two rattles used by the star-dancers among the northern Arapaho. Both are flat, rather small, and quite thin.   This appears to be the characteristic shape of the rattles used in this ceremony.   It is noticeable, however, that the two rattles differ considerably.   One (*a*) is painted red, the other (*b*) green.   The former has lightning painted upon it; the latter lacks this symbol.   The former is wound with fur, the latter has two thongs tied to it.   The star-dancers are described as carrying lances and rattles and wearing horned bonnets or other conspicuous regalia.   It seems that this company has no lodge, their dancing being on the open prairie.

FIRST DANCE (HIITCEÄOXA^{n}WU).

After the star-dance, the first dance (hiitceäoxa^{n}wu) begins the regular series of regulated ceremonies, being followed in its turn by the second dance (biitaha^{n}wu), that has already been described.   The general course of the first dance is very much like that of the second.   The elder brothers of the society select the recipients of honors.   The young men go to the tent of older men, who act as their grandfathers. These grandfathers are directed by the old men who have charge of the dance.   Three days are used for making the regalia. The young men look for sticks that are suitable for being made into representations of tomahawks, which they carry in the dance.   They collect the feathers, knife, sinew, and other implements and materials needed for making the object, and wrap them in a piece of cloth.   This they take to their grand-fathers, who keep the cloth, giving part of it to the old man who is directing them.   When the regalia are finished, they are hung on a pole in front of the tent-door, as in the second dance.

The lodge for this ceremony is like that in the second one. The pledger of the dance has his place in front of the screen at the eastern end.   The men of higher degrees sit in the lodge nearest the entrance.   The relative places of the rank and file of the dancers, of the grandfathers, of the old men, and of the fire, are the same as in the second dance.   The pledger carries a burning coal to one of the old men, who puts incense of sweet-grass on it, and then prays.   An old man has chewed häçawaanaxu.   The dancers receive a minute quantity from him in their mouths, and then rub it, together with a little earth and saliva, over their bodies. This prevents them from becoming tired.

As in the second dance, the pledger and his immediate companions are the first to dance. These young men dance opposite their grandfathers. In dancing they hop up and down, much as in the second dance. When they have danced, each of the young men approaches his grandfather, and, saying "hoiii," passes his hands downward close to his face. This is called ça^{n}xueiyaa^{n}t^i. Then they return to their places and sit down, to be followed by the four men of higher degrees. These also dance opposite their grandfathers, and, having thanked them, sit down. Then the body of dancers form a ring facing inward. The four men of higher degrees come farther into the lodge, to the west of the ring of dancers, and stand with their grandfathers, facing eastward. A song is sung, and they dance, standing in their places. To the second song the ring of dancers moves slowly from left to right, while the four men outside and their four grandfathers dance from right to left. To the third song the circle of men dance more swiftly. The four men outside again dance in the opposite direction, but their grandfathers now no longer dance with them. Presumably they dance to a fourth song before they stop. By this time it is night.

Following this evening, there are three days of dancing by the young men, who are no longer under the direction of their grandfathers. As in the second dance, they begin before sunrise, dance, and race. They dance all day as they like, and feast on what their grandmothers bring them.

The characteristic paint-design of the first dance is a figure representing a long burr, called by the Arapaho "they who go after women" (waniseinä^{n}hiici). This figure is painted on the forehead, the two cheeks, the chin, the upper and lower arm, the thigh, and the calf. The entire body is painted red, the figures being in black. There is also a black line around each ankle. The figures are made longer each day, until on the last day of the dance they form a continuous stripe around the face and down the length of the limbs. This, it will be observed, calls to mind the sun-dance painting. During the time that the dance lasts, the young men do not wash off their paint or touch their bodies with water. It is believed that if they did so, it would rain.

The dancers of the first dance carry as regalia sticks whose upper end is bent at an angle and carved into a rude representation of an animal's head. There appear to be no regalia for this dance that are worn on the body. There are only

Fig. 56 ($\frac{50}{405}$). Model of Sword of Dancer of First Degree, First Dance.

two higher degrees. Each of the four men constituting these carries a flat board or wand, called kakaox, which is the term for "sword."[1] Of these four dancers, one is of the first degree; the three others, of the second.

First Degree. — The board carried by the dancer of the first degree (Fig. 56) is about three feet long, straight along one edge, and notched in curves along the other. It is painted black with about seven green semicircles across its flat sides, each of these semicircles corresponding to a pro-

---

[1] All four objects are called kakaox; the black one of highest degree, honaunaa^{n}huu; the four dancers of these two degrees, hiikakaoxuiçi; the rank and file, hiitceãoxuiçi.

jection on the edge. Along the wavy edge are bunches of crow-feathers, which, like the feathers in most ceremonial implements, may be tipped with dyed plumes or horse-hair. The upper end of the board is cut off diagonally. The lower end is sharpened so that it may be stuck into the ground. Between this point and the main portion of the wand is a somewhat narrower part forming a sort of handle. This is wound with a thong of quill-work, under which are the usual

Fig. 57 ($\frac{50}{1003}$). Sword of Dancer of Second Degree, First Dance.

strip of red cloth and braid of sweet-grass. From this handle hang also a large brass bell and several eagle-feathers.

The specimen here figured is a model said to have been made for use in the ghost-dance revival. The sharp point below the handle has been cut off in this specimen. Two pendant pieces of skin, the ends of which are slit into a fringe, to which hoofs are hung, have been attached to this particular piece in place of two buffalo-calf tails, which it was impossible to secure at the time of making.

Second Degree. — The board of the second degree (Fig. 57) is somewhat similar to that of the highest degree. It lacks the notches, however, both edges being straight. The feathers are white and dark. In the specimen figured the white feathers are of swan or pelican; the dark, mostly of eagle, with a few hawk and crow feathers. In place of being painted black with green arcs of circles, this board has from six to eight [1] square or rectangular areas on its flat surface, painted alternately green and a light-reddish color. Each of these squares contains four dots of the opposite color. The squares are separated by yellow stripes, the stripes being longitudinally divided by a red line. The strip of skin to which the row of feathers is attached is painted green, red, and yellow, to agree with the board. The upper end of the board is cut off diagonally, as in the sword of the first degree, the acute angle being on the unfeathered edge. The lower end is sharpened. To the handle at this end is hung a bunch of objects similar to those on the wand of the first degree, — a buffalo-tail, seven eagle-feathers, a bell, and a bunch of loose buffalo-hair.

Lowest Degree. — The sticks (Fig. 58) carried in the lowest degree (naçan[i]) are about 1 m. long and about 2.5 cm. in diameter. The lower end is sharpened to allow of their being stuck into the ground, like the lances of the second dance. The upper end of the stick extends nearly at right angles to the main portion. To effect this, a stick with a sudden bend or an angular root is selected. The upper portion is carved into what has the appearance of being a horse-head, but is said to represent a buffalo. The mouth is indicated by carving, and the eye at the present day generally by a brass furniture-tack. The lower jaw is generally cut into a number of small notches. At the upper end of the straight portion of the stick, just below the head, is a wrapping of quill-covered thong. This holds in place a bunch of buffalo or horse hair standing upright at the back of the animal head. Two other longer and thinner bunches of hair fall downward from this wrapping, as if from both sides of the head. These are wrapped or tied with a bit of whitish fur. The arrangement of the hair closely resembles a method of wearing the

---

[1] Six in a specimen from Oklahoma, eight in the northern Arapaho piece figured.

hair practised on the Plains. The upright bunch of hair on
top of the figure's head is trimmed off square above. It may
be trimmed only by a man who has taken a scalp. A grandfather who has not won this distinction must secure another

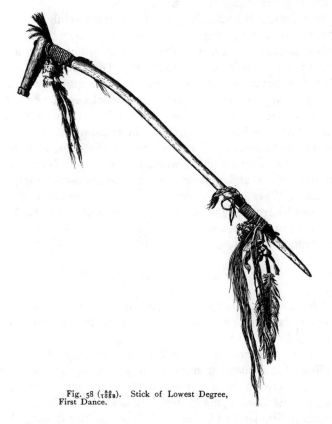

Fig. 58 ($\frac{50}{1008}$). Stick of Lowest Degree,
First Dance.

man to do this. The entire stick, including the head, is
painted red. At the lower end of the stick, just above where
it begins to taper to a point, is another wrapping of quill-
covered thong. This holds in place a strip of red cloth and
a braid of sweet-grass, as on the lances used in the second
dance, while from it hang a buffalo-tail, or strip of buffalo-skin
with hair, a bunch of rattles, loose buffalo-hair such as is blown

over the prairie, seven thongs wound at intervals with quills, buffalo-fur wrapped with quilled thong, and a wing-feather of an eagle.

The stick carried by the pledger of the dance is said to be painted green under the jaw.

These sticks represent the war-spike or war-club (tceäox) of the Plains tribes, generally called "tomahawk." The first dance is said to have reference to the buffalo, just as the second dance refers to the thunder. The sticks are said to represent buffalo as well as weapons. The quill-work on the thongs that are wrapped around the sticks is of two colors. On some sticks it is white; on others, yellow. The sticks with the white quill-work represent buffalo-bulls; those with yellow, buffalo-cows. The same distinction, more elaborately carried out, is found in the women's dance. In Navajo ceremonies, white and yellow are used to represent male and female. There is also a symbolic reference to the buffalo in the sand-burr designs which are represented in the body-painting of the first dance, as the burrs constantly stick to the buffalo's hair.

THIRD DANCE (HAHA^{n}KA^{n}WU).

The fool or crazy lodge is the next ceremony after the second dance. The participants seem to be about forty years old.

The regalia of this dance consist primarily of a cape of buffalo-skin somewhat more than a yard square, and worn with the hair inside, over the shoulders and back. The upper half of this skin is painted red, the lower half white. In the centre a circular flap is nearly cut out, so that it hangs loose. At the corners of the cape are small bunches of crow-feathers. This cape or robe is held in place by a string around the neck or breast. From its upper part hang two strips of skin about two inches wide, and somewhat longer than the cape. These are painted red, and have a few crow-feathers at the ends. In addition, the crazy-dancers wear a head-band, across the front of which is a bunch of owl-feathers. They wear also a leglet [1] of raccoon-skin around the ankles and a narrow strip of skin covered with porcupine-quill work below each knee. Around the neck, on an embroidered thong, hangs a bone whistle. In place of the clubs of the first and the lances of the second dance, the weapons carried in this ceremony are small bows. Four arrows are used with each. One arrow has an iron point, another a rounded knob of wood at the end, the third is chewed soft, while the fourth is split and has inserted in it a small quantity of a supposedly powerful root which is used in this dance. After the dance, this medicine is taken out and the bow and arrows are thrown away.

There is only one dancer of higher degree in this ceremony. He is called the "white crazy man" or "white fool" (na^{n}k'ha-ha^{n}kä^n). His regalia differ from the others in being almost completely white. His cape is entirely white instead of being half red, and light-colored owl-feathers are attached to it in place of the black crow-feathers. This dancer is painted white over his entire body. As the dancers move about the camp-circle, he always goes last, being markedly slow in his actions in contrast with the lively and untiring movements of all his companions.

The general course of this ceremony is much like that of the two that precede it; the elder brothers, grandfathers, and grandfathers who direct the ceremony, playing the same parts as in the dances already described. Three days are also used in making the regalia, the third of these days being at the same time the first day of the dance. On the morning of this third day, the regalia, being completed, are given to the young men, who are dressed in them by their grandfathers. Holding their bows, they stand abreast in front of the old man who directs their grandfather. This old man does not move. Then the grandfather recounts a coup. As he says the last word, the men all shoot at a buffalo-chip lying just inside the door, shouting and jumping toward it. It is said that this is not done by the entire company of participants in the dancing-lodge, but by each group of dancers in their grandfather's tent,

---

[1] In one specimen obtained the leg-bands are of raccoon-skin; in another, of badger; those of the white-fool are of young wild-cat.

where their regalia have been made. After shooting at the buffalo-chip, the dancers proceed to make the circuit of the camp-circle in single file. On returning they undress again.

In the dancing-lodge the pledger of the dance is the first to dance, standing opposite his grandfather, who dances with him. Then the white fool dances opposite his grandfather. Then the entire company dance in a circle. This order is entirely analogous to that followed in the preceding ceremonies. The dancers also jump up and down, as in these dances, but the position taken in dancing differs from that in the first and second dances. The crazy-dancers hold one hand over the eyes, and the other extended out from the body and somewhat down, and blow their whistles.

The ceremonies of this day are concluded with a spectacular dance through the fire with bare feet. Two elder brothers of the company and their wives go to two grandfathers of the company and their wives, and are taught by them how to build the fire. The two older women instruct the two women, and the two older men, the men. They receive property for this. The elder brothers and their wives split tent-poles and build the fire. The two grandfathers then show them how the glowing coals are to be spread. After having given this instruction, they take away the horses or other property that they receive in payment. The dancers now dance again, and at the conclusion rush into the fire, stamping or dancing on it until they have trampled it out. Then they run about the camp-circle.

For the night after this fire-dance, and for the three succeeding days, the dancers are supposed to be crazy. They act in as extravagant and foolish a manner as possible, and are allowed full license to do whatever they please anywhere through the camp except within the tents. A root which they have attached to one of their arrows, to their owl-feather head-circlets, and to their capes, is supposed to make them extraordinarily active during this period, and to give them the power of paralyzing men and animals. This root is called tcetcäätcei. Only very small pieces of it are used.

These could not be identified. The Gros Ventres use a root, which they call by a dialectic form of the same name, for similar purposes. They declare that this root is the well-known poisonous wild parsnip. It seems very probable that the same plant is used by the two tribes. It is believed that if a living thing is touched with this medicine after it has been prepared by the older men and given to the dancers, inability to move will result. It is thought that the same effect can be produced by a dancer sweeping his cape, which has the root attached to it, over the tracks of a person or animal. It is said that birds, which leave no tracks, are the only beings that cannot thus be paralyzed. Much is told about the power of the crazy-dancers when armed with this medicine. One narrator, when a boy, saw a hunter driving a buffalo-bull toward the camp during the crazy-dance. The hunter, on seeing the dancers, dismounted and walked off to his tent, afraid of being paralyzed together with the buffalo. The dancers brushed their medicine over the buffalo's tracks. The bull was only able to walk. The dancers came up to him, sat on his back and on his head, pulled his beard, and dragged him into the camp-circle, where he was killed. Before paralyzing the bull, the dancers were playing with a large rattlesnake. It is also said that they take a stick with a little grass on the end of it, spit their medicine on this, and then allow a snake to bite it. Then, striking it with the stick along the length of its body, they make it unable to coil, so that they can handle it with impunity. They paralyze dogs by striking them, and give them to their grandfathers for food. If a dog runs away from them, they cause it to fall down, unable to move, by merely sweeping their capes over its tracks. The dancers are unable to paralyze or injure one another, because they are protected by the same root that gives them their power. When they desire a woman, they go around her tent, spitting on it. When they enter, the inmates are so fast asleep that they do not awake.

It is evident that suggestion is an important factor both in the efficiency of the tcetcäätcei-root and in the performance of the fire-dance.

The crazy-dancers act as ridiculously as possible, and annoy every one in camp. Sometimes one of them will act like a bird. He will climb up a tent-pole and sit on top of the tent, like a bird. The rest, coming up, shoot at him, aiming their arrows backward over their shoulders. The dancer on the tent-pole then falls down, rolls over, and lies dead. After this he may impersonate a buffalo or some other animal, and his companions shoot him again. The dancers pursue every one who ventures out of his tent, and do all the mischief they are capable of. If another tribe, such as perhaps the Cheyenne, are camped not far away, the crazy-dancers may run several miles to kill dogs there. If a chief or other distinguished man, becoming angry at their provocations and liberties, should take his bow to shoot at them, the dancers by a single motion would paralyze his arms. It is said that if a man from fear should refrain from entering this dance with his proper company, he would be particularly persecuted during the entire dance. Of all the people in the camp-circle, only the crazy-dancers' grandfathers are exempt from annoyance.

On the last day the dancers rub their hands over the bottoms of sooty kettles, and then slap themselves over the body and face.

The crazy-dancers do whatever they can in reverse fashion. They "talk backward," as the Indians say; that is, they say the direct opposite of what they mean. When their elder brothers summon them to a feast, they say, "Do not come!" If they should say, "Come!" the dancers would not come. When one of the dancers is carrying a comparatively heavy load, such as a dog, he acts as if it weighed almost nothing; while, if he is carrying a puppy, he pretends that it is exceedingly heavy. The shooting-backward over the shoulder that has been mentioned is done for the same reason.

The foolishness of the dancers is connected with their owl-feather circlets. When they enter a tent for a feast, they take off these head-bands and give them to a man, presumably one of the servants of the company, standing at the door. As they go out, the circlets are returned to them. If they should not take off the circlets, they would act as foolishly in the tent as out of doors. If a person not a dancer has been paralyzed, he can be made well again by being rubbed with one of the circlets, especially that of the white fool.

In the dancers' ears are put mushrooms. Their hair is said to be drawn over the head and fastened at the ear.

In this ceremony, as in all the others, the häçawaanaxuroot is used to prevent the dancers from becoming tired. The crazy-dancers receive this from one of the old men in the following way: At night the old man goes out from the camp-circle with the dancers' wives. The women lie down on the ground naked. The old man bites off a piece of root and gives it backward to one of the women without looking at her. It is said that if the old man is unable to restrain himself, and looks at the woman, it is bad for the tribe. He gives each woman a piece of root. The women return to their husbands and kiss them, transferring the small piece of root from their own mouths into their husbands'.

First Degree. — As stated before, the dancer of the first degree is called the "white crazy man" or "white fool" (nank'hahankän). His regalia are shown on Plate XXXIV. It will be observed, that, apart from being whitened everywhere, the chief difference between these and the ordinary fool-dancer's regalia is in the bow or stick which he carries. This seems to be a sort of lance, and was described as being about 120 cm. long. The stick itself had been thrown away by the owner, and a restoration is shown here. At one end a knife is inserted. The other end is pointed. At the knife end hangs a bunch of red-tailed hawk wing-feathers and eagle tail-feathers. About 30 cm. from the opposite end is a similar bunch; while at the extreme end, opposite the knife, is a single black eagle wing-feather. There are four other long, narrow, black feathers tied to the stick, — two extending in one direction, and two in the opposite direction. These are tied in the middle with a buckskin thong painted green. Under the windings of this thong are sweet-grass and sage. This part of the stick serves as a handle. A white string extends the length of the stick. It is intended to represent a

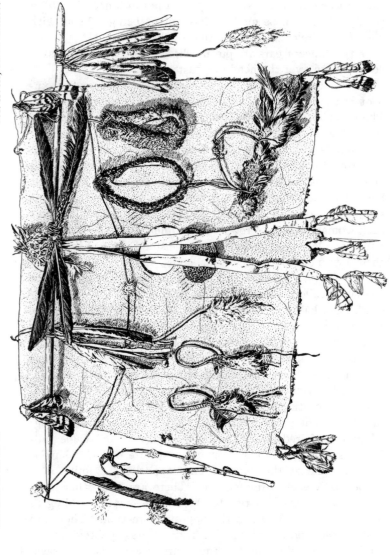

REGALIA OF THE WHITE-FOOL.

bow-string. On this are two small bunches of down. On one side of the knife was said to have been painted a small circle, on the other side a crescent, representing respectively the sun and the moon, presumably to symbolize, in this case as in others, day and night. At present only a small speck of green shows on one side of the knife.

The head-band of eagle-thigh plumes and great horned-owl feathers includes a bluebird's skin. The plumes indicate lightness; the white color of the feathers, cleanness. The head-band contains tcetcäätcei. In case of illness, it is some-times passed across the body a number of times, and then in the same way down the body, being given a sort of rotary or elliptical motion. A small mushroom on the head-band rep-resents the human ear. As the crazy-dancers carry a small mushroom in their ear, it is probable that this is intended for such use.

As to the circular flap in the cape, and the cuts in it, the owner of the regalia knew nothing. He said that the feathers at the corners of the robe represented the people holding to and living in accord with the injunctions of the father. The human race lives over the entire world, and this is indicated by the fact that the feathers are at the four corners. The two long loose strips of skin attached to the cape are those by which Indians and whites hold to the father. This latter interpretation is probably due to the influence of ghost-dance ideas.

Marks cut on the bone whistle symbolize a strong breath; that is, vitality. Leg-bands of thongs wrapped with whit-ened corn-husk fibre, with attached red-tailed hawk feathers, are tied just below the knee, while bands of young wild-cat skin are worn around the ankles. The regalia are kept folded in a rectangular buffalo-skin case opening along the top. Sim-ilar cases are used for the regalia of all the crazy-dancers. They are scarcely distinguishable from the cases used to hold the regalia of the women's dance.

In connection with these regalia, the owner said that the father made man and woman to live on the earth in order that the human race might grow. These regalia would make part of human life as long as men survived. The father said to men, that, if they did no evil during their life, life would continue as it was; but if they did wrong, there would be a change. However, when men were more numerous, they disobeyed the father and killed each other. Then he told them that there would be a change of life (their race would be superseded by another). Then a new life began. These regalia were then given to the new life. They are day, night, wind, rain, human beings, and all animals, and have existed among the people since they were given.

Before parting with his regalia, the owner prayed to them. He said they should remember that he was selling them not only for money, but because they would be kept in a better place. Their shadow would remain in his tent, and their teachings in his mind. Therefore he asked that he himself and his relatives might remain well and have good fortune.

The white-fool regalia are supposed to be very powerful, and there is thought to be considerable danger that those who remove them from their buffalo-skin case and handle them, or even see them, will become temporarily paralyzed in consequence. This of course does not apply to the white-fool himself. To prevent any such effect, hãçawaanaxu-root is used. Before the case is opened, the hand is touched to the ground, a little of the root spit on the palm, and the body is then rubbed over with the hands. The regalia are laid on sage, and not allowed to come in contact with the ground.

Lowest Degree. — The ordinary crazy-dancer's apparel has been described. Plate xxxv shows a figure dressed in this costume, and in what is described as a characteristic dance position.

FOURTH DANCE (HEÇAWA^{N}WU).

The fourth dance, or dog-lodge (heçawa^{n}wu), follows the crazy-lodge. The participants are men about fifty years old. Like all other lodges, it can be held only when an individual of the proper age has made a pledge to make the lodge in order to avert personal danger or death. The lodge itself, the securing of older men for grandfathers, the making of the

CRAZY-DANCER OF THE LOWEST DEGREE.

regalia, and the three days' preparation, are analogous to what occurs in the preceding ceremonies.

There are three higher degrees in the fourth dance. The highest is called "furry or shaggy dog" (tciiyanehi). As in other ceremonies, there is only one dancer of this highest rank. He wears a shirt covered with crow-feathers. This dancer must have some one to drive him, before he will move. He must be struck like a dog. He does not even eat of his own accord.

Four men called hiina^{n}tceiyaniςi constitute the second and third degrees. They wear long scarfs reaching to the ground. These scarfs are slit along the middle near the upper end, and the head and one arm are inserted through the opening. The scarf then passes over the other shoulder and hangs down at the side, the end reaching to the ground. At this end there is an eagle-feather. These scarfs are called "ropes" (säna^{n}k^u). In battle the men wearing them fasten the ends to the ground with an arrow or a stick. When they are thus fastened, they do not flee, however great the danger, until a companion releases them and orders them away. The shaggy dog follows a similar practice. He remains in his place, even at imminent risk of death, until he is driven away. Owing to these restrictions, a man is always left with such of these dogs dancers as are present in a fight, in order to enable them to escape if necessary. The four ropes (säna^{n}k^u) are of two ranks. Two are red, and their wearers are of the second degree of the dance. The other two are yellow, and regarded as not so high in rank, forming the third degree.

The ordinary dancers of this society wear an upright bunch of turkey-feathers on their heads. This is not worn by the shaggy dog or the men with scarfs, who have only a horizontal eagle-feather and a hanging plume at the back of the head. All the dancers, both rank and file and those of higher rank, have whistles of eagle-bone, and rattles consisting of a skin-covered stick along which small hoofs are attached. All the dancers also wear leggings painted alternately with red and black stripes and fringed with hair. No implements suggesting weapons are used in this dance.

A grandfather who has not scalped an enemy may not make or touch the leglets fringed with scalps. He must employ some one else in his place. When the regalia are completed, they are hung on a pole in front of the tent-door, as in the other ceremonies. In the lodge the pledger takes his pipe to the fire and lights it. He then smokes it while he is going to his grandfather. Having passed his hand in front of the old man four times, he gives him the pipe, holding it with both hands, the bowl being upward. When the grandfather has smoked it, he returns the pipe, and the dog-dancer says "hoiii" three or four times, and again passes his hand over the old man's face. Then, laying the pipe across each shoulder twice, he goes back to his place. The other dancers follow in the same way. After this the regalia are given them by their grandfathers, who, as in the preceding lodges, recount coups and place each object on the dancers' bodies after the fourth motion. If several members of the society have gone together to one old man for their grandfather, he has secured other old men to help him, one for each of the dancers. In this way each dancer has his own grandfather to make his regalia and give them to him in the lodge; and to him the dancer gives property.

The dancing in this ceremony differs somewhat from that in the preceding lodges. When the participants have received their regalia, the lodge is taken down. They dance for four nights after this, in each case for the entire night. These four nights do not follow in succession, but occur at intervals as there is occasion. The dancers go to some tent in the camp-circle, and, forming a ring in front of the tent, whistling, and shaking their rattles, they dance. At the back of the circle or semicircle, facing the tent, stand the elder brothers, and behind these their wives. At the sides of the circle, behind the dancers, stand their own wives. Some of the dancers enter the circle and dance. In dancing, the feet are barely raised from the ground. The four men wearing scarfs have the ends of these regalia held up by other men, so that they do not drag on the ground. The owner of the tent goes out and lays down a gift. If he gives a horse, he lays down a stick, mentioning the name of the recipient, who takes the stick and thanks him. Sometimes he merely lays down the stick, and the dog-dancers themselves select the one of their number who is to receive the horse. Four servants accompany the dancers to carry the gifts and the food to the tent used by the company. The dancers follow the camp-circle from left to right, stopping at whatever tents they like. They do not, however, solicit presents from their grandfathers. Dancing with this object is carried on in much the same way in the younger lodges; but there it occurs for three successive nights, and forms only part of all the dancing in the ceremony, since the company dances inside the lodge on the first evening and the succeeding mornings. In the morning the dog-dancers have a feast and distribute the property they have received during the night. They are then painted by their grandfathers. After this they go to their tents, and, rubbing off the paint, go to sleep. They are not allowed to sleep while painted, and are also forbidden to wash off the paint.

The painting in this dance consists of long black lines crossed by shorter ones. The face is painted red, and over this are painted the lines. One passes around the face. Another reaches from ear to ear, extending across the nose. There are also black stripes on the forehead. The act of painting constitutes an important part of this ceremony. The painting is continued for some time after the making of the regalia and the first night's dance. Every morning each dancer, accompanied by his wife, repairs to his grandfather. His grandfather has a string with a number of knots tied in it, representing the number of times he was painted when he went through the ceremony. This number is often about forty, but sometimes runs as high as ninety. Too great a number is thought to be undesirable. Every time the grandfather paints the dancer he unties one knot in his string. At the same time the younger man makes a knot in a string which he brings. At the end of the painting the grandfather has thus untied all the knots in his string; and his grandson's string now contains the same number, which, when he in turn becomes the grandfather of a later dancer, will be untied in the same way. The dancer's wife is painted by the grand-father's wife. Every morning that the dancer is painted he takes food and his pipe to his grandfather.

The collection in the Museum contains a dog-dancer's paint-bag. It consists of a plain bag of skin, in which the other objects are kept. It is painted red. In it is a knotted string containing about fifty knots. It is covered so thickly with paint as to redden the fingers when touched. Two small bags, containing respectively black and red paint, and a small stone, are also contained in the paint-bag.

During the period in which the dancers are daily painted, they go every night, accompanied by their wives, to their grandfathers' tents. The grandfather and the woman leave the tent and go off some distance. The woman lies down. The old man sits and prays, and then, biting off a piece of häçawaanaxu, gives it to her backward. Then the woman returns alone to the tent, where she is met by her husband, who utters the ceremonial word for "thanks" and kisses her. She spits the medicine from her mouth into her husband's. The grandfather must be given a present each time. A gun, however, counts for four presents. This is continued until the dancer has been painted the full number of times that his grandfather's string calls for. This ceremony, and the painting of the dancers' wives in addition to the dancers themselves, occur in the crazy-lodge and the dog-lodge, but apparently only in these two.

Anything lent to the dog-dancers during the ceremony be-comes their property. They may also eat food belonging to any one without interference. With the men of higher de-grees these practices are said to continue until their next dance. The shaggy dog must also follow the restrictions which he observes during the dance until the next ceremony performed by his company. If any of the five men of higher rank should be unwilling to accept these honors, on account of the dangers or the restrictions involved, the elder brothers who have chosen them would force a pipe into their hands,—an act that compels them to comply. This forcing a per-son to take a pipe is practised on other occasions by the

Arapaho as a means of compelling acceptance of something undesired.[1]

First Degree. — The dog-dancer of highest rank, the tcii-yanehi, has been mentioned. No example of the shirt covered with crow-feathers, which is characteristic of this degree, could be secured. The leggings shown in Plate xxxvi were said to have been worn by a tciiyanehi, but are probably not different from the other dog-dancers' leggings.

Second Degree. — Plate xxxvi shows the regalia of the second degree, the red scarfs (säna^{n}k^u or tayaa^{n}tceiya^n). As a second set of the regalia of this degree was obtained with fuller information, this will be described first. A scarf is worn, as shown in Plate xxxvi, over the left shoulder. At the upper end of the scarf is a short fringe made by slitting the end of the buckskin strip into forty narrow pieces, each of which is wound with corn-husk as a substitute for porcupine-quills. This fringe indicates that the dancer is painted a considerable number of times by his grandfather, but the number of pieces in the fringe is not intended to give the exact number of times. This is indicated only by the knotted string described. Near the upper end of the scarf are six eagle-feathers. These, it was said, should properly number seven, and should be lightly painted red to correspond with the color of the buckskin. Where these feathers are attached to the scarf, there is tied also a piece of root, called niäätä^n, which is said to mean the "foremost" or "principal." As the dancers go about the camp to sing, or before going into battle, they bite off a small piece of the root. It is also used as incense.[2] In four places on the long red scarf is a set of transverse bars of embroidery. Each bar is white, and is divided by small black portions into five divisions. This design represents the four hills or ridges of life.[3] On the sides of the scarf, eagle-plumes were attached at regular intervals, and some of these remain. They represent dog's hair. They serve to make the wearer of the scarf light and quick in battle. If he is pinned

---

[1] A company's elder brothers can be made to accept their positions in this way; and a young man may compel a man with whose wife he has eloped to accept reconciliation by procuring this man's ceremonial grandfather to place a pipe in his hands (p. 13).

[2] Cf. p. 32.

[3] Symbolism of the Arapaho Indians, op. cit., p. 78, Fig. 117.

down by the lower end of the scarf during the fight, he moves around the stick. As he does so, the light eagle-down sways. If he continues to move, he will not be shot, just as the moving feathers are not struck. At the lower end of the scarf is a gray feather of an eagle, called an old bird by the Arapaho. The feather is gray, like the hair of a man beginning to age, and therefore appropriate to this dance.

On the rattle of this set of regalia, which does not differ essentially from the rattles of other dog-dancers, there are bands of embroidery, broad crosses on which represent the morning star. A head-dress, tied to the scalp-lock, is worn with this scarf. This consists of a plume of eagle-down, the lower end of which is thickened by a winding of red cloth. Over the cloth is wound a string of blue beads. The red cloth symbolizes blood; and its being covered, or nearly covered, with beads, indicates the absence of wounds. The beads, being smooth and hard, symbolize invulnerability. The blue color of these beads represents the smoke which in battle conceals and protects the fighter. The whistle of this set of regalia is missing. The leather string to which it is attached consists of a single strip of buckskin slit at each end for the greater part of its length into seven strands. The middle portion, which is undivided, passes around the back of the neck. The seven strands of buckskin hang down in front of each shoulder. Each string is wound in seven places with corn-husk. The seven strings on each side, as well as the seven ornamented spots on each, refer to the seven old men at the head of the Arapaho ceremonial organization. The strings as a whole represent the old men's hair hanging over the chest; and the ornamented places, the matted or gummy spots in their hair. The smooth wider portion of skin in the middle represents the back of the head or skull. The leggings that were worn with these regalia during the ceremony had not been preserved by the owner, but had been cut up for other purposes. The scalps with which they were ornamented had been furnished by various prominent men in the tribe.

The regalia of this degree shown on the figure of the dancer

DOG-DANCER OF SECOND DEGREE.

represented in Plate xxxvi have the required seven eagle-
feathers attached near the upper end of the scarf.   The embroidery on the scarf was given the same interpretation of the
four hills of life as in the last piece.   There are seven feathers;
and the pendants on each side of the string by which the
whistle is hung number seven, because, as the wearer stated,
in the lodges of the older men everything is done seven times.
The pendants in this set, however, are embroidery-wound in
only four places, instead of the more usual seven.   These four
places, again, designate the four hills of life.   The scarf has
niäätä[n] attached to it, and sweet-grass is attached to the rattle
which represents a snake.   It is incensed with this grass before
being used.   An eagle-feather should be worn horizontally
at the back of the head with this scarf, and a down head-
dress should hang from
the same spot, so that
the two form a cross.

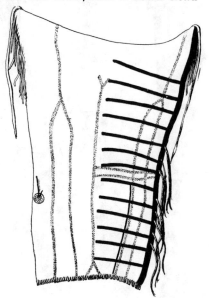

The leggings on this
figure (Fig. 59), though
properly part of another
set of regalia (see first degree), are characteristic
of all the dog-dancers.
They are of deerskin
painted yellow, and are
fringed.   Small bunches
of hair are attached to
them.   Transverse black
lines across the leggings
represent coups.   Those
on the right leg indicate
the most honorable ones,
those on the left repre-
sent deeds of less dis-

Fig. 59 ($\frac{50}{660}$).   Legging of Dog-dancer, opened out.

tinction.   A long red line, forked for the greater part of its
length, represents the course of life of man, who is at first
alone, but later married.   At the upper end of the leggings
are two small, loose flaps of skin.   One is painted green;

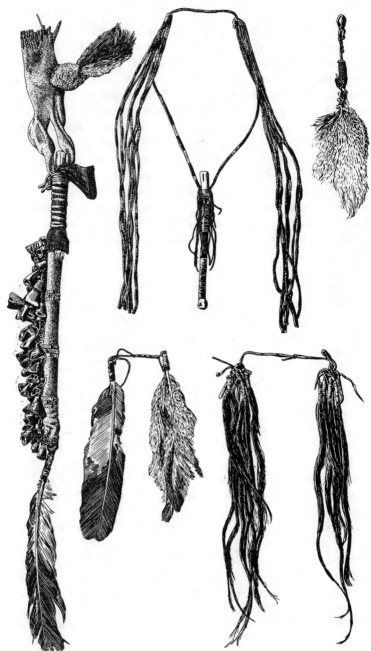

REGALIA OF DOG-DANCER OF THIRD DEGREE.

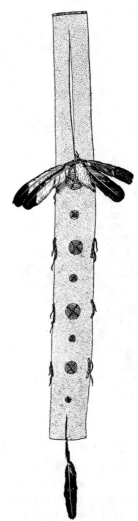

Fig. 60 ($\frac{60}{698}$). Scarf of Dog-
dancer of Third Degree.

the other, yellow. This duality also represents husband and wife.

Third Degree. — Plate XXXVII and Fig. 60 show the regalia of the third degree, which are similar to those of the preceding. The most striking difference is that the scarf (Fig. 60) is painted a light yellow instead of a dull red. The ornamentation of the scarf differs also in that the quill-embroidery consists of four circles, each with four black radii, and of intervening smaller circles, in place of the four sets of four bars that are the ornamentation of the red scarf. The signification of these ornaments was given as the four generations of the world. It is not certain that the other small differences between the yellow and the red scarf are indicative of the difference of degree.[1] This yellow scarf has five eagle-feathers and a plume attached to it, in place of seven feathers on the red scarf. There are both niäätä^n and häçawaanaxu roots on it. The rattle represents a snake. The head-dress of eagle-down is worn hanging at the back of the head.

Lowest Degree. — The regalia of the ordinary dog-dancers are comparatively simple. Most conspicuous is the large head-dress of upright turkey-feathers (Fig. 61). No scarf is worn.

[1] There are many individual variations in Arapaho regalia, due to the fact that each set is made by a different person. The differences arising from the absence of certain portions or ornaments in some objects are also not intentional. Certain parts of regalia, such as whistles, seem often to be merely borrowed for the occasion. Lance-shafts and bows are usually thrown away after the ceremony, only their attachments being kept. Feathers, medicine-roots, and other parts appear at times to be taken off in order to be attached to another ceremonial object, owing to lack of material. Very few sets of regalia except those of the highest rank in the higher ceremonies are therefore found in a state of entire completeness.

The rattle, and the whistle with the thongs to which it is attached, are identical with those of higher degrees. Bunches of human and buffalo hair are fastened as fringe to the dancer's leggings.

FIFTH DANCE (HINANAHA^{N}WU).

In the fifth dance, the members of which are old men, no regalia are worn nor do there appear to be any degrees of

Fig. 61 ($\frac{50}{3884}$d). Head-dress of Dog-dancer of Lowest Degree.

rank. The participants sing for four nights in the lodge. They sit in a circle. No drums are used, but the old men of the sixth society rattle for them. The participants are painted red over the entire body. They are naked except for a buffalo-robe painted red. The fourth night they sing until twilight. Then, taking their robes and squatting low, they form a circle and hop about, imitating prairie chickens, and calling as the prairie chickens do. One or two dance inside the ring. While they dance they sing a song that has reference to prairie chickens. When the sun rises, they leave the lodge in all directions and shake their blankets, just as birds stretch and shake their wings in the morning.

This ceremony is highly respected, and young people do not enter the lodge or go near it. The old men are said to be questioned by the still older ones as to their knowledge. They are also given the häçawaanaxu-root which the dancers in all the preceding lodges receive from their grandfathers. One informant stated that the members of the fifth lodge danced, butting and hooking each other like buffalo-bulls.

SIXTH DANCE (TCIINETCEI BÄHÄEIIHA[N]).

The last lodge, the members of which are the oldest men of the tribe, differs still more than the fifth from the earlier ceremonies. It is said to consist of only seven men. It is not clear just how this statement is meant, nor what arrangement is made when the company that has passed through the fifth dance numbers more than seven men. It would appear that membership among these seven old men is determined by the possession of one of seven sacred tribal bags or bundles of buffalo-skin. Each of these bags contains a rattle, a buffalo-tail used for sprinkling or whipping the body while sweating, and presumably paint and other objects. The seven rattles are described as simple round rattles of rawhide containing gravel. They were painted red with a black crescent representing the moon, and therefore the night, on one side, and on the other a circle symbolizing the sun and the day. At the top was tied a reddened down-feather. These rattles were handed down to succeeding generations, new ones not being made for each ceremony. The best of care was taken of them, so that they were never lost or destroyed. Only if one wore out completely was a new one made. The sacred bags containing these rattles were never buried at the death of the owner. They were given to the old men to keep, but were not regarded as private property. They belonged to the tribe. All of them are said to be still in existence.

These seven old men embodied everything that was most sacred in Arapaho life. They directed all the lodges. The actual part they played in these consisted chiefly of directing the grandfathers, often only by gestures. The grandfathers, in turn, instructed the dancers. This oldest society is therefore said to contain all the others. Every dance, every song, and every action of the lodges was performed at the direction of these old men.

The extreme sacredness of this lodge makes it difficult to secure information in regard to it except on acquaintance with the older Indians. The young and middle-aged people

Fig. 62 ($\frac{50}{848}$).　Rawhide Bag.

are almost completely ignorant of it. The seven old men are said not to dance. They sing for four days in a large sweathouse. This is said to be made like the ordinary sweathouse,—that is to say, domed, instead of conical like a tent,—but to be larger. In this they sweat once each day. During this period they fast and do not drink. They sing many different songs, accompanying them with their sacred rattles. They have no regalia and are entirely naked. They paint only in red. Black is said to belong to all the preceding lodges, but not to this. Ever after having performed this ceremony they must paint with red daily.

Fig. 62 shows a rawhide bag said to have belonged to one of the members of the sixth dance. It does not appear to differ from the ordinary square bags of rawhide, and is painted with a customary design. The flat isosceles triangles containing a rectangle were said by the elderly man from whom the bag was obtained to represent the mountain from which the buffalo issued.[1]

WOMEN'S SACRED BAGS.

The seven sacred bags owned by women and regarded as corresponding to the seven sacred bags of the sixth lodge

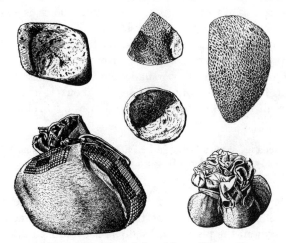

Fig. 63 ($\frac{50}{7713}$). Woman's Sacred Bag and Contents.

have been mentioned previously, and an account of the ceremonies at the transfer of such a bag from one possessor to another owner has been given.[2] Fig. 63 shows one of these bags and its contents. The bag is small, being less than 30 cm. long. It is made of skin, and is painted red. Near its opening it is ornamented with red, blue, and white beads. These beads are larger than those now used by the Arapaho. The bag contains pieces of cloth; four small skin bags tied together, each containing a broken or powdered part of a

[1] Symbolism of the Arapaho Indians, op. cit., p. 77, Fig. 87.
[2] See pp. 30, 70, of this volume.

plant used as incense; two small stones, naturally hollow, serving as paint-cups ; and two bones said to be made from the knee-joint of a buffalo, ground to an edge, used for marking the outlines of embroidery. The bones do not differ from the bones formerly always used for this purpose.

WOMEN'S DANCE (BÄNUXTAᴺWU).

The only women's dance corresponding to the series of men's dances is the bänuxtaⁿwu. The meaning of this term is not known, but it is generally translated "buffalo-dance." The participants represent buffalo.

Like the men's ceremonies, the buffalo-dance is made by reason of the pledge of an individual. The woman who has made the vow goes, accompanied by her husband and bearing a pipe, around the camp-circle from left to right, entering each tent and trying to persuade the women therein to participate in the ceremony. As she is about to start out on her circuit of the camp, her husband cries out, riding around the camp,

| "Nänäⁿtcaaⁿa | waⁿwaⁿhotaniinitciiinisänaⁿ | bänuxtiseinaⁿ." |
| "Get ready | now are ready to go around | the bänuxtaⁿwu women." |

There appears to be no restriction or limitation as to the age of the dancers, but most of them are young women. The women whom the pledger asks do as they think best. Some agree to take part in the dance, others refuse. It is often difficult to persuade them to enter the ceremony, on account of the payments that must be made by the dancers. As the pledger of the dance goes from tent to tent, she is accompanied by those whom she has persuaded to participate. The women are accompanied by their husbands.

The lodge is put up in the centre of the camp-circle. It is made of tent-poles and tent-skins contributed by the people of the camp. It is said to be similar to the lodge of the fifth dance, and resembles in certain respects the sun-dance lodge. Seven tent-poles tied together with a rope of buffalo-skin are set up in the middle. Across these near the top is tied a digging-stick (biinahaa^n) painted red. Against this rest the other tent-poles. One pole each at the northeast and southwest are painted black; one each at the northwest and southeast, red. The two colors, as so often in Arapaho ceremonials, represent night and day. Three or four skin tent-coverings are used to cover the poles. The entrance is at the east.

Degrees in this dance are comparatively numerous. Highest of all is the "white-woman" (na^{n}kuuhisei), who appears to be the pledger of the dance. Second in rank is the "owner-of-the-tent-poles" (hiitaka^{n}xuinit^i), who represents an old bull. The insignia of the third degree are called "red-stand" (bääkuu); those of the fourth degree are similar except in color, and are called "white-stand" (nana^{n}kaäkuu). Two little girls, called "calves" (wouu), are also regarded as of high rank. The rank and file (naçan^i) are distinguished according to the sex of the buffalo they represent, the bull regalia being whitened, those of the cows painted yellow. The dancers of all degrees except the red-stand and white-stand wear a head-dress of buffalo-skin falling over the back of the head and the shoulders and surmounted with horns. The red-stand and white-stand head-dresses consist of a narrow band passing around the head, in which red and white feathers are stood upright. All the dancers wear belts that resemble the men's belts for the second dance, and all have whistles.

The general course of the ceremony is much like that of the men's ceremonies. For two days after the lodge has been erected in the centre of the camp-circle the regalia are being made, and the participants dance in the lodge without them. On the third day they put on their full regalia, and what is considered the first of the four days' dance begins. Each of the dancers has a grandmother, a woman who has been through the dance, and who fills exactly the place of a grandfather in the men's dance. These grandmothers are under the direction of old men, or of one old man, who takes the place of the man who first obtained the ceremony, having seen it supernaturally performed by the buffalo.[1]

---

[1] Traditions of the Arapaho, op. cit., p. 49.

After the lodge has been put up, the old man who directs the ceremony enters, followed by the women participants. These are led by the owner-of-the-tent-poles. Singing, they march around the tent. The old man, holding a pipe, moves it four times toward the ground, each time spitting häça-waanaxu on the ground. On the fourth motion he touches the ground where he has spit medicine. Then the owner-of-the-tent-poles strikes the ground with an axe four times, and cuts out the ground.

The regalia are made in the dancing-lodge, not in the tents as in the men's dances. The grandmothers make the regalia, their husbands advising them. When they do not know how to proceed, one of the old men is asked, receiving payment for the information.

The white-woman has a bed made for her at the western end or back of the lodge. There she lies down, not to move during the entire ceremony unless ordered. Whenever she wishes to change her position, her relatives must make gifts to the old man in charge of the dance. She abstains from food and water while the ceremony lasts. The two calves are at the two ends of the semicircular line of people at the back of the tent. They also are not allowed to change their position during the ceremony; and if they wish to move, their parents must make a payment to the old people in charge of the dance. It is said that the parents of these calves are often completely stripped of property at the end of the ceremony. For this reason it is very difficult to persuade people to allow their children to take these parts.

On the third day, when the regalia have all been made, the dancers put them on. They dance facing their grandmothers, who dance first, and whom they imitate. Both the dancer and her grandmother each blows a whistle. At first all those of the higher degrees dance, the members of each degree separately. They turn or twist their heads to the left with a regular movement, blowing their whistles each time. After the dancers of higher degrees have danced, the ordinary dancers form a ring with them, and all dance in a circle. The servants of the society, who are a man and a woman, meanwhile

drive away dogs, and, as during the entire ceremony, in other
ways attend to the dancers' wants. After this dance the
women walk off from the lodge to the camp-circle, strung out
like a herd of buffalo. They walk around the camp-circle
four times from left to right, and then back into the lodge,
where they return to their places. In this procession the
owner-of-the-tent-poles goes first. At the end of the procession come the two calves. They hold two sticks in each hand,
which they use like canes, though with an exaggerated motion. Behind the calves, the last of all, comes the white-
woman, who walks very slowly. She also has two sticks.
As they march, all blow their whistles with a long, continuous
sound. While the women are marching, the old men at the
back of the lodge continue their singing and rattling. When
the dancers return to the lodge, they take off their regalia.
The skin coverings of the walls of the lodge are now raised on
all sides, and the people come from all parts of the camp-
circle to watch. The old men sing to the women's dancing.
The women walk about in a circle. To a second song they
move faster. To a third song they begin to run in a circle.
At the fourth song they run fast. At the end of the song
they rush off to the stream near the camp. The one who
reaches the water and drinks first is thought to have made
the greatest effort, and is called a good cow. From the water
the women all run back to the lodge, and the one who arrives
first is also highly thought of. The women's action in this
part of the ceremony represents the buffalo lying, standing,
walking on the ground, going to water and returning, and
raising the dust as they march.

Another part of the ceremony consists of the dancers leaving the lodge and going outside the camp-circle. There they
"sit" (lie) and walk like buffalo. They continue to do this
until they smell some buffalo-dung that has been lighted.
Then, still imitating buffalo, they become frightened and run
back to the lodge. Two men with bows follow them, and,
having entered the lodge, each counts a coup. Then they
shoot one of the buffalo women. This woman has a piece of
fat under her belt. She appears to die, and they go through

the motions of cutting her up and taking out the buffalo-fat. These two men are called "buffalo-hunters" (tcäbiheihiha^n).

The buffalo women dance also at night, but no precise accounts of this have been obtained.[1] During the night, as at the time when the women race to the water and back, men are allowed to come to the lodge and watch; but during the day no men, excepting the old men directing the ceremony, are permitted in the lodge, as the women seem to take off their clothes in order to paint.

The dancers have the face painted red. The chin is blackened. Around the corners of the mouth rise small black horns. This entire painting represents a horned buffalo-head. On the centre of the nose is made a black dot, which symbolizes a buffalo-calf. The painting is done every morning during the dance. The white-woman is painted white; the calves are painted yellow.

The head-dresses for this dance (see Figs. 64, 66, 69) have the form of a kind of cap of buffalo-skin, which covers the forehead and falls loosely over the back of the head to below the neck. Most of these head-dresses are made of buffalo-fur; that of the white-woman, however, is covered thickly with white plumes. In front, directly over the forehead of the wearer, is a rectangular piece of dressed buffalo-skin, notched along the upper edge. The lower part of this piece of skin is embroidered with horizontal stripes, the number and coloring of which varies in different head-dresses. From the sides of the top of the head-dress rise two buffalo-horns, which, when the piece is worn, are held upright by means of strings drawn through to the inside of the head-dress. The ends of the horns are tipped with plumes, and the horns are painted either white or yellow to correspond to the color of the rest of the head-dress. On one side of the head-dress, just below the horn, is tied a small ring wound with embroidery and with two transverse strings and four plumes tied to it.

As has been mentioned, the head-dresses known as red-stand and white-stand (see Figs. 67, 68) differ altogether from

[1] It is perhaps to this dancing that the statement given in Traditions of the Arapaho (op. cit., p. 49) refers, that the buffalo women danced to four songs, standing in their places and changing their position at the end of each song.

these buffalo head-dresses, being merely head-bands stuck full
of large feathers. The belts of all degrees (Figs. 65–69), including those of the red-stand and white-stand, are essentially
alike, however, differing only in color and in minor details.
In a general way the belts are similar to those of the second
dance, being made of painted skin nearly a foot wide, notched
along the lower edge, and ornamented in certain respects like
the belts for the second dance. In place of the red cloth
bordering these waist-pieces, however, the women's belts have
narrow strips of quill-wound rawhide. These run along the
top of the belt and down the two ends, being white or yellow,
according to the color of the belt, with small black areas at a
few points. At four places on the belt there are vertical bars
of quill or fibre embroidery. These are about half as long as
the belt is wide, so that they do not extend altogether across
it. They are also white or yellow, and each one is crossed by
four small black marks. In the spaces between these vertical
bars there are embroidered crosses. These bars and crosses
resemble the green painted lines and crosses on the second-
dance belts. The wavy lower edge of the women's belts is
embroidered. In addition to this, the belts are ornamented with three sets of attachments hung from near the
top in three places. Often these attachments are so placed
as to cover three of the embroidered crosses. The middle set
consists of a buffalo-tail, some loose buffalo-hair, and two or
sometimes three pendants. These pendants resemble somewhat the ornaments hung in a row over the doors of tents,[1]
but are shorter; they consist of from two to four strips of
quill-wound skin, at the lower ends of which there are small
hoofs and quill-wound loops. The two other attachments also
contain a buffalo-tail, and are similar to the one in the middle,
but their pendants are different. They have only one pendant, consisting of a pair of thin strings wound with embroidery, and bearing the customary hoofs and loops. These thin
pendants seem usually to have also down-feathers at their
lower ends. At one end of the belt there is usually a small
hoop like that on the head-dress. In complete sets there is

---

[1] Plate IX, also Fig. 10, of this volume.

usually also a third ring (Fig. 68), which is carried in the hand
and moved so as to describe a circle each time the whistles are
blown.   This, however, lacks the strings and down-feathers
attached to the rings on the head-dress and belt.   A pair of
skin bracelets or leglets wound with quill-work are also worn
by the buffalo women.   At the place
where the ends of these are tied together
there are one or two small hoofs and
loops.   An eagle wing-bone whistle completes the women's dance regalia, which
are carefully kept folded in a rectangular
case of buffalo-skin.   These cases are
about 60 cm. wide, and 30 cm. high, or
a little smaller, and open along the top.
They are almost indistinguishable from
the cases for the regalia of the fifth
dance.

First Degree.—The regalia of the first
degree—of the white-woman—may be
seen in Figs. 64 and 65.   The head-dress
(Fig. 64), in its general shape, is similar to
the majority of head-dresses worn in the
dance, but is somewhat larger and longer,
falling well below the shoulders.   Its
chief difference from the other head-
dresses is that it is not made of buffalo-
fur, but of a piece of dressed skin covered
with a large number of plumes of swan
or goose down.   The feathers are attached to thongs that pass through the
skin to the inside of the head-dress.   A
white weasel-skin is attached to the head-
dress.   There is on it also one of the
small hoops described, together with

Fig. 64 (₄₅₀). Head-dress of
White-woman.

häçawaanaxu-root.   The white embroi-
dery on the front of the head-dress bears four black vertical
marks, tapering downward.   These black marks were said to
represent buffalo-horns.   On the belt (Fig. 65), which is shown

doubled over, are embroidered five crosses and four white bars
marked with black. The middle cross is nearly covered by
the middle buffalo-tail and attachments. There are three
pendants, each of three strips, attached to this tail. The thin
pendants on the two other tails also number three, whereas

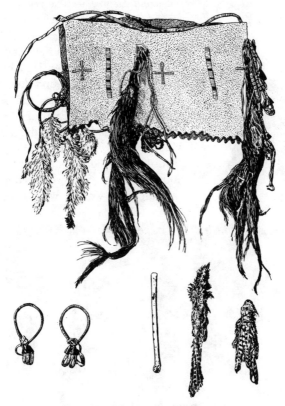

Fig. 65 ($\frac{50}{748}$–$\frac{50}{752}$).   Regalia of White-woman.

in most other belts there are only two. At one end of the
belt are two hoops. Two bird-skins, identified as those of
the whip-poor-will and poor-will, shown at the bottom of
Fig. 65, are tied to the belt when it is used. Two embroidered
strips of skin with attached small hoofs and loops, also shown
in Fig. 65, were said to be worn around the leg under the

knee, but appear rather like wristlets. Two small embroidered loops with white and brown feathers are put on the two sticks with which the white-woman walks. The wearer of these regalia may not eat either the heads of horned animals or any birds.

Second Degree. — The regalia of the second degree — of the owner-of-the-tent-poles — are represented in Fig. 66. They do not seem to differ very much from the regalia representing a buffalo-bull among the rank and file of the dancers. The head-dress and belt are entirely whitened. Even the buffalo-hair of the head-dress is dusted with white paint. On the front of the head-dress, at each side of the rectangular piece of embroidered skin, is a small loop wound with corn-husk

Fig. 66 (⁴⁰⁄₇₀₀). Regalia of Owner-of-the-tent-poles.

embroidery. These loops represent eyes. Between them there is a loosely attached thong, also wrapped with embroidery. Below this loose thong are three other stripes of ornamentation. Each of these four stripes of white has four black marks on it. This ornamentation represents the four hills of life.

The belt is about 25 cm. wide. Along its top runs a fibre-wound thong, white, with small black marks at regular intervals. It represents a snake. At the right side of the belt is a small ring wound with corn-husk. This represents the sun. White morning-star crosses are embroidered on the belt. Of the three bunches of pendants, the middle one consists of a piece of yellow buffalo-calf skin, a buffalo-tail, a piece of loose buffalo-hair as it is found on the prairie, and two ornaments of hanging thongs wound with corn-husk. On these are black marks which represent hiiteni.[1] At the ends of these ornaments are small hoofs, the rattling of which is symbolic of the tramping of a herd of moving buffalo.

Accompanying the belt is a small ring similar to the one attached to the head-dress. A third ring is carried in the hand. All three rings have four small black marks upon them, which, in the two that are fastened to the belt and the head-dress, are connected by strings and have white plumes tied near them. These four marks at opposite sides of the rings represent the ends of the earth (häneisa^n biitaawu). The blowing of the whistle that belongs to these regalia indicates the roaring of buffalo.

The owner-of-the-tent-poles represents a buffalo-bull leading his herd. During the ceremony the wearer of these regalia acts like such a bull, for instance, driving back cows that leave the herd. After the race of the buffalo women, she makes a tea or drink of red paint and ashes. Those who are tired from the race drink this to refresh themselves. Like all other regalia of high degree, these are handled with much reverence and care. They are hung up so as not to touch the ground. Children are forbidden to be noisy where they are kept. Occasionally they are taken into the open air, and, after being spread out, are prayed to. This is to see that they remain in good condition. Before this can be done, the owner must rub her body with häçawaanaxu. Before the regalia may be repacked, this root must again be chewed and spit on the objects. Only the owner herself may take them from the case or put them back. While the regalia are in the

---

[1] See p. 40 of this volume.

tent in which they are kept, no ashes may be taken from it. Before the ashes are removed, the owner of the regalia must leave the tent. If this is not done, it is thought that ashes may be blown into her eyes and she may loose her eyesight. If this should happen, she would use häçawaanaxu to cure herself. Four horses, two cattle, and other property were paid by the owner of these regalia to her grandmother.

The case in which these regalia are kept is made of buffalo-skin, and represents a buffalo-calf. At one of its lower cor-

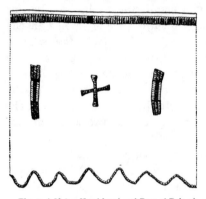

Fig. 67 (₁⁶⁰₂). Head-band and Part of Belt of Red-stand.

ners there is a small hole through which a small piece of yellow buffalo-skin projects. This represents the buffalo-calf's tail.

Third Degree.—The regalia of the third degree — the red-stand (bääkuu) — are not illustrated in detail, since they are the same in form as those of the white-stand (see Fig. 68). The head-dress consists of a piece of skin shaped like a tube, into which feathers are stuck (Fig. 67). This head-band has been stuffed with tobacco, and is tied around the head. The feathers, which are mounted on sharp sticks, are set into holes at regular intervals. The head-band represents a rattlesnake. At one end it is horizontally divided for a short distance, resembling the open jaws of a snake. At the other end there is a stiff projection wound alternately with white and black rings of quills. This part resembles the rattle of the snake. The skin of the entire head-band is painted red. It is ornamented with quill-embroidered bars. The color arrangement of these bars is similar to the one frequently used on objects

that have a tribal style of ornamentation,[1] being yellow, red,
yellow, the colors being separated by transverse stripes bordered by black.   Between the bars are small crosses.   In
the very front of the head-dress are stuck two long black
eagle wing-feathers (see Fig. 68).   Where these are attached
to the stick on which they stand, a split red-shafted flicker
feather is fastened to them.   These two upright black feathers
seem to represent buffalo-horns.   All the other feathers in
the head-dress are fluffy plumes of the great horned owl, and
are painted entirely red.

The belt accompanying this head-dress (Fig. 67) is also
painted red.   Otherwise it does not appear to differ much
from other belts for the women's dance.   Instead of the usual
four vertical embroidered bars and five crosses, it has only
three bars and four crosses; so that the attached buffalo-tails
cover the bars instead of the crosses.   This difference may
be due to the fact that this piece came from the northern
Arapaho, whereas all the others shown are from the southern
branch of the tribe.   Three sets of pendants are attached to
the middle buffalo-tail.   The three embroidered vertical bars
are yellow at the ends, while the middle portion is white and
light red.   The yellow and the red-white portions are separated by transverse red stripes.

A small loop consisting of a thong, part of which is covered
with quill-work, is worn as a finger-ring with these regalia.

Both in the red-stand and white-stand there is no small
hoop on the head-dress.   There is one on the belt; and another, without strings or feathers, is carried loose.

Fourth Degree. — Fig. 68 shows a white-stand (nana^{n}kaäkuu).
This is an almost exact counterpart of the red-stand, except
for its color.   The total number of feathered sticks in the
head-band is eighteen.   The head-band represents a snake, and
has embroidered crosses upon it; but the horizontal bars between the crosses do not show the same arrangement of colors
as the red-stand described.   They are white stripes crossed in
four places by black lines, and are thus identical with the vertical bars embroidered on most of the belts.   The middle

---

[1] See pp. 64–67, also Fig. 12, of this volume.

buffalo-tail of the belt of this apparel has only two sets of pendants attached to it.

Fifth Degree. — It is not certain of which degree the two calves (wouu) are regarded to be. They are said to wear an

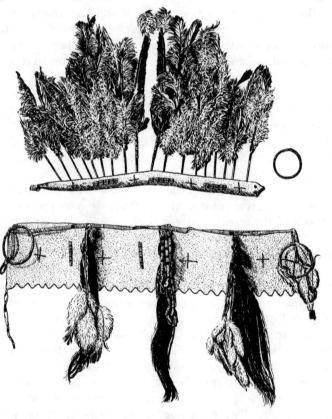

Fig. 68 ($\frac{50}{384}$, $\frac{50}{385}$). Regalia of White-stand.

embroidered head-band representing a snake, in which stand white feathers. It would therefore seem that they wear a miniature white-stand, just as the two boys in the second dance carry black lances like the dancers known as hiiwao-tänaⁿxäyaniçi. The calves walk with two sticks. They are painted yellow to represent yellow buffalo-calves. Their mothers enter the ceremony with them, taking the parts of buffalo-cows that have calves.

Lowest Degree. — Fig. 69 shows the regalia of one of the rank and file (naçan[i]). As these regalia are those of a cow, they are painted yellow. Those indicating bulls, like the owner-of-the-tent-poles, are white. It will be seen that the piece of skin on the forehead of this head-dress is quite narrow, and its orna-mentation somewhat simpler than is usual. The embroidery on the belt presents no unusual features, but it seems that the attachments are not quite what they should be. Strips of buffalo-skin with long hair have been used in place of buffalo-tails, perhaps on account of lack of the latter. Attached to the middle one of these strips of skin

Fig. 69 (₅₀/₈₈₅, ₅₀/₈₉₆).   Regalia of Lowest Degree of Women-dancers.

there is only a single pair of thin pendants, of the kind belong-ing properly to the buffalo-tails on the sides. A pair of bracelets or leglets belongs to this set.

Fig. 70, *a*, shows part of the embroidery from another speci-men of buffalo-cow regalia. This ornamentation is somewhat different from that on most of the regalia. On the belt the four vertical bars are each closely flanked by two crosses. Each bar is not in white or yellow, divided by four black marks; but its two ends are yellow, and its middle portion red without any black. The embroidered piece of skin on the head-dress was said to represent the brain and eyes.[1] Fig. 70, *b*, shows still another form of embroidery on a head-dress.

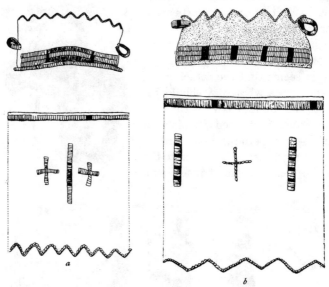

Fig. 70, *a* ($\frac{50}{741}$, $\frac{50}{742}$), *b* ($\frac{50}{868}$, $\frac{50}{868}$). Designs from Head-bands and Belts of Women-dancers.

This is from a bull head-dress. This embroidery, consisting of a white stripe transversely divided by four black marks, is identical with the bars embroidered on the belts.

Place of the Women's Dance. — It is quite clear that the women's dance corresponds very nearly to the series of men's dances. In certain details, however, it resembles the sun-dance. Though the lodge in which it is held is made of tent-poles, and not of forked trees cut for the purpose, it has a centre pole like the sun-dance lodge; and four of its poles are

---

[1] Symbolism of the Arapaho Indians, op. cit., p. 72, Fig. 16.

painted, as in the sun-dance.   There is also a similarity to the
sun-dance, in that the pledger, the white-woman, is painted
white, and has her place at the middle of the back of the
lodge.   In the men's dances the pledger is not necessarily of
the highest degree.   Several other features of the women's
dance, such as the cutting of the ground and the mimic shooting of the buffalo preceded by recounting of coups, resemble
certain parts of the sun-dance.

In the majority of its characteristics, however, the women's
dance resembles sometimes one and sometimes another of the
series of men's dances.   The symbolizing of buffalo, and the
classification of the dancers into buffalo bulls and cows, are
analogous to the first dance of the men.   The two calves
call to mind the two boys in the second dance, and the
number and variety of degrees suggest the same ceremony.
The belts worn by the women are also very much like those
used in the second dance.   There is a similarity to the crazy-
dance in the buffalo-skin cases in which the regalia are kept.
These are nearly identical for the two ceremonies.   That the
single dancers of highest degree, the white-fool and the white-
woman, are painted entirely white and are respectively very
slow in movement and not allowed to move at all, is another
point of similarity.   Whistles like those of the women are
used by the men in the crazy-dance and in the dog-dance.   In
the use of these whistles by the dancers, and of rattles by the
singers, the women's dance resembles the older societies of the
men; but in the racing of the dancers there is a similarity to
the first and second dances.   In the estimation of the Arapaho, the women's dance is more sacred than the dances of
the younger men, ranking in this regard probably at least as
high as the dog-dance.

SUMMARY.

The Arapaho bäyaa^{n}wu consists of a form of the widely
spread sun-dance and of a series of men's ceremonies graded
by age, and a single but analogous ceremony for women.   The
men's ceremonies are performed by groups of men of the
same age.   These companies are not voluntary organizations,

226 Bulletin American Museum of Natural History. [Vol. XVIII,

but consist of all the individuals of a certain age in the tribe. There is a symbolic reference to war in most of the ceremonies; and the companies, or sometimes certain members of them, have social and warlike functions. All the ceremonies are under the direction of the members of the oldest society. Intermediary between these and the dancers are men known as the dancers' grandfathers, who instruct them in the parts to play in the ceremony, and provide them with regalia. The ceremonies are held in a lodge in the centre of the camp-circle, and consist of a three-days' period of preparation and a four-days' period of dancing. Very characteristic of these ceremonies are the numerous degrees of rank, which are indicated by differences in regalia. These differences in rank do not depend at all upon any previous religious experience or training. They have little purpose except their own existence, and are bestowed as marks of honor. While there are many similarities of detail between the sun-dance and the age-ceremonies of the bäyaa^{n}wu, due to their being ceremonies of the same tribe, there is nevertheless a fundamental difference in scope and character.

SYSTEM OF THE BÄYAAⁿWU.

	Approximate Age.	No. of Degrees.	Fixed Regalia of Dancers.				Symbolic Reference.	Lodge.	Characteristic Action of Participants.
			Warlike.	Musical.	On Body.	On Head.			
Sun-dance........	Any	—	—	Whistle.	(Sage.)	(Sage.)	—	Of brush; centre pole.	Dancing, fasting, torture.
Kit-fox dance....	18	—	—	Rattle.	—	—	—	None (?).	—
Star-dance.......	20	—	—	Rattle.	—	—	—	None.	—
Tomahawk-dance..	25	3	Tomahawk.	—	Belt.	Feathers at occiput.	Buffalo.	Skins; no centre pole.	Dancing, racing.
Biitahaⁿwu.......	30	6	Lance.	—	Belt.	Feathers at forehead.	Thunder	"	"
Crazy-dance......	40	2	Bow.	Whistle.	Cape.	Feathers on head.	—	"	Dancing, fire-stamping, extravagance.
Dog-dance........	50	4	—	Whistle and rattle	(Scarf.)	—	—	"	Dancing, painting.
Hinanahaⁿwu.....	60	—	—	(Rattle.)	(Robe.)	—	—	"	Singing, one dance.
Water-sprinkling old men........	70	—	—	Rattle.	—	—	—	Sweat-house	Singing, sweating.
Women's dance...	Any	6	—	Whistle.	Belt.	Buffalo head-dress.	Buffalo.	Skins; centre pole.	Dancing, racing, representing buffalo.

SYSTEM OF DEGREES OF THE BÄYAA^{n}WU.

	NUMBER OF INDIVIDUALS.	CHARACTERISTIC REGALIA.	COLOR OF REGALIA.
Tomahawk-dance.			
First degree.........	1	Kakaox (sword).	Black.
Second degree.......	3	Kakaox (sword).	Red, etc.
Lowest degree { bulls.	indef-	Tceäox (tomahawk).	Red and white.
{ cows .	inite.	Tceäox (tomahawk).	Red and yellow.
Biitaha^{n}wu.			
First degree.........	1	Tawa$_n$hä^n (straight club).	
Second degree.......	2	Crooked fur-wrapped lance.	(Otter-skin).
Third degree.........	2	Straight fur-wrapped lance.	(Otter-skin).
Fourth degree.......	2	Boy's lance.	"Black."
Fifth degree.........	4	Beaded lance.	"Black."
Lowest degree.......	ind.	Lance.	Red.
Crazy-dance.			
First degree.........	1	Bow and cape.	White.
Lowest degree.......	ind.	Bow and cape.	Red and white.
Dog-dance.			
First degree.........	1	Feather-covered coat.	(Crow-feathers).
Second degree.......	2	Scarf.	Red.
Third degree.........	2	Scarf.	Yellow.
Lowest degree.......	ind.	Upright feather head-dress.	(Turkey-feathers).
Women's dance.			
First degree.........	1	Swan-down buffalo head-dress.	White.
Second degree.......	1	Buffalo head-dress.	White.
Third degree.........	?	Head-dress of standing feathers.	Red.
Fourth degree.......	?	Head-dress of standing feathers.	White.
Fifth (?) degree......	2	Head-dress of standing feathers (?).	White (?).
Lowest degree { bulls.	ind.	Buffalo head-dress.	White.
{ cows .	ind.	Buffalo head-dress.	Yellow.

LIST OF DEGREES AND ILLUSTRATED REGALIA.

	Regalia	*Page*
Kit-fox dance (members, nouhinena^n).........	—	—
Star dance (members, haçaahouha^n)...........	Fig. 55	181

Hiitceäoxa$_n$wu (first dance).

			Regalia	*Page*
First degree	(hiikaka-	with black sword.	Fig. 56	184
Second degree	oxuiçi)	with colored sword.	Fig. 57	185
Lowest degree (naçani hiitceäoxinena^n or hiitceäoxuiçi).......................			Fig. 58	187

Biitaha^{n}wu (second dance).

	Regalia		*Page*
First degree (hiitawa^{n}hä^{n}hit^i)..............	Fig. 49		170
Second degree (hiinousäeitciçaniçi).........	Pl. xxxii	opp.	175
Third degree (hiibiixa^{n}uçi)...............	—		—
Fourth degree (biitaheisana^n)..............	Pl. xxxiii		177
Fifth degree (hiiwaotäna^{n}xäyaniçi).........	Fig. 53		179
Lowest degree (naçani biitaheinena^n).......	Fig. 54		180

Haha^{n}ka^{n}wu (third, crazy, or fool dance).

	Regalia		*Page*
First degree (na^{n}k'haha^{n}kä^n)..............	Pl. xxxiv		194
Lowest degree (naçani haha^{n}kä^{n}nena^n)......	Pl. xxxv	opp.	196

Heçawa^{n}wu (fourth or dog dance).

			Regalia	*Page*
First degree (tciiyanehi)..................			Fig. 59	203
Second degree	(hiina^{n}tcei-	with red scarfs .	Pl. xxxvi opp.	203
			Fig. 59	203
Third degree	yaniçi)	" yellow "	Pl. xxxvii	204
			Fig. 60	205
Lowest degree (naçani heçäbinena^n)........			Fig. 61	206

	Regalia	*Page*
Hinanaha^{n}wu or fifth dance (members, nanaanä^n-heiçi).................................	—	—
Tciinetcei bähäeiha^n (sixth dance)............	Fig. 62	208

Bänuxta^{n}wu (women's dance)...............

	Regalia	*Page*
First degree (na^{n}kuuhisei).................	Figs. 64, 65	216, 217
Second degree (hiitaka^{n}xuinit^i).............	Fig. 66	218
Third degree (dancers with bääkuu)........	Figs. 67, 68	220, 222
Fourth degree (dancers with nana^{n}kaäkuu)..	Fig. 68	222
Fifth degree (?) (wouu, calves)............	—	—
Lowest degree (naçani bänuxtiseina^n), bulls (waxaçou), cows (bii).................	Fig. 69	223

THE ARAPAHO.

By Alfred L. Kroeber.

IV. — RELIGION.

Plates LVII–LXXXVIII.

Introduction.

Part IV, "Religion," completes that portion of " The Arapaho" which deals with the Arapaho proper. Like the preceding parts, it is issued as the result of investigations made through the generosity of Mrs. Morris K. Jesup. It includes all the information obtained on this phase of Arapaho life, with two exceptions. The first of these is the ceremonial organization, which has been described in the preceding section. The sun-dance, which by the Arapaho themselves is included in the enumeration of their tribal ceremonies, but which is fundamentally different, is treated in the present part. This ceremony has been recently described with great thoroughness as it is practised by the southern Arapaho.[1] The present much briefer account applies to the northern Arapaho. The second exception is the myths and traditions. These have been published conjointly with a more extensive collection subsequently made along the same lines in the same tribe by Dr. G. A. Dorsey.[2] The present section of "The Arapaho," besides treating of the sun-dance, includes information on religious customs of a tribal nature, modern ceremonies and the objects used in them, and personal supernatural powers.

THE SUN-DANCE.

The following brief account of the sun-dance of 1900 among the Wyoming Arapaho is a record of casual observations during a week spent in the camp and given over primarily to other purposes. It is about what any one in the camp would witness, both within the camp-circle and in the dancing-lodge,

[1] G. A. Dorsey, The Arapaho Sun-Dance (Field Columbian Museum Publications, Anthropological Series, Vol. IV).
[2] G. A. Dorsey and A. L. Kroeber, Traditions of the Arapaho, ibid., Vol. V.

without entering the ceremony, or being directly connected with it.[1]

Opening Day. — By noon of June 14, the tribe had gathered and the camp-circle was practically complete, although a few tents were put up subsequently. About the middle of the day, the old men — including the head priest, the keeper of the sacred pipe — were gathered under a shelter in the middle of the camp-circle. The men of proper age to be members of the second of the tribal series of dances, the biitaha^{n}wu, charged on the camp from behind a hill to the west, shooting and crying. All were mounted. They carried rude shields of willow brush, and lances made of willow poles on the ends of which the leaves had been left. Many had guns, and some flags. Some had leggings of bagging or of green calico around their horses' front legs. This was to indicate unmounted men. West of the camp they stopped and stood for a while. Then they rode entirely around the outside of the camp-circle anti-sunwise. Then, passing inside through a gap at the western end, they rode around the interior of the camp-circle in the opposite direction, two, three, four, and sometimes five abreast. Behind them rode two men who were either the head men of this company or more probably their ceremonial elder brothers. After completing the inner circuit, these two men joined the old men under the shelter in the centre of the camp-circle, while the company of mounted men went to their place, just opposite the west end of the camp-circle, and there drew up abreast in three lines with a few stragglers. After a few minutes they dispersed. Some of the horses were painted with mud on the forehead and from the hind quarters down to the hoofs.

The same night, about ten o'clock, the people gathered for what was called the "stirring-up singing," for practice, as it were, evidently of sun-dance songs. The singing took place in a tent, no doubt the rabbit-tent or the tent of preparation

---

[1] The sun-dance is called by the Arapaho "haseiha^{n}wu," which is translated sacrifice-lodge or offering-lodge. The individual directly responsible for the perform-ance of each ceremony is called "yanahut,"— as in the age-society ceremonies, — which has been rendered here by " pledger," the equivalent of Dorsey's " lodge-maker." See p. 152.

for the ceremony; but no note of this was made by the writer. The singing here continued until four next morning. Then the biitahaⁿwu company again rode around the camp-circle, three or four abreast, with much shooting and yelling, as on the previous day. They carried no willow shields, except in a few instances, where they were obviously left over from the preceding day. The course now was somewhat different. Starting from the interior of the camp-circle at its eastern end, they rode out, and then three-quarters of the way around it, from left to right. Turning north of the camp-circle, they retraced their course in the opposite direction, and entered the camp-circle again at the east, riding to the middle, where they disbanded.

The slight shelter in the middle of the camp-circle appears to have been in the place later occupied by the sun-dance lodge. It was erected before noon of June 14, the first day of the ceremony. On the evening of this day, the rabbit-tent appears to have been set up. It stood during the next three days (June 15, 16, 17) about halfway west of the centre of the camp-circle, between it and the circle of tents. West of the rabbit-tent — almost in the line of tents, but a little nearer the inside of the camp-circle than the others — was the painted tent of the keeper of the sacred pipe.

The tent for the keeper of the sacred pipe is shown in Plate LVII. It is at present made of canvas, and the painting is as follows: The lower edge of the tent for two or three feet up is blue. There are eight different sections of this, each having five horizontal rows of yellow suns, represented by solid circles. Each row contains seven of these circles, except in one section, where there are eight in a row. The parts of the tent surface which separate these sections of circles are painted each with seven vertical zigzag red lines forked at the top, apparently representing lightning. Above this lower band of sun and lightning symbols, the body of the surface of the tent is occupied by horizontal stripes, alternately orange-red and green. There are fourteen of the red stripes, and thirteen of the green. The very uppermost portion of the tent is again blue, with five horizontal rows of yellow circles.

In front, the strip where the tent is pinned together is painted red. At the lower end, at the top of the door, this red band expands into a circle. Down the middle of the back of the tent, from the top as far down as the lowest of the red horizontal stripes, is a green line. At the very top this is crossed with a horizontal green bar; near the lower end, where it intersects the next to the lowest red stripe, two green horns branch out, forming a horizontal crescent.

This tent is discussed later in connection with the tribal pipe.

First Preliminary Day. — About eleven in the morning of June 15, four good warriors went out as scouts or "wolves" to find suitable trees for the dancing-lodge. An hour or two later the young men gathered on horseback again, and rode around the camp-circle, as they had on the previous day. It was said that this ride represented a ride customary before a war-party started out. After they had made two circuits, the company gathered near the shelter in the centre of the camp-circle. After a time they sent out scouts. These met the four "wolves" who had been sent out earlier in the day. These four men cried "Wuuuu!" imitating wolves; thus announcing that they had seen the enemy. Thereupon the entire company of young men rode out of the camp and then charged on it. After this they drew up, still mounted, west of the shelter in the centre. The four scouts came riding slowly one behind the other. Women were singing, and drums beating. The women stood in two rows; one in front of the shelter, looking west, and the other in front of the rabbit-tent, looking east. In front of the row of women at the shelter stood the drummers. The mounted young men were in three rows, south or southwest of the shelter. They also faced about west. The four scouts came from the direction in which the selected trees were, to the west of the camp-circle, or, more exactly, somewhat northwest. The young men now wheeled three times in a body around the shelter in which the old men were. Then the scouts, one after another, advanced and told war-stories. Thereupon the gathering broke up.

Soon after this, three elderly men went off in a southerly

direction to hunt buffalo. One or two of them carried bows and quivers. At some distance out on the prairie a buffalo-skin had been laid. They shot this and then loaded it on the horse of one of them. In the old days, of course, a live buffalo was shot. As they returned, a drum was beaten in the rabbit-tent. They came quite slowly, walking their horses. Stopping in front of the rabbit-tent, they counted their coups one after the other. The keeper of the sacred pipe came out of the rabbit-tent, and going to its rear, where a small cedar-tree leaned against it, took some buffalo-chips. One of the three hunters took the buffalo-skin from the horse. Two of them took hold of it, and, after moving it four times, stretched it out by a little pile of dirt (Plate LVIII). The keeper of the sacred pipe took a little of the earth, and at the head of the skin made a pile of it. A glowing coal was brought out from the rabbit-tent on a forked stick and put on this heap of earth. Then incense was put on it. The women of the camp now brought all the small children to touch the buffalo-skin four times. After this the men went up to touch it. Finally two of the hunters took the skin again, and, after moving it four times, raised it up and walked to the rabbit-tent, taking about five minutes to cover the short distance. Taking four slow steps, they stopped while a song, accompanied by rattling, was sung in the tent. When the singing ended, they were near the door, and took the skin inside. Then a man and a woman inside, evidently the pledger of the dance and his wife, said "Hoiii!" several times in thanks.

During the day, "medicine was boiled" in the rabbit-tent, the medicine being sung over with drumming.

Second Preliminary Day. — On the morning of June 16, about sunrise, all the children, it was said, were brought to touch a piece of calico which had been " given away " or sacri-ficed (haseïyaa^n) to the supernatural beings (tcäyatawuneni-ta^n, untrue person), and was now being held out toward the east. The man who "gave away" this cloth sacrificed it on account of his wife who had been sick. After the children had all touched it, it was hung up over the door of the largest tent in the camp, which was at the southeast of the camp-circle.

It is not certain whether or not this man was the pledger of the dance. The man "gave away" considerable property, and furnished food. Other people also contributed. The gifts were made to old men. On this morning about forty women brought food to the tent.

Later in the day a sweat-house was put up. In the morning the willows for this sweat-house were lying back of the tent in which the gathering took place. Some of the willow poles for the framework were put in place by four women together holding a stick. One woman went about the framework before it was covered with blankets, and passed her hands down along each of the poles toward the ground. On a little mound of earth east of the entrance lay a buffalo-skull.

This skull faced the east, and was painted red and black. Between the horns it was black. The left or southern horn was painted black; the right or northern, red. Down the median line of the skull ran a black and a red line, the black on the south, the red on the north. There were also four short black lines extending toward the nose from the black area between the horns. The nasal and orbital cavities were stuffed with vegetation, perhaps sage. This appears to have been the skull later used at the "altar" in the main lodge.

All the morning and afternoon of this day, singing went on in the large tent, where at intervals the people "gave away" their property. The singing was accompanied by rattling. The songs were all begun by an old man in a loud voice and at a high pitch. After a few notes, other men joined in the singing, and, towards the end of each song, one woman or more. The song gradually fell in both pitch and volume until it died away. Thereupon the leader in the singing began again. The pledger of the dance and his wife were said not to be in this tent, but in the rabbit-tent, fasting.

Early in the afternoon a hole was dug for the centre pole of the sun-dance lodge and a small cottonwood-branch stuck into it. Sixteen holes were dug in a circle around this centre hole for the outside forks of the lodge, and a similar branch put in each.

Before sunset, long stripped pine-trees were brought on

wagons. These were to be the rafters for the top of the lodge. They had been brought about twenty miles from the mountains. All the young men now rode into the camp-circle; then, dividing into two parties, they went through a sham battle, each side alternately pursuing the other. After this the two parties rode around the camp in opposite directions; one inside the camp-circle, the other outside, and then respectively outside and inside. After this they drew up around the shelter in the centre of the camp-circle, and dismounted. Food was then provided for them by the elder brothers of the companies that had taken part in the ride.

On the evening of this day, two young men who were going to take part in the dance came into the tent of an old man who was to be their grandfather. They touched both him and his wife on the forehead, saying "Hoiii, hoiii!" One of them prayed as they sat at the back of the tent. They again said "Hoiii!" twice. Food was prepared and set before them. Each of them said "Hoiii!" twice again, and then ate. They left the tent without having spoken another word, taking with them the food that they had not eaten.

Third Preliminary Day. — June 17 was the day on which the centre pole for the lodge was to be brought to the camp-circle. About nine in the morning the majority of the people of the camp rode around the camp once slowly, and singing. The women followed the men: the dog-company, and perhaps others, brought up the rear. Then they rode to where the tree intended for the centre pole stood, about four miles up stream in a northwesterly direction. Several wagons accompanied them to bring back brush to form the walls of the lodge. The women gathered large, leafy branches for this purpose, and put them on the wagons. Some would take one or two cottonwood-branches, and, tying them to ropes, fasten them to their saddles to drag home. A large crowd gathered in groups among the timber and brush of the river-bottom about the main tree. This was cut down, and as it fell the people shouted, shooting at it; and certain men ran to count coup on it, striking it with whatever they held in their hands. One branch of the fork was broken by the

fall of the tree, but after some consultation it was decided that
the tree would answer. It was cut off and stripped, and four
horses tied to it. They hardly succeeded in dragging it through
the brush out on to the prairie. There it was put on a wagon.
The wagon started for the camp, and the people went with
it amid some excitement and much merriment. The women
rode ahead, while the men followed in two parties. On arriving at the camp, these two parties engaged in a sham battle.[1]
Then they rode to the centre of the camp-circle. After this
they again rode, two abreast in two companies, twice around
the camp-circle in opposite directions, inside and out. Meanwhile about fifteen old men and women were dancing shoulder
to shoulder, the men holding hand-drums.

It was on the morning of this day that the old man made
the speech to the people given on p. 15.

While the people were away bringing the centre pole, the
pledger of the dance made the circuit of the camp-circle from
left to right, asking the people who had remained for contri-
butions of food. He wore a buffalo-robe to which pieces of
rabbit-fur were attached, and which, later in the ceremony,
lay at the foot of the centre pole.

A stick about four feet high with a fork at the top had been
set up west of the incompleted dancing-lodge, between it and
the pile of brush later used for the walls of the lodge. This
stick had sage at the top, similar to the bundle of willows that
later was put into the fork of the centre pole of the lodge,
and in addition to the sage something red, apparently cloth.

Late this afternoon the important ceremony of the erection
of the dance-lodge took place. The pledger and his wife, the
keeper of the sacred pipe, and other people, including three
of the dancers, came out of the rabbit-tent bearing the sacred

---

[1] It was said that among the southern Arapaho the dog-company takes charge of the
bringing-in of the centre pole, the younger companies fighting a sham battle on the way
home. In this battle the stars and biitaha^{n}wu company are opposed to the kit-foxes
and tomahawk-men; that is to say, the second preliminary and second full company
against the first preliminary and first full company. Dorsey, however (op. cit. 80, 84),
states, that in 1901 the battle was between the dog-company as against stars, kit-foxes,
and biitaheinena^n (the crazy-company having failed to arrive), and in 1902, between
the dog-company, the kit-foxes, and the biitaheinena^n, against the stars and crazy-men.
Thus in 1901 the fourth society would have been opposed to the second and the two
preliminaries; in 1902 the second and fourth societies with the first preliminary company
would have been against the third society and the second preliminary. It will be seen
that all these accounts conflict considerably.

paraphernalia, consisting of a buffalo-skull, the buffalo-skin shot the preceding day, a buffalo-robe, a stick that was apparently a digging-stick, with buffalo-fat, a rawhide rope, the sacred wheel, a pipe, a knife, and black and red paint (Plates LIX and LX). After emerging from the tent, the people carrying these objects proceeded to the dancing-lodge to paint the rafters, after which the centre pole was put up. Sixteen forks around the periphery of the lodge had been previously put up, as well as the short rafters connecting them.

The pledger's wife, carrying the sacred wheel, was the first to emerge from the tent. She was followed by her husband with the pipe. After him came three men; the first carrying the knife, the second the black paint in a bag, and the third the red paint. These three dancers, as well as the pledger, were painted with white paint, with a black circle on the breast, and lines extending from this over the shoulders and arms. They wore also a white plume erect at the back of the head. The pledger's wife wore a blanket from her waist down. She was painted red over the body, and her hair was loose. On her chest was painted a blue circle. Her wrists had black bands, and below her eyes were black lines. A red feather hung down from the back of her head. After coming out from the tent, these five people stood and waited; whereupon the old men bringing the buffalo-skins, the digging-stick, and other objects, came out. They proceeded very slowly in single file toward the dancing-lodge. Three men in advance carried the buffalo-skin shot on the preceding day, and perhaps a buffalo-skull. They were followed by two men with a buffalo-robe. After them came a man with the badger-skin, then one with the stick and the fat, and after him the one with the rawhide rope. The keeper of the sacred pipe was sometimes behind this line of men, and sometimes in advance. Evidently he did not form part of the procession. After a little interval came the pledger's wife, then the pledger, then the three dancers with the knife and the paint, and finally two men to paint the pole. The progress of these people was very slow and impressive, and great silence was maintained in the camp. A number of people, especially old men, were gathered near the dancing-lodge, while others of all ages sat in the open space of the camp-circle or at their tents.

In the slow circling that now took place around the half-erected dance-lodge to paint the poles, not all of the people that had emerged in procession from the rabbit-tent took part. There were now only seven. They still marched in single file, but not quite as slowly as before. First came the ceremonial grandfather of the pledger, carrying sage. He was followed by the keeper of the sacred pipe with an eagle-wing fan, which he carried with him throughout the ceremony, and some sage. Third was the pledger with his pipe; next, his wife, still with the wheel; then the dancer with the knife; and, sixth and seventh, the two men to do the painting. The rafters were lying outside the lodge, on the ground. The seven people went four times around the lodge, touching the rafters with their feet. They did not quite complete the fourth circuit, but stopped south of the pole, raising what they carried, except two men with the paint. Then they bowed their heads, sang softly, and prayed. They were standing abreast along the rafter. The pledger now touched the pole seven times, cutting it twice on the right, twice on the left, then on the right again, and then drawing from the right to the left twice. Then the woman touched the pole with her wheel, and the dancer carrying the knife cut the rafter four times, first cutting, and then drawing the knife across. After this, the first of the two men carrying paint, the one with black, stooped down and began painting the rafter. He first painted the pole in the places where it had been cut, and then filled in all the intervening spaces, making a band of paint extending around the tree. The keeper of the sacred pipe stood about, directing the cutting and the painting, pointing out the places. The seven people then continued to proceed around the dancing-lodge from left to right, four poles altogether being painted, — one at the southeast and southwest, each black; and one at the northwest and northeast, each red. In painting the first two poles black on the south of the lodge, the seven people stood facing the east; in painting the last two poles red on the north side of the lodge, they faced westward.

After this, they entered the half-completed lodge from the east and stood abreast in the middle, facing north and praying. The members of the biitaha^{n}wu[1] now drew up north and south of the lodge; the "stout men" on the south, the "short men" on the north. With the latter half of the company were two drummers. The members of the company carried tent-poles the tops of which were connected in pairs by short ropes. They sang a biitaha^{n}wu song referring to the thunder. It began with gentle drumming, then a hard crack on the drum represented a flash of lightning and sharp thunder. Toward the end of the song the drumming became soft again.

The keeper of the sacred pipe now began to fasten the various objects to the centre pole. Two men lifted up the bunch of willows. The centre pole, which was lying on the ground, was turned so that the plane of its forking branches was vertical, and the willows were tied to it. Then came women and a number of visiting Crees and a few Arapaho men, bringing calico and other objects to be fastened to the centre pole. The woman for whom the dance had been pledged now kissed all the people who gave things to tie to the pole, in thanks for her restoration to health. At this time about ten elderly men, said to belong to the dog-company, were sitting close to the lodge (west of it), and drumming. The rawhide rope carried in the ceremonial procession was used to tie the various objects to the tree, Then a man told a war-story, and, taking the digging-stick painted red at the point, stuck it into the bunch of willows and other objects to hold them in place.

The centre pole was now lifted a short distance seven times amid shouting, while it was motioned to with the wheel to rise. The seventh time it was lifted up, and by means of the joined tent-poles pushed into place (Plate LXI). All this time the dog-dancers were drumming and singing. The pledger, his wife, and the three other dancers, had retired to the west of the lodge, facing the east. It was now perhaps three-quarters of an hour before sunset. The young men with

---

[1] It is not certain that the information given as to the part played by the biitaha^{n}wu here, before, and subsequently, is exact. It is possible that several of the younger companies should have participated. but that the disorganization of bäyaa^{n}wu at the present time caused a modification, or that several companies did take part and only the biitaha^{n}wu was mentioned. See footnote on p. 286.

tent-poles continued to hold the centre pole in place until it was firmly set in the ground. Then the long horizontal rafters from the centre fork to the periphery were slid into place while the dog-dancers continued their drumming and singing. As soon as these rafters were in place, young men climbed up on the forks at the edge of the lodge to tie the rafters in place with thongs. The pile of cottonwood-branches was then distributed and the branches set up around the lodge, leaning against the polygon of horizontal beams. The lodge was herewith completed (Plate LXII).

Not long after, "the dancing-in" took place. The people had returned to their tents, but now gathered rapidly. The young men collected in two or three parties at various places in the camp-circle, and ran to the lodge, two abreast, shooting and shouting. They came into the lodge by the entrance at the east. Everybody in the camp came into the lodge, which was much crowded. The young men and women stood in a ring, facing the centre pole; behind and around them, just inside of the brush wall of the lodge, stood other people, mostly older; in the centre were the old men. The people danced, standing and singing, some of the men shooting at the fork· In the intervals between the songs, horses and calico were given away. The visiting Crees especially received these gifts. Then this formation broke up. The old men and women now danced a few times, standing shoulder to shoulder, the men carrying drums. Practically all the old men of the tribe took part in this, for the dancers were so numerous that they formed two concentric circles.

This evening or night the rabbit-tent was taken down.

First Day of the Dance. — On June 18 the dancers were painted by the old men. About one in the afternoon they had been painted white, but with no designs, and were resting. At half-past seven in the evening they were dancing, fully painted. Most of them were white, some yellow, some buff, and some pink. Each of them had on the breast a circle. From this, two lines extended downward, and two others upward, on the shoulders and along the arms. They usually had a line around the wrists and a line enclosing the face. In

many cases, perhaps in the majority, the lines were replaced by
a double row of dots.   They danced standing in their places,
merely raising the heels from the ground, the toes remaining
entirely stationary.   Each time the heels came down on the
ground, the body seemed to be dropped into the pelvis.   The
upper part of the body was also thrown a little forward.   The
arms were hanging and the head up, with a bone whistle in
the mouth projecting straight forward or upward.   The
dancers looked to the top of the centre pole.   At this time
eighteen were dancing.   Later on, they dropped out one by
one, and rested.   At half-past ten in the evening, only four
were dancing.   The dancers wore blankets from their hips,
and long breech-cloths (most of them red), and had three
bunches of sage stuck in the fronts of their belts.   At the ends
of their bone whistles were feather plumes, and all wore a
plume upright at the back of the head.   The pledger's hands
were painted black up to his wrists, looking like gloves.   He
was holding the wheel, and with each dance-movement raised
it to about the height of his head, occasionally passing it
behind his back to change it to his other hand.

About half-past seven of the evening of this day, a stand
of four sticks was brought.   The keeper of the sacred pipe
set the stand up in front of two of the dancers in order to
help them, and then hung the bundle containing the sacred
pipe upon it.   The buffalo-robe trimmed with pieces of rabbit-
skin, which had been previously worn by the pledger and had
been carried in the ceremonial procession from the rabbit-
tent to the dancing-lodge, now lay west of the foot of the centre pole.   The dancers, while erect, had the blankets on which
they reposed when resting, lying before them at their feet.
In the southeast part of the lodge sat the drummers, all young
men, beating a bass drum hung from sticks set in the ground,
most of them using sticks the ends of which were not wrapped.
At this time, fourteen were drumming at once, sitting crowded
very closely in a circle.   All around them the women sat on
the ground in their blankets, holding up branches of willows,
raising them in time to the drumming and their own singing.
In concluding a song the drummers struck about four hard

blows at intervals twice as great as the beats accompanying the song. The women continued to sing two or three phrases after the stop of the drum, and then allowed their voices to die away. The men, on the other hand, began each song, and continued to sing only as long as the drumming lasted. The dancers blew their whistles each time that they raised themselves on their toes.

At half-past ten the scene was much the same, except that there were fewer dancers. A fire was burning in the lodge, the bundle containing the sacred pipe was on the stand in front of one or two of the dancers, the drumming was going on, the singing-women were still about the drummers, while about the lodge, mostly outside, stood young men concealing their faces behind their blankets, and watching. The dancing appears to have continued all this night.

Second Day of the Dance. — About sunrise on June 19, all the dancers are said to have faced the east and danced, after which the four rafters that had been painted were motioned to with food.

By eight this morning, this being the second of the three days of the actual dance, the relatives of the dancers brought food for the young men's grandfathers into the lodge, in return for their painting the dancers. The old men distributed this food to their relatives. It is said that on the last day the giving was reversed, the grandfathers presenting food to their grandchildren, the dancers. On this morning a rod, apparently a tent-pole, painted red, with a small crossbar at the top from which hung feathers and two blue handkerchiefs, was put up for a young man who had made the dance two or three times, having on each occasion fasted for the entire period.

Several tents or shelters had been taken down and their canvas used to cover the western half of the dancing-lodge to shelter the dancers. This canvas was stretched inside of the brush wall along the entire western half of the lodge. Where the spectators looked in, the wall consisted only of cottonwood brush. On the morning of June 19, tent-canvas was also put on the rafters overhead, along the western part of the circumference of the lodge, to form a shade for the grandfathers and dancers. Other men variously occupied other places in the lodge. The middle of the back or western end of the lodge was occupied by the pledger and his wife, and was screened with six deciduous trees and with the small cedar-tree that previously had been leaned against the back of the rabbit-tent. The pledger's wife did not come forward like the men dancers, nor dance. From this place a small trench extended in the direction of the centre of the lodge, bordered on each side by a small log and by seven upright sticks tufted with bunches of rabbit-fur. These logs and sticks were painted respectively red and black on the two sides of the trench. At the rear or western end of the trench a painted buffalo-skull lay, apparently the one used two days before for the sweat-house. Near this skull stood a forked stick, mentioned before as having stood, at the time of the cere-monial procession, outside of the sun-dance lodge, with sage and a red object on it. It was now used to hang the wheel from, when this was not held by the pledger. In front of the skull, between it and the rear of the trench, or perhaps cover-ing the rear portion of the trench, were small arched sticks or wickets in a row. Nearly at each side of these sticks was a small mass of low shrubbery stuck into a round piece of soil or sod which had been cut out of the ground. These two pieces of earth and shrubbery had been brought in the morning of the first day of the dance by old men and women who had gone to the near-by river for the purpose. The seven small trees formed a sort of screen parallel with the outside of the lodge at the middle of this western end. Just to the south of the rear end of the trench was the cedar, south of this was a row of three cottonwood trees or branches, making a total of four trees south of the trench. The three trees on the north side of the trench were of three different species; the first one nearest the trench being again a cottonwood; the second, a tree called by the Arapaho ha^{n}wa^{n}wubiic ("praying-wood"); and the third and farthest, a willow.

The centre pole, about ten feet above the ground, was encircled by a band of black and red paint, the black below. Between these bands a piece of light-colored calico a foot or more in width, encircled in the middle by a yellow ribbon, was tied around the tree so that the red-painted portion of the trunk was immediately above it, the black just below. From the fork of the tree hung a buffalo-robe, to the lowest end of which were attached a bunch of eagle-feathers and gorgets (beii).

About nine or ten in the morning of this second day, singing began in the lodge preparatory to the painting of the dancers. The grandfathers now sat in a semicircle at the eastern end of the lodge, the end opposite to that in which the dancing went on. In front of them were sitting their grandsons (the dancers), twenty-four in number. At the end of each song the old men touched the dancers on the face with wet sage, and the last time on the back. After this the old men got up, went to the west end of the lodge, and sat down. The dancers stood up, and washed themselves with water brought to them in buckets, and then sat around the middle of the lodge to dry.

When they were dry, they came up to the old man, the keeper of the sacred pipe, and he touched them with paint. Taking paint of the color with which they were to be covered, he rubbed it in his hands, and made a mark on each hand with the other. Then he passed his hands up from the feet of each young man to his body; from his hands up his arms, to his shoulders, and to his head, touching him lightly with the paint. The young man sat before him with his knees drawn up, and his hands over his shins. Then the old man passed his hands along the dancer in reverse direction, taking hold of several fingers of his hands, and pulling them downward. To some dancers he did this twice, to others four times. Then the young man turned around, presenting his back, which the old man rubbed rather heavily with paint. After this the young men took cups of paint, and rubbed themselves uniformly over the entire body. Fewer of them were white, and more of them yellow, than on the day before. The pledger of the dance and his father, who had gone into the dance with him and constantly stood beside him, were again painted white. Then the grandfathers came, and sat or knelt before the keeper of the sacred pipe, who described to them how to paint the dancers. Thereupon the old men proceeded to do the painting. Using black paint, they enclosed the face in a line, made a circle on the breast, bands around the arms just above the wrists, and around the legs just above the ankles, and a horizontal arc of a circle on the back over the left shoulder-blade. Then they drew lines from the circle on the breast, downward along the legs, and up over the shoulders, down the arms, to the lines at the wrists. In most cases a row of black dots bordered the black lines on each side, or entirely replaced them. The pledger and his father had two diamond-shaped areas on each leg and arm wiped clear of paint to be later painted over in dark red. The pledger and his father, while being painted, sat just north of the ceremonial trench. The old man in charge of the ceremony sat just south of this trench in front of the cedar-tree. Four dancers, all of them with a ground-color of yellowish buff, were not painted with lines or dots, but had, instead, two eagles painted on each arm and leg, one on the breast, and four or five small eagles on the face. These four dancers also showed certain differences in their apparel. The majority wore wreaths of sage on the head, with the down plume that had been previously worn at the back now standing up in front. The four men painted with eagles wore no such wreath, and had the down plume at the back of the head. They also wore bunches of sage in their belts, as on the preceding day; while the majority of the dancers now had a wreath or belt of it around the waist. All the dancers wore anklets and wrist-bands of sage, held in shape with sinew.

About half-past one, with a large crowd in the lodge, and after a number of horses had been given away, the pledger took a piece of white skin, and moved along slowly, holding it a foot or less above the ground, going along the lodge from left to right until he came to where the drummers and singers were. He passed the skin to them, and they began the drumming, whereupon dancing commenced. The pledger thereupon laid the skin down at the foot of the centre pole. The drum, although made like a bass drum, with double head and lacings, was of native manufacture, about two feet in diameter and a foot high.

At first little interest was shown in the dancing. Many horses were given away at this period and the ears of a number of children were pierced. Three young men, all of them dancers, changed their names at this time, each giving away a horse. An old man, speaking over them, stood behind them, holding a bunch of sage over their heads, and touching them with it at the end of his speech.

Early in the afternoon a number of dancers, first of all the pledger and his father, took a twig of sage, dipped it into food, and then, standing under the four painted rafters; motioned toward them. Then, standing east of the centre pole, they touched this with the food-dipped sage; and finally, going to the pipe-bundle hanging on its stand west of the foot of the centre pole, they touched this in the same way.

A tent-pole painted yellow had been set up in the lodge for one of the dancers. Another one was now brought in. This was painted red with a green band nearly halfway up, and an eagle-feather tied on it somewhat higher. At the top was a crow. Later in the afternoon a third pole, which had been erected on the preceding day some distance outside of the entrance to the lodge, was also set up inside. These poles were set in the ground just in front of the dancers for whom they were erected, so that they could hold them while dancing.

The old man in charge of the dance moved the sacred-pipe bundle with its stand several times in the course of the afternoon, setting it up before different dancers.

During the day the larger wood-fire of the night was replaced by a small fire of cow-dung used in place of buffalo-chips.

About six or seven o'clock in the evening of this second day, somewhat before sunset, the dancers rested, and were repainted; but the singing and drumming continued without intermission. Some of the dancers at this time, especially about the time the sun went down and for some time afterward, took blankets and lay down on the ground outside of the lodge. They were now repainted somewhat differently. The pledger and his father were still white; but in each place where before they had had a large red diamond they now had two small ones. One other dancer was painted white. These three and six other dancers wore neither head-wreaths, anklets, nor wrist-bands of sage. Among these six other men were the four dancers who earlier in the afternoon had been painted with eagles. Of these four, three were painted a dull red; the fourth was light yellow, and he had a red circle on his breast. The three others were painted with green figures of animals shaped somewhat like turtles, but narrower, and with horns on the head. Of the remaining dancers, more than before were painted with dull yellow-buff. Some of them still had the lines and rows of dots extending from the circle on the breast down the arms and legs, while others had the entire breast covered with red dots on the yellow ground. A small upright mark was generally made at the upper end of the circle on the breast.

About nine in the evening it was fully dark, and a wood-fire was lighted in the lodge. Few of the participants in the ceremony were now dancing. Most of them were in the lodge, in their places, sleeping. Generally not more than from one to four were dancing at one time, and these were not always whistling. One man and three women had lain all day in the southern part of the lodge at one end of the row of dancers, fasting. About sunset, or soon after, the women went off. About ten o'clock the keeper of the sacred pipe and the grand-fathers were not in the lodge. The singing-women sat around the drummers; and all about the inside of the lodge, as well as outside, lay, sat, and stood young men wrapped up in their blankets. Once or twice a dancer went to the pipe-bundle, laid his head on it, and cried or prayed.

Third Day of the Dance. — At a quarter after four on the morning of June 20, the third and last day of the dance, very few of the dancers were standing. All the women had left the lodge; but twelve men who were drumming were singing. Just before sunrise, twenty-two of the twenty-four dancers got up. Facing the spot on the horizon where the sun was about to rise, they danced without intermission five or ten minutes, until the sun was completely above the horizon; then they all lay down. No old men were present. The pledger danced in the trench, but without his wheel. The sacred-pipe stand was in front of a dancer whose place was a few yards to the right of the pledger. All the dancers whistled.

About seven in the morning, all the grandfathers and old men were in the lodge again. A great quantity of food was on the ground around the centre pole. Smoking was going on, the keeper of the sacred pipe giving pipes to the dancers to smoke. Taking a little tobacco from the pipe, and laying it on the ground, he motioned with the pipe in the four cardinal directions, then up, and then down, evidently praying. A young man kneeling in front of him then received the pipe in his left hand, passing his right hand down over the old man's arm four times, and saying "Hoiii!" twice. Other old men gave pipes to the dancers to smoke in the same way. Sometimes the old men, before motioning with the pipe, held it with the bowl up, passing each hand down it twice, and then held it horizontally, again passing the hands along it. The bundle containing the sacred pipe was now hanging on its stand west of the foot of the centre pole, the stand being above the buffalo-robe trimmed with rabbit-fur.

The dancing on this last day began about noon, or soon after. The four dancers painted with eagles the preceding day were now painted in 'green, their faces red, and their hands and forearms yellow. They were painted with dragon-fly designs, consisting of a line knobbed at one end and forked at the other, and crossed near the former by two short bars. These designs were yellow except where, as on the forearms, the background was yellow, in which case they were done in red. These four men danced four songs in four different places around the centre pole. The pledger and his father were painted in a purplish or pinkish white with a double row of dots down the arms and legs. Of the other dancers, some had these rows of dots, some red or green circles on their breast and around their nipples, and one was painted with what looked like a lightning design. On this day all danced with much gesticulation. One man fell to the ground from thirst. He was covered with a blanket, and soon got up again. One jumped wildly about, and then leaned against the centre pole, hugging it. Several dancers at times laid their heads on the sacred-pipe bundle, and wept aloud. One or two cried in this way while leaning against the centre pole. About half-past two the pledger's father took sage dipped into food, and motioned from the four painted rafters toward the ground, then to the centre pole, and then touched the sacred-pipe bundle. After this the other dancers did the same. Much food was brought into the lodge. Some of it was given away by the grandfathers to the visiting Crees and to other people. In the intervals of the dancing, horses were given away.

After five in the afternoon, dancing began again, the dancers having been once more repainted. All except three were now painted in some shade of yellow-buff. Of the three exceptions, one was painted red, and two (the pledger and his father) were still in the purplish-white in which they had been painted earlier in the day. The majority were painted with rows of spots, some with large ones, and others with many small ones. The colors of these spots were various, — red, green, blue, or black. One man was painted with a tree on his forearms and legs. The pledger and his father had a lightning-mark extending down the arm. The crowd of spectators was much larger than before and the scene was very animated. All of the twenty-four participants in the ceremony were still in the lodge. The bundle for the sacred pipe was still on its stand at the foot of the centre pole; the sacred pipe itself, it was said, having been during the dance at the very back of the lodge behind the pledger. Again one of the dancers, after beginning to swing his arms wildly, fell down, or rather threw himself down, but soon got up and rested. Later on, fewer of the dancers were dancing. Some went out of the lodge a short distance to rest, and one was washed off. Near sunset they gave away their blankets, apparently to their grandfathers. When the sun had set, part of the canvas wall at the western end of the lodge was removed. Seven dancers, including the pledger now (for the only time in the ceremony), stood in the eastern part of the lodge, facing the west, dancing against the sun. One song was repeated without intermission for nearly half an hour, the pledger as he danced swinging his wheel heavily downward. The scene was full of excitement. All the dancers but the seven were sitting about. When finally the old men had given the signal that the last red glow had disappeared from the sky, there was a rush to drink the goose-water (hitêçounetc) behind the ceremonial trench. The dancers did not appear to whistle or utter a sound before drinking of this, as they were said to do among the southern Arapaho. Many of the spectators also crowded to this water and drank of it. The dancers now drank water, vomited, and, some having bathed, ate for the first time after their three-days' fast. The people of the entire camp were scattered about the open space around the lodge, sitting on the ground in groups, and eating, making a most pleasing picture in the dusk. It was about half-past eight when the last song of the dance was concluded.

Before the end of the dance, the keeper of the sacred pipe had taken all the sacred objects from the back of the lodge and laid them at the foot of the centre pole, under the stand for the pipe-bundle. He took in this way the pipe itself, the badger-skin, two bundles of skin and sticks, or rattles, as well as the forked stick on which the wheel had hung, which was set in the ground west of the foot of the centre pole. At the conclusion of the ceremony the drum was picked up and carried, and beaten in a circle from left to right once or twice, those carrying it dancing with it, and the women forming in dense circles around.

Supplementary Day. — None of the supplementary ceremonies on the following day, June 21, — such as the "dancing-out" in the morning and the tying of children's worn-out clothing to the lodge-poles, — were witnessed; but they took place according to custom. The camp began to break this day, and by evening comparatively few tents appear still to have stood.

About two months before the ceremony, the keeper of the sacred pipe was said to have prayed on behalf of the tribe at a gathering of the people at a place down stream from where the dance was later held. Among the southern Arapaho, it is said, this prayer is made after the tribe has gathered in

the camp-circle at the site of the dance.   In walking across
the camp-circle this man should have moved exceedingly slow.
A sudden and violent wind-storm on June 14, after the camp
had assembled for the dance, was attributed to his having
walked too carelessly and fast on the earlier occasion.

It is said that during one sun-dance in the past it became
so hot that the pledger was unable to continue the ceremony,
and left the lodge.   The other dancers followed, as they could
not continue the dance without him.   On another occasion
the sun, in the final "dancing against the sun," to deceive the
people, came up again after it had set.

COMPARISON OF THE SUN-DANCE OF THE NORTHERN AND SOUTHERN ARAPAHO.

A comparison of this more or less casual account with the
studies made by Dr. George A. Dorsey, of the southern Arapaho sun-dances of 1901-02, brings out great similarities, but
some interesting minor differences.   The general plan of the
ceremony, and the duration and sequence of events, are identical among the two parts of the tribe.   Dr. Dorsey's scheme of
the eight days applies exactly to the northern Arapaho.   It
would seem, however, that a clearer conception of the relation
of different portions of the ceremony is gained by a somewhat different arrangement.   This is briefly the following: —

Opening Day (First Day): —
   Gathering of the camp, and formal announcement of ceremony.
   At the end of the day, erection of the preparatory or rabbit tent,
      followed by singing in this during the night.

First Preliminary Day (Second Day).   Rabbit-tent : —
   Singing and rites in the rabbit-tent.
   Scouting for the centre pole.
   Killing the buffalo.

Second Preliminary Day (Third Day).   Rabbit-tent : —
   Rites in the rabbit-tent.
   Making and use of the sweat-house.
   Lodge-rafters brought.

Third Preliminary Day (Fourth Day).   Rabbit-tent : —
   Felling and bringing of the centre pole.
   Procession abandoning the rabbit-tent, and painting of the lodge-
      poles.

Erection of the lodge.
" Dancing-in."
Beginning of the dancers' fast.

First Day of the Dance (Fifth Day).   Dancing-lodge: —
Cutting sods, and construction of the altar.
Painting of all the dancers.
Dancing.

Second Day of the Dance (Sixth Day). Dancing-lodge: —
Painting of all the dancers.
Dancing.

Third Day of the Dance (Seventh Day).   Dancing-lodge: —
Painting of all the dancers.
Dancing.
Formerly, torture of the dancers.
Dancing against the sun, drinking of the sacred water, breaking
of the dancers' fast, end of the ceremony.

Supplementary Day (Eighth Day): —
" Dancing-out."
Sacrifice of children's worn clothing in the dancing-lodge.
Abandonment of the lodge, and breaking of the camp.

The main ceremony thus lasts three nights and three days.
It is held in the completed dancing-lodge, and the participants fast and abstain from drink, dance and are painted,
during this time.   Formerly the self-torture characteristic of
the sun-dance also took place during these three days.   This
chief portion of the ceremony is preceded by a period of three
days of preparation, during which the rabbit-tent, an ordinary
tent temporarily set apart for the purpose, is used.   In this
are the pledger of the dance and his wife.   The rites in this
tent are comparatively secret.   They include singing on the
first day, and the preparation of various ceremonial objects.
The public ceremonies during these three days relate mainly
to the securing of the materials for the dancing-lodge.   There
is no dancing during the rabbit-tent period: the ordinary
participants in the ceremony as yet take no part.   The
rabbit-tent is erected in the evening preceding the three days
during which it is used.   At the end of the third of these days
it is abandoned.   An impressive ceremonial procession leaves
it for the dancing-lodge, which is then erected.   A few minutes'
dance by the people (the "dancing-in") on this same evening
resembles a dedication of the now completed dancing-lodge.

Just three days later, almost at the same hour, the arduous ceremony is ended. Next morning, on the supplementary day, a few minutes' "dancing-out" marks the ceremonial abandonment of the lodge, which is further signalized by the leaving in it of all the worn-out clothing of the children in the tribe. The opening day preceding the three preparatory days is even more devoid of ritual actions, these being practically confined to the formal announcement of the beginning of the ceremony, and riding by the members of the younger age-companies. The erection of the rabbit-tent at the end of this opening day, and the singing in it during the night, should be regarded as marking the beginning of the three preliminary days; for it is evident — from the fact that the erection of this tent as well as of the dancing-lodge, and the conclusion of the dancers' fasting, painting, and dancing, all occur about sunset — that each of the periods of three days includes the preceding evening.

This division of the sun-dance agrees exactly with that existing in the age-company ceremonies, in which there is also a three-days' period of preparation, more or less private or secret, and a three-days' period of public spectacular performance. The Indians generally speak of both the bäyaa^{n}wu and the sun-dance as four-day ceremonies. They include with the latter the evening which terminates the three preliminary days and begins the ceremony proper; so that this actually occurs on four consecutive days. Altogether, however, it occupies only three nights and three days.[1]

The sun-dance lodge of the northern Arapaho differs considerably in appearance, due chiefly to varying proportions, from that of the southern Arapaho, as a glance at the figure here shown, as compared with the photographic illustrations in Dr. Dorsey's work on the sun-dance, will reveal. The northern Arapaho lodge is much greater in diameter, and correspondingly flatter in proportion, than that of the southern Arapaho. The northern Arapaho lodge in the present figure (Plate LIX) was that of 1899, which was said by the Indians to have been too low or flat; but that seen erected in 1900,

---

[1] See pp. 152, 153, 166, 226.

which was declared to be of proper proportions, was but very little higher. The difference between the shape of the lodge in the two parts of the tribe seems to be due to geographical location. The Oklahoma people are on the Plains, with little timber available other than cottonwood, which is short, heavy, and crooked. The Wyoming Arapaho are at the edge of the mountains, from which they easily obtain straight, long, slender pines or conifers, which enable them to increase the diameter of their lodge, and give it a clear-cut look that is entirely wanting about the tumble-down southern lodge.

For all uprights and the short beams, the Wyoming people use cottonwood. The southern people rest the long inclined rafters on the horizontal cross-beams forming the periphery of the lodge; the northern people attach them to or lay them into the upright forks that support these cross-beams. The southern Arapaho continue the cross-beams entirely around the lodge; those in the north omit the one at the easternmost side of the lodge, thus more definitely marking an entrance opposite the "altar."

As regards the interior of the lodge, the general plan of the "altar" at the middle of the back is identical among the two groups. There is, however, considerable difference in the proportions of the objects composing it and the distances between them, much as in the shape of the lodge. Thus the seven arched sticks appear to be much larger among the northern Arapaho. Unfortunately, the loss on the prairie of a note-book containing memoranda as to the "altar" makes it impossible to speak more definitely. The impression produced by the excellent model of the southern Arapaho sun-dance "altar" at the Field Columbian Museum, after the northern "altar" has been seen, is, that it would be an entirely complete but somewhat distorted representation of the latter.

That there may be minor differences other than of proportion between the two "altars" is made probable by the differences in the species of trees used for the screen just behind the "altar." In order from north to south, these seven little trees are respectively: —

Southern Arapaho.	Northern Arapaho.
Red-painted cottonwood.	Willow.
Red-painted cottonwood.	Praying-wood.
Red-painted cottonwood.	Cottonwood.
(trench)	(trench)
Cedar.	Cedar.
Willow.	Cottonwood.
Black-painted cottonwood.	Cottonwood.
Black-painted cottonwood.	Cottonwood.

The present account being so much less full than Dr. Dorsey's,
and neither secret rites having been witnessed nor any special
study of the ceremony having been made on the spot, omis-
sions in the foregoing description, when compared with Dr.
Dorsey's, must not be regarded as indicative of the absence
of such features in the northern ceremony. The chief positive differences that have been observed are the following: —

On the opening day, the ride of the young men about noon
was lacking in the Oklahoma ceremonies. The singing in the
rabbit-tent this night appears to have been continued longer
in the north.

The ride around the camp before sunrise next morning
has not been mentioned in the south.

The cedar-tree at the back of the rabbit-tent appears to
have been put in place in the north on the first preliminary
day; in the south, on the second. In the north it was four or
five feet high; in the south, about twenty.

After the buffalo (represented at the present time by
a skin) had been killed and the hide brought in, it was
touched, among the northern Arapaho, by the children of the
camp (brought by their mothers), and then by a number of
men. It seems that the southern Arapaho also formerly had
this practice; but it was not observed in the two ceremonies
described.

The singing all day in the large tent, with the sacrifice of
cloth and the feast on the second preliminary day, by the
northern Arapaho, appears to have had no parallel in the two
southern ceremonies. This ceremony was not held in the
rabbit-tent, and was perhaps entirely accessory or intrusive.

The sweat-house of this day is made by men in the south,

by women in the north. It is used by men in the south; nothing was observed as to its use in the north.

The ceremonial procession from the rabbit-tent to the lodge-rafters to be painted, at the end of the third preliminary day, differs considerably in the north and south. In the south it includes nine people besides the old man directing the dance, who generally does not walk in file with the others: in the north, it includes fifteen. The order of the persons and objects in the procession also varies.[1] The following is a comparison of the northern Arapaho procession of 1900 and the southern of 1902: —

Northern.	*Southern.*	*Southern Equivalent of Northern Agent.*
1 man with buffalo-skull	1 man with skull	1
2 man ⎫ with buffalo-skin 3 man ⎭	2 woman with wheel ⎫ 3 man with buffalo-skin ⎭	3
4 man ⎫ with buffalo-robe 5 man ⎭		0
6 man with badger-skin	4 man with badger-skin	4
7 man with digging-stick		9
8 man with rawhide rope		0
9 woman with wheel		2
10 pledger with straight pipe	5 man with pipe	5
11 dancer with knife		8
12 dancer with black paint	6 pledger with red paint	7
13 dancer with red paint	7 man with black paint	6
14 man to paint rafters	8 dancer with knife	0
15 man to paint rafters	9 man with digging-stick	0

At the conclusion of the ceremony, the northern dancers were not heard to whistle, or utter a cry, before drinking the sacred water.

A great proportion of the children's sacrificed clothing was hung by the northern Arapaho on the forks of the sixteen uprights at the periphery of the lodge, as can be seen in Plate LXII. The southern Arapaho tied the clothing mainly to the centre pole, and what was on the outside uprights was half-way up, not at the fork on top.

The body-painting used varied considerably, although the general type — consisting of an oval on the face, a circle on the

---

[1] Compare Plates LIX and LX with Dorsey, Arapaho Sun-dance, Plate XXXII.

breast, lines around wrists and ankles, and lines, rows of dots, or series of figures, from the breast-circle to the wrist and ankles — persisted with hardly an exception.   The sun-dance paintings are so largely individual in their nature, that they differ in successive ceremonies among the same people.   There is, however, a marked difference in the number of paintings observed in the north and south.   Dr. Dorsey distinguishes four paintings; the first occurring on the evening of the last preliminary day, in the very first hours of the seventy-two that the dance lasts; the second, third, and fourth, on the three succeeding days.   As to the first painting, no observations were made among the northern Arapaho.   During the following day, the first of the dance, the dancers were painted in the afternoon.   It is not known whether they were painted in the morning also.   On the second and third days, they were painted twice, — once in the morning and once in the afternoon. As opposed to the total of four paintings among the southern Arapaho, five were observed in the north, though six undoubtedly took place, and there may have been a total of seven.

The pledger's paint in the south is white.   An oval area on the face, including the eyes and mouth, is colored.   On his breast, and on each thigh, calf, upper arm, and lower arm, are colored diamonds connected by lines.   On the first day, this oval and the diamonds are red; on the second, yellow; on the third, green.   In the north, the pledger's paint was also white.   On the first day he appears to have been painted only with lines, or rows of dots, from a circle on the breast to the wrists and ankles.   His hands were black.   On the second day he was first painted with red diamonds; later, with smaller red diamonds, — four, instead of two, on each leg and arm. On the third day he was first painted with double rows of dots.   The second paint on this day was zigzag or wavy lines from breast to wrists and ankles.   Neither he nor any other dancer appears to have had the circle on his breast replaced by a diamond at any time.

The small figure surmounted by a tree-symbol, usually painted by the southern Arapaho on top of the breast-circle,.

is generally reduced to a smaller and simple upright mark, painted solidly, in the north.

Of the southern Arapaho paints described, the pink calf paint and the striking yellow-hammer and thunder paints were not seen in the north. The observations recorded were not sufficiently detailed to say how exactly the other southern paints — the pink, yellow earth, first yellow, and second yellow — were represented. At least, one remarkable northern paint has not been described in the south. In this the dancers were painted at different times with figures of dragon-flies, water-monsters, and eagles. The ground-color of one of their paints was green. Four men wore this painting, which was considered particularly hard to endure, and were further distinguished from the other dancers by variations in the sage apparel.

It seems probable that the few features here recorded, but not yet observed in the southern Arapaho sun-dance, were originally common, but have been retained in the north while already lost or abridged in the south, chiefly through contact with civilization. The other differences between the two ceremonies are due in part to habitat, such as the form of the lodge, or rest largely on the room left to individual action in certain aspects of the dance, such as the paintings. Finally, there are certain direct discrepancies which cannot be explained. These, though interesting, are entirely minor: fundamentally, the two ceremonies are identical.

TRIBAL RELIGIOUS CUSTOMS.

The great tribal fetish of the Arapaho is a sacred pipe. This is called säeitca^n ("flat pipe"). As the pipe is not flat, but cylindrical, the reason for the use of this name is not clear, unless the word denotes that the pipe is tubular without a bowl at an angle to the stem. The pipe is in the keeping of an old man among the northern Arapaho. Its sacredness is equally recognized by the northern and southern Arapaho, though obviously it can play but little direct part in the religious practice of the latter. The pipe is cylindrical, about two feet long, an inch and a half or two inches in diameter, and without taper. The stem is as thick as the bowl, and is white, apparently of wood. The bowl, whose length is perhaps half a foot, is black, probably of the soapstone often used by the Plains tribes for small pipe-bowls. Strings of some kind hang from the stem, but there are few appendages. The pipe is kept wrapped in a large bundle of many separate pieces of cloth, one around the other. This bundle is hung near the top of a stand of four sticks to keep it from touching the ground. It is kept in a painted tent. This tent, which is now of canvas, but probably preserves the old painting, has been described in the preceding section (Plate LVII). At present the keeper of the pipe lives in an ordinary tent, but during the sun-dance he erects the painted tent, and inhabits it. Whether this was also formerly the case, or whether the painted tent was then continuously used by the keeper of the sacred pipe, is not known. The symbolism of this tent recalls that prevalent during the ghost-dance, and may be partly or entirely influenced by the movement. The official origin or tribal myth of the Arapaho is in the keeping of the individual who has the sacred pipe in his possession. The tradition can be told only with the observance of certain regulations and ceremonies, and occupies four entire consecutive nights for its narration. It has never yet been recorded by a white man even in fragments of any amount. The majority of the Arapaho, even of those who have heard it related by the proper keeper, know it very imperfectly, and have been forbidden to tell it. In addition to being the maintainer of the sacred tribal myth, the keeper of the sacred pipe seems to have the chief direction of important ceremonies among the northern Arapaho. At the sun-dance in 1900 he supervised and ordered the entire ceremony, and was treated with the greatest respect and awe.

There seem to be several sacred wheels in the tribe, as the southern Arapaho have at least one, and the northern Arapaho use another at the sun-dance. Owing to the presence of the sacred pipe among the northern Arapaho, the wheel is relatively of more importance among the southern half of the tribe. The wheel is a hoop, perhaps a foot and a half across, sometimes used for a game (see Fig. 139). The hoop of the wheel represents a snake (biisä^n), literally " insect, vermin." Among the southern Arapaho it is kept enclosed in a bundle, and is ceremonially wrapped and sacrificed to for the good of the giver. Like the sacred pipe in the north, it is in the keeping of a special individual, whose approval must, of course, be secured before this ceremony can be made. The keeper of the wheel sits at the middle of the back of the tent, and is the one to handle it. The ground in the tent is covered with sage, and cedar is used as incense. Silence is observed, except where prayer or speaking forms part of the ritual. Usually, cloth is given to the wheel, and at the conclusion of the ceremony is wrapped around it, the earlier wrappings remaining outside. After this, food is eaten, presumably furnished by the person wishing the ceremony made. The wheel might be thus wrapped on account of the sickness of a relative. The wheel and its ceremonies have been more fully described by Dr. Dorsey in his account of the sun-dance.

There are a number of sacred bags in the tribe, and one was obtained, through inheritance, by a young woman shortly before the summer of 1899. In Plate LXIII the bag is shown unpacked, and its contents in the position in which they are set in the tent. The upright cylindrical leather object is a person, apparently the spirit of the bag. Food and gifts were given to the bag on the occasions on which it was opened. The food, or part of it, was then kept in the bag. The object of these gifts was to secure prosperity and an abundance of food to the giver.

The disposition of the contents of the bag during the ceremony is as follows: —

The owner of the bag sits at the rear of the tent. In the middle is a small fire of coals. Directly before the owner is the outer bag, now holding only the various gifts of food contained in small bags and pieces of cloth. The outer bag itself is still covered, to a large extent, with the calico with which it is ordinarily kept wrapped, and which presumably has been given to it. The smaller longitudinal bag is removed from the inside of the large bag, and put in front of it, nearer the fire. In front of this are placed grizzly-bear claws. To the right of these claws is a small bag of incense called "man," and to the left a similar bag called "woman." Immediately in front of the grizzly-claws are four small sticks of unequal length, which are leaned up together like tent-poles, and which represent a tent. In front of these sticks, and not far from the fire, is the cylindrical leather case representing the "owner" of the bag. By the side of this object and the four sticks, another stick, ordinarily kept inside of the cylindrical case, is laid on the ground. This represents the gift of a horse.

A middle-aged northern Arapaho has in his possession two pieces of buckskin on which are painted in three or four colors pictographic designs referring to myths of creation and the tribal ceremonies. These pieces could neither be secured nor reproduced at the time they were seen, and only fragmentary information was obtained in regard to them. The designs are, however, comparatively simple, and are reproduced here from memory, with probably approximate correctness (Plate LXIV). The first of the two strips of skin is several inches wide and a foot or more long. Its end is cut off rudely and irregularly. Near this end are figures in blue with two red spots. A straight line diagonal to the length of the buckskin strip represents the extent of the world and the course of the sun. On it are shown both the sun and the moon; the former, by a small solid circle, the latter by the arc of a circle. Four blue dots, two on each side of the line, represent the "four old men." Beyond the end of this line is a painted ovate figure drawn in blue outline, and representing a mountain-goat horn spoon from which old men are fed. Near this a red spot denotes paint. To the side of the line on which are painted the sun and the moon, is a third group of figures. The centre of this is a blue spot, or solidly filled circle, representing the heart. Around this are four short lines or bars forming a square in outline. These four lines represent the bands or lines painted around the wrists and ankles of the old men in the tribal ceremonies. These old men are said to maintain the life of the people. These four bars also denote the four old men themselves. Just beyond them is a small crescent, the half-moon, and near it a hollow circle representing either the sun or a sun-dog, while an oval red spot denotes paint. The central circle, with the four surrounding bars and the crescent, also represent sun-dance body-paintings; the circle being the circle painted on the dancers' breasts; the bars, the lines encircling their wrists and ankles; and the crescent often painted on the back at the shoulder-blade.

The symbols just described constitute the painting of only one end of the larger strip of skin. The rest of this piece is executed in a design of red and yellow lines, small solid circles, smaller triangles, and broken semicircles, to which two or three blue semicircles, called "black," are added. The meaning of this part of the pictograph is not known. Its fourfold arrangement is no doubt significant. On the back of this strip of skin there is painted only a single figure in blue, consisting of a hollow circle bisected by a line extending beyond it on both sides, and containing four spots, — two on each side of the bisecting line.

The second piece of skin was also painted on both sides, one representing the earth, the other the sky. On the side representing the sky was a long wavy red line. Near one end of this was a figure of the thunder-bird in blue; beyond it, also on the line, a half-moon; and beyond this the sun, also in blue. Near the opposite end, this red line was crossed by two blue bars, while at the end was an ellipse solidly filled in with green. On the middle of the line, and parallel to it, were four figures, — two blue on the right, and two green or red on the left. These consisted of wavy lines forked at the upper ends. It will be noticed that this part of the painting contains green, but no yellow. It has been reproduced in the plate. In addition, this strip contains two human figures in brown at the side of the long red line, and four others, one above the other, painted in yellow. On the other side, which represents the earth, this piece of skin was painted with eight figures. Each of these consisted of two lines somewhat resembling a pair of legs, the upper parts of the two lines being close together and parallel, and the lower ends diverging. Above the upper end of each line was a dot.

The earth is sometimes spoken of as woman, the sky as man, as shown in the phrase "biitaawu^n neina^n hixtçäba neisana^n" (" the earth my mother, the above my father").

The beings addressed in certain prayers are, in order, first our father, second the sun, third hiiteni, fourth hitaxusa^n (or last child, equivalent to hiintcäbiit, "water-monster or owner of water"), fifth the thunder, sixth the whirlwind, and seventh the earth.

According to one account, the persons sometimes addressed in prayer were successively, Above-Nih'ä^{n}ça^n,[1] the four old men, and then the sun.

The following is a free rendering of a hypothetical prayer or speech made by an old man at a young man's change of name.

"This is what I mention. On the Cimarron River near the Turkey hills I brought back black paint. May children grow well! The seven old men and the seven old women, Found-in-the-grass (biaxuya^n), and the myths, may they be for the good of the people of all ages! This is another that I mention: At sand creek. I mention when there were seven sweat-houses, and the day and the rivers and the earth made sickness be far away. My grandfather, the sun, you who walk yellow, look down on us. Pity us. Pity us. May this young man facing straight be helped to walk for his life! Those that shine above at night, and the animals of the night, we pray to you. The morning star and my father, listen. I have asked for long breath, for large life. May this young man, with his people and his relatives, do well, walking where it is good, obtaining food and clothing and horses of many colors, and where there are birds that are crying and the day is long and the wind is good! Animals that move on the surface, animals

---

[1] Nih'ä^{n}ça^n (spider, also white person), etymology still uncertain, is the trickster-culture-hero of Arapaho mythology (see Traditions of the Arapaho, op. cit., pp. 6, 7, footnotes). Hixtcäbä-nih'a^{n}ça^n, Above-Nih'ä^{n}ça^n, or Above-White-man, is the term for the God of Christianity. Nih'a^{n}ça^n seems to be more or less hesitatingly identified with heisanäni (our Father), the vague supreme deity above: how much Christian notions have had to do with this is not certain. By the people of the present day, Above-Nih'N^{n}ça^n is quite frequently mentioned; but in ceremony " our Father" seems to be the name still customary. Compare in Traditions, op. cit., p. 16, "After this, Nih'ä^{n}ça^n ived in the sky, and was called our Father."

under ground that inhabit the water, listen, be attentive. This one standing here asks of you a name that is good. Children of all ages, young men and young women of all ages. old women and old men of all ages, all look at him. Do well to this young man, and be kind to him. He wishes to become an old man. Bäiinena[n] of whatever company, look at this young man. Call him Sun-child when you give him commands, when you invite him to give him food, when you look at him, when you meet him. — Sun-child you will be called. This is your name. Now take it. Rainy-mountain remains here. With Sun-child your name, go away. Father-above-white-man, you who are nailed down flat, and Father Crow, and Large-nose (thunder), and the birds, — now they have all heard it. Well, now at last, my friend, you are known."

The following is a prayer such as might be spoken before eating.

"Our father, hear us, and our grandfather. I mention also all those that shine (the stars), the yellow day, the good wind, the good timber, and the good earth. All the animals, listen to me under the ground. Animals above ground, and water-animals, listen to me. We shall eat your remnants of food. Let them be good. Let there be long breath and life. Let the people increase, the children of all ages, the girls and the boys, and the men of all ages and the women, the old men of all ages and the old women. The food will give us strength whenever the sun runs. Listen to us, father, grandfather. We ask thought, heart, love, happiness. We are going to eat."

When a young man desired to live to be old, he would go to an old man, especially to one of the seven men of the oldest society, and begin to cry, generally outside of his tent, perhaps at the door, perhaps by the wall of the tent where the old man's bed was. The old man would wait a long time to see if the young man was really in earnest. Then at last he would get up from his bed, and pray for him. After mentioning the beings addressed in prayer, he would say, —

" Häyuni'çi	haçoutii	hätiitetaⁿ	hanaxaaha
" Four	ridges [1]	may you pass over,	young man,
nihiiçãⁿçi	tc iinetcei	bä häeihahaⁿ."	
said	the sprinkling (?)	old men." [2]	

The following is a hypothetical speech of a man at the
marriage of his daughter.

"I have thought of this occasion before, just as others
have, since I have had a daughter. I used to plan that my
daughter when married might have good land to sit on. That
is what I wished for. That is why I took pains to look for a
place that was good where this tent now stands. 'May my
daughter live safely in this house that I am making,' I have
said to myself. It is a custom for men who are fathers to
welcome the son-in-law because of marriage. This young man
pleases me. I am satisfied that he unites with my tent.
That is why I spoke to my daughter. Now her other relatives
have not come, because they live scattered and away. My
son-in-law, here is your tent. This is your pipe. Here is
your water and your food, together with your wife. Now eat."

The following is a hypothetical speech of the father of a
young man at his marriage to a Cheyenne woman.

" My chiefs, my friends, women, I am deeply glad that you
have come here on account of my son who is to marry. It
is the wish of men when their sons marry, for I and my son
are poor. My son has chosen well for his union. He has
made his own selection. Even though the distance is great
where my son will belong, nevertheless many Cheyenne are
married with the Arapaho. I am glad where my son is mar-
rying. Thanks. I say it to you, her parents, who treated
me and my son well, who are people that I am fond of, who
try to be agreeable. — My son, it pleases me much where you
found a woman. My son, disregard it, even if there is something unpleasant for you to hear. Even if your own wife
strikes you, disregard it, and even if the others say what you
do not like to listen to. Where you are a servant, you must
not mind it. Try hard, my son, not to become discouraged
too quickly. Do not be bashful, but be kind. Do good where

---

[1] Or hills. [2] The members of the old society.

you are united. Whatever your father-in-law orders you to do, my son, or your mother-in-law, or your brother-in-law, do that for them. Do not go away without the consent of your wife. Do not roam about without purpose, my son, but do your best where you offered yourself as servant. In the former life of the people it was good to be a servant. If I might be young, I should be providing food for all; but what we lived on is gone. Do your best in planting, which we are shown by the whites, my son. Do whatever you are told, and water your animals carefully. Love your wife's parents, and love her people. Be pleasant to persons who come to your tent, my son. When friends come where you are serving, they will be Cheyenne who come. When the Cheyenne arrive, say to them, 'Well, come in.' Do not be bashful, for you are now united to them. Do not scold your wife. Always treat her well and pity her. Those who try to be good are treated well and are pitied. Do your best, and do not become tired. And now look at your tent, your pipe, your food, and your friends.''

Fig. 103 ($\frac{50}{385}$). Switch of Horse-tail. Length, 64 cm.

Buffalo-tails mounted on a short stick, and in recent times horse-tails, are used by the Arapaho in the sweat-house to switch or whip the body. This practice seems to be in large measure ceremonial, but is no doubt founded on a practical purpose. A specimen from the northern Arapaho consists of a white horse-tail, about three feet in length, wrapped to a stick handle about an inch in diameter, by a thong painted red. A dozen long iridescent magpie-feathers are attached to this handle by red-painted thongs (Museum No. $\frac{50}{1118}$). A specimen (Museum No. $\frac{50}{52}$) from the southern Arapaho is a yellowish white horse-tail or cow-tail much shorter than the preceding. It is wrapped to a thinner but longer stick handle by twine. Another specimen (Fig. 103) is a black buffalo-tail. It is mounted on a stick about one-third of an inch in diameter and two-thirds of a foot long, apparently painted red. The skin of the tail is tightly sewed over the stick with diagonal stitches of sinew. For the upper half of the stick the tail is cut free from hair, thus forming a distinct handle: below this, the outermost hair is allowed to extend about an inch, when it is cut off. The hair under this extends to its full length, so that where the outermost hair is cut off there is a notch-like depression extending around the tail.

Screech-owls (bääçeinaⁿ) are ghosts. When quiet or timid people die, their spirits are noisy and troublesome; but the ghosts of people who in life are loud and active are harmless after death. The property of the dead, including clothes and bedding, is burnt, as it is thought that the dead spirit will revisit the locality if this is not done. For the same reason, cedar is thrown on the fire before the relatives of the dead go to bed at night.

The rainbow is the fishing-line of the thunder for the hiintcä-biit. Lightning is generally thought to strike in the water, being aimed at this monster. Springs are inhabited by these beings. When a spring dries up, the thunder is thought to have taken away the water-monster inhabiting it. The spring is sometimes thought to issue from the monster's mouth. Near a certain spring, numerous snakes were seen projecting their heads. Clothes and offerings were frequently tied to a tree near this spring, and people were afraid to go to it alone. The flashing of the eye of the hiintcäbiit can be seen, especially in the morning or evening.

The Arapaho do not count the stars, as it would cause misfortune.

When there was a fog, a figure of the turtle would be drawn in the soft earth, and then beaten with a stick. "Now it is killed, the fog will clear off," it was said. The Omaha-Ponka had much the same practice. The custom is no doubt connected with the identity of the words for fog and turtle (bäänaⁿ) in Arapaho.

The meadow-lark's song is supposed to be hinênitäⁿ tcei-

taksa^n ("a person is crawling toward me"). Children sometimes imitate this song, though forbidden to do so by their
parents. The song of this bird is thought to be evil. Sometimes it is also interpreted as obscene.

When stories are told during winter nights, the listeners
must constantly say "Hi!" to show that they are awake. If
any of them fall asleep, the narrator takes a stick from the
fire, and touches them with it on the finger-nail.

Men say "Haa" for yes; women, "Aa." For thanks, men
say "Hahou;" women, in former times, "Hahoukac;" though
at present "Hahou" is used by both sexes. "Hoii" is a more
distinctly ceremonial word of thanks.

An entertainment practised at night is called "tcâoçoçihiit."
Two parties of men sit on opposite sides of a tent, the older
being nearer the door. In the middle, at the back, sits a
questioner. Between the two sides is placed food, to be consumed during the night. In front of each side, near the questioner, four sticks are set up in the ground. The questioner then
states hypothetical cases of deeds of war or of generosity.
These are always quite specific and detailed. The following
are characteristic examples.

"Your father-in-law gave you a tent with black ornaments,
and you gave him a white horse with black ears."

"You went to war, starting from such a place and going
to such a one."

"While travelling, you met a friend and gave him your
horse."

"When you possessed only one horse, you gave it away."

Any man who can say that he has performed the particular
feat that is mentioned, speaks, and relates it at length. If
this statement is accepted, a counter is put down for him. The
side for which the most counters are laid down on any one question scores one point, and one of its four sticks is laid down.
When all the four sticks on one side have been laid down, that
side has won, and one of its old men selects four men from the
other side to provide breakfast. The questioning and relating occupy the entire night. Very often a hypothetical deed
is proposed which no one present has accomplished. For a

man to be accepted, it is necessary for him to have performed exactly the conditions of the case stated by the questioner: even a slight deviation in circumstances rules him out. A pipe passed around and smoked during the contest serves to cause the truth to be told. Those who are present deny or affirm a man's statements about himself. Sometimes a man when thus challenged will at once give a horse to a doubter in order to prove his manliness. At other times, statements are challenged in joke, especially between brothers-in-law.

When men dispute as to deeds of honor in war, the misunderstanding is sometimes settled by their whipping each other; the one who first becomes angry being considered unmanly (tciineniīnit).

MODERN CEREMONIES.

Several modern ceremonies, belonging to at least two different cults, have obtained a foothold with the Arapaho; and among the people at large, especially among the younger members of the tribe, these now occupy a much larger part in their life than the virtually extinct ceremonies of the bäyaa^{n}wu or the sun-dance.

The more important of these ceremonies are the result of the ghost-dance movement of fifteen years ago. This has been elaborately treated by Mooney, who has given special attention to the cult among the Arapaho.[1] The ghost-dance proper is no longer practised; but the beliefs of the movement have left a considerable influence on the minds of the people. A number of objects made for use in the ghost-dance at the time of greatest activity in its agitation are described in the following pages, with special reference to the symbolism shown by them. It will be seen that while this symbolism is always more or less decorative, and often so to a considerable degree, it is in most cases primarily pictographic. Many of the figures are semi-realistic, and where there is a conventionalization it is in the meaning rather than in the designs.

Many old games were revived during the ghost-dance, and assumed a religious aspect. A number of objects made for

---

[1] Fourteenth Report of the Bureau of American Ethnology.

such games, most of them more or less symbolic, are described in the following pages. Accounts of several games not particularly connected with the ghost-dance have also been included.

The so-called "crow-dance" is the dance most commonly practised by the Arapaho of to-day. It is chiefly the younger people who take part in it; but the older do not look upon it as in any way an intrusion or innovation, and give it full approval. At present the ceremony is permeated with ghost-dance ideas. Its basis seems to have been a widespread dance, half social and half religious, attributed to some of the eastern Plains tribes, usually the Omaha. At the time of the ghost-dance movement, this seems to have been taken up by certain tribes, such as the Arapaho, and to have had a lively growth under the new influences. A brief description of this ceremony is given.

Entirely distinct from the ghost-dance cult is the peyote worship. This cult rests on the mental excitement produced by the eating of a small dried cactus commonly called by the Indians "mescal," or "mescal bean," and known in literature as "mescal button" and "peyote." It is not known how accurate the latter term is, as the Aztec peyote may have been a different plant. It affects the heart, produces muscular lassitude, is a strong stimulant of the nervous system, and has a marked effect on the general feeling of the person, giving the impression of stimulating especially the intellectual faculties. In most cases it produces visions of a kaleidoscopic nature. Its emotional effect varies greatly, being in some cases depressing or intensely disagreeable; in others, which are the more frequent, producing quiet but intense exaltation. There is little subsequent reaction.

The religious ceremonies connected with this drug have been previously described by Mooney as witnessed by him among the Kiowa.[1] They are said to have been introduced among the Arapaho by the Kiowa. A number of young meu

[1] J. Mooney, The Kiowa Peyote Rite (Am Urquell, N. S., I, 329; Therapeutic Gazette, Jan. 15, 1896). See, also, Prentiss and Morgan (Therapeutic Gazette, September, 1895, February, 1896; Medical Record, Aug. 22, 1896), J. Ramirez (Anales del Inst. Med. Nac., Mexico, IV, 233, 1900), S. Weir Mitchell (Brit. Med. Jour., December, 1896), L. Lewin (Arch. f. Experim. Pathol. u. Pharmak., XXIV, 401, XXXIV, 374), A. Hefftner (ibid., XXXIV, 65), H. Ellis (Contemp. Review, January, 1898)

now follow the cult with assiduity among the Arapaho. Middle-aged men and women are not rare among the participants, but there are very few of the older men. The plant is not ordinarily eaten, even by the devotees, except during the ceremonies, which take place at irregular intervals of weeks, though sometimes it is used without any formality, as medicine.

GHOST-DANCE. *Head-dresses.*—A great many feather objects, especially head-dresses, are made by the Arapaho in connection with their ghost-dance beliefs. These, of course, resemble in certain respects the feather-work of their older tribal ceremonies, but on the whole have a distinct character of their own. The head-dresses are characterized especially by the frequent use of plumes and of hanging feathers, by a frequent and often exceedingly beautiful use of dyes obtained from the whites, and by a certain method of trimming and cutting feathers. The last two characteristics are almost wanting in the feather-work of the older ceremonies of the tribe. Eagle-feathers continue to be freely used in ghost-dance objects. The same is true of owl and hawk feathers, which occur in all classes of Arapaho deco-

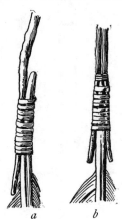

ration. It is possible that the connection believed to exist between owls and spirits of the dead contributed to the use of owl-feathers on ghost-dance objects. Crow and magpie feathers are more frequent than owl-feathers. Magpie-feathers appear not to have been more used, only because they could not be secured. Pheasant-feathers are not uncommon. Other feathers are rare. These characteristics of feather head-dresses are found also in the feather portions of other ghost-dance objects, including games.

Fig. 104 (a,$\frac{50}{97}$; b,$\frac{50}{1074}$). Feather Attachments.

Several methods of attaching feathers to thongs are in use in such modern ceremonial ornaments. The most common is the simple laying of the end of the thong along the base of the quill, and then wrapping them together with sinew. This is the usual method for small feathers, and it is not rare for the large ones (Fig. 104, *a*). In a few instances the base of the quill is halved or slit so that the thong fits into it: more often the base of the quill is somewhat flattened. There are a few instances of large feathers with square quills being attached to a two-strand thong. The two thongs are laid along opposite sides of the quill, and wrapped to it with sinew (Fig. 104, *b*). Again, large feathers are sometimes, though not often, attached by means of a hole made through one side of the quill, just above the base (Plate LXV). The thong enters at the cut-off end of the quill, and passes out of this hole. It is then either knotted so that it cannot slip back (1), or laid

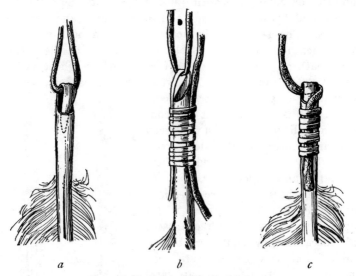

a b c

Fig. 105 (a, ₅₆/₈₈a; b, ₅₀/₃₉₉b; c, ₅₀/₁₁₀). Feather Attachments.

along the quill and wrapped to it (2), or brought back to itself and there tied (3). A variation of this method of piercing the quill is to pass the thong through two holes made into the quill on opposite sides (4). This practice seems to be followed chiefly with feathers the butt-ends of whose quills have been shortened by wear or accident. A third method is the well-known one of bringing the end of the quill back on itself, thus forming a loop through which the thong passes (Fig. 105). This is done in two ways, in each of which the end of the quill is cut down to a comparatively narrow strip. According to the first method, this narrow strip is simply inserted in the quill (*a*), which may in addition be bound with sinew. According to the second method, it is laid against the outside of the quill, and then wrapped to it with sinew (*b*). A variation, consisting of a combination of this method and of wrapping the thong to the quill, is shown in *c*.

A combination of methods of attachment is shown in Fig. 106. One feather is attached to a thong by being wrapped to it. The end of the quill is split, whether with intent or not is not clear, and the thong is almost enclosed by it. Over the same thong is looped the narrow end of the quill of another feather inserted in itself. Wrappings on both feathers hold the bases of dyed plumes decorating the lower portions of the two feathers.

Fig. 106 ($\frac{50}{552}$). Combination Feather Attachment.

The ghost-dance head-dresses of the Arapaho are principally of the following types.

Dyed plumes mounted on small sticks inserted in the quill, and worn upright at the back of the head, constitute one type. Occasionally they are fastened to the hair by a thong attached to the stick, but more usually the stick is pointed, and simply stuck into the hair. It seems that the wearing of head-dresses of this type was associated with the expected return of the dead. These were usually thought to be wearing such head-dresses; and a spirit as opposed to a living person is often represented on ghost-dance pictographs by a human figure with an upright feather at the back of the head. In most cases the head-dresses of the present type contain a number of plumes, often of different colors. They are attached to the stick on which they are mounted by having the base of the quill wrapped to it with sinew. The feathers at the upper end of the stick are attached first; and those below successively overlap the wrapping of those above, so that nothing is visible in the head-dress but the downy feathers and the pointed end of the stick. Usually these head-dresses are erect and slender; occasionally, as in Fig. 1, Plate LXVI, they are fuller. In a few cases a wrapping of a string of beads covers the sinew wrapping at the base. Sometimes small feathers of different character are attached to the base of a head-dress. Fig. 2, Plate LXVI, shows a head-dress consisting of purplish-blue plumes. At the base are three small black feathers covering the wrapping of the plume. Fig. 3, Plate LXVII, shows a head-dress of the present type with a thong for fastening it to the hair. This head-dress is also unusual in having few feathers, so that the stick on which they are mounted is visible, and in the fact that the top of the lower plume is tied to the stick with the bottom of the upper feather, whereas ordinarily the plumes are fastened only at the base. Fig. 3, Plate LXVI, shows a form lacking any unusual characteristics. The plumes at the base are bright red; those above, white. The feathers in Fig. 1, Plate LXVI, are light-colored plumes dyed in soft shades of light red, blue, yellow, and green, which blend with very beautiful effect. At the base is a black plume.

A second type of head-dress characteristic of the ghost-dance consists essentially of several feathers, usually of crows, mounted upright on a pointed stick, and in part cut away to the quill. The lower part of the vanes may be cut off entirely, or only in parts. The uppermost portion of the vanes is in all cases left on the quill. Sometimes the lower portion of the vanes is not entirely removed, and the quill is slit, so that the lower part of the quill stands up, while the two vanes fall downward, giving the feather a slashed effect. This general method of cutting and trimming feathers is not confined to crow and magpie feathers, nor to this specific type of head-dress, but occurs also in hanging head-dresses and in other feather objects. In such other objects, short hanging crow-feathers are often cut off across their ends; but this mutila-

FIG. 107 ($\frac{50}{6371}$). Ghost-dance Head-dress.
Length, 45 cm.

tion is found also in certain of the older tribal regalia. In the case of the upright head-dresses under present consideration, the black feathers are usually rubbed over with red paint. In order to keep the upright feathers apart, the end of the stick, or, in longer head-dresses, several portions, swell into a sort of head, arouhd which, or just below which, the feathers are fastened with sinew wrapping. The swelling of the stick gives the feathers an inclination to separate from one another. The head-dresses of this type are usually worn by the leaders of the ceremony.

Fig. 107 shows one of seven head-dresses of this type made, together with seven painted shirts or dresses, by Sitting Bull, the most influential Arapaho ghost-dance apostle. The stick on which the feathers are mounted has three successive knobs or swellings, at each of which upright feathers are attached. There are four medium-sized feathers in the lowest of these tiers or circles, three medium-sized feathers in the second, and four long and two short feathers in the uppermost tier. All the feathers are cut into the vane in two, three, or four places on both sides of the quill, and are more or less reddened with paint.

Fig. 3, Plate LXVIII, shows a simpler head-dress. From the end of the stick rise four feathers entirely trimmed away, except for the tip. Even the quill has been mostly cut away, and barely enough left to enable the feather to stand without drooping. The interior side of the four cut quills is painted respectively blue, red, yellow, and green. The remaining portions of the vanes are reddened. In the middle of the top of the stick is set a small black wing-feather, which appears to have been nearly cut in two, but is not cut away.

Fig. 1, Plate LXVII, shows a similar head-dress, in which both feather and quill have been cut away still more than in the last piece, so that nothing remains of the quill but a thin strip resembling whalebone. The inner side of these strips of quill is painted red. At the mounting of the four trimmed feathers, blue and yellow plumes are inserted. The four black tops are reddened with paint.

Fig. 108 shows a simple head-dress somewhat resembling

the multiple crow-feather head-dress just described. It consists of a single brownish feather mounted on a stick which
appears to be inserted in the end of the quill; and
the vanes are cut away, except at the top. At the
mounting, three small hawk-feathers are wrapped
on with sinew.

A third type of upright head-dress consists of
a pair of long narrow feathers mounted on a stick.
Occasionally, single feathers of this character are
thus treated, and sometimes three feathers are
mounted together. The favorite feather for this
type of head-dress is the long tail-feather of the
magpie. The feathers are usually ornamented either
at the base or at the tip, or in both places. The
ornamentation is usually dyed plumes, which are
either fastened to the feather with cement, or, at
the base, are included in the wrapping of the feather.
Fig. 1, Plate LXIX, shows a typical head-dress of this
type. It consists of two magpie-feathers and a few
small orange-yellow plumes. Another specimen
(part of Museum set Nos. $\frac{5\,0}{1\,0\,2}$—$\frac{5\,0}{1\,1\,2}$ consists of a single
magpie-feather mounted on a stick without any
adornment. Fig. 2, Plate LXIX, shows, a three-
feathered form of this type of head-dress. The
feathers in this case are of a pheasant. They are
ornamented just below their pointed tips with red
plumes, and at their bases with a pair of small black-and-
white woodpecker-feathers.

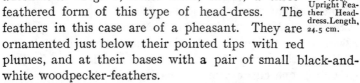

Fig. 108 $(\frac{5\,0}{2\,9\,3})$. Upright Feather Head-dress. Length, 24.5 cm.

Another type of head-dress that is common consists of a
cross of stiff skin either painted, or covered with bead-work,
and in most cases with a hanging attachment of feathers or
embroidered strings. Plate LXX shows one form, the use and
symbolism of which are described in another place in connection with the remaining objects obtained from its owner.
Fig. 138, and Fig. 1, Plate LXXI, show two other cross head-
dresses, which, like the last, form part of a larger group of
objects, in connection with which they, also, are more fully
described. Fig. 2, Plate LXXI, shows a somewhat different

form of these head-dresses. The skin is in the shape of a simple cross, without appreciable taper towards the middle, and is covered with bead-work instead of painting. The feather attachments, which are more elaborate than in the preceding cases, consist of two eagle-feathers, along the quill of each of which is tied a strip of skin completely wrapped with red, yellow, and green quill-work. The feathers are tipped with red plumes, and attached to the middle of the cross by strings of red beads. The four ends of the cross are also tipped with red plumes. Like the preceding piece, this specimen also forms part of a group, the pieces accompanying it being a whistle, and pendants for tying the hair (Museum No. $\frac{50}{114}$, *b, c*), which are described elsewhere.

In the collection is another bead-covered cross (Museum No. $\frac{50}{409}$) with slight taper towards the middle of the arms. The beading is red, except that at the ends of the arms there are four small lines of blue beads. From the centre of the cross hang the usual attachments, which in this case consist of five thin thongs wrapped with red quill-work. On each thong are five places where blue quill-work replaces the red. Pendants of this nature occur on ghost-dance head-dresses of other types; and similar pendants are found in regalia of the older tribal ceremonial organizations, as in the whistle ornaments of the dog-dance.

Specimen Museum No. $\frac{50}{53}$ is a Maltese cross of painted rawhide, resembling the body of the piece shown in Plate LXX in having the centre of the cross circular. Half of this cross, including one entire arm and half of the adjacent arms, is painted green; the other half, red. These colors represent respectively sky and earth. The whole cross is the morning star. A white eagle-feather hangs from the end of one arm. Such attachment of feathers to the ends of the arms seems usual in painted crosses, whereas beaded crosses ordinarily have the attachments made to the middle. The white feather is painted in part with red and green. A narrow strip on each side of the lower part of the quill is reddened; beyond this there is a narrow green stripe on each side of the quill to the tip of the feather, where the green area spreads out fan-shaped. A red and a dark band pass transversely across the feather near this end.

Another type of head-dress somewhat resembles the beaded cross head-dresses, but replaces the cross with the figure of a bird. Fig. 109 shows such a head-dress, which, like the cross head-dresses, is worn attached by thongs at the back or side of the head. The bird — which probably represents the crow, or perhaps the thunder-bird — is covered with blue beading. From the centre of its body issues a thong to which is attached a feather, apparently of a hawk. The base of this feather is covered with a piece of bird-skin, apparently from the head or neck of a duck.

Specimen Museum No. $\frac{50}{88}$, *a*, is a similar piece. The figure of the bird is somewhat smaller than in the last specimen, and is covered with blue beads with a crescent of red, green, and yellow beads at the centre of its body. Two black feathers, ornamented at their bases with red-dyed plumes, hang from this crescent ornament.

Still another type of head-dress resembling the cross and bird head-dresses — in that its body is of wood or skin, and its feathers are primarily attachments to this — consists of a small ring or hoop. Usually these rings are covered with bead-work of one color, and have

Fig. 109 ($\frac{50}{88}$, *b*). Head-dress representing a Bird. Length, 26 cm.

four small areas of another color on them. They are also traversed by two bisecting strings of sinew. Feathers may be attached at the four colored spots, or at the bisection of the strings. These head-dresses represent the sacred tribal wheels and the game-wheels used by the Arapaho. The symbolism of the sacred wheels — which refers to the world, the snake, and other ideas — is therefore more or less transferred to them. Fig. 111 shows such a head-dress, one of a pair which are more fully commented upon elsewhere. Another such object is shown attached to the crow belt shown in Plate LXXIV. A third piece approximating this

type is shown in Fig. 110, one of a set of ghost-dance objects.
It consists of a small hoop wrapped with a dark-green thong.

From the hoop hang, by yellow-painted
thongs, five tips of black feathers, and
by longer thongs (which are yellow,
green, and red), two other such feather-
tips. Two still longer thongs probably
serve to fasten the ornament to the head.
A fourth piece, resembling the last, has
been illustrated in Fig. 3, Plate VI.

A somewhat divergent type of head-
dress is shown in Fig. 112. A hoop of
rawhide is covered on one side only with
blue beads. From it hang two strings
of blue beads
and two twists
of brown fur,
which appear to
have been
partly painted
green. This
head-dress, like
the ordinary
head-dress, is
worn attached
by two thongs.
A type of
ghost-dance

Fig. 110 ($\frac{50}{109}$). Head-ornament used in the Ghost–dance.
Length, 22 cm.

Fig. 111 ($\frac{50}{592}$, ^{h}). Head-ornament used in the Ghost-dance.
Length, 19 cm.

head-dress different from all the preceding, in that it
is a realistic representation instead of a merely symbolic
ornament, consists of a small bow and arrows, usually
ornamented with feathers. Such a head-dress (forming
part of a larger group of objects belonging to one man, and
described elsewhere) is shown in Fig. 113. The bow is painted
red on one edge, green on the other, and dark green on the
outer side: the inner side is half green, half yellow. Two arrows
are tied to the middle of the bow. These are carved so as to
show triangular feathering and a notch at the end. The forward

half of each arrow is yellow; the rear half, dark green.   The
arrows are tied against the bow, so that their yellow halves
are near the green portion of the inside of the bow, their green

Fig.   112
(⁵⁰⁄₃₂₅).
Head - orna-
ment used in
Ghost-dance.
Length,21cm.

Fig. 113 (⁵⁰⁄₁₁₂,ᵃ).   Head–dress of Small Bow and Arrows.   Length
of bow, 23 cm.

halves along the yellow portion of the bow.   Seven short
crow-feathers hang from thongs at the place where the arrows
are tied to the bow.   Five of these thongs are short, two are
considerably longer, so that the feathers at their ends fall below the others.   Two additional thongs fastened at the same
place serve to tie the head-dress to the hair.   This arrangement of seven small black feathers on thongs of unequal
length occurs on another object belonging to the same owner
(Fig. 110), described under the hoop form of head-dress.

Other head-dresses consist of combinations of two or more
of the types described.   Fig. 114 shows such a specimen.   It
consists of two magpie-feathers mounted on a stick, of a hoop
head-dress with four quill-covered pendants, and of a miniature
bow and arrows.   The entire object is profusely ornamented

with green and yellow quill wrapping and with green, yellow, and red plumes. The bow is painted green, as are the two arrows, which are feathered with trimmed magpie-feathers. One arrow is blunt as if for play, the other pointed. These two arrows are said to represent the sun; the quilled pendants, rain. Such head-dresses as this are worn upright at the back of the head, the hoop and bow hanging from the lower part of the upright head-dress. This object belonged to the same person who owned the specimens Museum Nos. $\frac{50}{312}$ — $\frac{50}{316}$

A head-dress similar to the last specimen is Museum No. $\frac{50}{125}$. It lacks the bow and arrows of the last piece, but has the pair of mounted magpie-feathers ornamented along the shaft with a strip of quill-work, and the quill-covered hoop, from which hang quill-covered pendants. At the ends of these pendants are feathers. The quill-work on the magpie-feathers is alternately red and yellow. At the base of the feathers are red plumes; at their tips, blue plumes. The ring is half red and half yellow. From it hang, besides a single plume, five thin thongs completely wrapped with quill-work. Four areas of the quill covering of each of these thongs are red, and three black. At the end of each thong is an iridescent black magpie-feather, at the base of which are red and yellow plume-feathers. The yellow quill-work on this double head-dress is said to represent the earth, more, perhaps, because it occurs on the circular hoop than on account of its color. The red denotes people; the blue, the sky. The feathers represent birds.

Another form of head-dress consists of a pair of hanging eagle-feathers. This type has already been met with as a

Fig. 114 ($\frac{50}{125}$). Head-dress with Wheel and Bow. Length, 75 cm.

constituent of the cross head-dress. Fig. 115 shows such a head-dress taken from a group of ghost-dance objects. The feathers are nearly perfectly white eagle-feathers somewhat stained with paint, which may not have been intentional. They are tied together by a thong passing through the loop formed by the trimmed end of the quill doubled, and inserted into itself. Like most other head-dresses of this class, this one is worn hanging from the back of the head.

Fig. 116 is a head-dress accompanying the feathered belt or scarf shown in Plate LXXIII. It is a spotted eagle-feather more or less stained with red, and tipped, at the end and at a short distance below the end, with yellow down attached to the feather with red cement. Contrary to the most common usage, this feather lacks any thong for attachment. A little of the feathering is removed on one side of the base, and the end of the quill is sharpened, so that it seems to have been intended to have been stuck into the hair.

Head-dresses consisting of entire or partial bird-skins are not rare. There

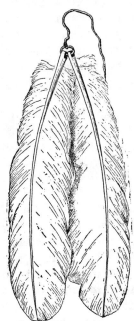

Fig. 115 ($\frac{50}{110}$). Simple Head-dress of Feathers. Length, 29 cm.

Fig. 116($\frac{50}{121}$,*b*). Feather worn in the Hair. Length, 34 cm.

are two such skins — one an entire crow-skin, the other a partial one — in the set of the ghost-dance objects (Museum Nos. $\frac{50}{102}$—$\frac{50}{112}$). Specimen No. $\frac{50}{98}$ is another crow-skin, kept wrapped in red flannel. The eyes have been painted red. It is not certain whether or not this bird-skin was removed from its red-flannel wrapping when worn. Two ends of thong attached at the neck of the bird serve to fasten the head-dress to the back of the dancer's head. Plate LXXII shows a head-dress consisting of a black and a red bird-skin tied breast to breast. The birds appear to be a black-bird and a tanager. This head-dress is also worn fastened to the hair by two thongs.

Specimen Museum No. $\frac{50}{6\,2\,2}$ is a head-dress belonging to the class of bead-covered rawhide head-dresses with attached feathers, but cannot be included under the related types of cross, bird, and hoop head-dresses. It is a crescent forming the greater part of a circle, with its ends downward. Half of the crescent is beaded yellow, and half light blue. Red and yellow plumes are attached respectively to the blue and yellow ends of the crescent, and from the middle there rise larger red, green, and yellow plumes. This form of head-dress does not seem to be common.

One of the simplest forms consists of a number of hanging feathers. These are usually wrapped with sinew against thongs, the thongs knotted together, and two of them extended beyond the rest; or perhaps, more frequently, two additional thongs are inserted for tying the head-dress to the scalp-lock or to the hair at the side of the head.

Specimen Museum No. $\frac{50}{5\,5}$ is such a head-dress, consisting of twenty-four iridescent magpie-feathers, some of them being the long tail-feathers of the bird. There is also attached a black-and-white eagle or hawk feather. This specimen was secured for the Museum by Rev. W. C. Roe, and, according to the information given him, was worn in war to turn away the enemy's missiles. It thus appears that this form of head-dress is not especially associated with the ghost-dance movement.

Fig. 117 shows another such head-dress, consisting of twelve crow-feathers, the number being determined by the number of feathers in the bird's tail. The thongs and sinew wrappings are painted red. The thongs are knotted together into a round lump of considerable mass. This feature is often found on head-dresses of this type, including those used in the peyote worship.

This simple form of ghost-dance head-dress, the hanging bunch of feathers, does not occur among the regalia of the Arapaho tribal ceremonial organization, just as another common form — the thick bunch of feathers worn upright on the head among the Shoshoneans,

Fig. 117 (⅘). Head-dress of Crow-feathers. Length, 22 cm.

the Californians, and other Indians — is lacking altogether among the Arapaho. The bunch of hanging feathers is a frequent head-dress in the Arapaho peyote ceremony. The peyote head-dresses, however, differ from those of the ghost and crow dance in being smaller, and from other species of birds.

An unusual form of head-dress, worn by a boy, is shown in Fig. 118. It consists of a long tuft of twisted white hair from a cow's tail, representing a snake. At the top are attached two brass clock-wheels, the larger flat one representing the sun, and the other, it is said, food.

Fig. 118 (⁵⁰⁄₃₁₄). Head-dress of Unusual Form. Length, 32 cm.

Specimen Museum No. ⁵⁰⁄₁₁₄, *c*, is a pair of hair-ornaments, each consisting of two thongs painted red, ornamented about the middle with red, white, and green quill wrapping, and divided each at the lower end into four fringes. These hair-ties form a group with a feather-ornamented whistle and the cross head-dress shown in Fig. 2, Plate LXXI.

Fig. 119 shows a flat piece of bone used as a base for an upright feather arising from one of the deer-tail head-dresses of familiar type. The bone is cut into the shape of a woman.   Several holes in the face indicate spots of paint.

A number of head-dresses and other objects of wear made in connection with the ghost-dance, and kept together by one man, who was also the owner of the painted tent described below, comprise the following: a shell gorget (called "beii," or

"moon-shell," when the Indians speak English) representing a part of the buffalo's throat, and hence the buffalo (Fig. 120); an entire crow-skin worn tied to the back of the head; another crow-skin, split, and lacking the head, similarly worn; knee-bands of bells; armlets of porcupine-quills; a pair of white feathers of the bald eagle; a head-dress (Fig. 115); a head-dress of four upright trimmed black feathers, to be worn by the leaders in the dance (Plate LXVIII); a long single-mounted magpie tail-feather; four upright plume head-dresses of the type first described; a miniature bow and arrow head-dress (Fig. 113), to be worn by a drummer; the hoop head-dress of Fig. 110.

Fig. 119 ($\frac{50}{306}$).
A Piece of Bone from a Head-dress.
Length, 13.5 cm.

Feather Necklaces and Belts. — Necklaces and belts or scarfs ornamented with feathers were frequently made in connection with the ghost-dance movement.   With but few exceptions, these consist of a two-strand twisted cord of skin or cloth to which are attached numerous feathers ornamented at the base or tip with the usual dyed plumes or hair.   In one specimen in the Museum a single partly twisted strand of fur is used; in another, a somewhat wider flat strip of otter-skin; and in one case the feathers are attached to the two edges of a silk handkerchief folded diagonally.

A necklace or scarf consisting of two black-painted thongs twisted together, to which crow-feathers and four eagle-feathers are tied by red-painted thongs, is shown in Plate LXXIII.   The crow-feathers are ornamented at the base by red plumes; two of the black-and-white eagle-feathers have green plumes at the base; and all four have red plumes at the ends.   The white portion of these eagle-feathers has been rubbed with red paint. All four of them are much worn, especially along one side. To each of the thongs, from which hangs an eagle-feather, are attached four other thongs, at the ends of which are crow-feathers without plume ornamentation. It was stated that each of these eagle-feathers, with its four crow-feathers, represented five successive lives or worlds, the eagle-feather being the last.

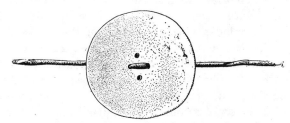

Fig. 120 ($\frac{50}{102}$). A Gorget of Shell. Diameter, 6 cm.

Specimen Museum No. $\frac{50}{92}$, *a*, was said to have been worn as a scarf over one shoulder. Its body consists of a cord of two strands of twisted red calico. The pendant attachments are in part weasel-tails more or less ornamented with red and purple and green plumes, and long tufts of green horse-tail ornamented with red and blue plumes. One yellow tuft of hair is ornamented with green and purple. A number of small belts are also attached to the scarf. The fur and other pendants were said to represent people in the new world. The green of the horsehair tufts denoted the earth, the yellow the sky.

Specimen Museum No. $\frac{50}{324}$, altogether about three feet long, seems to have been intended primarily for wear from the back of the head, but resembles the scarfs. It consists of a cord of two strands of twisted black silk, from which hang five bunches of black-and-white magpie-feathers and two bunches of black crow or magpie feathers. From one end hang three pheasant-feathers and a white weasel-skin. Near the middle is attached a small rawhide cross, about an inch in size, wrapped with red, white, and blue quills. This was also worn separately as a head-dress, being tied to the hair by two thongs.

Specimen Museum No. $\frac{50}{408}$ is one of the largest of these feathered scarfs. The feathers are attached by thongs to two cords of braided rawhide. One half of these two rawhide ropes is painted red; the other half, green. According to customary ghost-dance symbolism, these represent earth and sky. The feathers attached to the two halves of the scarf are dyed red and green to accord with the color of the rawhide braid to which they are fastened. The green-dyed feathers are adorned with green plumes at the base, and yellow at the tip. In the middle, at the junction of the red and green halves of the scarf, is a red ribbon, an eagle-feather dyed purple and ornamented with yellow plumes at the base and tip, a long grayish-white feather dyed yellow and tipped with a red plume, and five red-tipped black feathers attached to green thongs. At one end of the scarf a somewhat similar bunch of pendants consisting of a gray-and-white feather dyed yellow and of four red-tipped black feathers, is attached to the scarf by green thongs. The opposite red end of the scarf shows no such attachments; but this half of the scarf has fastened to it, at some distance from the end, a single yellow-tipped white feather. About two dozen small brass bells are attached to this scarf in addition to the feathers. These bells were said to represent hail. The red covering of the feathers on the scarf denoted the sun; the yellow, the water of a lake in the world to be.

Specimen Museum No. $\frac{50}{100}$ is an unusually graceful necklace of black-and-white magpie-feathers ornamented with orange, green, and yellow plumes of delicate shades. The body of the necklace is a light-brown fur somewhat twisted, and lightly painted red. The two ends of this hang down for nearly a foot beyond where they are joined. From the point of the junction there hangs also a bunch of six black-and-white magpie-feathers without colored plumes, together with a fringe of green thongs.

Specimen Museum No. $\frac{50}{40}$ consists of feathers hanging from a strip of otter-skin about an inch wide. The bare side of the skin is painted yellow. From the hair side proceed thongs to which black feathers are attached, for the most part in pairs. These feathers are ornamented with red plumes at the base and with yellow plumes at the tip.   At one end of the piece there is a length of more than a foot of twisted otter-skin without any feather attachments.

The one scarf or belt consisting of feathers attached along the two outer edges of a folded silk handkerchief contains crow, magpie, pheasant, hawk or owl, and perhaps other feathers, dyed red, yellow and green, and ornamented at the base with red, yellow, or green plumes.   The plumes are always of a different color from the feather to which they are attached. The feathers are tied to the handkerchief with red thongs.

A necklace of rabbit feet and feathers (specimen Museum No. $\frac{5}{330}$) was worn during the ghost-dance or crow-dance to prevent the dancer from becoming tired.   Similar rabbit-foot charms seem to be sometimes put on horses to enable them to run better.   An additional motive for the selection of rabbits' feet in this case was the fact that the Piute origina-tor of the ghost-dance movement was reported to the Arapaho to live largely on rabbits.

Crow Belts. — The most conspicuous pieces worn in the crow-dance are common to the Arapaho and to almost all of the Plains tribes.   They consist of a belt from which hang two long and sometimes wide strips of skin ornamented with feathers, paintings, and sometimes bells.   These strips fall from the back of the waist of the dancer nearly to the ground. At the upper part of the back of the belt there is a piece of rawhide, usually cut into the shape of a bird.   This serves to give support to various ornaments.   The most conspicuous and frequent of these are two projecting arms attached to thongs which are drawn through the rawhide, and which, being pulled tight and knotted behind, cause the ornaments to stand out horizontally, at right angles from the rest of the piece.   Sometimes a row of feathers between these two arms is made to project in a similar manner.   As the crow-dance belts are worn, these projecting ornaments stand out from the back below the waist in a very striking manner.   It will be seen that, while these specimens are nominally belts, they actually ornament only the lower part of the wearer's rear.

A specimen of this class, which was made by the owner as

the result of his belief that he visited the sky as a "shadow," and was there instructed to make the belt, is shown in Plate LXXIV. The two hanging strips of skin which form the body of the specimen are together somewhat over a foot in width. The one on the left is painted yellow; the one on the right, red. To each strip are attached four rows of about four plumes each, alternating with rows of about four tufts of wool. These plumes and tufts of wool are wrapped with sinew to thongs passing through the skin, and knotted on the other side. The plumes and wool are dyed yellow and red to accord with the painting of the skin to which they are attached. Halfway down the length of the strip of skin, a skin fringe is sewed on. To this skin are attached two horizontal rows of small bells. The lower ends of the two strips are also fringed, and just above the fringe are ornamented with horizontal stripes of blue, red, and yellow bead-work. The yellow and red ground-color of the two strips has been painted over with six wavy vertical lines extending the length of each strip, and applied in a more intense shade of the color of the background. In addition, two red horizontal crescents are painted on the yellow strip, two black ones on the red strip. The backs of the two strips are painted over very lightly with red and yellow. On the yellow side of the back are painted four black and three red crescents; on the red strip, four red and three black crescents.

The piece of rawhide at the top has in this specimen been cut into the shape of the upper part of an eagle. It is pierced with many small holes, and is edged with red, blue, and yellow beading. The body of the bird below the wings has not been represented, and almost all there is of it projects above the two hanging strips. To the eye of this rawhide figure of a bird is attached a small head-dress, probably usually removed from this belt, and tied to the wearer's hair. This head-dress consists of a bunch of half a dozen crow-feathers that have been rubbed with red paint. These feathers have been slit in the customary ghost-dance style, so that the quill remains bare, except at the tip; while the lower part of the feather, much slashed, remains hanging loose at the base of the quill.

The two projecting arms are in this specimen made of wire

entirely wrapped with bead-work, — red on the right arm, and blue on the left. At the base of each arm are a few owl-feathers cut like the crow-feathers just described, and dyed respectively red and yellow on the right and left arms. At the outer end of each wire arm is a black feather trimmed so as to resemble the vane of a two-feathered arrow. At the base, this feather is ornamented with yellow-dyed plumes; at its tip, with a tuft of dyed wool wrapped to the pared quill with sinew. Between the two projecting arms are six large eagle-feathers, each attached to thongs passing through the rawhide. The base of the quills of these feathers is wrapped with yellow ribbon, from under which hangs a red ribbon several inches in length. The tips of the six feathers are orna-mented with yellow-dyed plumes fastened to the feather with cement; while a few inches below, a red plume is similarly fas-tened. As the specimen is worn, these six feathers project at an angle downward. Under their bases is a large braid of grass, apparently the sweet-grass used for incense. Below the sweet-grass are two rows of hawk or owl feathers partly trimmed from the quill. They are dyed red and yellow to accord with the side of the piece to which they are fastened. Just above the six large feathers there are attached two rawhide horns painted black. These also project from the piece, much as did the two arms and the row of feathers.

The belt-straps of this specimen are formed by a strip of skin little more than an inch in width, which is fastened by thongs to the back of the rawhide bird. This belt is orna-mented with vertical strips of blue, red, and yellow bead-work, in several places with bells, and with several bunches of crow-feathers hanging from thongs a few inches in length. These crow-feathers have had the upper half cut off. From one of the belt-straps hangs a small ring wrapped with red quill-work. In two opposite places, yellow wrapping replaces the red on the ring; and in two other places, also diametrically opposed, there is blue quill-work. These four points are con-nected by strings. From the intersection of these strings hangs a long thong wrapped in three places with red quill-work. It is possible that this small hoop was intended to be detached from the belt on certain occasions, and worn as a head-dress.

The symbolism of this piece is the following. The entire object represents the thunder-bird. The six eagle-feathers projecting from the lower part of the rawhide figure are to be considered as its tail. The two bead-covered projecting attachments are lightning: they also represent arrows, as indicated by the feathering at their end. The two black horns of rawhide indicate buffalo, and therefore subsistence. The yellow strip of skin denotes life in heaven; the red one, life on earth. The blue, red, and yellow stripes of bead-work on the lower ends of the main skin-strips and on the belt-straps represent the rainbow. The ceremony in which these pieces are worn, not only refers to the thunder, but is sometimes called "rain-dance." The owl-feathers at the base of the two projections denote ghosts, which owls are supposed to be. Their trimming, which leaves only the tip of the feather on the quill, was said to represent arrow-feathering. The numerous small holes in the rawhide bird represent the metallic sheen of the thunder-bird. The red and yellow ribbons at the bases of the eagle-feathers 'are flashes of lightning. The bells on the specimen represent thundering, and, as they are round, hail. The red crescent denotes the sun; the black, the moon. The small hoop attached to the belt-strap represents the sacred wheel. The entire object is called niihina^{n}ka^n ("bird-tail" or "eagle-tail").

Accompanying this specimen is a head-dress, the body of which consists of a wooden arrow with a barbed point and a wooden representation of feathering (Fig. 121). Three feathers appear to have been represented; only two now remain. The shaft of the arrow is wrapped with a string of red beads on sinew. At the base of the wooden feathering, bits of plumes dyed dark blue are attached by sinew wrapping. The shaft is painted red; the point, dark green or black; and the feathering, red on one side and dark green on the other. At the end of the wooden feathering an eagle-feather is attached by a string. This string passes through the doubled quill. The lower portion of the feather is notched. This arrow is worn as a head-dress with the point downward. It represents the thunder's arrow, — lightning. The eagle-feather and bits of plume were interpreted as arrow-feathering; the red beads were said to represent each a person; and the string along the wooden feathering, serving as a means of attachment for the hanging eagle-feather, was said to be the course of the owner, or of his prayer to heaven before he predicted rain.

Another crow belt (Museum No. $\frac{5}{3}\frac{0}{8}$) is green on one side, yellow on the other. The green represents the earth; the yellow, the sky. The feathers attached to each side are dyed in the same color, and the belt strips are painted in the same color as the hanging strips. From the middle of the top, where a magpie-skin lacking the head is attached over the red-painted figure of a bird, there hang two long thin strips of skin, one green, and one yellow. In addition there are two yellow ribbons. From the sides of the red figure of the bird a red line

Fig. 121 ($\frac{5}{3}\frac{0}{0}\frac{}{1}$, c). Head-dress resembling an Arrow. Length of arrow, 28.5 cm.

extends on each side down to the lower end of the speci-men. The two ornaments made to stand out from the upper-most piece have for their main part an eagle wing-feather, the quill of which has a wrapping of porcupine-work laid over it and tied on. Small bells are strung along the back of the feather. At the base of the eagle wing-feather, where this is apparently stiffened by the insertion of a stick into the quill and by wrap-ping with thong, about eight feathers, apparently of an owl, are attached. The quills of these have been split to the base.

These feathers are attached by reducing the base of the quill to a flat strip, bending this around the thong and back upon the entire quill above, where it is fastened by a wrapping of sinew. These owl-feathers are dyed respectively green and yellow on the two sides. Where the projecting ornaments which they encircle are attached, small five-pointed stars of rawhide intervene between the body of the piece and the ornaments. At the top of the back is a piece of rawhide cut out into the shape of a bird, presumably the thunder-bird. This piece is attached so that, when the specimen is worn, it is entirely hidden from view, except for the head of the bird, which projects above the top of the soft skin of which the main portion of the specimen consists. This head is painted with red and green vertical stripes. When the specimen is spread out so that the belt-straps are horizontal, the entire piece resembles in outline a bird; the head being made by the head of this bird-form piece of rawhide; the wings, by the fringed and pointed belt-straps; and the tail, by the two long feathered hanging strips. On the back of these two main strips of skin are painted irregular dots of green and yellow. The green dots are on that one of the two strips which in front is yellow, and *vice versa.* With the yellow dots are a few in light blue. This specimen was obtained by Rev. W. C. Roe.

A simpler piece (Museum No. $\frac{50}{39}$), obtained by the Rev. Mr. Roe, lacks the rawhide figure of a bird at the top of the back. Instead, there is a rectangular piece of stiff rawhide doubled on itself, from the lower part of which two triangular pieces have been cut, giving the whole piece the angular outline of the body, wings, and tail of a bird. While no information was obtained as to the symbolism of this specimen, it seems very probable that this piece of hide represented a bird to its maker. Through the upper part of this hide is passed a horizontal stick to support the entire specimen. The soft skin forming the body of the specimen appears to have been painted over very lightly in green. The uppermost portion of this soft skin, about where it covers the stiff rawhide, is painted green more distinctly. In this green area is a dark-blue horizontal crescent. On each of the two hanging strips

of the soft skin is painted a long dark-blue arrow, the point
upward.   The back or inside of the soft skin is roughly painted
dark blue.   The feather ornamentation of this piece consists
principally of pheasant-feathers, which are attached in five or
six horizontal tiers of about five feathers each.   These pheasant-
feathers have been lightly dyed blue.   The uppermost tier of
feathers is, as usual, attached to a strip of skin distinct from the
body of the piece, and shows some tendency to stand out at an
angle.   The feathers are all attached by the method of turning
the quill upon itself over a thong, and have small red-dyed
plumes fastened to their bases by the same sinew wrapping
which holds the doubled-over end of the quill.   A few pheasant-
feathers are also attached to the belt-straps.   They are fastened to bunches of short thongs, which are tied into one knot.
The two stiff projecting ornaments are in appearance quite
different from the customary form, in that they consist of
slender rods covered with rabbit-skin.   The interior of these
rods, however, appears to be nothing but a long eagle wing-
feather which has been folded closely around its quill; so that
actually the usual type is adhered to.   The ends of these
projecting ornaments are tipped with bunches of red-dyed
plumes, and at the base each ornament is encircled by owl
or hawk feathers dyed green.   These have been cut off square
at the ends, and the entire lower portion of each feather has
been slit from the quill on each side, remaining attached only
at the base.

Specimen Museum No. $\frac{5\,0}{2\,9\,3}$ is made of cloth instead of deer-
skin, and is somewhat smaller and simpler than the preceding
pieces.   It is entirely supported by a square piece of rawhide doubled upon itself over a horizontal stick at the top.
From each side of this hangs a comparatively narrow strip of
blue-edged red cloth to which are attached six eagle-feathers
in pairs.   Just above the place where these two hanging strips
are fastened to the rawhide, are the two projecting attachments, which, in this piece also, consist essentially of a long
eagle wing-feather.   Over the front of this a smaller feather,
apparently also from an eagle-wing, has been laid: along the
under side of the quill there is a strip of red and black quill-

wrapped rawhide. Four or five small brass bells are attached to a string running along the feather and this quilled strip. At the base, each of the two eagle wing-feathers is encircled by about eight owl or hawk feathers dyed green. The quills of these have been slit, so that the body of the feather hangs loosely in two portions from the base; only the quill itself, with the small tip, remaining stiff. The belt-straps consist of a woven woollen band the middle of which has been tied to the rawhide backing. At the middle of the front of this rawhide is attached a bird-skin, apparently of a hawk, so that it comes between the pairs of projecting ornaments and hanging strips. Below this, from the middle of the lower part of the rawhide square, hangs an ornament roughly resembling the head-dresses worn in the second dance of the ceremonial series. It is a trapezoidal piece of skin doubled on itself, in one end of which are inserted five eagle-feathers. It seems probable that this piece is also a head-dress, and has been attached here for safe-keeping.

Women's Dresses. — A woman's deerskin dress made for the ghost-dance, and seen among the southern Arapaho in 1899, was painted over from the waist up. The ground-color of the painting was blue. Across the dress were two rows of thirteen suns (yellow circles), and, below these, two rows of seven large morning-star crosses. These crosses were yellow with red edges. The back of the dress showed the same painting. For the middle star of the upper row on the front of the dress was substituted a large red crescent moon: the corresponding place on the back of the dress was filled with a figure of the thunder-bird (also in red), four red lightning-marks proceeding from its eyes to the side of the dress.

A little girl's buckskin dress ornamented with beads, painted with symbolic designs, in accordance with several dreams, by a young man who was her relative, is shown in Plate LXXV. Over the shoulders of the dress, on the part of it that is worn highest, is painted the thunder-bird, with lightning issuing from its eye. In the middle of one side of the dress is painted a large red Maltese cross, the morning star. The ends of this cross are green. This green denotes the freshness of the new

world to be.   Below one shoulder is a buffalo, the means of subsistence; below the other shoulder, a magpie in green.   Flank-
ing the morning-star cross are black trapezoidal figures, the familiar hiiteni life-symbols.   A figure of a turtle below the cross
refers to the origin of the earth.   The turtle is painted in a gray-
ish-blue intended to give the effect of fog or mist, the word for
turtle (bääna^n) being the same as that for fog.   Other figures on
this side of the dress are a five-pointed star and the new moon.
At the bottom of the dress, a green strip represents the earth
in spring.   A symbol of a tree with leaves represents a deciduous tree, no doubt the cottonwood, with fresh leaves.   The
rainbow is represented by an arch of colored bands.   A dark
cloud is enclosed by it.   Another figure of the thunder-bird
and of the lightning issuing from it symbolizes early summer,
the time of the first thunderstorm.

On the opposite side of this dress there are pictures of the
turtle, of two pipes, of two buffalo, and of the crow, the messenger and guide to the new world.   A red sun below refers
to the new sun that will be.   The bottom of the dress is
painted dark blue, which indicates the sky, as the corresponding green band on the opposite side indicates the earth.
Above this blue are painted two cedar-trees, indicated by
tree-symbols without leaves.

To the shoulders, front, and back, are attached several small
representations of the netted hoop-wheel used as a game, and
more or less revived at the time of the ghost-dance.

Another painted deerskin ghost-dance dress for a girl was
obtained, with information as to its symbolism, by Rev. W.
C. Roe.   The symbolic decoration is the following: On one
side (Plate LXXVI), below the throat, a Maltese-cross morning
star in green; five five-pointed stars on each side; below these,
two figures of crows or magpies (to judge from the painting, the former); — below a horizontal beaded band (which
is decorative), in the centre, a pipe, bowl down; on the two
sides, a red sun and a buffalo; — at the waist, a crow and
three small solid circles representing the heated stones used
in the sweat-house to produce steam; below, two crows, a
tent, and two trees.   The symbolism on the other side

(Plate LXXVII) is the following : A hollow circle below the throat is the full moon; a half-circle in green, below this, the new moon; — to the sides, stars, and crows or magpies; below, two sweat-house stones and (a small solid oval with a line at one end) a buffalo seen from above; — at the bottom, a turtle, a tent, a red semicircle denoting a sweat-house, and a high quadrilateral representing a mountain. Down the shoulders is a stripe of bead-work. Under this on each side, and for the greater part covered by it, is a circle, said to represent the game-wheel, but resembling the usual symbols for the sacred hoop-wheel. The game-wheel, however, is itself regarded at times as a symbol of the latter.

In the Museum collection is a painted canvas tent (No. $\frac{50}{411}$) ornamented in accordance with a dream, and used for the crow-dance. It is decorated as follows: The upper part of the tent is painted green as far down as the ears or upper flaps extend. The lower border of the tent, for about four feet up from the ground, is also painted green. The green area at the top is bordered by a red line; the one below, by an orange line. Down the front of the tent, where the two edges are joined when it is erected, is an orange border. On the sides and back of the tent are five red stripes, each about a foot wide, extending vertically from the upper green portion of the tent to the lower green portion. These red stripes have each seven blue circles painted in outline upon them, and, like the two orange stripes down the front of the tent, are edged with blue.

The door of this tent has painted on it a green bird, apparently a crow. The heart of this bird is represented in yellow, and from it a yellow line issues through the mouth of the bird, and upward to the edge of the door. Under the bird is a figure of a buffalo in green; and beyond this, outside of the hoop forming the frame of the door, is a drawing in outline of a rider with bow and arrow, apparently pursuing the buffalo. At the two corners of the door and in the middle of it, between the crow and the buffalo, there are attached a few crow-feathers and small bells; at one place on the side, a few crow-feathers.

A large number of crow and some magpie feathers have been tied into bunches for attachment to this tent. The wooden pins used for fastening the front of the tent together are painted red, and ornamented with small black feathers wrapped by their bases to the wood in two places near one end. One of these pins is painted green instead of red.

Drums and Accessories. — Fig. 122 shows a hand drum. It is somewhat more than a foot across. It consists of a circular piece of skin stretched over one edge of a hoop of wood, and brought around over its other edge. The hoop is

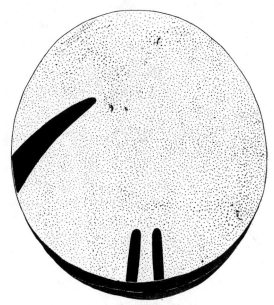

Fig. 122 ($\frac{50}{937}$).   A Hand Drum.   Diameter, 41 cm.

pierced with holes an inch or more apart; and a thong passing through these and the skin on the inside and outside of the hoop stretches the drum. From four opposite points of the hoop, on the back or bottom, thongs extend toward the centre, where they are fastened together and wrapped with cloth, to afford a handle. This bottom, or inside of the drum, is said to resemble the sacred wheel, because this is also crossed by two bisecting strings. The inside of the hoop itself is painted dark green. The under side of the skin is painted red. The inside of the drum is called hääⁿtetc ("the ocean"). The upper side, which is shown in the figure, is also painted red, and is said to represent the sun. A large black figure denotes a buffalo-horn; two smaller black marks, about the size of fingers, represent man and woman.

Fig. 123 shows one of four sticks used to suspend a large drum. The painted ends of the sticks are stuck in the ground, and the drum is hung from the forks at the top. Two of the sticks are painted yellow at the bottom, and two black. The forks at the top of the sticks are so that one branch comes at almost right angles to the straight stem, which gives the entire stick the character-istic shape of the

Fig. 123 (₃₉₉⁄₉, a). Forked Support for a Large Drum.
Length, 86 cm.

Fig. 124 (₁₈₅⁄₈₈). A Drum-Stick. Length, 59 cm.

Plains pipe. The sticks are therefore said to be pipes. The squarely cut ends of the transverse branches are painted red to represent red catlinite. Of the colors with which the sticks are painted, black represents night; yellow, daylight; and green. the earth. Near their upper part the sticks are wound with transparent beads, said to indicate the sun. Eagle, magpie, and other feathers are also tied to them near the top. These

refer to people sitting closely around the drum when it
is beaten. The eagle-feathers on each stick (one or two), perhaps through association of the eagle with the thunder-bird,
were said to represent clouds.

An object very similar to that in
Fig. 129, but quite different from
it in use, is shown in Fig. 124. The
present piece was obtained from a
northern Arapaho, and is a drum-
stick. The wooden handle is uncovered or unornamented; but the
stuffed head is of green-painted
skin with a black eagle (quill-
embroidered) on one side and a
white one on the other, very similar
to the crows on the head of specimen Fig. 129. The drumsticks
of the Arapaho are not often as
thickly padded as this piece, and
are not usually ornamented. Sometimes an entirely bare stick is used,
and sometimes a stick with a few
turns of skin wrapped around one
end.

Whistles. — Wooden   whistles
were made in connection with the
ghost and crow dance. The whistles
typical of the older tribal ceremonies are of bone, often ornamented with a partial wrapping of blue
beads, and usually they have no
feathers, other than a single projecting plume, attached to them.
The ghost-dance whistles are of
wood, considerably larger, painted,

Fig. 125 ($\frac{50}{296}$). A Carved Wooden
Whistle. Length, 48 cm.

often carved in relief or outline, and ornamented with pendant
feathers at the end.

Fig. 125 represents a whistle, carved, painted, and decorated with feathers. The carvings consist of a cross, which is as usual the morning star, a vertical line from it representing its course as it rises; above it, the figure of a person with a red upright head-feather, representing the sun; above this, the thunder-bird. A straight line issuing from its mouth represents rain; wavy lines are lightning. Of the colors painted on the whistle, red is the blood of humanity, blue the sky, and green the earth. The black and white of the magpie-feathers attached to the whistle represent clouds; and small plumes dyed red, and attached to these feathers, represent lightning. Of the feathers on the whistle, those of the magpie refer to the thunder-bird, on account of the swift flight of this bird. The use of a primary wing-feather of this bird further refers to the flight of the thunder-bird. The blowing of the whistle when it is used represents thunder.

Another whistle of wood (Museum No. $\frac{50}{880}$), painted green, is ornamented along the upper side by a straight line which runs the length of the piece, and has been painted red and blue. On the other side of the whistle are four zigzag incised lines. The lines are symbols of roads. Around the end of the whistle is a strip of otter-skin. From this hang an eagle-feather (stained reddish at the base, and ornamented there with a blue plume), a small barred feather, a few small trimmed iridescent magpie-feathers much worn, a thong ornamented with three small wrappings of red quills, and four thongs each ornamented with quill-work of one color, and tipped at the end with a feather or plume. Two of these quilled thongs are white, one yellow, and one red.

A whistle (Museum No. $\frac{50}{114}$, *b*) forms part of a set that includes the cross head-dress shown in Fig. 2, Plate LXXI, and a pair of hair-ties described elsewhere. This whistle is smaller than the others, free from carving, painted red, and ornamented with a single large eagle-feather from which a large section has been roughly cut on one side.

Objects carried in the Hand. — Figs. 1 and 2, Plate LXXVIII, represent two ceremonial whips or wands used in the ghost-dance or crow-dance. It will be seen that they resemble somewhat the kakaox, or swords (Fig. 56), of the first of the tribal series of ceremonies. The flat sides of the wands are carved in low relief, and the incisions are painted. One wand (Fig. 1, Plate LXXVIII) shows on one side a figure representing a "shadow," or spirit. He wears an upright head-dress at the back of his head. Above him is a crescent moon from which grows a cottonwood-tree. This side of the wand is red; the incised lines and areas, mainly blue and black. On the other side of the wand, which is black, is a cedar-tree in red. The other piece (Fig. 2) is black on both sides. It shows on one side two red circles, the sun, towards each of which are directed five or six parallel blue lines, kakaûçetcaⁿ ("thoughts" or "wishes"). Between the two circles are a red and a blue line, just failing to meet. On the other side are incised similar lines at each end, directed toward a crow and a Maltese-cross morning star, between which is a single line. All the carvings on this side of the wand are red.

From the end of the first wand hang two eagle wing-feathers, a long thong with a yellow-dyed plume, a short thong with a yellow plume, short red and yellow ribbons attached to the bases of the eagle-feathers, a bunch of small bells, and below these a bunch of pheasant and black magpie feathers. The attachments at the end of the other piece are similar. They consist of two eagle wing-feathers with red and yellow ribbons at the base, two long red ribbons, a long thong at the end of which is a red-dyed plume, a bunch of bells, and below this a bunch of about fifteen black-and-white magpie-feathers dyed red.

At the handles of the two wands there are also feather attachments: these are attached to a skin cover slipped over the handle. A few feathers are attached at the forward end of this cover. The hind end falls in a streamer of some length, to which feathers are attached that are lashed with sinew wrapping to thongs passing through the skin, and knotted behind. The first wand has at the forward end of the handle two thongs, ten small crow or magpie feathers, and two tufts of green-dyed horsehair. The skin hanging from the handle is painted dark blue, and ten or a dozen green-dyed feathers are fastened to it. The second wand has at one end of the handle-cover three large white feathers trimmed to the quill

along the lower half of their length, and ornamented with
yellow and green dyed plumes wrapped to the quill with sinew.
The hanging skin-strip is painted red; from it hang about ten
red-dyed feathers, and at the end a bit·of blue ribbon and a
small purple-dyed plume.

Fig. 126 shows a form of quirt more or less typical of the
ghost-dance. As in most Indian whips, the handle is much
more prominent than the whip itself. In ceremonial whips
such as this, the handle is of course by far the most important

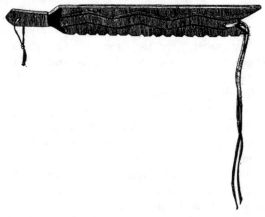

Fig. 126 (₃₈₀₀). A Quirt used in the Ghost-dance. Total length, 98 cm.

portion. This piece suggests the feathered board wands carried by the dancers of the two highest degrees in the first of
the series of tribal ceremonies. Such imitations were not
rare. The black sword (Fig. 56) described in connection with
the regalia of this first dance is actually a ghost-dance model
made in imitation of the proper regalia.

The present piece has a different handle. The body is a
board about three inches wide and a foot and a half long.
The end has one large notch. One edge is grooved, the other
notched. The whip proper consists of a thong passed through
a hole in the board near the large notch at the end, and then
passed twice through a split in itself; so that both ends, which
are of equal length, hang loose. The board portion of the
implement is painted red on both sides. On one side there is

at the bottom a somewhat irregular area adjoining the handle, which is painted black. This represents a cloud. From this issue three wavy incised lines, two painted black and one yellow, which extend to the opposite end of the board. These are lightning-symbols. On the opposite side of the quirt is a large cross painted black, at the foot of which are several irregular and, in part, bifurcated lines. This pictograph represents the Christian cross with grass growing at its base. Along one edge of the board are notches, which were called both "teeth" and "steps to the sky." A yellow-painted groove along the opposite edge was called a "lightning-flash." The relation of quirts of this type to the feathered wands of the tribal ceremonies is made still clearer by the fact that the owner of this piece stated that an eagle wing-feather should be tied to the end of the implement.

A quirt (Museum No. $\frac{50}{312}$) has a twisted wooden handle, two leather thongs as whip, and a beaded loop of skin to pass around the wrist. The stick is painted red, with green lines following its spiral twist. The red represents lightning; and the green, clouds. The bead-work on the loop is chiefly white, and represents snow. Small ornaments on this are stars. Triangular figures in black, blue, and red beading, represent the sky and clouds. The blue is the sky; the red, the evening sky; and the black around the outside of the triangle, clouds.

A fan of brown hawk-feathers (Museum No. $\frac{50}{323}$) used at the crow-dance and on similar occasions is made of eight feathers set into a trapezoidal piece of rawhide bent on itself, recalling the construction of the upright head-dresses used in the biita-ha^{n}wu dance. This piece of rawhide forms the handle of the fan. It is covered with soft skin painted red, is embroidered with beads, and is slit into a short fringe above. From the bottom a few longer thongs hang down; at the ends of these thongs are a few white beads. The bead-work on both sides of the handle is approximately heart-shaped. On the back it is light blue with a red-and-white border. In the centre is a dark-blue Maltese cross. On the front is a light-blue area in which there are represented in dark-blue beads a bird and two small crosses. Across the breast of the bird is a crescent of red beads, the ends of the crescent pointing downward. From the lower end of the handle there hang, besides the half-dozen thongs mentioned, two spotted eagle-feathers ornamented at the base with bits of red and yellow ribbon. The edge of one of these feathers is cut into notches a few inches up from its base. The heart-shaped figures of bead-work are said to represent the heart. The bird is said to be the crow. The crosses are no doubt the morning star. The thongs are said to represent rain; and the white beads at their ends, hail.

Hand mirrors, usually mounted in carved wooden frames, are used by the Arapaho, as by the Assiniboine and by other Plains tribes, in connection with the ceremonials that have

originated in recent times from or as the Omaha, crow, or grass dance, and which also received new impetus at the time of the ghost-dance. A southern Arapaho specimen obtained by Rev. W. C. Roe is shown in Fig. 127. The wooden frame has much the shape of a bootjack. A circular mirror about three inches in diameter occupies the middle of the side not shown in the illustration. Two areas, one circular and one crescentic, are cut through the wood. The mirror and the round hole represent the sun; the crescent, the moon. From the hole a wavy incised line painted green issues, passes by the side of the mirror, and thence in an irregular course down one of the forked ends of the piece. Below the mirror, a Maltese cross is cut in low relief, and painted yellow. This is the inevitable morning star. Between each two of its arms, two or three lines radiate, no doubt indicating its shining. Along the edge of the inside of the fork, on one side only, is an incised

Fig. 127 ($\frac{50}{878}$). Wooden Frame for a Mirror. Length, 45 cm.; width, 11 cm.

line painted yellow, the end of which touches the morning-star figure. This line is the path of the morning star. On the opposite side of the object, which is the one shown in the illustration, is a heavy incised line painted white, and nearly surrounding the crescentic portion cut out of the wood. From one horn of this surrounding crescentic line a smaller wavy, somewhat irregular line, painted white and green, extends diagonally a short distance downward. On the opposite side of this crescentic figure the two lines do not quite meet. One of them ends in an incised line painted blue and extending down the entire length of the following edge. This is the course of the moon. Roughly parallel to this green line, but wavy instead of straight, is an unpainted line, which touches the end of an arm of a human figure in the centre of the board. This human figure, which is in low relief and painted red, represents the owner of the implement; and the line in contact with the end of his arm is the path of his life. The figure holds in the other outstretched arm a pipe with bowl upward, and on its head is a green-painted symbol representing a cedar-branch worn on the head. Along one edge of the piece are a number of notches, painted green and representing steps to heaven. From the top of the frame hang two ribbons and two strips of white fur, apparently of a horse. These, perhaps, are substitutes for weasel-skins.

A feathered stick (Plate LXXIX), xawaa^n, — used in the crow-dance as a signal to start the dance, and stuck into the ground in the intervals between dances, — is covered with skin painted blue or green to represent the sky. The magpie, and, perhaps, crow feathers fastened to it, are people dancing. Dyed bits of plumes and feathers, attached to the ends of the feathers, represent the head-dresses worn by the dancers. Small bells attached at each end of the stick are breath or shouting (niitouhuut). The feathers are attached by thongs passing through a pair of small holes in the skin, and knotted. One end of the thong hangs free, the other is lashed to the quill of a feather by a wrapping of sinew.

An interesting cane was obtained among the southern Arapaho (Museum No. $\frac{50}{743}$). It is said to have been carved in accordance with a vision, and it is therefore probably more or less connected with the ghost-dance. It does not seem to have had any special purpose, or to have been used only on certain occasions, but to have been carried whenever there was suitable opportunity, as at gatherings or dances. At such times, it was said to have been generally repainted. At the top of the cane is a brass cap, and from this hang a number of magpie and other feathers. These are the only ornaments of the stick, other than the carving. The lower third of the cane is carved with four parallel lines winding in a spiral six times around the stick. These are said to represent lightning. Above these spiral lines are two figures of fish, on opposite sides of the cane, so arranged that the tips of their fins and tails are in contact. This arrangement holds also for the figures on the remainder of the cane, which are always in pairs that are in contact. Above the fish come deer-heads without horns, representing does; and above these, in relief, is a plain band about an inch in width. Next follow deer-heads with double-branching horns, kit-foxes, deer-heads with once-branched horns, and again kit-foxes. The feathers hanging from the top of the stick are said to denote people and clouds.

Forked sticks of some length, pointed at the bottom, are used in the crow, and perhaps in the ghost, dance to take meat from kettles. Two specimens from the northern Arapaho are in the Museum. One of these (Museum No. $\frac{50}{1083}$) is higher than a man, and it is wrapped for the greater part of its length with woolly buffalo-skin. Near the point of the fork, and at each of the ends of the fork, an eagle-feather is attached by a yellow thong. The white portion of these feathers is stained somewhat yellow. The three feathers are tipped with red plumes attached with brown cement. From one end of the fork there hangs also a tuft of green-dyed horsehair; from the other, green and red horsehair. Near the lower end, the stick is wrapped with blue cloth instead of with buffalo-hair. At each end of this cloth-wrapped portion of the stick are tufts of red-dyed horsehair. The very lowest end of the stick is painted yellow.

Fig. 128 shows a fork of about half the length of the preceding. The stick is painted orange-yellow, and about the middle, including the entire length of the shorter prong, is wrapped with light-blue beads. Yellow and green bands on this light-blue ground-color are said to denote songs. From

each end of the fork hang two
brown-and-white hawk or eagle
feathers tipped with unusually long
tufts of light-blue hair.

Fig. 129 shows an implement
used in the ghost-dance, apparently
to aid in the act of hypnotization
of the dancer. It consists of a
longer and a shorter stick enclosed
in a single covering of skin, which
holds them together, and forms a
joint where the ends of the two
sticks meet. At the opposite end
of the smaller stick, the skin covering is stuffed to form a head for
the implement. It is said that
when the object is held at the
joint, and a dancer is tapped over
the body with it, it makes him
dizzy. From the lower end of the
specimen hang a few strips of skin.
The skin covering is painted dark
green. On each side of the head is
embroidered a rude representation
of a crow. On one side, this embroidery is red for the head and
body, and white for the tail and
wings. On the opposite side of the
head, the two colors are reversed.

Model of Sacred Pipe. — Fig. 130
shows a wooden model of the sacred
tribal flat pipe with accompani-
ments, as it was seen in a dream
by the maker, and made by him in
connection with the ghost-dance.
This man, though elderly, had
never seen the sacred pipe itself,
as he is a southern Arapaho: con-

Fig. 128 ($\frac{50}{1087}$). Pointed Stick used
in serving Meat. Length, 95 cm.

sequently his pipe differs materially from the actual sacred pipe, which is tubular. On one side of the present pipe is

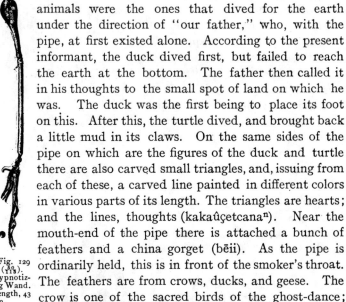

carved a turtle; on the other, a duck. These two animals were the ones that dived for the earth under the direction of "our father," who, with the pipe, at first existed alone. According to the present informant, the duck dived first, but failed to reach the earth at the bottom. The father then called it in his thoughts to the small spot of land on which he was. The duck was the first being to place its foot on this. After this, the turtle dived, and brought back a little mud in its claws. On the same sides of the pipe on which are the figures of the duck and turtle there are also carved small triangles, and, issuing from each of these, a carved line painted in different colors in various parts of its length. The triangles are hearts; and the lines, thoughts (kakaûçetcana^n). Near the mouth-end of the pipe there is attached a bunch of feathers and a china gorget (bēii). As the pipe is ordinarily held, this is in front of the smoker's throat.

Fig. 129 (₁₁₃).
Hypnotiz-
ing Wand.
Length, 43
cm.

The feathers are from crows, ducks, and geese. The crow is one of the sacred birds of the ghost-dance; the duck is connected with the sacred pipe; and of the geese it is said, that, at the beginning of the world, they flew about looking for land on which to settle, to which action there is also a reference in the sun-dance.

With the pipe are four flat sticks, each somewhat over a foot in length and an inch in width. These are painted, covered with incised carvings, and the incisions are also painted. The pipe is carried in the hand during the ghost-dance, with two of the sticks (which are green) held alongside of it, and the two others (which are red) outside of these. The pictographic carving on both sides of the four sticks is interpreted from below upwards, on each stick, in the following order : —

At the bottom of the first stick (Fig. 1, Plate LXXX) is a picture of the father who directed the duck and the turtle to dive. Following him are figures of the duck and the turtle, and then of a person representing mankind. Above him is the crow, then there is a rosebush (yēiniici), the first plant on earth.

On the opposite side of this stick is represented the sacred tribal pipe. A black oblong figure is the life-symbol, hiiteni. Then follows niihi (" bird," or sometimes specifically " eagle ").

Fig. 130 (³⁰⁄₃₉₇, *a*), Model of the Sacred Tribal Flat Pipe. Length, 39 cm.

On another stick (Fig. 2) are two figures of women, one yellow and the other red, praying while holding shinny-sticks. A green oblong figure represents the earth; the birds are crows; and a green triangle in a black rectangle is a woman's heart. A woman's figure in green and yellow represents the mythical character Whirlwind-Woman, who assisted in the making of the earth. Above her are four lines of different colors, — black, yellow, green, white, representing four winds; and a black area at the end of the stick denotes the sky.

On the other side of this stick are represented successively a person; a tent; a buffalo, signifying the sun-dance; a white buffalo, signifying the women's buffalo-dance; a magpie; a crow; a spirit, literally, shadow (bätääçä^n), wearing an upright bow at the back of his head in place of the ordinary feather; and a black heart (denoting sleep and dreams) in a green rectangle.

The third stick (Fig. 1, Plate LXXXI) shows in sequence the moon; a bird painted red; a black tent, supposed to be in the sky; a person, denoting mankind; a bow and arrow; the moon; the morning star and a line from it, which denotes its course as it rises. The first moon is circular; the second, an inverted crescent.

The opposite side of this stick is green, and denotes the earth. There is painted on it a yellow arrow, the means of subsistence.

The fourth stick (Fig. 2) is carved on one side with the figures successively of a weasel; a cedar, which is used for incense; a bird painted yellow, and indicating paint; a yellow and a green wavy line, representing the bird's sight (çana^{n}); the moon, represented by a solid black circle; the stars, indicated by small dots; and the sky, represented by a rectangular black area.

On the opposite side is a black figure of a pipe. Seven holes at the upper end of this side of the stick denote the seven old men. This side of the stick has a number of notches drawn transversely across it. Some of these pass entirely across the stick, and are painted so as to be red and white; but the majority are smaller. The notches denote lapse of time, — the larger ones, the time of which there is knowledge; and the more numerous ones, the time previous. It does not appear that the notches were intended to represent years or other definite periods. The total number on the stick is a hundred and ninety; but the maker was under the impression that the number was larger.

The owner of this model of the sacred pipe possessed also a guessing-game set with numerous accompanying head-dresses (partly shown in Fig. 1, Plate LXIX; Fig. 1, Plate LXXI; and Fig. 138) and the ceremonial quirt of Fig. 126.

The following is an approximate translation of a prayer addressed to this model of the sacred pipe by its owner's wife on parting with it: —

"Through reverence I have never given you up. I have kept you pure. I have prayed to you. I wish to live in happiness while the sun travels and runs. I wish for long breath while the tent stands fast. I went with you, and you went before me. Pity me, with my dear children and the man, my husband, who lives with me. I know it will be a good and safe place where you will be, my grandfather. My father, we part from you that it may be good. Remember us. Every morning we will be poor. It is not we who give you up, it is our father. From this time on there may be long life, and a tent, and happiness, and a good heart, until the time made by our father for meeting again with all my children and my relatives, when they will smile on account of the food, and as they meet one another and are together. We have told of your directions to us that are powerful and above us. Pity us, and let the way we travel on the earth be clear, and let it be smooth before our walking. May our life be good and easy during the day; let sickness be far away. This person [the interpreter] who is serving, may he travel where it is good during the day, and sleep at night. I ask this for him. Your body is going away with this white man. Thanks. It is well. I think of you, and shall never forget your purposes and your instructions, my grandfather. My father, it is well. I am glad for food and clothing and horses of different colors. Thanks. I say to you, Pity us. Do not forget us, for I with my children am poor. I do not think too much of myself, therefore I pray to you. Thanks, thanks, my grandfather and my father. During day and night a lasting life — that I ask of you."

THE CROW-DANCE. — The following is an account of part of a crow-dance seen in September, 1899, among the southern Arapaho.

The dance was held in a confined camp-circle near the north fork of the Canadian River. The dancing-place was in the middle of this camp-circle, the ground of which was not quite level. Two or three sides of the dancing-place were surrounded by shelters of sticks and canvas. The old and middle-aged men sat on the west; the dancers, to the south and the north of the dancing-place, spectators standing behind them. At the eastern end was the drum. Here there were four women who acted as servants for the dance. Most of the women were on the eastern side of the dancing-place. The songs were comparatively short, and the intermissions at first of some length, especially when horses were given away, or announcements made. Toward the end of the dancing, however, late in the afternoon, the intermissions grew shorter and shorter. The dancing did not begin until about the middle of the afternoon, and lasted perhaps three hours. The drum hung over four sticks; and about eight men sat crowded closely together around it, singing, and all beating it in unison, with sticks the ends of which were wrapped with cloth. In beating the drum, they moved their entire body. Their singing was in the throat, but very much constrained, and without an attempt at producing a clear sound. As is customary, they also did not sing loudly. They looked either at the drum, or straight in front of them, without watching the dancing. The drummers were all comparatively young men. The drumming and singing for each dance began low. As the drumming rose in volume, the dancers got up from their places.

The dancers were very variously dressed. Some of them wore crow-tails, and others had other feather ornaments. Some were entirely naked, except for a breech-cloth; but these generally carried something in their hands. Knee-bands with rattles, and especially with bells, were worn by many. A large proportion carried ceremonial objects of some kind. One man was painted entirely red over the body; some, yellow; some, chiefly black. One man had hand-marks in red and black slapped over his body. One man was painted black on one side and yellow on the other; another, red above, and blue below. The painting was quite different from the sun-dance painting in its general lack of character. Every man dressed differently, apparently merely following his choice; and there was an almost equal difference in the painting and in the dance-steps.

The dancers moved about at random and irregularly within the square dancing-space, passing one another in all directions. Some of the dancers moved rather violently; others, rather slowly and quietly. The only feature common to the dancing of all was the double-step, with a greater or less forward inclination of the body, familiar from Indian dances. The degree of this inclination and of the gesticulation varied in great measure with the rapidity of the songs and drumming. The arms were carried at pleasure. A middle-aged man who was regarded as the best dancer was one of the most sedate, and his dancing differed less from ordinary walking than that of the others. He put down his foot almost flat, and raised it only slightly at the heel for the second part of the step, but then set it down on the ground with great tension and some tremor. Some men swung their feet, and others shuffled them; some, after putting the foot down, merely raised themselves on the toe for the second part of the step. The women danced much more slowly and heavily than the men; the second part of each dance-step being only a sinking-down of the body on the foot. One old woman, however, raised her feet, and skipped along with a little swing.

After a few songs, horses were led into the dancing-place, all of them loaded with property. A crier, who wore a sort of flag as blanket, called out the names of the recipients, who received a stick from the donor. In some cases, the horse was not actually brought to the dancing-place. The recipient then thanked the donor and his wife, or, if it was a woman, her and her husband or her children, by passing his hand down in front of their foreheads and faces. Sometimes the donor was kissed, and occasionally embraced. After this, the recipient went back to his place among the spectators. Several old women, after receiving gifts, stood up in the dancing-place, and sang. Many of the horses were given away for ear-piercing or hair-cutting performed on children. The children were brought in and the motions of piercing the ear were gone through with a stick; but the piercing was not actually done until subsequently. The man to do the piercing stood before the drum, facing it, and told a war-story, generally in a low voice, but with gestures. At the mention of the deed, the drum was struck sharply two or four times, and the women cried "Niiiii!" Young men who had not been to war, and were given a horse for piercing a child's ear, got an older man to count coup for them, and subsequently gave him some of the property received with the horse. One young man changed his name. As he stood at the western end of the open place, facing westward, an old man stood behind him, and spoke loudly for some time, part of his speech being a war-experience. One man gave a horse and buggy for the ear-piercing of a grandchild only a few days old. Three visiting northern Arapaho from Wyoming received many gifts, especially of money, in order to enable them to return home. When the crier himself received a stick indicating the gift of a horse, and called out "Hahou" (thanks), there was a general laugh. Most of the horses brought into the dancing-place to be given away were painted in yellow with spots on the shoulders, a stripe down the back and sometimes across the hind quarters, a circle around the eye, and with the mane and tail yellowed. A few horses of dark color were painted in green.

Within the dancing-place were three poles to which flags were fastened. The middle of these was a favorite place for middle-aged and old women to stand and cry, raising their right hand. The crying was ceremonial, resembling a chant. A Cheyenne woman provided food for all the dancers and spectators, and, in return, property was contributed for her. She received several large bundles of calico and blankets. Altogether, about forty horses were given away. The four women who acted as servants for the dance sometimes drove away the dogs that found their way to the dancing-place.

Toward the end of the afternoon there were several more special dances, — one for food, another with bows and arrows, and a third with spoons. A kettle of food was brought in. The front row of people around the dancing-place rose and danced in their places, thus forming a hollow square. Then three or four crow tail-pieces were laid on the ground to the north and south. At the east, four men stood up in front of the drum, and danced standing there. About ten men got up on the northern and southern sides of the dancing-place, facing each other. These two bodies danced standing. Then each body followed one or two leaders, turning about. Three or four of the leaders took up the crow tail-pieces, and put them on. The singing now became much faster and more excited. The two groups now danced around the dancing-place to meet each other. On coming together, the leaders of each line would recoil somewhat, and make a gesture, whereupon the two lines would pass each other. At the western end of the dancing-place, one of the lines passed outside of the other. At the eastern end, where they met again in the same way, the outside line would pass inside. This was done four times. After this, the two lines formed at the north and south again, still dancing. Two of the dancers now brought the kettle into the middle. Both the lines now advanced toward it, stretching out their arms, and returned four times. The fifth time they made a rush, and all dipped their fingers into it. Thereupon they returned to their seats. It seems that in this action the dancers represent magpies. The three visiting northern Arapaho were showing this particular dance to the southern Arapaho, and led one of the two lines.

After this, four men made a dance with bows and arrows, only the two leaders, however, carrying bows. The general course of this was much the same as in the preceding food-dance, except that there were only two men on a side. In finally approaching the kettle, the four men stood abreast to the east of it, whereas previously the two lines had been to the north and south.

Four men then danced, carrying spoons. They faced one another, advanced, passed one another, making a gesture toward the kettle of food, and then occupied one another's places. After thus passing one another several times, they stood abreast east of the kettle, moved to it, dipped their spoons into it, and then poured the contents of the spoons on the ground, saying "Hahou" (thanks). Thereupon they took their seats.

Another dance, similar to the last, was then made by four men. The song sung at the beginning of this dance was to the words, "I am holding the sky standing on the earth, says our father."

At the conclusion of this special dance, a few more of the general and more irregular dances that had characterized the first part of the ceremony were held, and food was passed to the spectators by women. Thereupon the gathering broke up. The dancing was resumed again in the evening.

According to an account obtained from an elderly man in

Wyoming, the Arapaho believe that the so-called Omaha dance originated with the Pawnees and the Osages. Both tribes were connected by means of it, and it was a dance signifying friendship. The dance was then brought to the Omaha, and they practised it until one of them was told by the Thunder that the dance belonged to him. He said, since the people were practising it, he would show them how to hold it right. He told them to make tails of eagle-feathers and owl-feathers. The owl-feathers were to be red. The dancers were also to carry a wooden whistle to represent a gun. A man who had been wounded in battle was to carry such a whistle, and wear one of the feathered tails, the red of the feathers symbolizing blood. The Thunder directed that these objects were to be made as he said, and nothing further was to be added to them. A grass was to be used as incense. The Thunder directed, that, when the people were going to eat food at the dance, they were not to hide anything. If a man had slept with his wife since the dance began, he was not to take any of the food. The others were to eat. When a man passed by the food, the spoon was motioned with to the four directions, and then held up. The Thunder also directed that the people should not cohabit during a thunderstorm. A man who disobeyed him was killed by lightning. The Omaha brought the dance to the Sioux. The Sioux brought the dance to the Arapaho and other tribes. They brought it in connection with the tceäk'çan, a sacred bundle offered to friendly tribes, and which, if refused, would cause defeat in war. The Arapaho had the dance until, at the time of the ghost-dance, the older limitations as to the kind and color of feathers and the accompanying regulations were given up or modified; and the ceremony was called "crow-dance."

THE GUESSING-GAME. — Rather elaborate sets of a form of guessing-game were made in considerable numbers at the time of the ghost-dance movement. These sets consist of buttons hidden in the hand, of sticks used as counters, and usually of other sticks and feathers which are used as pointers, as symbols of gifts or of food, and in other semi-ceremonial ways. All the sticks not actually used as counters, and many of those so used, are ornamented with feathers, or otherwise. In addition, head-dresses of the various types described were not infrequently made specifically to be worn in connection with the game. As these do not differ in any way from ordinary ghost-dance head-dresses, they will be mentioned here, only to illustrate the degree of elaboration with which such game-sets were made.

The buttons hidden in the hands, and guessed at, form pairs, or multiples of pairs, up to eight. The pointers form a pair, and the counters and other sticks form two sets of equal numbers, distinguished from one another by their ornamentation, and used respectively by the two sides of players. One set of sticks is usually black; the other, red. The players using the black sticks are called "magpies;" those with the red sticks, "crows." The number of such stick counters seems to be most frequently ten. In one set there are twenty; but the ten sticks used by each side are of two kinds. There is a secondary tendency toward twelve sticks. One set (Museum No. $\frac{50}{893}$) has ten plain counters and two ornamented singing-wands. Another set (Museum No. $\frac{50}{57}$) has ten counters and twelve ornamented gift or food sticks used in connection with gifts and invitations. A northern Arapaho set of invitation-sticks has twelve sticks, besides special ones for the host and the singers. The head-dresses used at these games are frequently made in pairs, and worn by people on the opposite sides.

While there is a general similarity running through all the sets that have been seen or obtained for the Museum, the uses to which similar pieces, especially the sticks, are put, are quite different. One set (Museum No. $\frac{50}{96}$) has feathered sticks which are used as counters; but, as they have small bells attached to them at the top, it is not unlikely they were used also as rattles during the singing accompanying the game. One odd stick in this set, similar to those used as counters, is held by a person who prays during or before the game, and who apparently, therefore, acts as director. In another set (Museum No. $\frac{50}{55}$), the most elaborate in the Museum, and obtained for it by Rev. Walter C. Roe, there are three kinds of sticks, — plain sticks merely rubbed over with paint, and used as counters; similar sticks ornamented with feathers and fur, and given to women who cook for the gathering; and two sticks considerably longer than the others, and forming a third class. These two are more elaborately decorated than the others, and are used as pointers when a player signifies in which hand he guesses that a button is held. In another set (Museum No. $\frac{50}{302}$), sticks ornamented with feathers, fur, and skin fringes, are used as counters; whereas one longer stick in the form of a cross, ornamented with skin fringe, and somewhat recalling the pair of sticks in the preceding set used as pointers, is set in the ground between the two lines of players, in front of the person directing the game. A fourth set comprises plain sticks painted over, and two similar sticks to the ends of which a few feathers are attached. The plain sticks are counters: the feathered ones are shaken as singing-wands by the leaders of the two sides. The set of invitation-sticks mentioned as obtained from the northern Arapaho (Museum No. $\frac{50}{1097}$) closely resembles in appearance the sticks used in connection with the present game among the southern Arapaho. Plain sticks painted over are ordinary invitation-sticks in this set. They are also used to indicate the presentation of a gift, in the way in which any stick is thus frequently used to express the gift especially of a horse. Two similar sticks in this same set are forked at the upper end, and ornamented with feathers and fringes. These are given to the singers, and appear also to be shaken by them during the singing. A single stick of a third class is ornamented like the two singers' sticks, but is unforked and longer. This stick is kept by the host of the occasion, who, of course, directs the gathering. It will be seen that in this respect, as well as in its greater length and in being the only one of its kind in the set, it resembles the longer cross stick mentioned in the third set.

The different classes of sticks thus have, in all, the following uses, — plain sticks, counters, food or gift sticks; feathered sticks, counters, food or gift sticks, singing-wands; pair of forked sticks, pointers, singing-wands; one special stick, direc-

tor's or host's stick.   A full set of objects for the game would
seem to consist of hiding-buttons in pairs, a pair of feathers for
pointers, sticks for counters, ornamented sticks as food-sticks,
a pair of specially ornamented sticks for two singers, and a
single longer stick for the host, besides accessory head-dresses.
Most of the objects would be in two sets of different colors,
sometimes red and yellow, but usually red and black.   Actually no set has been found so complete as this.

Various sets of this game will now be described separately.

Museum set No. $\frac{50}{592}$ consists of two buttons, ten plain
sticks used as counters, two similar ornamented sticks used
as singing-wands, an eagle-feather used as a pointer, a pair of
circular beaded head-dresses, and a number of head-dresses,
not, perhaps, so directly connected with the game, and of
several different types.   Of the two hiding-buttons, one is a
stone found on a hill where the maker of the set had gone to
fast and on which he had seen a vision.   It has rudely the
shape of a foot or moccasin, and he regarded it as a direct
gift to himself.   The other counter is a leg-bone of a turtle
which he killed on this hill.   Around each end of this bone is
tied a thong.   Of the ten stick counters, the five red ones were
said to denote crows, or to be used by players called " crows; "
the five black ones, magpies.   The red and black sticks are
painted respectively black and red at the ends.   The two feathered sticks held by the leaders of the two sides during the
game, and shaken no doubt as an accompaniment to the singing, are identical with the plain sticks, but for their feather
attachments.   These consist on each stick of five small black
feathers ornamented with red-dyed plumes at the base, and
each attached to a red-painted thong.   The eagle-feather
used as a pointer is ornamented with red plumes both at its
base and at its tip.   The two circular head-dresses, one of
which is shown in Fig. 111, are worn by a certain player on
each side, apparently the same man who holds one of the
feathered sticks.   The framework of the hoops is wood,
around which a string of beads is wound.   There are four
spots of beading of a different color; and two thin sinew
strings bisect the interior of each hoop.   Four plumes are

attached to each ring, and a thong serves to tie it to the hair. One hoop has yellow plumes and yellow beads, with the four smaller beaded areas in red; and the thongs attaching its plumes are red. The other hoop is dark blue with light-blue beads in four places. The plumes attached to it seem to have been faintly dyed green, and the thongs attaching them are also green. The yellow hoop represents daylight. The four red areas on it denote paint and mankind. On the other hoop the dark-blue beading represents the highest sky, the future world. The four areas of light-blue beading represent the lower sky, apparently the atmosphere. The green of the feathers denotes this world. While this symbolism is entirely one of colors, the two head-dresses are no doubt also world-symbols as regards their shape. Six other head-dresses obtained from the same man, and more or less connected in his mind and in their use with the objects described, are the following: Two head-dresses of trimmed feathers mounted on sticks — one of four crow-feathers (Fig 127) and the other of a single hawk-feather with a few small owl-feathers at the base — appear to have been worn by the leaders of the two sides of players. A pair of head-dresses consisting of dyed and mounted plumes were also worn, each by one player on a side. One of these is white above and red below (Museum No. $\frac{50}{393}$): the other is red above and green below. The colors of these two plumes were said to denote the various colors of the world. The fifth head-dress consists of an eagle-feather similar to the one used as a pointer (Fig. 132). It is ornamented with a red plume at the base, and appears to have lost a similar ornament at its tip. A thong passing through the base of the quill is all that designates this feather as a head-dress, and not a pointer. The sixth head-dress consists of the skins of a blackbird and of a smaller redbird, tied breast to breast, and attached to thongs for wear on the head. A seventh head-dress, which the owner refused to part with, consisted of a white eagle-plume mounted on a stick, and ornamented at the base with red plumes. This owner had been the white-fool in the crazy-dance, and had had a dream in which he saw people passing, and himself following last, wearing this white plume on his head, just as the white-fool always follows the crowd of dancers.

In the set $\frac{50}{96}$, shown in Fig. 131, there are four counters. The first button (*a*) appears to consist of wound and

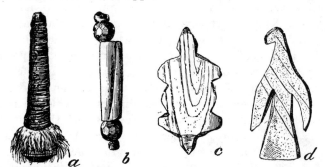

Fig. 131 ($\frac{50}{96}$, *a–d*). Counters for a Guessing-game. Length of *a*, 5 cm.; of *b*, 4.5 cm.; of *c*, 3.5 cm.; of *d*, 4 cm.

knotted thong. At the upper end a bit of rabbit-fur is attached. This end of the object is wound with porcupine-quills dyed yellow; the remainder of the surface, with quills dyed light green. The entire object represents the whirlwind, which, it will be remembered, plays a part in Arapaho mythology in the making of the earth. A piece of eagle-quill (*b*) about an inch long, through which a thong is passed, at each end of which is a light-blue bead, symbolizes a white eagle in the sky. The blue beads denote the sky or clouds. A figure of a turtle (*c*) — cut out of a flat piece of wood, and painted red, yellow, and green — refers to the world. A small bird (*d*) — cut out of rawhide lightly painted green, the edges being red — represents a white crow in the sky. It is evident that one pair of the buttons refers to the earth, the other to the sky; also that, in shape and appearance, the four buttons divide into two pairs, one flat and one long, each pair consisting of one earth and one sky symbol. Two dyed feathers are used as pointers in the game-set. One of these is shown in Fig. 132. Both of these feathers have a second narrower undyed black-and-white wing-feather tied over them. The quill of the main feather and that of the superimposed feather are tied together at the base with wrappings of sinew, and the tops of their quills are tied together with a thin string of sinew. The narrower upper feather is ornamented at the base with dyed plumes. Where the bases of the quills of the two feathers are joined, a braid of sweet-grass is attached to them by a sinew wrapping near each of its ends. The main feather in the pointer shown in the illustration is dyed red, and the plume at the base of the superimposed feather is also red. The principal feather in the other pointer is blue; but, instead of there being a small plume, the base of the superimposed feather seems to have been dyed light

green. The sticks in this set, of which there are eleven (ten used as counters and the eleventh held up by a person who prays), are thicker in proportion to their length than is customary in these game-sets. Five of the counters are painted dark green, which to the Arapaho is the equivalent of black, and five red. The sticks of both colors are ornamented at the top by a wrapping of fur (apparently of rabbit-skin), by a small brass bell, and by two black feathers (probably of a crow) the bases of which are ornamented with red-dyed plumes, and which hang from thongs passing around the top of the stick just above the fur. Across both transverse ends of each stick are two intersecting notches. These notches in the green-black sticks (Fig. 133) are painted red; in the red sticks, blue. All the sticks are ornamented with carving in low relief. On the red sticks there is at each

Fig. 132 (⁵⁰⁄₉₉). *f.* Feather used as a Pointer in a Guessing-game. Length, 34 cm.

end a figure of a bird and a Maltese cross, representing the crow and the morning star. The heads of the birds are towards the middle of the stick. The bird at the lower end is painted green; the morning-star cross near it, yellow. The bird at the upper end of the stick is blue, and the cross near it green. On the dark-green sticks (Fig. 134) there are at each end similar figures of the morning-star and the crescent moon. In the middle of these green sticks a pointed figure forms a scroll of a single turn around the stick. All the carving on the green sticks seems to have been painted red, and then dark blue over the red. While nothing was said in connection with this set as to any reference of the sticks to crows and magpies respectively, it will be noted that the red sticks are ornamented with figures of crows.

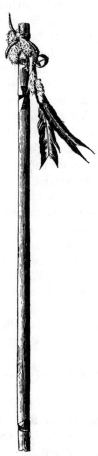

The guessing-game set Museum Nos. $\frac{50}{55}-\frac{50}{58}$ has been mentioned as the most elaborate of this kind in the Museum. There are two hiding-buttons somewhat more than an inch long, and nearly cylindrical. These are made of skin wrapped with red and blue beads, forming transverse stripes. Two sticks, each about three feet long, are said to be pointers; but their sharpened ends and their elaborate decoration make it appear probable that they had also some other use, which included their being set up in the ground. One of these sticks is shown in Fig. 135. It will be seen that near the base it has a short fork. Above this is tied a strip of fur and a small hoop of wood wrapped with dyed corn-husk, recently used by the southern Arapaho as a substitute for porcupine-quills. This wrapping is yellow,

Fig. 133 ($\frac{50}{55}$,9). Counting-stick for a Guessing-game. Length, 46.5 cm.

Fig. 134 ($\frac{50}{58}$, *l*). Counting-stick for a Guessing-game. Length, 46 cm.

except in four places, where it is red. These red areas are bordered by black. Such a hoop is almost invariably a world-symbol among the Arapaho, but may have other signification in addition. The stick itself is painted red. Near the upper end of the stick are attached two pheasant-feathers and ten small

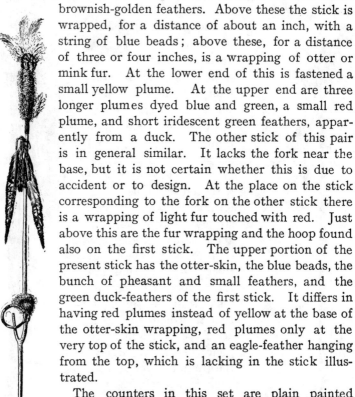

brownish-golden feathers. Above these the stick is wrapped, for a distance of about an inch, with a string of blue beads ; above these, for a distance of three or four inches, is a wrapping of otter or mink fur. At the lower end of this is fastened a small yellow plume. At the upper end are three longer plumes dyed blue and green, a small red plume, and short iridescent green feathers, apparently from a duck. The other stick of this pair is in general similar. It lacks the fork near the base, but it is not certain whether this is due to accident or to design. At the place on the stick corresponding to the fork on the other stick there is a wrapping of light fur touched with red. Just above this are the fur wrapping and the hoop found also on the first stick. The upper portion of the present stick has the otter-skin, the blue beads, the bunch of pheasant and small feathers, and the green duck-feathers of the first stick. It differs in having red plumes instead of yellow at the base of the otter-skin wrapping, red plumes only at the very top of the stick, and an eagle-feather hanging from the top, which is lacking in the stick illustrated.

The counters in this set are plain painted sticks, ten in number.

Fig. 135 ($\frac{5\,9}{5\,8}$, *b*).
Pointer used in a Guessing-game. Length, 99 cm.

The feathered sticks used in this set are twelve in number, and, which is unusual, are of four or five different types. Four of the sticks are painted red; eight, dark green, which is no doubt, in this case as in others, the equivalent of black. One pair of red sticks is wrapped at the upper end with fur, perhaps of a rabbit, touched with red paint. From the upper

end of each stick hang a crescent-shaped piece of hide covered
on one side with beads, and a bunch of feathers. On one stick,
the beading on the crescent is red and the feathers are red
with yellow plumes at the base: on the
other stick, the crescent is beaded yellow
and the four feathers are dyed yellow.
The two other red sticks of this set
appear to have a somewhat darker fur
wrapping at the top. Attached to one
are six small barred feathers, a plume
dyed orange with a small barred feather
at its base, and part of the wing of a
magpie, consisting of four or five feathers
ornamented with red plumes at the base.
All these feathers are attached to the
stick by thongs painted yellow. The other
stick appears to have lost most of its
feathers, but to have been similar. One
of this pair of sticks has near its base
the remains of white plumes attached by
sinew wrapping. The other shows no
signs at the present time of such ornaments. The eight green-painted sticks
are of three types. The most elaborate
pair is ornamented in the middle and at
the lower end with gray down feathers
wrapped to the stick with sinew; another
type, comprising four sticks, has such
down ornamentation only at the base (Fig.
136); and a third type, again consisting
of a pair, lacks such down attachments.
The two green sticks with double down
ornamentation are painted green (only
over the upper half), and have attached
at the upper end a small eagle or hawk

Fig. 136 (⅔₉, *d*). Feathered
Stick for a Guessing-game.
Length, 51 cm.

feather, four black feathers, and one other feather, as well
as a few gray down feathers of the same kind as those
wrapped on farther down the stick. The four sticks with

gray down only at the base are painted distinctly green, only over the upper third of their length. The middle third appears to have been lightly painted red; and the lower third, again, lightly green. Four grayish-black feathers are attached by yellow-painted thongs to the upper ends of these sticks. On two sticks of these four there are iridescent white-edged magpie-feathers; on two others, dark-green feathers, appar-

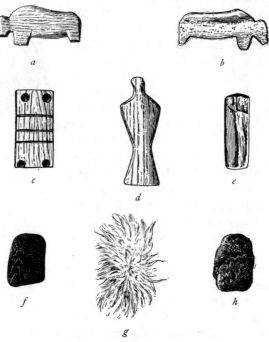

Fig. 137 (¼⁹₂₉₃) Hiding-buttons. Length of *d*, 3.5 cm.

ently also from the magpie. The two green sticks without any down on the handle are exactly like the four last described, except in this particular and in the fact that one of them has a weather-beaten white plume tied to its top. From information furnished with this valuable set by Rev. W. C. Roe, its collector, it appears that these twelve feather-ornamented sticks were invitation-sticks, either to receive or to prepare food.

Museum set No. $\frac{50}{393}$ lacks the counter-sticks, but is rich·
in hiding-buttons and accessory head-dresses. An eagle wing-
feather is used as a pointer. It is mounted on a pointed stick
ornamented at the base with one gray and one blue feath·
er and a red plume, and is tipped with a red plume. The
buttons used in this game are eight in number, and are shown
in Fig. 137. They consist of a figure of a buffalo cut out
of wood (*a*); a similar figure cut out of bone, and representing a white buffalo (*b*); a small oblong slab of stone
of natural shape, given the name of the life-symbol, hiiteni (*e*); a rectangular piece of wood, also a hiiteni symbol,
which on one side is bisected by a red-
painted line, on the other side by three
such lines, besides having two pits at each
end (*c*); a figure of a bird cut out of wood,
called simply niihi, "bird," or specifically
"eagle" (*d*); a small weathered stone (*f*);
another similar stone (*h*); and a bit of sage
covered with rabbit-fur (*g*), referring to the
Piute originator of the ghost-dance, who is
sometimes called " he who has a jack-rabbit
blanket." This set of objects was owned
by the same man who made the objects

Fig. 138 ($\frac{50}{393}$, *b*). Ornament worn by a Player
in the Guessing-game.
Diameter, 10 cm.

illustrated in Fig. 1, Plate LXXI; Fig. 2, Plate LXIX; and
Fig. 138.

The head-dresses accompanying this game-set consist in
part of feathers mounted on sticks, and in part of rawhide
crosses. The former class comprises a head-dress of four
trimmed crow-feathers, similar to the one shown in Fig. 2,
Plate LXVIII; a head-dress of three upright pheasant-feathers, shown in Fig. 2, Plate LXIX (both of these worn by
old men); and six head-dresses of down feathers, three
dyed red and three yellow (Fig. 111), worn by players on opposite sides. The rawhide head-dresses are all Maltese-cross
shaped, painted, and in part ornamented with feathers.
Three are of one size, two smaller. The three larger are worn
by the drummers in the game, the smaller by the leaders of
the two sides, who guess where the buttons on the opposing

side are held. One of the larger crosses, which is painted white (Fig. 138), was made in consequence of a dream or vision in which the owner entered a tent where gray-headed men were sitting smoking the sacred flat pipe. Being intended to be worn by the oldest men, or because it refers to old men, it is unornamented with feathers: old people dress more simply than the young. The entire ornament, because cross-shaped, of course represents the morning star. Three of the arms, however, the lower one being disregarded, have the shape of the characteristic catlinite pipe-bowl. It will also be observed that two of the arms are in addition so cut at the ends, and painted, as to show an entire pipe bowl and stem. Another of the five ornaments is similar in general shape, but uncolored instead of white (except at the ends, which are yellow), ornamented with a feather plume hanging from the end of one arm, and somewhat different in the details of its painting. A third cross is black with red across the ends of its arms and a yellow spot in the middle, near which a red-dyed down feather is attached. This piece lacks the small pipe of the two preceding specimens. Its black color was said to represent the night, during which the morning star is invisible; the red at the ends of the arms, the morning, when the star begins to appear. The yellow spot in the centre was called the heart. The two smaller crosses are painted to resemble the last two pieces, and similar feathers are attached to them. Where the fastening thongs are attached at the centre of each of these two smaller crosses there is a small stick painted red, representing the sacred straight pipe. The feathers in these small crosses are attached to the middle of the sticks, not to the rawhide itself.

Museum set No. $\frac{50}{302}$ consists of two buttons, twenty feathered sticks used as counters, and one longer stick set in the ground. The buttons are similar in shape to those of Museum set Nos. $\frac{50}{88}$–$\frac{50}{88}$, and perhaps represent an older type. They consist of sticks a little more than an inch long, and wrapped with thong. One button is painted red, the other black. In the bead-covered buttons of the previous set, red and blue beading are used in the same manner, though diversified by bands of the opposite·color. The stick — which in the present set is set up in the ground between the players, at the ends of the two rows, before the person directing the game — is more than three feet long, and painted red. A few inches from the top a small crossbar is tied to it. The ends of this, as well as the top of the stick and a place a few inches below the crossbar, are ornamented with skin fringes painted red. Both the stick and the crossbar are painted dark blue near the point of attachment of these fringes. It is not improbable that Christian motives have influenced this portion of the specimen. The stick counters in this set are twenty in number, and their lower ends are sharpened, as if for setting into the ground. The sticks are long and slender. The upper fourth of each is wrapped with sinew. Near the lower end of this sinew wrapping, a tassel of a few red-painted thongs is attached. Below this fringe, the sticks are painted, — ten of them red, and ten black. The sinew wrapping is painted of the opposite color from the stick. Each stick is ornamented at the very top with a tuft of dyed wool and with a thong wrapped in several places with porcupine-quills, and having a single sharp broad feather at its end. Of the ten black sticks, five have the tuft of wool dyed red, the quill wrappings of the thong alternately red and green, and a crow-feather hanging from the end of the stick. Five of the sticks have the tuft of wool dyed yellow; the quill wrappings of the thong are alternately red and white; and at the end of the stick is a barred hawk or owl feather. The ten black sticks are ornamented in two sets in exactly the same way. The players using the black sticks, and to whom the black button belongs, were called " magpies; " those using the red sticks and the red button, " crows."

The set of northern Arapaho invitation-sticks (Museum No. $\frac{50}{1097}$) were used to send to guests who brought food with them. On arriving, the guests each laid their sticks across the vessel of food brought by them. Twelve of the sticks in the set are perfectly plain and straight, except for a very small knobbing at the end, due apparently to their having been cut off at a joint. They are painted red. These

twelve are the sticks sent to the guests. Two sticks of equal
length with these, used by the singers, have small branches
projecting at an angle for a short distance near their upper
ends. The upper ends are ornamented with a hanging magpie
tail-feather and with five thongs wrapped with red and white
porcupine-quills. The fifteenth stick of the set, kept by the
host, has exactly the same ornamentation as the two singers'
sticks, but lacks the fork, and is a few inches longer than either
these or the plain sticks. The forked sticks (perhaps because
they are given to the singers, who also drum) were said to
represent the forked sticks on which a drum is often hung.
The quilled pendant thongs attached to the three special
sticks in the set represent water-snakes; and the wood of
which all the sticks are made is called in Arapaho "water-
snake wood." The bundle of sticks is kept together by a
thong to which a bit of whitish fur is attached.

The Hoop Game. — Another form of game prominent in
ghost-dance times consists of a hoop at which two players each
throw a pair of joined darts. Points are scored as certain parts
of the hoop, marked by ornaments, lie in contact with the
darts after the throw. The hoops are about a foot and a half
in diameter; the darts, about two feet and a half in length.
The thong connecting the darts of each pair is about half a
foot in length. About one-third way from the front the darts
are tied with this thong, and the portion of the stick forward
of the tying is usually flattened on two sides. The darts are
unpointed.

Figs. 139–141 represent models of such a game-set obtained
by the Museum through the courtesy of Rev. Walter C. Roe.
The hoop is painted red, and where it is joined it is wrapped
with fur. There are eight marks on each side of the hoop, produced by incised carving, and painted. On one side, these
ornaments are as follows. Two shallow triangular notches—
one painted blue, the other green, and forming together an hour-
glass shaped figure — were given the name hunch-back. Two
incised lines crossing at an acute angle, and painted dark blue,
represent a pair of the joined darts used with the hoop. The
third ornament, whose symbolism is unknown, is a dark-blue

rectangle notched on one side with five short yellow lines, and on the other with green lines. The fourth is a blue Maltese cross, the morning star. The fifth is again the hunch-back design; and the sixth, a dark-blue crescent moon. The seventh is similar to the third; and the eighth, painted green, is a symbol of a cedar or cedar-branch. On the opposite side, the figures are the following, — a dark-blue arrow, a hunch-back design in dark blue, a light-blue arrow, a light-blue rectangle traversed near its end by two notched white lines, a green

Fig. 139 ($\frac{50}{879}$, *a*). Model of a Game Hoop. Diameter, 43 cm.

arrow, another dark-blue hunch-back, a yellow arrow, and a light-blue rectangular figure identical with the preceding one. It is not improbable that the rectangular figures on both sides of the hoop were the hiiteni symbol. It is noticeable that the hunch-back and rectangular figures, which occur in

Fig. 140 ($\frac{50}{879}$, *b, c*). Pair of Red Darts for the Hoop Game. Length, 83 cm.

Fig. 141 ($\frac{50}{879}$. *e, d*). Pair of Blue Darts for the Hoop Game. Length, 85 cm.

pairs, are placed opposite each other on the hoop, and that the four arrows on one side are painted in four colors, and are situated at four opposite sides of the circumference.

Of the darts in this set, one pair is painted red, the other blue. The red pair is connected by a double-twisted thong painted red (Fig. 140). Where this thong is attached, the stick is wrapped with black fur. For a distance equal to about one-fourth the length of the stick, backward from this wrapping, the stick is flattened on two opposite sides, and these painted dark blue. The blue pair of darts (Fig. 141) is joined by a double-twisted yellow thong, at the attachment of which the sticks are bound with white fur. The flattened portions of this pair of darts are less than half as long as in the other pair. In one stick they are painted red; in the other, green. Two small flattened areas on each stick, about the size of a finger-nail, are painted yellow.

Museum set Nos. $\frac{5\,0}{6\,4\,4}$, $\frac{5\,0}{6\,4\,5}$, has seen use. One side of the hoop is painted red, the other side lightly with dark green. This is the familiar red and black color-dualism of the Arapaho. The red side of the hoop has carved on it two figures of birds and two rectangles with projecting acute corners, which look as if they might be turtle or more probably buffalo symbols. The birds are painted dark green; the quadrilaterals, red. On the dark-green side of the hoop are two birds and two green rectangles, each crossed by five notched lines painted red. The darts in this set are plain, — one pair red, the other dark green, — connected by twisted double thongs of the same color. The flattened portions are forward of the thongs, and are of the same color as the remainder of the stick.

In Museum set Nos. $\frac{5\,0}{6\,8\,2}$, $\frac{5\,0}{6\,8\,3}$, the hoop is blue. The outer periphery is slightly flattened, and painted green. Where it is joined are tied two small bells and two feathers, one dyed, the other cut across the end, and both ornamented with dyed plumes attached by a red-painted thong. On one side, the hoop has four marks; on the other, six. On the former are a pair of figures like the hunch-back symbols of the piece first described. One is painted yellow; the other, blue or green. The other figures on this side are a pair of rectangles, one painted red the other green. The red one is crossed by seven notched lines: the green one has cut in it a longitudinal zigzag painted blue. On the opposite side of the hoop are the same figures with two added figures of birds, one painted green or blue, the other red. The darts in this set are one pair blue, and one green, with connecting thongs of the same color. The flattened sides forward of these thongs are red. A single feather is attached to each pair where the thong joins it. This feather is dyed red, ornamented at the base with red and yellow plumes, and tipped with a blue plume.

The carved figures on these hoops are much alike in character, consisting chiefly of the hunch-back design, of rectangles with incised lines, and of bird figures. Other designs are less common, and are usually realistic. It appears that, but for lacking feather attachments, these gaming-hoops are virtually identical with the sacred tribal wheel several times referred to, and described by Dorsey.[1]

THE WHEEL GAME. — Netted hoops thrown at with arrows are made by grown-up people for boys. They are properly made of a green stick and a single long thong of buffalo-skin. The wheels are used in several ways, sometimes by two parties of boys drawn up opposite, and sometimes by a smaller number. One way of playing is to throw the wheel so that it will roll over another player's bent back. This player then runs after it to spear it.

Such a netted hoop thrown at with darts is shown in Plate LXXXII. It has a large centre mesh painted red, and called the "heart," which counts four points, if speared. All the remainder of the netting is painted blue. There are two rows of large oblong meshes intersecting at the "heart," and called "buffalo-bulls." The small hexagonal meshes occupying the body of the network are called "buffalo-cows." No points are counted, if either the buffalo bulls or cows are speared. Between the buffalo-cow meshes are small triangular interstices called "buffalo-calves." If one of these is speared, one point is scored. Along the inside of the wooden rim there are hexagonal meshes, called "wolves;" and, where the rawhide thongs turn to pass

---

[1] Arapaho Sun-dance, *op. cit.*, p. 12, Plate I.

around the wooden rim, they form small triangular openings which are perpendicular to the plane of all the other meshes, and are called "coyotes." Both wolves and coyotes count one point, if they are speared. The arrangement of meshes in this piece is entirely typical. The darts thrown at this hoop generally have several points, their ends being split.

A game was played by boys by fastening a bow, slanting diagonally from the ground, to a notch in a tree, which held it in place. The taut string was touched with an arrow, which flew back some distance. Another player then struck the string with his arrow, trying to make it fall on the first one thrown. If his arrow fell across the shaft of the first, nothing was counted; if it touched the feather, he made one point; if it touched the head or the sinew binding, it counted two points; while if it touched the notch, he made four points.

DICE. — The dice games played by the Arapaho are of two kinds. One form is played with bones or seeds, the other with sticks. The former will be considered first.

The bone or seed game consists of two or more sets of either two or three dice, and often of a basket in which these are tossed. The dice are sometimes made of plum-stones or similar seeds; in other cases, of bone. Whatever the material, they are usually marked by burning on one side only, though occasionally they are incised, or bored with rows of holes, such marks being then filled in with paint. The shape of the bone dice is most frequently circular, rectangular, or rhomboidal. Sometimes the ends of the rhombus are cut off, resulting in a hexagonal die; and not infrequently the rounding of the rectangle or rhombus gives rise to oval forms. The number of dice in a set, a set being the number of identical dice in a game, is either two or three. The number of sets constituting a game is from two to five, though only two sets seem generally to be used at one time. The count depends on the combination of marked and unmarked sides as the dice fall.

According to a method of counting obtained, the stakes are won when all the dice in both the sets used fall alike, either the marked or unmarked side being up; or when the dice of each set fall alike, even though the sets differ. When one die alone falls (marked or unmarked), and all the rest are different, one point is scored.

Fig. 142 shows four seed dice. A dragon-fly and a bird symbol are readily recognizable. The fourth die represented is ornamented with a pentagonal figure. It is not certain whether this shape is unintentional, or due to white influence. Fig. 143 shows the five kinds of bone dice forming another game. These are all marked by burning, except the nearly square die with three transverse lines and two rows of dots, the lines in which are filled with red paint, the dots with blue. Fig. 144 shows examples of the three sets, also of bone dice, constituting another game. The larger die in the middle has been marked by burning; the two others, by rows of small holes filled in with paint. Fig. 145 shows three further forms of bone dice from two games, all more or less diamond-shaped, and marked by burning. Fig. 146 shows the forms of the two sets of another game. One of these is cut with transverse diagonal lines in two directions. These lines have been filled

Fig. 142 ($\frac{50}{98}$, *a, c, h , f*). Seed Dice. Length of *a*, 2.5 cm.; width, 1.5 cm.

in with red paint. It is probably only on account of this intersection that the name na^{n}kaox (meaning both morning star and cross) was given to these markings. The other die of this game is somewhat larger, and its upper surface is drilled with five longitudinal rows of small holes. These were said to represent rows of buffalo travelling. The holes, being of some depth, look dark, so that this symbolism is entirely analogous with that of certain paintings on parfleches that have been discussed. Dice from five sets of another game, all of them of bone marked by burning, are shown in Fig. 146, *c*, and in Fig 147. Symbolic interpretations for the markings on these dice were obtained from two individuals at different times, — one an old woman, and the other a younger woman, the owner of the set. The older woman called the

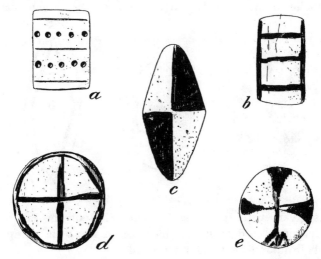

Fig. 143 (⅘⅝).   Five Kinds of Bone Dice.   Length of *c*, 4 cm.

design on the round die with the hour-glass markings, a "tent-ornament;" that of the long oval die with four transverse lines, the "four hills of life." The younger woman called both the latter and the other oval-shaped die, "moccasins." Her

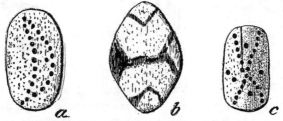

Fig. 144 (⅘⅝, *f*, *h*).   Sample Dice from Three Sets.   Length of *b*, 3 cm.

interpretation for the hour-glass figure on one of the rectangular dice was a "butterfly," and for the H-shaped figure flanked by two parallel lines, a "swing between two poles," with persons at each side. While the interpretations from these two informants do not agree, and the last one given is quite fanciful, so that it is very probable there was no symbolic intent when the dice were made, yet the explana-

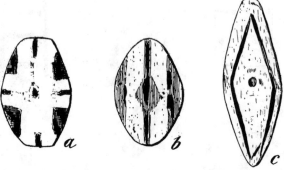

Fig. 145 ($\frac{50}{3985}$,*a*,*b*; $\frac{50}{127}$,*c*) .Three Forms of Bone Dice marked by Burning. Length of *c*, 4.5 cm.

tions given, with, perhaps, the exception of the last, are entirely in accord with the character of the usual Arapaho symbolism, and are no doubt typical.

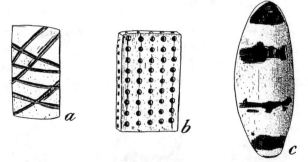

Fig. 146 ($\frac{50}{1048}$, *d*, *a*; $\frac{50}{1088}$, *g*). Dice from Two Different Sets. Length of *b*, 3 cm.; width, 2 cm.

It will be observed from the figures, that there are never in any one game two sets of dice of the same shape and size. There are not frequently two round or two rectangular sets; but in this case, as shown by Figs. 143 and 146, they differ considerably in size. In Fig. 147, *c* and *d*, the dice are very nearly of the same superficial shape and size; but the dice of Fig. 147, *c*, are somewhat convex as compared with the flat

pieces of Fig. 147, *d*. It is obvious that this differentiation
in size or shape between the dice of different series is brought
about by considerations of convenience during play, so that
the dice of different sets may be distinguished at a glance, on
their unmarked as well as on their marked sides.

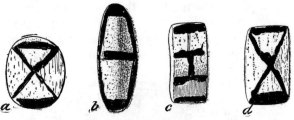

Fig. 147 ($\frac{50}{1008}$).   Bone Dice with Symbolic Ornamentation.   Length of *b*, 4.5 cm.

There are two dice-tossing baskets in the collections of
the Museum. In general appearance they are very similar,
but in detail of construction they differ in several points.
Both baskets are about eight inches in diameter, two inches
in depth, with a flat bottom and with sides rising without cur-
vature at an angle of from 50 to 70 degrees from the bottom.
In both baskets, the technique is primarily a one-stick coiling,
which leaves the centre of the basket open; and in both, the
border is a simple wrapping enclosing two rods of the foundation. The two baskets differ as follows. The one shown in
Fig. 148 has a one-rod foundation, which is, however, split to
have the woof passed through it, each woof-strand itself being
split by the woof-strand of the following coil. At the origin
of the basket is an opening about a quarter of an inch in
diameter. The rod of the outermost coil is considerably
heavier than any other in the basket. It is wrapped to the
rod of the coil below it, apparently without the splitting of the
latter, by a wide and heavy woof-strand, which is, perhaps, of
the same material as the woof of the rest of the basket, but
contrasts with it in appearance, owing to its greater mas-
siveness. All the rods used for the foundation in this basket
appear to be unpeeled. The other basket (Museum No. $\frac{50}{73}$)
is a one-stick coiled basket executed without splitting of the
warp, and in most cases without splitting of the woof, though

there are some stitches that split the woof-strand below them. The foundation-rods are for the most part peeled, though, near the beginning of the basket, they are unpeeled. The upper and outermost foundation-rod is not markedly heavier than the others. The wrapping which binds it to the rod below is a light-red fibre differing from the woof of the remainder of the basket, and apparently dyed. The bottom of the basket is covered with a piece of skin sewed on by stitches of sinew thread. The centre of the basket is without coiling for a

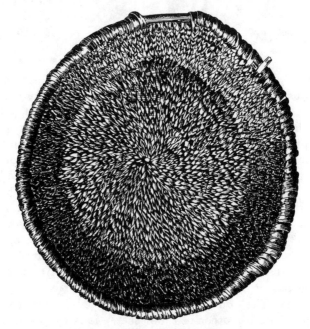

Fig. 148 ($\frac{50}{297}$). Basket for Tossing Dice. Diameter, 21 cm.

space about an inch in diameter. The coiling begins apparently on a rod bent on itself in a hoop of this diameter. The space within this hoop is filled in with an interlacing of strands, which in part pass over the neighboring warp, and in part under the woof. These strands appear to be drawn so that they complete a circumference of the hoop in three stretches. The number of strands in this filling-in of the central opening is not certain. Two ends are visible in the very centre. The woof-stitches in the body of this basket have some inclination against the direction in which the coil runs. The ends of the woof-strands are turned in the opposite direction, so as to more or less follow the coil, and are held down by from one to four or five wraps of the new woof-strand. The same method of holding the ends of the woof-strand appears to have been followed in the other basket, but, on account of the splitting of the stitches, this is not so strikingly apparent. The materials of these two baskets are not known, except that willow enters into them. The warp of the one shown in the illustration is an ordinary wood; the woof is coarse and fibrous. The warp of the other piece may well be willow, and its woof has all the appearance of being so. These two baskets differ so much, in spite of their superficial resemblance, that it is not impossible that one of them is not of Arapaho origin. It is very curious that basketry should not be made or used by this tribe, except, apparently, for the single purpose of playing dice.

The second form of Arapaho dice, used, like the preceding game, by women, consists of slender sticks from half a foot to a foot in length, split longitudinally, and with the pith removed. The flat side is then painted, the outer (convex) side left white. A game consists of two sets, each of four sticks, of one color. Sometimes a game contains three or four sets; but only two appear to be used at one time in playing (Fig. 149). As only the flat sides of the sticks are colored, the backs are marked, to distinguish the sets, by a simple burnt figure, such as two or three diagonal lines, or a cross. Usually only one of two sets is thus marked. The game itself is much like the game played with bone dice. The eight sticks are thrown, and points are scored, according to the combination of faces up and faces down. If all the dice of each set fall alike, whether the two sets agree or not, the stakes are won. If one is either face up or down and the other seven are respectively down or up, either one or seven points are scored. Other combinations, according to some, earn nothing; according to others, a certain number of points. One game of such stick dice in the Museum consists of four sets. One set of the four is painted green, another yellow, and two red. The green sticks are marked on the back by two diagonal crossed lines; the yellow set, by two diagonal parallel lines. The red sticks are marked on the painted side by two trans-verse lines on each side. The entire face or flat side of these

Fig. 149 ($\frac{50}{310}$, *c*, *f*). Stick Dice. Length, 27.5 cm.

sticks, including the channel left by the removal of the pith, is painted. In game Museum No. $\frac{53}{310}$ there are eight dice, forming two sets, one painted red, the other bluish-green. In both sets the painting is confined to the pith groove. The red set is unmarked by burning; the green set is marked on the back by three diagonal lines in the middle, on the front also by three diagonal lines, and at both ends by two trans-verse lines.

BALLS. — Stuffed deerskin balls are used by women and girls in another form of game revived at the time of the ghost-dancé. They are attached to a string, by which they may be held while being kicked. It would seem that these balls are as much implements for some form of juggling as they are balls to be actually thrown. They are made of two circular pieces of skin. These are apparently stuffed into hemispheres, and then their edges are sewed together by a back-and-forth stitching of sinew. Along this seam, the ball is often painted of a color different from the remainder of the surface, which appears to be almost always colored. Sometimes there are spots of paint on each hemisphere. One specimen has, in-stead of spots, a hand and five groups of three parallel bars on each side of the ball, the general effect being quite similar to that of the spots. Another specimen has the two hemispheres painted in different colors, with the middle border along the seam of still another color. Each hemisphere has a large symbol painted in the middle. At what may be called the upper of the seam of these balls, a string, of either single or double twisted thong, is attached. It is by this that the ball is held when it is kicked. At the end of this thong there is often a dyed plume. Sometimes an additional plume is attached to another thong issuing from the lower end of the ball or from the middle of one of the sides. In this case the plume at the upper end of the main supporting thong may be either retained or omitted.

One ball (Fig. 150) is yellow. It has painted on it on each side a black hand, the ball being thrown by the hand. Five groups of three small parallel black bars near the seam of the ball represent face painting.

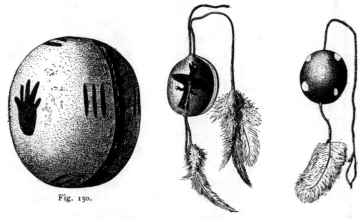

Fig. 150.

Fig. 151. Fig. 152.

Fig. 150 ($\frac{50}{311}$). Ball used by Women. Diameter, 9 cm.
Fig. 151 ($\frac{50}{363}$). Ball with Appendage. Diameter, 7 cm.
Fig. 152 ($\frac{50}{899}$). Small Decorated Ball. Diameter, 5.5 cm.

Another ball (Fig. 151) is blue on one side, red on the other, and yellow along the dividing seam. These three colors represent sky, earth, and daylight. On the blue half is painted a red cross, on the red side a dark-blue crow. From the middle of the figure of the crow issues a short thong, at the end of which is a red-ornamented blue plume representing breath. The ball is attached to a larger thong, to the end of which is fastened a group of dyed plumes. This larger thong was said to represent old age or long life.

One ball (Fig. 152), smaller than the others in the Museum's collection, is painted dark blue, with five yellow spots on one side, and five red on the other. These spots denote the striking of the ball. The red color represents dawn, the yellow daylight. The ball is hung from a two-strand twisted thong about a foot long, looped above for the insertion of the finger. From the opposite end of the ball proceeds a very short twisted thong ending in a plume. It was said that, in using this ball, the player or dancer turned himself about, swinging the ball. Then he struck it against the ground so that it rebounded.

A ball (Museum No. $\frac{50}{316}$) attached to a plume-tipped string, and accompanying an armlet shown in Plate VI of this volume, is yellow, with the seam reddened and a red spot in the centre of one hemisphere. This ball was used as follows. After being whirled about the head, it was struck against the head, on the ground, against the right knee, the left knee, over the heart, and was then thrown, and caught by another player.

OTHER GAMES.—The bull-roarer is a toy among the Arapaho. It is also thought to produce wind. A model (Fig. 153) is attached to a thong about two feet long tied to the end of a stick of equal length. The bull-roarer itself is of bone, a little more than an inch wide, and only four or five inches long. Neither end is pointed. The end to which the string is attached is cut off squarely, and the opposite end is deeply notched.

Fig. 153
($\frac{50}{1581}$).
Bull-roarer.
Length of
handle, 61
cm.

Along each side there are about a dozen notches. If this specimen is typical of the Arapaho bull-roarer, the implement is quite different in form from the longer, pointed wooden bull-roarer of the Gros Ventre.

A bone buzzer made of the foot-bone of a cow, and called, like a bull-roarer, "hateikuuca"," is sometimes used in the ghost-dance to start the singing. One specimen (Museum No. $\frac{50}{3110}$) has a few small holes in it. Three of these in a row were said to represent the three stars of Orion, called by the Arapaho "buffalo-bulls."

Tops — some of them flat-headed, and others pointed at both ends — were whipped. The game was called "going to war." Any top that was brought through still spinning, without having fallen, was regarded as victorious in war.

Fig. 154 shows a cup-and-ball game consisting of four hollow deer leg-bones, each about two inches long, strung in sequence and caught on a needle; the bones caught counting two, three, four, and five respectively, according as they are more or less distant. At the end of the string are several loops of beads, each of which, if caught, counts one point. If several bones are caught on the needle at one throw, the number of points is not the total of the separate value of each, but only as many as the number of bones caught. The sides of the bones are pierced with several small transverse holes. If the needle penetrates one of these, the game is said to be won. From the way the game is counted by other tribes, it is probable that this statement refers only to a certain hole near the end of the last bone. Each player continues to play until he misses, or has missed twice, as may be pre-arranged when his opponent receives the implement.

Another cup-and-ball game (Museum No. $\frac{50}{974}$) is similar to the last, except that small hoofs replace the bead loops at the end of the string. The bones in this

Fig. 154 ($\frac{50}{943}$). Cup-and-Ball Game. Total length, 49 cm.

set count respectively from one to four; and the hoofs, if caught, one point each. In this set, it is said, there was no way in which the game could be won by a single throw.

THE PEYOTE WORSHIP. — The peyote ceremony is comparatively brief.   It is held in an ordinary tent, and lasts through
a night.   After dark the participants enter the tent, and each
eats four of the small plants.   They may follow this first
quantity during the course of the night with as many more as
they wish.   The night is spent in singing around a small fire.
Between this fire and the back of the tent, where the leader of
the ceremony sits, is the equivalent of a simple altar on the
ground.   Only one participant sings at a time, accompanying
himself by a rattle.   The man next to him drums for him.
After four songs, the rattle and the drum are respectively
passed to the next participant; and in this way the songs make
the round of the tent during the night.   The conclusion of the
ceremony is marked by certain symbolic actions about sunrise, and the participants then leave the tent, and eat.   The
day is spent in company at rest in the shade, with occasional irregular singing, but with no ceremonies.   The action of the drug lasts until night, at which time the company
breaks up.

The peyote cult is not tinged appreciably with ghost-dance
beliefs.   It contains many Christian ideas, but they are so
incorporated that fundamentally the worship is not dependent
on Christianity.

The leader of each ceremony is sole director of it.   He may
make his ceremony in accordance with dreams which he has
had, or base it partly on visions during previous ceremonies.
In other cases, he follows ceremonies that he has participated
in, changing or adding details to suit his personal ideas.   No
two ceremonies conducted by different individuals are therefore
exactly alike; but the general course of all is quite similar.

The following account of the peyote worship is based on a
description obtained from a worshipper and on two ceremonies
seen.   These three sources of information have been com-
bined in a single description, which may be regarded as
applicable to the ceremonies typical in the tribe about 1899.
The informant from whom the account was obtained took
part in both the ceremonies seen.   The first of these ceremonies had only three participants, besides a woman.   In

the second there were about a dozen men (some of whom were Cheyenne, and all considerably younger than on the previous occasion) and again a woman.

The course of the ceremony is as follows.

Toward evening the man who is to conduct the ceremony selects a suitable place for a tent. He stands facing westward of where the centre of the tent will be. Raising his right hand, he prays. The grass is scraped from the ground, being cut first from west to east, and then from north to south. The tent is then put up, facing, as usual, the east. The wood that is to be burned during the night is stacked inside the tent to the south of the door. Small sticks of a wood that will burn without sparks are used. The leader of the ceremony takes a blanket, and, gathering red or reddish-brown earth or sand, brings it into the tent, or perhaps sends some one to do this. This reddish earth is put in a semicircle around the fireplace in the middle of the lodge, the centre of the crescent being toward the back of the tent, opposite the door. The diameter of the semicircle is perhaps four or five feet. Sage is pulled out, and laid on the ground around the inside of the tent, to be sat upon. The men sitting on this can stretch forward and reach the semicircle of soil. Sometimes the participants bathe just before making the ceremony. In the water they make one plunge against and one with the current of the stream. On coming out of the water, they may rub themselves with sage. The clothing and head are sometimes rubbed with teaxuwine[n] or waxuwahan, scented plants that are chewed.

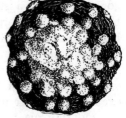

The mescal-plants, hahaayā[n]x, which are wooden-looking disks an inch or more across, tufted with dull white (Fig. 155), are soaked in water. When the

Fig. 155 ($\frac{2\,9\,9}{2\,7\,7}$). Mescal prepared for the Ceremony. Diameter, 4 cm.

dry plants are very hard, the soaking renders them sufficiently soft to be chewed, but with some difficulty. Before the tent is entered for the ceremony, the plants are taken from the water, which has become brownish, and are laid in a cloth. The dirty and very bitter liquid remaining is passed around to the participants, each of whom takes two sips of it, though this is not obligatory.

The drum consists of an ordinary small earthenware pot over which is stretched a piece of buckskin, or sometimes canvas, which is kept wet through the night by a little water inside of the jar. The skin is stretched by a rope. This rope, however, does not pass through holes in the skin, but is wound around seven glass marbles which have been rolled up in the skin. This device prevents the stretching of the skin, or the tearing out of perforations in it when the string is tightened. The seven glass marbles also play a part in the symbolical rites the next morning. The drum is made on the evening of the ceremony, and hours are sometimes consumed in adjusting it. When at last the right degree of tension is secured, together with the proper saturation of the skin, the effect is a tone moderately loud and deep, and very resonant. The drum is usually beaten very rapidly so that the reverberations from the separate blows fuse.

Inside the drum are a small quantity of ashes and three small billets of pine-wood. The introduction of these is purely for ceremonial reasons.

The rattle which is held by each man as he sings is a small gourd stuck on a stick, and containing ordinary small glass beads. As compared with the clattering sound produced by the gravel contained in some Indian rattles, the noise of these peyote implements is a swish rather than a rattle.

Pocket-knives and other sharp instruments must be left outside the tent in which the ceremony is conducted. Not even forks may be used with the food eaten in the tent, or at the mid-day meal on the following day out of doors. The symbolism of this observance seems to be the idea that the ceremony is an occasion of peace and good-feeling, which must not be disturbed. For the same reason, perhaps, all food eaten in connection with the ceremony must be cooked entirely without salt. This ceremonial idea is, however, found in many regions without being based on any specific reason.

The participants in the ceremony gather outdoors; and the

leader of the ceremony, the one in whose tent it is held, selects a fire-tender, called hictänä^{n}tcä ("fire chief"), silently pointing to him with an eagle wing-feather. This feather the fire-tender uses as a fan for the fire during the ceremony. The place of the fire-tender is just inside of the door, to its left or north. The fire chief goes first, and starts the fire inside the tent. When this begins to be illuminated, the other worshippers gather their blankets about them, and in single file walk to the tent. The fire chief kneels or stands on the prairie, outside the door, with his head bowed, facing the tent, or, according to one account obtained, in the opposite direction. The conductor of the ceremony, who has led the row of men, stands, and prays in a low voice, and then enters. He is followed by the others singly. The fire chief goes last, and closes the door of the tent. The worshippers then sit down, the director of the ceremony always at the middle of the back of the tent.

Usually corn-husk cigarettes are first smoked, and are lighted with a stick taken from the fire by the fire-tender. The leader of the ceremony then produces from a small beaded purse or pouch a mescal-plant, which he keeps permanently, often carrying it on his person. The plant selected is usually large, round, and even. He carefully smoothes a little space at the middle point of the crescent of reddish earth before him. Breaking eight short stems of sage, he lays them on this spot in the form of two superimposed crosses, the ends of the stems pointing in the cardinal directions and between. On this sage his mescal-plant is then laid (usually a head feather plume, which may have been worn in the hair on entering the tent, is stuck in the ground so that its tip nods over the plant); then, starting from the plant, the leader makes a crease along the top of the crescent of earth, first to the right, then to the left. This is continued at its two ends by the worshippers sitting on each side of the leader, and their neighbors carry it farther until the end of the crescent is reached. This crease or line is made by pressing the thumb into the loose earth. It represents the path by which the thoughts of the worshippers travel to the mescal-plant.

After this altar, as it might be called, has been completed, the peyote is eaten. The director gives to each of the participants four of the plants, which he takes out of the cloth or handkerchief. They are exceedingly bitter, and still quite hard. They are ground between the teeth, one at a time, until they crumble; and the chewing is continued until they are fine. The mass is then pressed by the tongue into a round ball, which, being soft, is easily swallowed. Most of the furry tufts on the face of the plant are spit out during the chewing. In a tent full of worshippers, a constant sputtering breaks the silence for a few minutes. After these first four plants have been eaten, more can be called for in the course of the night, whenever any one wishes them. Four are generally eaten at a time. The average number taken varies considerably, but seems to be about twelve. Sometimes more than thirty are eaten.

Sometimes, just before receiving the plants, the worshippers chew sage, and rub themselves with it. The director passes the cloth of soaked plants four times over cedar incense. He takes one himself, and gives one to the man on his left, who will drum for him. After they have eaten these, the director gives each of the participants four plants, first stretching his hand toward the east.

After the first four plants have been disposed of by all, the leader takes up his rattle and begins to sing. Sometimes he rests his left hand upon a staff, holding in this hand an eagle-feather fan. Such a fan is quite commonly used in the ceremony. The man at his left drums for him. Just before the singing, the drum, rattle, fan, and staff have been passed four times over cedar incense. The leader passes the rattle to his left-hand neighbor, and drums. After four songs, the third worshipper takes the rattle. It goes about the tent from left to right, from right to left, as the worshippers sit, making circuit after circuit, each man singing four songs. Except in the case of the singing of the leader, the man on the singer's right always drums for him. About midnight, on the completion of a round of singing, the woman present, who is usually the wife of the leader of the ceremony, leaves the tent.

She soon returns with a jar of water, which is placed before her husband. He then, at least on some occasions, takes an eagle-bone whistle with which he imitates the cry of an eagle as it gradually descends from a great height to the ground in search of water. The gradual approach of the bird from a distance is very vividly indicated, ending with a climax of shrill cries. The end of the whistle is then dipped into the water. After this the leader drinks from the jar. The water is then passed about the tent from left to right in regular ceremonial order, and every one drinks four swallows. The effects of the peyote make the participants very thirsty, but this occasion is the only interruption in the ceremonies of the night. From this time on until sunrise, the singing and the drumming go on continuously.

Sometimes, it is said, the leader goes out of the tent before the water is brought in at midnight, the worshippers remaining in the tent, and praying. Facing the east, he prays to the morning star; then, facing west, he prays to the peyote, which is in the tent, west of him. On his return, cedar is put on the fire as incense, to carry the prayers up. The fire-tender scrapes the ashes into a crescentic shape, inside the crescent of earth, and then stands and dances. His dancing consists of a shaking. The leader of the ceremony sings and rattles; the man at his left drums; and a third participant, it is said, blows the whistle, imitating a bird. At the end of four songs, the fire-tender, still carrying his eagle wing-feather, goes out. He returns with the water, which he sets before the director.

During the night, the songs usually refer to the peyote itself, to the birds regarded as its messengers, and to the long duration of the night. In the morning, as the tent begins to become diffused with light, the songs refer to the morning star and the end which it brings to the ceremony. At sunrise the woman leaves the tent, and after a short time re-appears with four dishes of food and drink, which she places in a row on the ground, between the fire and the door. On one occasion, the woman on this re-appearance wore a symbolically painted buckskin dress. Soon after her entrance, the last round of singing is completed, the rattle is laid aside, and the fire is allowed to burn out. The drum is then loosened and taken apart; and each portion of it is passed around the ring of participants. A little of the water still remaining in the jar is drunk by each worshipper. Every man, in turn, wrings the wet skin, and, as the rope with which it was stretched is passed to him, he throws a loop of it over his foot, and tugs at it. This is a symbol of the roping of horses. The seven glass marbles are pressed by each man against his chest, his shoulders, and other parts of his body, in order to ward off disease. One man has been seen to roll all seven out of his palm into his mouth, and then drop them back one by one. The leader's fetish, which has lain all night at the back of the crescent of earth, is passed by each man to his neighbor, and is held and looked at for a short time. When it has made the circuit and returns to the leader, he puts it back carefully into his pouch. He distributes to the participants the bits of sage-stems on which the plant has rested The worshippers then wash the paint from their faces, and comb their hair; water, a towel, a mirror, and a comb also making the round of the tent. Then at last the drinking-water is passed around the circle, and is followed by the dishes of food, one after the other. After the food has gone around several times, and none of the dishes are any longer touched by any one, the worshippers rise. stretch themselves, shake their blankets (which have usually lain behind them during the night), and, one behind the other, leave the tent in the same order in which they entered it the night before.

It is perhaps eight in the morning when the tent is left. For the rest of the day the worshippers lie on blankets in a pleasant spot under trees, under a shade, or in the house. From time to time one of them sings, shaking the rattle softly. The drum is no longer used. Occasionally more than one man will sing different songs at the same time. The effect of the drug is still very strong. The physiological discomforts have usually worn off, and the pleasurable effects are at their height. It appears that new songs, inspired perhaps by the visions of the night, are often composed during this day. At noon a meal is again served, most of the food at which is sweet. At this meal only one spoon is allowed in the company, and food requiring the use of this is therefore passed around from one participant to the other. At dark the worshippers saddle their horses and ride home, or go to bed if they live at the leader's house.

One of the recent modifications of the peyote ceremonial was devised by a firm devotee, to cure a sick person. The originator of this new form of the worship believes himself to have been cured by the drug. In this ceremonial, which was repeated four times, the tent seems to have represented a sweat-house, and a path led from the entrance to a fire outside, as before a sweat-lodge. The ritual, while remaining a peyote ceremony, conformed more or less to the ordinary processes of doctoring a sick person.

The objects used in connection with the peyote worship have a distinct decorative character of their own. The most typical color on them is yellow, with which their wood and skin portions are almost always painted. The feathers most frequently used are those of the yellow-hammer and other species of woodpeckers. The bead-work on peyote objects is on the whole predominatingly yellow, but most frequently consists of a mixture of small areas of different colors. Very frequently there are bands of different color encircling stems and similar objects. In almost all cases the ornamentation is geometric.

The objects most used in the peyote ceremonies are gourd rattles, fans, pouches for the peyote-plant, head-dresses of yellow-hammer or woodpecker feathers, and wrist-bands.

The peyote rattles are made of small gourds, which are usually painted yellow. The stick handle projects through the gourd, and is ornamented with dyed horsehair at the top. In some cases, the handle is wrapped around with beads, and almost always decorated with attachments at the lower end of the handle. Small glass beads are used to produce the sound.

The fans are often quite elaborate. Plate LXXXIII shows a peyote fan. It consists essentially of a short bead-covered handle and of four eagle-feathers, which can be grasped so as to present a somewhat fan-like surface. The bases of the quills of these feathers are wrapped with beads, — one white, one green, one blue, and one yellow. On each of these ground-colors there are narrow bands of the three other colors. Above the bead-wrapping at the base of each feather proper are a red plume and a few fringes of skin. These four eagle-feathers are attached to the upper end of the handle in such a way that when this is held up they fall, and extend horizontally. Where they are attached to the handle are a number of trimmed yellow-hammer or similar feathers. These are ornamented with red and green plumes, — most of them at the base, but those that are longest, halfway up the feather also. The handle of the fan seems to be of skin. The beading enclosing it shows many bands, none of which is more than two rows of beads wide. There are all together six colors of beads on the handle. At the lower end of the handle is tied a strip of fur; and below this hangs a fringe of strips of skin more than a foot long, painted yellow.

The pouches used to contain the peyote-plant have room for only one of the disks, which is usually carried more or less as a personal amulet in addition to being the centre of worship during ceremonies. The pouches are beaded, and usually fringed and otherwise ornamented. Plate LXXXIV shows such a pouch. It is attached to a necklace of strings of black beads. The flap to the pouch consists of two strips of skin wrapped with beads at the end, and then fringed. The pouch itself is surrounded by a row of metal buttons and by a fringe of skin. This fringe, like all the unbeaded skin of the pouch, is painted yellow. A circular area of bead-work covering the front of the pouch itself, is said to represent the appearance of a peyote-plant while being worshipped. In the centre a cross of red beads represents the morning star. Around the edge of this circular bead-work are eight small triangular figures, which denote the vomitings deposited by the ring of worshippers around the inside of the tent in the course of the night. The yellow fringe around the pouch represents the sun's rays.

Accompanying this pouch are four bunches of small feathers of yellow-hammer, sparrow-hawk, and similar birds, containing each from one to three dozen feathers. These feathers are ornamented at their bases with dyed plumes or small barred feathers. They are attached to thongs, which are gathered into a single large knot, and enclosed by a covering of skin or wrapping of sinew. It is said that these bunches of feathers are hung on the tent-poles — at the northeast, northwest, southeast, and southwest — during the peyote ceremony, and that they are also used to brush the bodies of the worshippers when they are tired. It is not improbable that they may also have been worn as head-dresses.

Fig. 156 (⅘). Feather used to brush the Body. Full length, 22 cm.

Another bunch of feathers of this type (Fig. 156) was said to have been used both as a head-dress and to brush the body. The yellow parts are faded yellow-hammer feathers. Only seven remain on the specimen. Where the thongs to which they are attached are gathered together there is a bulb covered with skin. This bulb is further covered by red and yellow beads. As usual, two thongs are used to attach the head-dress to the hair.

Specimen Museum No. $\frac{50}{619}$ is another head-dress consisting of a bunch of feathers, and apparently intended for the peyote worship. To nine yellowhammer-feathers is tied a small eagle or hawk feather ornamented with a green plume at the base and with some red paint on the white portion of its surface. The thongs of all the feathers are painted red. Instead of the ball of knots there is in this specimen only a bit of weasel-skin. This head-dress would seem to have been

Fig. 157 ($\frac{50}{394}$, *a*). Head Ornament. Full length, 28 cm.

worn, at least in part, as an expression of a wish for the acquisition of a horse. When worn tied to the hair over the temple, it represents the blinders of a horse. The one larger feather, the upper end of which is black, is said to represent a black-eared horse; the bit of weasel-skin, horsehair.

Specimen Museum No. $\frac{50}{620}$ consists of a dozen yellow-hammer or similar feathers tied together by yellow-painted thongs. The large knot is lacking; instead, a small hemispherical metal button is attached, said to represent a peyote-plant.

Very similar is part of another head ornament (Fig. 157). This also consists of a dozen yellow-hammer or similar feathers on thongs gathered in a large knot, and ornamented with a curved metal button representing the peyote-plant. The yellow feathers are said to denote sticks in the fire during the ceremony. Perhaps originally a separate object, but now attached to this bunch of feathers, is a miniature fan of six bluish feathers wrapped with beads where they are gathered at their bases. Below this beaded handle is a fringe of a dozen thongs painted yellow, and at the base of the blue feathers a red-dyed plume. This red is said to represent the fire in the ceremony; the bluish feathers, ashes; and the approximately cylindrical bead-covered handle of the fan, a peyote-plant.

Another object was used as a bracelet (Fig. 158). It seems

originally to have formed the forked cover-flap of a peyote pouch, like that shown in Fig. 144, but to have been cut off and put to another use. The edges are bordered with green and yellow beads. At the end of each of the two strips is a large blue bead from which issue five loops of small beads. These bead attachments represent the hand with its five fingers.

Fig. 158 ($\frac{50}{314},a$).
Bracelet.   Full length, 37 cm.

Fig. 159 ($\frac{50}{120}$).
Bracelet made of Twisted   Cord.
Length, 18 cm.

Another such wrist-band (Fig. 159) consists primarily of two strands of thongs painted yellow, and twisted together into a single string. A thong fastens this together after it is passed around the wrist, and lets the two ends hang loose.

These ends consist of a cylindrical button covered with bands of beads, and of a yellow skin fringe. Attached to the fringe at one of the ends is a flat piece of pearl in the form of about two-thirds of the area of a circle. This was said to represent the moon, and to enable the wearer of the bracelet in the peyote tent, ceremonially of course, to detect the approach of morning by its reflection.

Specimen Museum No. $\frac{5}{7}\frac{0}{7}$, obtained from Rev. Walter C. Roe, is described as a bracelet made of hair taken from a captive. The specimen has every appearance of being a peyote object. The hair is light brown and braided, and in the middle bound with an ornament consisting of a cylindrical button of beads of several colors and a short yellow fringe. At the ends of the braid are similar smaller cylindrical buttons of light-blue beads, each with a yellow band at each end. From the lower ends of these bead ornaments hangs another yellow fringe. A two-strand yellow thong ties the bracelet together just above the two ornamented ends.

There seems to be considerable trading and giving of peyote objects. Many of the specimens described in different parts of this work might have been made by Indians of other tribes, and very probably some are of foreign origin. The possibility of this varies with the class of objects. The regalia of the age-societies are certainly always purely Arapaho, although many similar types occur among other tribes. Articles of clothing and implements may in some cases have been made outside the tribe; and the same holds true of the ghost and crow dance objects. The peyote paraphernalia are perhaps most likely to be imported. The ceremony is said to be derived from the Kiowa, and men of different tribes not infrequently now participate in the same worship.

CHARACTER OF CEREMONIAL OBJECTS.

Number and Color Symbolism.— It will be seen that the general character of the modern ghost-dance and related ceremonial objects is quite distinct from that of the regalia formerly used in the tribal age-ceremonies. The fundamental difference is, that the latter are fixed and the variations between individual pieces of the same kind are due to circumstances, and unintentional; whereas the modern ceremonies — not being based on established ritual to any extent, but dependent primarily on purely personal supernatural experience — impose on the objects used in them only a tendency to similarity, and in fact no two such pieces are ordinarily entirely alike even in intent. This difference is perhaps best exemplified by the coloring of the two classes of regalia. The tribal pieces are red, white, or yellow, with occasional small black or green embroidered or painted ornaments, or a little blue beading: the modern pieces are of all colors, used together indiscriminately without restriction. As regards form, many kinds of objects of each class are not found in the other. The two types of buffalo-dance head-dresses, belts of this and of the second age-dance, crazy-dance robes, dog-dance scarfs, the bunch-feather head-dresses of the dog-dance, the star-dance rattles, the wooden war-clubs of the first dance, and the bone whistles of several of the dances, — are all without parallel in the modern regalia. The board wands of the first dance, and perhaps in a degree the club of the highest degree of the second dance, the upright rawhide and feather head-dresses of the second dance, the quilled thong pendants of the dog-dance whistles and of other regalia, and the small quilled hoops of the buffalo-dance, have more or less close parallels or imitations, especially in the ghost-dance objects. The lances of the second dance, which have so wide a distribution on the Plains, especially the feathered crooks, do not seem to have close analogues in modern ceremonial objects, the only similar piece in the Museum collection being the short feathered stick shown in Plate LXXIX. On the other hand, practically every one of the many types of ghost-dance head-dresses, the crow-belts, the hand mirrors, the painted dresses, the feathered necklaces and belts, and other classes of objects, are, among the Arapaho, altogether modern.

From what has been said, Arapaho color and number symbolism, and their relations, can now be summarized. The Arapaho sacred numbers — as appears from innumerable references both in ceremonial and other connections, and from the traditions that have been published — are four, five, and seven. Six and ten do not occur. Seven is much less frequent than four. The Arapaho sometimes say that in certain matters, such as the membership of the highest age-society, four is the older number, seven the newer; but this is probably nothing more than a speculative supposition based on the greater inclusiveness of seven. Objects, names, and conceptions (ceremonial and mythological) are not infrequently seven in number, episodes in traditions occasionally, ritual actions hardly ever. Of the two other numbers, it may be said unqualifiedly, that five occurs only as based on four: it is, as an idea, the summing-up of the four, spatially the centre of the four. The idea of five as a significant number itself is as foreign to the Arapaho mind as that of three or of ten, except in so far as this is connected with the fingers and mathematical operations. On account of being the fulfilment of four, five is particularly common in ritualistic actions, perhaps exceeding four in frequency; but its relation to four is even then almost always clear to the Indian as well as to the white observer, especially in cases of visible spatial expression. Four, then, is the primary number with meaning to the Arapaho. They are unable to depart from this thought, and it enters into their life, even where there is no direct ceremony involved, to an extent and with an inevitability that may be equalled by certain peoples, but is perhaps scarcely surpassed by any, even in America. The material life of the Plains is probably not so conducive, directly and indirectly, to a concrete expression of this tendency as is that of the Southwest; but this is compensated for by the rigidity of the adherence of the Arapaho to four as compared with the great development in the Southwest of concepts also of six and seven. The difference in this point between the two culture-regions is evidenced in that the Arapaho begin and end with four, develop it frequently to five, and occasionally, by a leap, to seven. The southwestern Indians, with considerable frequency of four, seem to be trying always to reach seven, and their abundant six gives the impression of being only a step, a means of reaching seven more significantly. The Mexicans appear to agree more nearly with the Arapaho in having four as their primary number, but differ from them in the strong tendency to the use of higher numbers, such as thirteen, no doubt in connection with the greater development of their culture. It is remarkable how uniformly the exclusive significance of four as the lowest and most fundamental numerical base in the American hemisphere contrasts with that of three, or of numbers higher than four, in the Old World. Where the American Indian departs from four to five there is almost always a minimization of ritualistic and symbolic ceremonialism.

The connection of four with the conception of the circle is wonderfully deep in the Indian mind, and finds full expression with the Arapaho. Of course, this connection is given in nature by the four quarters determined by the sun, whose manifestations form the greatest visible phenomenon in the world, and there probably is more or less causal relation; but the connection extends to human matters not in any direct relation with nature. The idea of the circle as such, as we of Old-World civilization have it, is very slightly developed in the Indian; but it may safely be said that the idea of four is almost invariably inherent in the idea of the circle, at least in the mind of the Arapaho. A circle is to him a four-sided or four-ended thing: it is *per se* four-determined and four-containing. The rhombus, the rectangle, the cross, are all equivalents of the circle; and when, as often, the connection or identification is not directly made, it is almost always not far away.[1] Where we think geometrically, the Indian thinks symbolically; where we are realistically visual or spatially abstract, he is pictographic. Whether in North or in South America, this holds true, of course in varying degree; and in the Old World, savages and cultured nations — Europe, Africa, Asia, and Oceania — are in fundamental tendency a unit

---

[1] On p. 144 it is stated that, in the primarily decorative art of the Arapaho, the figure of a rhomboid has ten different significations. Six of these are of objects that are naturally round, or would naturally be represented by a circle by any people,—the navel, a lake, a turtle, a buffalo-wallow, the area of a hill, the floor of a tent. The seventh, a person, is no doubt an enlargement in idea of the navel; the eighth, the eye, is partly round, partly more realistic; the ninth, a star, is probably based on the cross, the rhomboid being a cross with its points connected; the tenth, the abstract symbol hiiteni, appears to have its primary significance in being four-cornered.

in this respect. Of course, the connection of this tendency as regards the conception of the circle, with the straight-lined character of American art (what we falsely call geometric) as contrasted with the overwhelming preponderance of the curve in the Old World, is not far to seek.

From the prevalence in North America of color-direction symbolism, and the extent among the Arapaho of direct color-symbolism, of world-quarter and of four symbolism, it might be expected that they, too, connected certain colors with certain directions. There is as yet apparently no trace of any such color-direction symbolism.[1] While there may be instances of it, they are certainly sporadic, and contrary to the general trend of Arapaho symbolism, and would only prove the innate deep-seatedness of such an association.

There is a certain connection of different colors with the number four, especially in ghost-dance ornamentation. A typical quill-embroidery in white, yellow, red, and black, has also been described (p. 65) as referring to the sacred four. In the few cases of ghost-dance objects observed, the colors have always been black, red, yellow, and green, blue sometimes replacing black. There is, however, no fixed order in which these successive colors come, so that it is evident, that, while taken collectively they may contain the idea of the four-directional world, there is no definite attribution of particular colors to certain directions. Taking the colors as they occur from left to right, or in sunrise circuit, their order in the several cases is black, yellow, green, red, black, green, red, yellow, with white as the central fifth; black, green, red, with white as the fifth; and blue, red, yellow, green. So that, whether the several series are read forward or backward, the same order cannot be obtained. One of these cases is that of four different winds represented by lines of different colors. The winds are often equivalents of the world-quarters in America, so that we are here apparently not very far from association

---

[1] The sun-dance connection of red and black with north and south is primarily a reference to day and night, not to directions. As matter of fact, the red (representing the day and the sun) is to the north; the black (standing for night, the moon, and winter) is south. According to Dorsey (Arapaho Sun-Dance, p. 125), the Arapaho state that the original symbolism was the reverse of this.

of colors with directions; but the only idea in the mind of the maker of this piece seems to have been that of four, and the colors served only to emphasize this idea as such.

Still less importance can be attached to the color-sequences as connected with directions when the technical and purely stylistic limitations of Arapaho art are considered. Mixed colors, such as the spotted or striped of the Southwest, do not occur; blue and dark blue are regarded as equivalents for black; light blue is comparatively little used, and was less so before the introduction of glass beads and civilized dyes, and, as if to still further minimize the rôle played by blue, it is sometimes the equivalent of green. This leaves only five colors, — red, yellow, green, black, and white; and as white is the normal color of the unornamented surface (whether skin, rawhide, wood, or quill), it is natural that it should be regarded as less distinctly a color than the others, and find its chief function in expressing the containing fifth, leaving the combination of red, yellow, green, and black as almost a necessity.

Decorative factors are also intimately connected with the white, yellow, red, black combination. A rich medium blue such as best brings out its quality as a distinct color is not used by the Arapaho, except in old blue-and-white bead-work in beads no longer employed, and to a certain extent in modern parfleche painting. Modern bead-work uses either distinctly dark or light blue; old rawhide painting lacked blue; wood and skin are not so often painted blue as red, green, or yellow, but if so, in dark blue; porcupine-quills for embroidery and modern ghost-dance feather-work are dyed in colors that are nearer purple than blue. It is in connection with this fact that blue is so neglected in color-combination, though whether technological reasons caused the stylistic development, and this affected symbolism, or the reverse took place, or the matter is stylistic in origin, cannot be said. Green is now frequently used as a well-marked color, though sometimes so dark a shade of the color is used that it is substituted for black. Green is at present not rare in objects ornamented in the tribal, that is, non-individual style, such as robes and cradles; but it is difficult to see how the native greens formerly available could have sufficed to produce a color artistically satisfactory, especially when they were applied to quills. In modern parfleches, green is one of the commonest colors; but in the old pieces — especially such as medicine-cases, where styles would be likely to be more conservatively adhered to than in household articles — the green is uniformly extremely dark. While this may be due in part to changes in the pigment, it seems that this old green must have been originally darker than that now used, and that it was employed as a more pleasing substitute for black, with red and yellow, on the naturally white background of rawhide. The tendency to use blue and green as substitutes for black goes very deep among the Arapaho. In all the regalia of the age-societies, there is scarcely a black line painted; and embroidery in black is limited to lines and small bars. Black beads are very unusual in any class of objects. There is scarcely an Arapaho article in existence painted with soot or charcoal. Outside of body-paint and certain ceremonial paintings, especially in the sun-dance, an actual black seems to have been avoided.[1] With blue and green so largely reduced in function to serve as its equivalents, especially in the older days, the white, yellow, red, black, blue, green, combination is also almost reducible to non-symbolic causes.

Along with these apportionments of colors into groups of fours, there is a color-dualism in certain circumstances, — the deep-seated contrast, which we, too, have not outlived, between black and red. This finds, perhaps, fullest expression in the sun-dance, so that black and red seem to be regarded as the distinctive sun-dance color-combination. Apparently it occurs also in the older age-society ceremonies, as in the body-paints used by the dog-dancers, and probably by the still older men. Sacred bags contain red and black paint. In the ghost-dance movement there seems to have been a new development of this idea in the division of the guessing-game sets into black and red halves. That blue or green replaces

---

[1] It is doubtful whether charcoal was ever used, except as a body-paint on the return of a victorious war-party. Black body and ceremonial paint was usually, if not always, mineral; black embroidery was by means of naturally black vegetable fibres; and the blackish outlines of rawhide paintings are made with vegetable juices.

black as soon as the artistic consideration takes a place beside the traditionary and old ceremonial, does not in the least impair the dualism to the Indian. It is curious that, in the ceremonial regalia of age-societies, the black and red combination is conspicuously wanting. There are frequent pairings of colors; but they are white and yellow, white and red, and yellow and red.

In connection with the ghost-dance movement there is a frequent color-dualism symbolizing heaven and earth, or the future or the present world; but the colors used vary. Blue and probably yellow denote only the sky; red, only the earth; green, both. When yellow and green are paired, the former is daylight and therefore the sky; green, vegetation and hence the earth. As between red and green, the former, denoting blood, man, paint, and earth, is this world; the latter, as an equivalent of blue, is the sky.

The average color-symbolism of the decoration of useful objects, which has been discussed on p. 149, is not very different from that of objects exclusively ceremonial, so that nothing need be added here to what has been said, except a few generalizations as to the scope of this symbolism. It will be seen that the significations of colors are taken from visible nature, — earth, sky, sun, night, light, rocks, water, snow, vegetation, blood, buffalo, sunset. There is virtually no designation of anything abstract; and any connection of colors with states of mind — such as grief, friendship, love, jealousy — is foreign to the aboriginal Arapaho way of thought. Black is a sign of victory, but expresses a fact rather than a feeling. It thus differs from our use of black as a mourning-color in dress: it is nearer the black crape on doors, which, whatever its origin may have been, is now not a direct expression of grief, but an indication of a fact. Like this, the use of black as a sign and then as a symbol of victory, and therefore of war, is entirely conventional; but its wide distribution in North America is remarkable. White is occasionally a symbol of old age; but here, however abstract the significance, the concrete visual basis of the symbolism remains clear. Red also sometimes implies age. The association of ideas in this case is through the use of the paint itself. Red is the paint *par excellence;* and it is the old people, who most paint themselves for religious motives, who direct the painting of the young in ceremonies and its use on objects. Then, too, old people, leading a simpler life, discard the other colors of youth, and paint themselves in red. Their clothing and their personal articles are usually unornamented with beads or embroidery, or anything but red paint. Here, again, a visible series of facts is the basis of the symbolism. The semi-abstract reference of red to man is similar in character. Red is blood: it is also paint, which man uses, and by means of which he lives. Even the designation of the earth by red is of this nature, though it is no doubt founded in part on the frequent redness of the soil in the Arapaho habitat. Red is paint, which comes out of the earth, and often is earthy: therefore it is the earth. It will be seen from this, that, where the representation of red is not of visible phenomena or objects, its symbolism is of the pigment and its uses, not of its color-quality; so that the symbolism is a matter of association of facts, not of a color as such with an abstraction as such.

PERSONAL SUPERNATURAL POWERS.

Supernatural power of whatever kind is believed among the Arapaho to be usually acquired at a time of fasting and isolation. The custom of more easterly tribes, for young boys to go out soon after the age of puberty, and fast in a given way for a certain number of days, is not known by the Arapaho. The men who go out to obtain supernatural power are usually fully adult, and sometimes of middle age. A man does not necessarily have supernatural experiences only once in his life. The places chosen are most frequently hills or mountain-peaks. The duration of the fast varies from two or three to, in some cases, seven days. Four days as the Indians reckon, which is perhaps usually seventy-two hours, seems to be the most common period. The being that appears to the faster, and becomes his guardian spirit, is usually an animal, most frequently, it would appear, a small animal. This fact is per-

haps connected with the practice in which a man uses the skin
of the animal, his supernatural helper, as his medicine-bag.
During the vision, when the worshipper is instructed, the spirit
most often appears in human form; only when it vanishes
is it seen to be an animal. Supernatural powers effective in
medicine or war, or of any other value, are not differentiated
in method of acquisition by the Arapaho. It appears that
the great majority of middle-aged men went out to receive supernatural communication, and were successful. Even at the
present day, this holds true of the men of some age. A distinct profession of medicine-men or shamans can therefore
not be spoken of with any approximation to correctness, any
more than can a caste of warriors. The differences between
individuals in kind and degree of supernatural power were
apparently not greater than in matters of bravery or distinction in war.

The following paragraphs give accounts of supernatural
experiences, descriptions of implements connected with such
experiences, of amulets, and of medicines, and statements of
a general nature made by Indians on such matters.

A man fasted on a hill for four days, crying. The fourth
morning, at sunrise, he saw a badger. The badger stood up on
his hind legs and turned into a naked man painted red over
his body. This badger-man looked like an image of the man
who saw him. He was, of course, an untrue person, or spirit.
He directed the faster to use a badger-skin for his medicine-
bag. To the badger belong all medicines that grow on the
ground. The man did not build a monument of stones on the
hill where he fasted, as is the common practice. He found a
buffalo-skull, and used it as a pillow when he slept. His
medicine-bag, which accordingly was of badger-skin, contained the following medicines: —

1. A red bag of niäätaⁿ-root, used against cough. Pinches
of the powdered root are put into a vessel of water at four sides,
proceeding in order from left to right. A fifth pinch of the
root is then dropped into the middle of the vessel, the fingers
being raised somewhat higher than before. The water is
then boiled, and the medicine drunk by the patient.

2. A little bag of medicine called waxubaa,[n] which is said to grow in the present habitat of the northern Arapaho. This is a medicine for stomach-ache.

3. A smaller yellow bag of häçawaanaxû, the root most frequently used in the tribal ceremonies of the Arapaho. By this man the root was mixed with earth when used. Five pinches were dropped into a vessel of water, boiled, and drunk. This was to cure pains in the back and in the chest.

4. A small red bag containing a pebble-like formation found by the owner in the side of the body of a buffalo, and called hänä[n]tcä[n] (" buffalo-bull"). This stone is laid on sores in order to cure them. The bag also contained a root, which, like the preceding remedies, is boiled in water and the decoction drunk. It is used as a cure for hemorrhages or lung-disease.

5. A turtle-tail worn as a head-dress by young men, being supposed to aid them in retaining good health. With this was the heart of a turtle, with which the owner refused to part. This heart is pounded fine, and drunk in water as a remedy for pain in the heart.

A well-known medicine-man, who, with much real devotion, has many of the qualities of the charlatan, told the following about his supernatural experiences.

Once he fasted four days. On the third day he saw fighting. A man painted green over his body, his hands red, and his face yellow with red streaks passing down from his forehead to his jaw, was on foot in the fight in the midst of the enemy. He wore a necklace from which hung medicine and an owl-feather, and which was swung around his back. This person ran be-tween the two fighting-lines four times. The enemy shot at him with arrows, but did not hit him once. Even when he was near them, their bow-strings would break. Then his dream or vision changed, and the people he had seen were small birds flying in flocks, called waotänictcēci; and the man running between them was a yellow-jacket or wasp, flying back and forth. After his fast and return home, the informant dreamed that he saw a man wearing on the front of his head a small figure representing the man he had seen in his vision.

After he had begun to have medicines, a person appeared

to him in a dream or vision, bringing him a badger-skin medicine-bag.

On another occasion he fasted on a hill near a lake on the Cimarron. It was the third night. As he was lying on the ground he heard footsteps. A man called to him to come to his tent. He thought some one was trying to deceive him, and he paid no attention. The person continued to call him. The fourth time he said, "Hurry and come. Other people are waiting for you." Then the informant consented. He went in his thoughts, but he himself did not get up from the ground. He went downward from where he was lying, into the ground. He followed the man who had called him, and entered a tent. On the right side in the tent sat four young men painted black with yellow streaks. On the left side in the tent sat three young men painted yellow with red streaks. The man who had possessed the medicine sat at the back of the tent. He himself sat down at the left side, so that there were four on each side of the man at the back. This person was painted red. In front of him lay a pipe with its head to the north (the left). The head of the tent put mushrooms on the fire as incense, and then shook his rattle, in imitation of a rattlesnake, while the young men sang. Then he passed the pipe, and they smoked. After this, he rubbed and cleaned the pipe, and told the visitor that he must do in the same way. Then he folded his arms, bent his head, and two snakes came from his mouth, coiled on the ground, and darted their tongues. Then the man who had vomited the two snakes blew on them, and they disappeared. At first the visitor did not know where they had gone. Then he realized that they were in his own body. He declares that he keeps them there now, one on each side. Through virtue of this dream he now cures rattlesnake-bites. A pipe is sent him, and after smoking it he goes to doctor the person that has been bitten. If he receives this pipe, he is able to effect a cure. While he is doctoring, the patient can see the two snakes projecting out of the medicine-man's mouth. When the medicine-man comes across a snake, of whatever kind, he catches it, strips off its skin, and eats its meat and internal organs raw.

It appears that the supernatural being that gave him his snake-medicine was the same that he had seen in a dream of the battle. Apparently this same person took him away in a dream and showed him the plant which he was to use when he doctored rattlesnake-bites. After having been shown the proper plant, he looked for it until he found it.

This man's medicine-bag was a badger-skin (Museum No. $\frac{50}{300}$), and its contents were the following: —

A small figure made of skin painted green, with a yellow head and with red hands, throat, and vertical stripes on the

face and legs, and with a small bag of medicine and an owl's feather attached, represents his supernatural helper as he saw him in the fight (Fig. 160). The small medicine-bag attached to the figure is painted with blue stripes, and contains a mixture consisting of a root called hiitcauxû- ûwaxu, of amalgam from a looking- glass, and of the excrement of wasps. A feather somewhat painted with green hangs from the medicine-bag. The body of the figure contains parts of two white plume feathers with quills. Hair is attached to the back of the head. The entire figure is worn on the head as a battle-amulet.

There is also in this collection of medicines and amulets a stuffed mole- skin to which are attached a bag of medicine and a small ring of red catlinite (Fig. 161). To touch a mole, or even the earth thrown up by one, gives the itch. The medicine kept with this mole-skin is used to cure this itch, as well as the bites of insects, or diseases supposed to be caused by them. It is therefore called biisänoxu (" insect medicine"). The medi- cine in the bag consists of scented leaves called tcaaxuwina[n],

Fig. 160 ($\frac{50}{300}$, *e*). Figure from a Medicine-bag. Length, 14 cm.

of charred tobacco, of hard red seeds called naⁿwubäei ("southern berries"), of the plant called biisänoxi, of the dust, probably the spores, of small mushrooms, which are supposed to fall
from the sky with the rain, and of powdered bone of hiintcäbiit,
the water-monster. Bones of a very large mammal or reptile

Fig. 161 ($\frac{50}{300}$, *d*). Stuffed Mole-skin. Length, 11 cm.

are not common on the river-banks of the Arapaho reservation
in Oklahoma, and are looked upon as the bones of this monster.
The small bag containing this mixed medicine has the shape of a
mushroom, it is said. Four small pits have been bored in the
catlinite ring, giving this the appearance of a world-symbol.

Another amulet worn in fighting consists of a bracelet or
armlet of badger-skin, painted green and yellow inside, to
which are attached a gopher-skin, an owl-claw, several bells,
feathers, some of the red seeds called "southern berries," and
a few skin fringes painted yellow, with green ends (Plate
LXXXV). The badger-skin wrist-band is used to increase the
speed of the horse that is ridden; the claw helps the wearer
to seize the enemy; the motion of the feathers drives away the

enemy; and the bells represent the noise of the fight. In case of need, one of the red seeds is broken open and chewed. Besides a battle-amulet, this object is also used as a rattle in doctoring the sick.

Two elk-tails on handles are used, first to point out the diseased spot while the doctor sings, and afterwards to brush away the pain in that part. They were both seen used in a dream. One of these tails is decorated with a small ring of catlinite, a brass clock-wheel representing the sun, and a piece of a Ute scalp (Fig. 162). To the other are attached several of the red southern berries. Water in which these berries have been boiled causes vomiting.

A small medicine-bag contains horse-medicine and amulets to cause mares to have colts of a certain color. The medicine in the bag is given to the mare, and she is then patted, and rubbed on the flanks with a bean of a certain color. The use of a red bean will make the colt roan or bay; of a white bean, white or buckskin. Others, spotted beans which the owner valued too highly to part with, are used to produce a painted colt. The medicine with these bean amulets consists of horse-fetlock used as incense and of the root of a plant called hiwaxuhaxhi-waxu ("horse-root"). This is given internally to a sick horse, or is rubbed on the nose of a tired horse to refresh it. The medicine used by this man to cure rattlesnake-bites consists of a root called ciiciiyenaxu ("snake-root"), of snake-scales, and of the red southern berry.

Fig. 162 ($\frac{50}{300}$, *f*). Tail of an Elk used in Doctoring. Length, 42 cm.

A one-legged man among the northern Arapaho, noted for his ability to do conjurer's tricks, said he thought the

time would come when the great beings would meet in the
new world and contend to see who could do the most.   He
thought that he would win with the feats he could do.

The paraphernalia of this man were the following.

Two stones used as amulets, representing, one the earth,
and the other meat.

A rawhide rattle, shown in Fig. 163, made of the scrotum

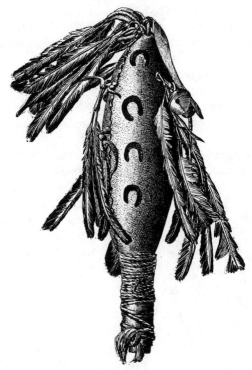

Fig. 163 ($\frac{50}{1011}$).   Rattle with Symbolic Decorations.   Length, 26⅛ cm.

of a buffalo-bull.   This rattle is elliptical instead of globular,
as is more often the case; but occasionally rattles of even
slender shape are made.   The owner was fasting on a hill.
Toward the end of his fast, his grandfather, the sun, directed
him to make this rattle.   The rattle is painted red, and marked
with dark horseshoe-shaped figures, symbolizing both the sun

and horse-tracks, and with small figures shaped like a 'Y bisected in the fork, which represent bird-tracks. Yellow-hammer or similar feathers and little brass bells are attached at four places, and again at four places below, this time without bells. At the top is a larger bunch of feathers and another bell· These attachments are made by a thong passing through a small raised area of the skin without perforating it to the interior. These thong-holes are perhaps made by a skewer left in the fresh hide. The handle of the rattle contains a stick, and is wrapped with twine. This rattle is used to cure the sick. It drives away the spirits, and aids the medicine that is administered.

A fossil shell found on the occasion of the owner's fasting on a hill represents a monument or pile of stones (çiäya^n). It is used to touch patients, and is also taken into the sweat-house. Incense of ibaa^{n}tou, fir (?) needles, is used with this stone.

A scaly turtle-tail or fish-back mounted on stuffed buck-skin, to one end of which are tied feathers, is used both as a

war-amulet and in doctoring (Fig. 164). In the latter case the sick person is fanned and brushed with the feathers. In going to war, the piece is worn on the head, on the chest, or on the side, hanging from a strip passing over one shoulder. The feathers produce swiftness, and the hard scales cause invulnerability.

A root called neniitcicaxaa^n, or pith-root, is used by this medicine-man as a cure especially for fits, but more generally for other illnesses. The root is eaten whole.

Fig. 164 ($\frac{8}{10}\frac{9}{13}$). A Turtle-tail, used as a War-amulet. Length, 27 cm.

A head-dress of split and in part trimmed feathers contains eagle and perhaps other gray-black feathers and a single plume dyed red (Plate LXXXVI). A small short stick is the foundation to which the ends of the quills are tied. Three central quills trimmed to the tip and the red plume are stiff, and stand when the head-dress is held up: the other feathers fall, because their quills have been split. It seems that the head-dress was worn in the ghost or crow dance, hanging down as illustrated. Feeble or weak people, and children, were brushed with it during the dance.

A man who at the time of the ghost-dance excitement fasted for seven days subsequently made the following objects, and told this story of his experiences.

The informant stated that he gave himself up to the ghost-dance, and tried to see visions. He put all his thoughts on the matter, but failed to have any visions. Then he made a vow to fast on Coyote Hills. He went up on the hills naked, except for a blanket, and during the night prayed and cried. For four days he saw nothing. He heard only the noise of the people talking near him and other things to distract him. But the last three days were more satisfactory. He saw super-natural things plainly, as if in full daylight, not as when asleep. A spirit came. He did not look at it; but it told him, "If you do as I tell you, it will be well." He continued not to look at it. It seemed to be bright day. The spirit directed him not to find fault, or be critical of other people, but to be generous and pleasant. It told him that the birds and animals would be his friends, and protect him; that, whenever there was a new moon, he would have a dream which would show him the future. It told him to have fortitude; for the sun would give him strength to complete the seven days of fasting which he had vowed. This spirit appeared on the fifth day. It brought nothing, but said that after the seven days were com-pleted, when he went back, the clouds would go with him, threatening rain. It told him then to think of the above, of the star exactly overhead, and of the morning star, which is the last to rise in the night. These would protect him while he was asleep. It told him also, that, when the day of the new world came, there would be signs in the morning, and the following colors would be visible at the rising of the sun, — black, green, red, yellow, and white. Finally the spirit told him to run when he went home after completing his seven days of fasting, but to stop if he met any one.

When the informant had fasted for seven days, he returned. As he ran it seemed to him that he was not touching the ground, but he saw that his feet were on the earth. As he ran he kept his hands open. Then there was an even, round hill in front of him. On it stood a man with a dark-blue blanket. Then he thought of what the spirit had told him, and stopped and went to this man. This person had one arm hanging out of his blanket. The arm was naked and fleshy. He held a black cane with a golden head, and stood facing the west. This person said, "I am not the father nor the messenger, but I am whom you have heard of and talked of, — the turtle. I own the rain. When you want rain, pray to me, for I am the fog. I know about your fasting, that you have a strong heart, and I will help you if you want rain. You have done well to fast for seven days, for Above-Nih'ā^{n}ça^n thinks well of that number. When you are at a feast, let the people take a little food and give it to me. Let them do this whenever they can, and I will remember them and protect them. You have done right to obey the spirit and stop here. Do not speak evil of people. You will have no difficulties hereafter. Everything will be pleasant." When the turtle spoke to him thus, it was a stout man, but, after it had finished, he saw it as a turtle.

It appears that there is a symbolic reference to the turtle in the round hill.

The following objects were made and kept by this man as the result of his experience.

A white flag or handkerchief (Fig. 165). The figure of a person painted on this represents the first spirit seen by the informant. This spirit carried a yellow and a green handkerchief, had his face painted yellow, and wore a red head feather. The turtle painted on this cloth is his real supernatural helper. The moon is represented, because the first spirit told him that every new moon he should dream of the future. The crescent is placed horizontally, which to the Arapaho is an omen of health and prosperity. When one horn of the moon is much higher than the other, it is believed that there will be general

sickness. The Maltese cross on this handkerchief represents
the morning star, which the spirit said would protect him. A
five-pointed star is painted in black, green, red, yellow, and
white, the five colors that were to be visible on the morning of

Fig. 165 ($\frac{50}{6327}$). Painted Cloth representing a Dream Experience. Length, 88 cm.; width, 91 cm.

the last day. Zigzag lines across the central portion of this
star represent its rays or twinkling. The white handkerchief
is bordered by margins of four different colors,—black, green,
red, and yellow; making, with the central white, the same five
colors prophesied.

A small human figure of buckskin (Fig. 166), with five crow-
feathers attached along one side of the body and a red-painted
fringe along the other, also represents this man's supernatural helper. It is fastened to strings so as to be worn as a
necklace. At the back of the head is hanging hair. At the tip
of the hair are red-dyed plumes. The body is painted yellow,
with red and green face and a red stripe down and one across
the body. The rear side is painted black and red.

The head of his supernatural being was further represented by this man in carving at the end of a club-shaped stick (Fig. 167). The greater part of this stick is wrapped with fur; and eagle, magpie, and perhaps crow feathers (some of them partly slit from the quills) are attached to the head. The being's hair is represented by furry buffalo-skin covering the

Fig. 166.   Fig. 167.

Fig. 166 ($\frac{50}{828}$).   Necklace bearing an Image of a Supernatural Helper.   Length, 72 cm.
Fig. 167 ($\frac{50}{355}$).   Carved Stick representing a Supernatural Helper.   Length, 58 cm.

back of the figure's head. Such three-dimensional carving as in this piece is very unusual among the Arapaho at the present day, and it is doubtful to what extent it was practised in aboriginal times.

A rawhide ornament in the shape of a Maltese cross represents the morning star. This cross, including a white china
disk (a modern substitute for the old shell gorgets) fastened to
its middle, is of the same five colors — black, yellow, green, and
red, with white in the middle — that appear on the handkerchief.
Shell gorgets of this type are used as offerings at the stone
piles on mountain-tops. This one is an offering to the morning
star. Attached to the ends of the cross by thongs are red,
yellow, and black down feathers representing the clouds, the
red in the morning and the evening, the yellow during the day,
and the black before rain.   The arrangement of colors of the
down feathers in relation to the colors of the cross-arms to
which they are attached, is the following: black arm, red;
yellow arm, yellow; green arm, black; and red arm, red.

A head-dress of long, black upright feathers attached to a
stick, the feathers being partly trimmed to the quill, is one of
seven made by Sitting-Bull, the originator of the ghost-dance
among the Arapaho, together with seven ghost-dance shirts
or dresses, some of which are still religiously preserved.

An iron chain to which a number of amulets and medicines
are attached is worn over one shoulder (Plate LXXXVII)·
The various objects on this are the following: —

A turtle-tail ornament at the base with a charm of blue
beads. This is worn as a head-dress when the owner sees a
cloud that appears dangerous, in order that the cloud, which
is the turtle (under the turtle's control), will not injure him.
The blue of the beads on this head-dress represents the sky.
The turtle-tail itself is said to be a cloud.

A horse-fetlock, with which the owner rubs his body when
he is about to break a horse.

A horse-tooth.

Another turtle-tail.

A piece of horse-hoof.   When one is kicked by a horse, this
is used to moderate the swelling.

A deer-tail.

Two deer-fetlocks.

Another deer-tail.   These last four pieces are all from animals that were hunted a long time before being killed.

Another turtle-tail, regarded as the foremost of all the objects on the chain. It is the largest piece attached to it, and the chain is worn so that this hangs at the bottom, "like a heart."

Another horse-tooth.

A horse-fetlock and a piece of otter-skin, worn as a head-dress in order not to be thrown in breaking a horse.

A red-painted turtle-tail and a slightly blue whitish plume mounted on a short stick, and worn at gatherings or feasts. The hardness of the scales of the tail represents the owner's health; and the feather plume, his lightness.

Another horse-tooth. The informant was once bitten through the finger by a horse, but a fresh nail grew over the wound.

Another deer-fetlock.

Another deer-tail.

Another deer-fetlock.

Strips of deer-skin.

A deer-tail secured when he was a boy or young man.

A deer-fetlock.

Another horse-tooth.

A man who was middle-aged at the time of the ghost-dance had the following dream: He saw himself standing alone on a green prairie, looking to the east. On his left, to the north, he then saw a person seated, dressed entirely in black silk. He thought that this was the messenger. The man wanted to approach him and touch him; but his thoughts were not strong enough, and he was unable to move. Then this person in black spoke to him. He knew all the man's thoughts. He told him of the new world that was to be, and that they were now on a cloud. Then the informant saw the earth below him and the sky above him at an equal distance. The person in black, who was the crow, then showed him a rainbow extending from east to west, and another from south to north. The informant was then taken by him to the spot where the two rainbows crossed one another. There he stood, and the crow told him to look up. He then saw where the father was, and saw the thoughts of all mankind reaching up to him. He saw also birds of all kinds. Two of these were the foremost, —

the eagle (niihi, literally, "bird") and the crow.   He saw also
the sun, the stars, and the morning star.

This dream was painted by the informant on a white sheet
worn as a blanket (Fig. 168).   The extremities of the two
lower corners are half filled in with red, representing the earth,
the rest of the sheet representing the above.   A pipe in one
corner, with a blue bowl, represents a black soapstone pipe; one
painted in red, in the other lower corner, a more ordinary, less
sacred, catlinite pipe.   Near the centre of the sheet is a red
circle from which yellow lines radiate.   This is the sun.   The

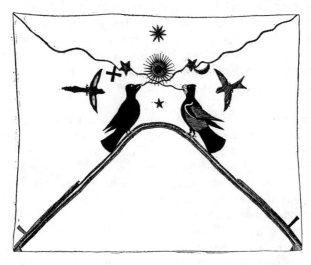

Fig. 168 ($\frac{50}{552}$). Painting representing a Dream Experience. Length, 2.13 m.; width, 1.68 m.

interior of this figure consists of several rings of different colors,
representing the rainbow.   The rainbow is also shown in a long
arch passing across the lower part of the blanket, painted in
stripes of four colors.   The upper and outermost color is blue.
It was on this, where the two rainbows crossed, that the informant stood and looked up to the highest heaven.   On each
side of the upper part of this rainbow-arch is the figure of a
large bird.   One of these is the crow; the other, which has
much the appearance of a parrot, represents niihi (" bird," or
" eagle").   This word here evidently denotes the thunder-bird.

This bird was said to be supposed to be in a cloud. Behind is a bull-bat, which is also indicative of rain, because this bird flies before rain. Behind the crow is a flying magpie. From the mouth of each of the two large birds a wavy line issues diagonally upward across the sheet. These lines are the voices of the birds. Each of the lines is in contact with a five-pointed star, which indicates that the birds' voices reach the sky, and are heard. The five-pointed star is evidently not aboriginal with the Arapaho. Above the figure of the sun is a ten-pointed star, larger than the others. This is, no doubt, merely on account of its size, the morning star. A yellow five-pointed star below the sun is an ordinary star. The two stars in contact with the voice-lines of the birds are surrounded by small lines indicating their shining. A cross behind the head of the crow represents the morning star, and a blue crescent in corresponding position behind the head of the other bird is the moon.

A man noted for his long hair was told in a dream to preserve all his hair as he combed it out. In consequence, he braided together all this loose hair until (at the time the specimen was obtained from him, when he was beginning to be an old man) the rope had reached a length of thirty feet, with a thickness of about half an inch.

An old woman stated that she had once been attacked and bitten by a bear. From that time on, she dreamed much of bears. In one of her dreams, a bear told her to wear bear-claws, to paint in a certain way, and to use certain plants for medicine and incense, and she would become a doctor; but she refused the supernatural gift.

A blind southern Arapaho, having been asked to show his supernatural powers, refused, on the ground that the people were then camped together for a dance, and that he would do nothing disturbing to good feeling and happiness. The following day he offered to vomit brass rings and bullets. Being refused, he offered to produce the bullets and some lime for a smaller payment. After some negotiations, this was accepted, and without preparation he began to cough and retch, finally spitting out four round bullets. Soon he began again, sucking inside his cheeks more than before. He then spat out a pink substance looking like wet slaked lime. After a short time, he began coughing, and sucking internally again, this time producing a blue substance in the same manner as before. The performance ended, he appeared to swallow the bullets again.

One of a pair of wristlets of otter-skin, ornamented with yellow-hammer or similar feathers and a plume, and possessing magical properties, belonged to this man, and is shown in Fig. 169. Attached to the wristlet is a small medicine-bag painted red. This was said to contain a mixture of powdered black iron ore, copper filings, gopher-eyes, snake-eyes, and the medicine tcetcäätcei-root, used in the crazy-dance, and thought to possess the power of paralyzing. With this small medicine-bag is a steel needle wrapped to a thong like a small feather. Some of the medicine being thrown on the ground, the needle at once pierces the heart of any one desired. The owner affirms that he once killed an antelope from a distance in this way. It fell down dead while running. Its heart contained his needle. At the other end of the wristlet are an iron and a catlinite ring.

Fig. 169 ($\frac{50}{710}$, b). Wristlet. Full length, 45 cm.

An elderly man among the northern Arapaho made the following statements in regard to the acquisition and transfer of supernatural power.

When such power was given by the spirit or some object in nature, certain restrictions were usually imposed. The supernatural being might say, "Do not eat the heart or the kidney, and do not pierce or stick any food that you are eating." Or, again, "There is one thing that I do not want you to eat, that is the head. If you do, your teeth will soon fall out, your strength will not last, and you will not become old." If a man who had received such powers supernaturally began to transfer them to others, he did not give them all away. After having begun to transfer his powers, he was even more careful than before to observe the restrictions. He would not drink from the same cup that other people did. Generally, when such powers were transferred, they were either sold, or given to sons or nephews. A young man might pray to an old man for his power. Then, instead of going out on the hills and suffering hardships to acquire it, he received his power by instruction. He paid the old man for each sitting with him. He learned the old man's medicine-roots and their uses, his way of painting, his songs, and so on. By the time the old man was dead, the young man had his power. A man's medicine-bag was generally repainted every year, when the new grass came up. Sometimes the supernatural power given to a person is bad for his family. The spirit does not mention this to him; but the recipient's family die off one by one, leaving him alone. Sometimes a man takes such power when he should refuse it on account of the effect on his relatives.

An old man who had horse-medicine taught it to his son and several other young men. In teaching it to them, he drew on the ground, with red paint, a horse facing to the left, and with yellow paint, another horse or a mule, somewhat smaller, facing the north. While this medicine was in a tent, no peg or other part of the tent might be removed, lest there should be a storm.

A famous medicine-man called Hänätcä^{n}hanaati, who died about twenty years ago, and who had particular power in bringing the buffalo, lived in a tent painted red, with black buffalo, the morning star, the sun, and other designs upon it. Children were not allowed to approach this tent for fear that sticks might be thrown against it. On his ceremonial rawhide medicine-case this medicine-man used the curious symbolic design of crescents and forked upright figures, that has been described on p. 134. He is said to have originated this design, but this seems improbable. He taught many men part of his medicine, among them being Little-Left-Hand, Sage-Bark, Young-Bull, Night, and Howling-Man. The ceremony of calling the buffalo was

called naⁿtanää.   Men stood in two long lines while the medicine-man went between them, leading the herd.   A certain
man tried to perform this feat, but failed.   His failure was
attributed to his making the attempt only in order to secure
a girl he wanted to marry; and the loss of an eye which he
suffered not long afterward was attributed to his failure.

After a certain chief, called Bänääseti, was buried, his grave
settled, until there was a depression in the ground.   It was
said that the thunder had taken him up out of the ground,
and thereafter people were not afraid to travel over the place
where he had been buried, whereas they always avoided other
graves.

A woman who was bitten by a rattlesnake was treated by a
medicine-man as follows.   He took the snake's head, chopped
it up, dried it and powdered it, mixed it with dried blood of
the snake, and added a medicine-root and some pepper.   The
mixture was then sprinkled over a cloth.   The medicine-man
abraded the skin in the wrist until it bled.   Then he tied the
cloth around it, put on a piece of fat, and kept the place warm
with a hot stone.

When persons, especially children, suddenly become sick
with pains in the side, or back, or neck, they are thought to
have been shot by a ghost.   The object which has entered the
body, and which may be a bone, tooth, hair, or piece of skin
of a dead person, is called a " ghost arrow" (çiikanaçi).   The
doctor says to the patient, "A ghost has shot you, çiiktcäbiin."
When the doctor sucks out the object, which sometimes proves
to be liquid or filthy, either he or the patient swallows it.   If
the doctor swallows it, it increases his power of sucking objects
of this kind.

People fasting on hills frequently set up piles of stone there.
It seems that these monuments are made either to symbolize
persons, or are thought to resemble them.

Children often wear a walnut on a string around the neck,
or, while they are very small, around the wrist.   This nut is
thought to resemble the face of a skull, and therefore to be
effective in keeping off ghosts.   The tree is called täbiiçabiic
(" cutnose-bush").

The root called niäätä[n], used otherwise as a component of incense and on the regalia of certain age-societies, is also put around children's necks as a general amulet.

A root called haakahaa (Museum No. $\frac{50}{991}$) is said to be used to put into the ears of crazy-dancers, making them deaf, it is thought, and at the same time crazy. Mushrooms are also used for this purpose by both the Arapaho and the Gros Ventre.

The bones of large mammals or reptiles, found especially on river-banks, and thought to be the bones of the hiintcäbiit or water-monsters, are frequently used by the Arapaho as ingredients of medicine, as well as for sucking out diseases, the porous bone being applied to sores or wounds.

For bites of centipedes or tarantulas, these animals are crushed and then mixed with a plant (after it has been powdered) known by the whites of Oklahoma as "shoestring" (Museum No. $\frac{50}{709}$).

Children's diarrhœa is thought to be caused by bad milk, and is cured either by sucking the breast or by drinking a decoction of a plant called beçenetcaana[n] ("breast-liquid," beçenetc being milk). This plant grows a foot or two feet high, has round leafless stems, and contains an abundance of white, thickish juice, which no doubt has been the cause of its use for this purpose. The woman drinks the medicine when stooping on her knees, so that it may run into her breasts. A mouthful of the decoction may also be sprinkled over the child by the medicine-man in order to cool it.

While the chief physical means of cure employed by medicine-men was sucking, bleeding was also practised. Pieces of "black glass" were fastened to sticks, and these were laid over a vein after the skin had been wet. The stick was then struck with another piece of wood, so that the blood spurted out. Bleeding was performed in spring and autumn, apparently for general indisposition rather than for specific pain.

Two small buffalo-horns in which are cut figures representing the sun, the moon, a star, and sun-rays, are used as points to throwing-sticks slid on the ice in play, as well as for doctoring. In case of rheumatism or similar ailments, a hole is cut in the

skin, and the hollow horn set over the cut The horn is then
supposed to suck the wound of itself, dropping off, like the last
specimen, when full of blood.   One of these horns, and the
designs carved on the other, are shown in Figs. 170, 171.

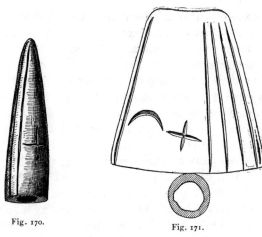

Fig. 170.

Fig. 171.

Fig. 170 ($\frac{50}{348}$).   A Cupping Instrument.   Length 8.5 cm.
Fig. 171 ($\frac{50}{329}$).   Design on a Cupping Instrument.

A similar small buffalo-horn used in doctoring (Museum
No. $\frac{50}{1093}$) is put over a hole in the skin in order to draw blood.
This horn is completely perforated, so that it can be sucked
through; but when it is in use the hole at the upper end is
plugged with medicine.   The horn is said to remain hanging
to the wound until it is filled with blood, when it drops off.
It is used especially on the head.

A woman's mortar and pestle (Museum No. $\frac{50}{940}$) were
used by the northern Arapaho for grinding medicine.   The
mortar consisted of part of a quartz-like concretion, the central concave portion of which held the medicine.   The pestle
was a smaller entire concretion, approximately globular, but
quite irregular.

In one family half a globular concretion, hollow inside, was
seen.   This was kept to be dipped into water containing
medicine, then to be put on the head of a woman about to
give birth to a child, in order to ease her delivery.

A river mussel-shell (Museum No. $\frac{50}{94}$) was used for various purposes, — to catch the blood of newly killed game to be cooked and eaten, as a spoon for medicine, and, on account of its smoothness or slipperiness, as an amulet to help a woman in labor.

A necklace worn as a charm in battle is shown in Plate LXXXVIII. The body of the necklace consists of large round beads which represent bullets. A brass ball strung on the necklace also represents a bullet. A number of pieces of iron, mainly hammers and triggers, are taken from various guns. Their purpose is to cause the enemy's gun to fail to go off. At the bottom of the necklace, over the breast of the wearer, is a ring three or four inches in diameter, and covered with white beads. This ring represents earthwork defences. There are four spots of blue beads among the white. These represent clouds of smoke from the guns, which serve to make the fighters invisible. Inside the ring, threads covered with white beads form a loose network representing a spider-web. The spider-web is so fine as to be often invisible. Beings can fly through it without injuring it, and it is a trap. From the ring hangs a little cluster of objects. In this there are several strips of weasel-skin or a substitute fur, whose yellowish color denotes smoke. There is also a piece of red cloth concealed by gray cloth. The red is completely covered in order that the blood of the person who wears the necklace shall not be shed. There is, further, a small bag of medicine. The medicine in this was said to contain a grain of gunpowder and a little dried flesh of a kingfisher. The kingfisher-flesh is used because this bird swoops and strikes. Actually the medicine consists, so far as can be seen, of a species of seeds. Tied to the medicine-bag is a piece of round pearly shell, which is held up against the light so as to reflect against the enemy. When the reflection strikes the enemy, they become unable to escape. Where the groups of objects are held together, there are a few turns of light-blue beads, indicating smoke, or haze, or fog.

Fig. 172 shows a necklace consisting of an iron chain to which are attached several red pear-shaped stones (apparently natural formations), two iron rings, and an arrow-head. The stones, being shaped much like small medicine-bags, are used as medicine. They are rubbed over the body, or, in case of intoxication, held in the mouth. The iron rings, because hard and indestructible, preserve the wearer in sound health. The arrow-head symbolizes the old life.

Fig. 172 ($\frac{50}{711}$). Necklace bearing Amulets.   Length of chain, 112 cm.

Specimen Museum No. $\frac{50}{851}$ consists of a piece of red sand-stone similar to those attached to the necklace just described, and, like them, apparently an unworked double concretion. In this case the larger portion of the stone far exceeds the smaller in size. A sinew is wrapped around the neck, and this holds in place the two ends of a thong which serve as a necklace for the amulet. The stone was called a turtle.

Specimen Museum No. $\frac{50}{950}$ is a small antelope-horn used as an amulet for children, to cause them to grow fast, and learn to walk. It is worn from a string around the neck. It is said to be used also to make horses run fast.

An elderly woman used as an amulet a number of small

pebbles, which she kept tied up in a cloth or bag. A few of them are shown in Fig. 173. Some of the stones are naturally pointed, others more round. The former represent canine teeth; the rounded ones, molars. The stones, being loose, represent teeth that have fallen out from old age, indicating the possessor's wish to reach that period of life.

Fig. 173 ($\frac{50}{349}$).   Amulets representing Teeth.   Length of *a*, 2 cm.

Three stone amulets of natural shape (Fig. 174), evidently kept on account of their resemblance to animals, were thought to be similar to a turtle (*a*), a bird (*b*), and a skunk or horse-hoof (*c*). The turtle stone was said to have been found inside

Fig. 174 ($\frac{50}{982}$–$\frac{50}{984}$).   Amulets representing a Turtle, Bird, and Skunk.   Length of *a*, 3 cm.;
b, 3 cm.; *c*, 5 cm.

a horse's body.   In case of diarrhœa, it was placed on the abdomen to warm the intestines.   The bird amulet was placed at the head of sick persons, while the skunk stone was held in the hand by sick persons while sleeping.

Two small translucent pebbles containing small black figures, and used as amulets, are shown in Fig. 175. Amulet *a* was said to have reference to water. The entire stone is thought to resemble a lake. The parallel lines were said to look like

a   b

Fig. 175 ($\frac{50}{926}$, $\frac{50}{927}$). Translucent Pebbles used as Amulets. Length of *a*, 2.5 cm.

waves, and a heavy double figure was called an island with trees on it, while near the upper end of the pebble a cross is regarded as the morning star, and above this are horizontal lines said to be clouds. Amulet *b* is fastened to a thong, so that it can be worn in the hair. It is worn when riding race-horses. Small black figures in the interior of this pebble are thought to resemble cedar-trees.

Fig. 176 represents one of two natural stones resembling the black fossils used by the Blackfeet as buffalo-stones. They were called centipedes. They are painted red, and were kept by the owner in a bag of incense. At the sun-dance he would take them out and lay them near incense.

Fig. 176 ($\frac{50}{1087}$,^{a}). Amulet representing a Centipede. Length, 2.5 cm.

Besides the two medicine-bags of badger-skin whose contents have been described, the Arapaho collections in the Museum contain medicine-bags of skunk, squirrel, prairie-dog, and beaver skin. The beaver bag is from a young animal. None of the bags are ornamented with embroidery, or in any other way, except that the portions of the skin free from hair, such as the inside of the throat and the tail (which some cases is split along the bottom), are painted red. The only one of these medicine-bags, other than the two previously described, that contains medicine, is Museum No. $\frac{50}{44}$, — a skunk-skin bag obtained through Rev. Walter C. Roe. This skin is filled with twenty medicine-bags, some of skin, some of cloth. These all consist of square or circular pieces of material, in the centre of which the medicine is gathered, and which are then folded around the medicine, and tied above it with a thong. Some of the bags are painted red. The medicines are in most cases ground or powdered, and are unrecognizable. None of the twenty bags contains a large quantity of medicine, and in many the amount is very minute. The owner of this bag having died before it was secured, no information was obtainable as to the composition and uses of the medicine.

Fig. 177 ($\frac{4}{8}$). Medicine-bag.
Height of bag, 7 cm.

Beaded medicine-bags similar to the small pieces of skin generally used as bags for holding medicine, but also different from them in more elaborate ornamentation and in holding a somewhat larger quantity of medicine, are sometimes made by the Arapaho. They seem to be used for what may be called " household medicines," in distinction from the medicines with more specifically supernatural connections, and perhaps for incense also. Such a bag (Fig. 177) was obtained through Rev. Walter C. Roe. The bag itself is a circular piece of skin painted red outside and yellow inside, and edged with a row of blue and a row of white beads. When the bag is gathered together over the medicine, this border is brought together at the top. At the very centre of the back, on the outer side, is an ornamented area about an inch in diameter. Around this are four concentric circles of bead-work in contact with each other, each about a quarter of an inch wide. Their colors are respectively greenish-blue, yellow, white, and a dark blue. The thong with which the medicine-bag is gathered has tied to it a ring of catlinite. The thong is wound several times around the bag. Its two ends widen out, and at the very end are notched once. These wider ends are edged by rows of greenish-blue and of yellow beads, and there is on each a small circle of greenish-blue beads. The contents of this bag consist of conifer-leaves, apparently fir-needles, which are used by the Arapaho as incense. There are also a small red pebble and a smooth orange-colored haw in the bag.

Another bag of the same type (Museum No. $\frac{50}{1019}$) was obtained among the northern Arapaho. This contains snuff made of lichen growing on conifer-bark, and used for headache. It is also circular, and little more than half a foot in diameter. The outside is painted yellow. One half of the circumference is edged with a row of red beads, the other half with blue beads. The blue was said to represent the sky, the red the clouds. Near the middle of the outside of the bag, in the portion which actually encloses the contents, are five small beaded figures, — two blue crescents, two red crescents, and a red cross. The cross is the morning star; the blue crescents, the moon; the red crescents, the sun.

Rawhide rattles of a shape typical on the Plains — consisting of a spherical or somewhat elongated head two or three inches in diameter, and a straight handle about six inches long — occur among the Arapaho. Rattles of this character seem to be used by the seven old men constituting the highest society in the ceremonial organization. On the whole, however, the use of rattles of this type is characteristic of the medicine-man and his individual supernatural powers, and not of the tribal ceremonies. In most of these ceremonies, rattles are either not used, as in the crazy-dance, or consist of bunches of hoofs attached to sticks, as in the dog-dance. Rawhide rattles are used in the star-dance, the first preliminary to the series of tribal ceremonies; but these rattles are small, kite-shaped, and flat, thus differing very distinctly from the globular or oval, or even sausage-shaped rattles, of the medicine-men. Among the Gros Ventre the same distinction exists between the star-dance rattle and the ordinary medicine-man's rattle,

Fig. 178 ($\frac{50}{3\,2\,4}$).   Rattle representing a Person.   Length, 52 cm.

though the Gros Ventre star-dance rattle is quite different from that of the Arapaho. The medicine-men's rattles under present consideration are made of two pieces of hide firmly sewed together, the stitched seam passing up one side of the handle and the head, over the top of the head, and down the other side. The head is apparently sewed when the hide is green, and dried over a filling of sand. The rattling is said to be produced by gravel. A stick is inserted in the handle, and the handle is almost always wrapped with cloth, skin, or thongs. Usually, feathers or similar ornaments are attached to thongs at the very top of the rattle; and in many cases cloth, skin, or other hanging substances fall from the lower end of the handle. Most of the globular rattles are streaked with vertical lines or incisions. It is not clear how these are produced. In some specimens they are sufficiently marked to cause the head of the rattle to have a distinctly corrugated appearance. In one case they would seem to have been burnt in.

The rattle shown in Fig. 178 was said to represent as a whole a person with a head-dress; the globular portion of the rattle, of course, forming the head, and the bells and feathers attached to the top, the head-dress. Among the feathers there are two white plumes lightly dyed red: these, because white and light, are said, as in many other instances, to represent cleanliness, and, because dyed red, to represent red paint. At the very top of the head of the rattle, where the bells are attached, is a circular area painted green: below this are concentric rings painted respectively red, blue, yellow, green, blue, and yellow. This painting represents the sun and rainbow, and occupies about the upper half of the head of the rattle. The lower half is occupied by vertical depressed lines painted yellow: these are sun-rays. The entire handle of the rattle is enclosed in a feathery owl-skin; two claws and the tail hanging below the end of the handle. Screech-owls are ghosts; and these feathers are here used in order to drive away ghosts when the rattle is used.

The specimen shown in Fig. 179 has a somewhat larger head to than usual. The top is ornamented with a bunch of thongs to which yellow-hammer or similar feathers appear to have been attached, and of which a few fragments remain. The handle is wrapped for the greater part of its length with thong, and this, again, has been wrapped for the greater portion of its length with string. The handle, as usual, contains a stick.

On one side of the rattle a depressed vertical black line or stripe, apparently produced, like all the other markings on this piece, by burning, extends from the middle of the top two-thirds or more of the distance down the head. Below this

stripe are three small circles in a row. On each side of the stripe is a similar single circle, and above each of these circles a horizontal line. Still farther to the sides, near the stitched edge, are two circles. This entire described half of the head represents a person's face; the vertical striping being the nose, the row of three circles the mouth, the pair of circles with lines above them the eyes and eyebrows, and the two sidemost circles the ears. On the opposite side, or back, are three straight vertical lines extending the length of the head of the rattle, and, on each side of these, two wavy lines, making seven in all. These lines represent hair. Still farther to the

Fig. 179 (⅝⅝). Rattle representing a Face. Length, 37 cm.

sides, near the stitched edges, are a number of small circles the significance of which is not clear. This valuable specimen, which is a medicine-man's rattle used in singing over the sick, is said to have been made of hide of a buffalo-calf, and was obtained through Rev. Walter C. Roe.

Specimen Museum No. $\frac{50}{854}$ is a plain rattle. The head is painted entirely red. It is streaked with the usual vertical depressions to a marked degree. The attachment at the top consists of a single feather at the end of a thong. The handle, which contains a stick, is covered with black cloth, the ends of which hang below the handle. This cloth is wrapped to the handle by cord.

Specimen Museum No. $\frac{50}{855}$ was obtained from the same individual, and is of about the same shape. The handle is very similar, being covered with black cloth, the end of which hangs free, and the upper portion of which is wrapped to the handle with white cord. The head of the rattle is painted red. Horizontally around its middle extends a green-painted ornament consisting of eight hanging loops or festoons. This rattle is further ornamented by four vertical rows, each of four thongs, fastened to the rawhide of the head. These thongs are passed under a small raised portion of the skin without appearing to pierce it entirely. They are knotted once after passing through the skin. The shorter of the hanging ends has a white plume tied to it. The longer end hangs free. The thongs are painted green.

The rattle shown in Fig. 163, and obtained from the northern Arapaho, resembles the last specimen in having feathers attached by thongs to its head. It is longer in proportion to its diameter than any of the preceding forms, being made of a buffalo-scrotum. It has been described in connection with the other implements belonging to the medicine-man who was its owner.

Specimen Museum No. $\frac{5\,0}{9\,3\,8}$, *a*, also from the northern Arapaho, is still more slender in proportion to its length than the last piece. The head merges imperceptibly into the handle. The total length is about the same as that of the southern Arapaho globular-headed rattles, but the transverse diameter is only about one-half as great. This rattle is entirely unornamented, except that it is painted red. A fossil univalve shell is tied to it by a red-painted thong.

Medicine-men's h o o f r a t t l e s, consisting of a number of hoofs separately attached to thongs, as distinguished from the hollow rawhide rattles, are also used. The specimen shown in Fig. 180 is from the northern Arap-

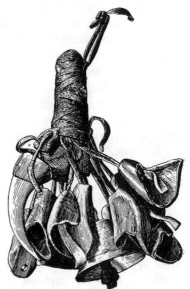

Fig. 180 ($\frac{5\,0}{10\,1\,6}$). Hoof Rattle. Length, 16 cm.

aho. This was said to have been used in the sweat-house. It consists of about a dozen elk-hoofs, a bear-claw, and a brass bell, attached to a handle by red-painted thongs. The interior of this handle, which is all together about three inches long, consists of a braid of sweet-grass. This is surrounded by folded skin painted red, and this, in turn, is wrapped with red-painted thong. A similar rattle, also from the northern Arapaho, is exhibited in the United States National Museum. It is, perhaps, more than a coincidence that both of these hoofrattles, and both the elliptical rattles in the American Museum, are from the northern Arapaho, and all that are globular-headed from the southern Arapaho.

Characteristics of Individual Supernatural Power. — As has been stated, the most characteristic way in which the Arapaho acquire shamanistic or individual supernatural power is by going out to seek it, more often as adults than at the time of puberty. To the seeker there appears a spirit, in the form of a person, from whom he receives instruction. As the spirit vanishes, it is seen to assume the form of some animal. Parts of this animal are often used as fetishes or medicine by the shaman. In many cases its skin is employed as his medicine-bag, and often there seems to be an idea that the peculiar powers of the animal have been acquired. The prospective shaman's purpose must, however, be serious and high-minded, and he must not be actuated only by desire or wish of gain; else his power may react for evil, as is evident from the instance given of the man who failed to call the buffalo. The appearance of the spirits takes place in waking visions as well as in dreams. While such is the most characteristic method of the acquisition of shamanistic power by the Arapaho, especially when they are compared with the people of different types of culture both in America and elsewhere, yet it is noticeable that this method is not the only one followed by them, and that the system of belief upon which these practicesare based is not consistently or rigorously followed out.

First of all it will be seen, from the instances given, that power may be sold or freely transferred to a relative. Then, too, animals and spirits visit people without solicitation, as appears from the case of the woman who dreamed repeatedly of bears. The offer of power that they bring may be rejected; or, on the other hand, power may be accepted, but may be so harmful in its effects on the recipient or his people, that it should be rejected by him, or would be, if he knew its danger. It is evident that these conceptions are quite at variance with the more fundamental one, that a man, of his own accord, seeks the aid of a spirit in order that he may acquire power that will be helpful to him.

It also appears, from the instances given, that, while the usual source of the medicine-man's power is his original communication with his spirit animal, yet there is at times a conception that his power lies in his keeping supernatural disease-objects within his own body. The shaman who cured rattlesnake-bites had two snakes in his body which he showed to his patients. A medicine-man who sucks ghost arrows increases his power, if he swallows and retains these objects after extracting them from the patient's body. It is probable that such beliefs are connected with the feeling that the ability to produce various objects at will, by vomiting, is an evidence of supernatural power. It has been stated in one case, and seems to be generally believed, that medicine-men with this power keep such objects permanently in their bodies.

Another principle that appears quite plainly is, that certain afflictions are cured by the homœopathic application of their cause. The rattlesnake itself is used as a medicine for curing rattlesnake-bites; centipedes and tarantulas, for injuries done by these animals; and a mole-skin cures the itch supposed to be produced by this animal. No cases are, however, yet known of this idea being extended to any causes of disease other than noxious animals.

Medicinal roots and plants are considerably used. Some of the most frequent of these are employed also in the tribal age-ceremonies. Such are niäätä^n, tcetcäätcei, and heçawaanaxû. It appears from several instances that the quantity of a medicinal root or plant given to a patient is often quite minute, so that its effect can be only through the imagination.

While the taking or application of medicines, and sucking by the shaman, are the principal means of curing disease, there are a number of other methods of an entirely different nature not connected with these more usual practices. Blood-letting and a form of cupping are performed. The sweat-house is used. Sometimes the medicine-man brushes the body with an object of fur. Porous bones are used to suck disease from the body; and warm stones are applied to swollen or diseased parts.

In addition to all these physiological, or supposed physiological, means of curing disease or accomplishing other results, amulets have an important use. Their employment may be designated as pure fetishism, though this fetishism is not of the direct kind,—in which the power of the fetish is simply inherent, or is derived from contact with some other object,— but is invariably dependent upon symbolism. It is in this symbolic resemblance, and association with something else, that the virtue of the Arapaho fetish chiefly rests, although in some cases rarety of the object, its curious shape, or its supposed supernatural origin, — as in the case of the pebbles believed to have been found in the interior of animals, — in other words, some abnormal feature, also contributes to the endowment of the fetish with power. It is noticeable, however, that even in such cases the symbolism is never absent, even though it may really be superadded and secondary. It is probable, for instance, that the black fossil-like objects described as having been used by a northern Arapaho were secured and kept primarily on account of their striking appearance; but it is significant that they were identified with centipedes on account of some slight resemblance. It is in symbolism, that is to say, the identification of distinct but similar objects, that the entire abundant fetishism of the Arapaho has its basis.

The instances of this fetishism are numerous. Beans of different colors are used to produce colts of certain colors; the horn of an antelope makes a horse swift; a nut which bears some resemblance to a skull keeps off ghosts; feathers and claws of owls, which are ghosts, also drive away ghosts;

a plant which contains a milky juice is medicine for milk; a shell that is smooth and slippery aids in delivery; triggers worn on a necklace cause the enemy's guns to fail to shoot; light-blue beads, whose color resembles that of smoke, make the fighters invisible; beads in the shape of a spider-web render the wearer, like the web, impervious to missiles, and at the same time insure the trapping of the enemy, as insects in a web. The covering-over of a bright-red cloth with that of another color prevents the shedding of the blood of the wearer. Pebbles resembling teeth are kept, so that the owner may live to an age when his teeth fall out. An iron chain or ring, being hard and indestructible, insures sound health. Reddish pear-shaped stones, resembling small buckskin medicine-bags painted red, are efficacious, if rubbed over the body, or held in the mouth.

It is interesting that some of this symbolic fetishistic power is positive in its supposed action, some negative. A red bean causes the color of a colt to be bay. On the other hand, a nut that resembles a skull does not bring, but drives away, ghosts; and the same is the effect of feathers of birds, that are supposed to be incarnate spirits. The horn of a swift-running animal makes a horse swift, and a plant with a milky juice is a medicine that improves milk. On the other hand, the wearing of triggers is not an amulet for better shooting, but for producing failure of the enemy's trigger to act. Logically there is in these instances a direct inconsistency. The principle underlying and uniting such opposite modes of thought seems to be that the fetish has the power of producing the desired end to which it has reference, though the means by which it achieves this purpose may be in one case causative and positive, and in the very next instance prohibitive and negative.

It is obvious that all this symbolism or fetishism is at bottom unconnected with shamanism, that is to say, the receipt of power directly from spirits. The two are based upon fundamentally different ideas. Still further, shamanism itself is of different kinds. While its power is usually sought, it may be received unsought. It may be received directly from spirits, or from living persons who are in possession of it. The guardian spirit naturally is in most cases helpful, but sometimes he is harmful. So the medicines that are used are sometimes pharmaceutical, sometimes of pharmaceutical effect only through the imagination, sometimes based upon crude supposed homœopathic principles, and at times purely symbolic. Even in this case their action may be either positive or negative. It is evident that analysis of the Arapaho concepts as to the source and operation of individual super-antural powers does not reveal a single consistent system of beliefs and practices, but a mixture of many unrelated and sometimes incongruous ideas.

TENT FOR THE KEEPER OF THE SACRED PIPE.

THE CEREMONY WITH THE BUFFALO-SKIN.

FIRST VIEW OF THE PROCESSION FROM THE RABBIT-TENT.

SECOND VIEW OF THE PROCESSION FROM THE RABBIT-TENT.

VOL. XVIII, PLATE LXI.

RAISING THE CENTRE POLE.

DANCE LODGE OF THE PRECEDING YEAR.

CONTENTS OF A SACRED BAG.

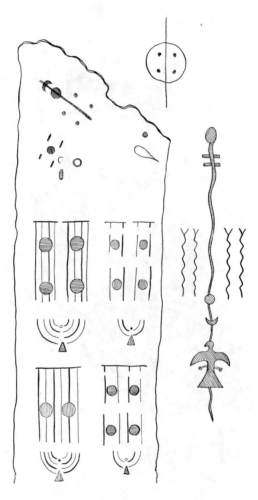

DESIGNS REFERRING TO MYTHS OF CREATION.

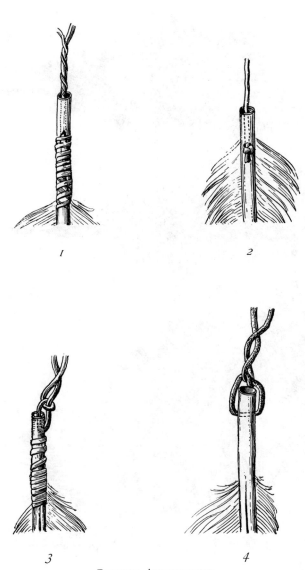

FEATHER ATTACHMENTS.

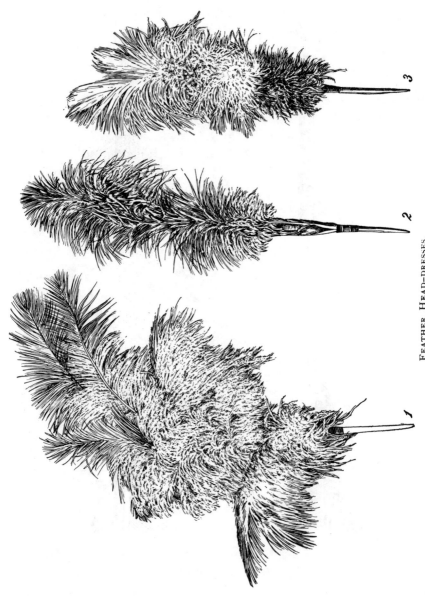

FEATHER HEAD-DRESSES.

FEATHER HEAD-DRESSES.

DETAIL OF ONE FORM OF HEAD-DRESS.

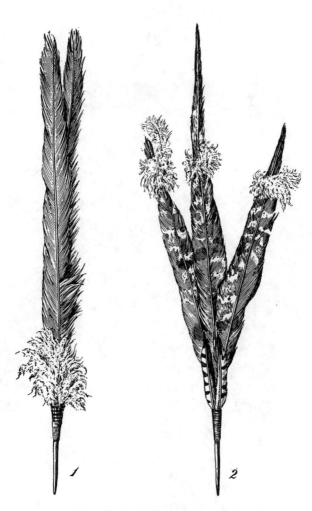

FEATHER HEAD-DRESS.

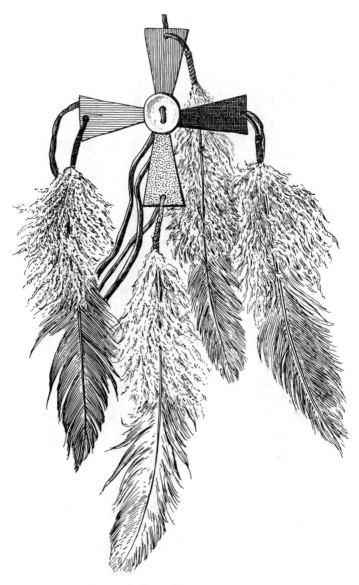

A CROSS HEAD-DRESS.

A CROSS HEAD-DRESS.

HEAD-DRESS OF CROW-SKIN.

Necklace of Feathers.

CROW BELT.

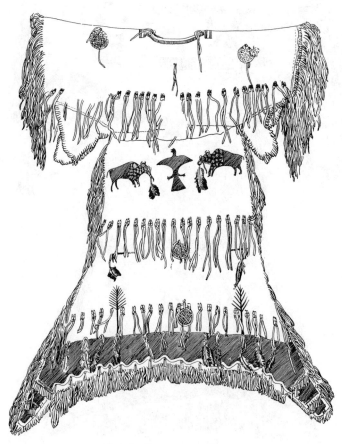

GIRL'S CEREMONIAL DRESS.

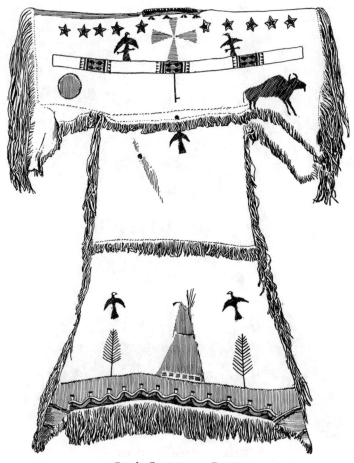

GIRL'S CEREMONIAL DRESS.

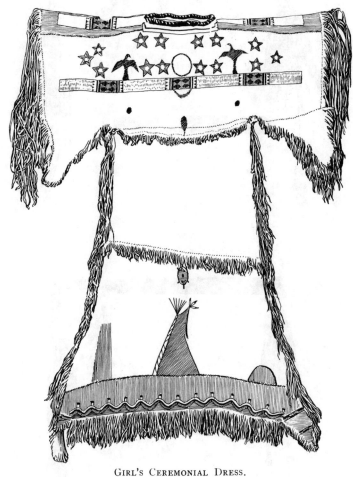

GIRL'S CEREMONIAL DRESS.

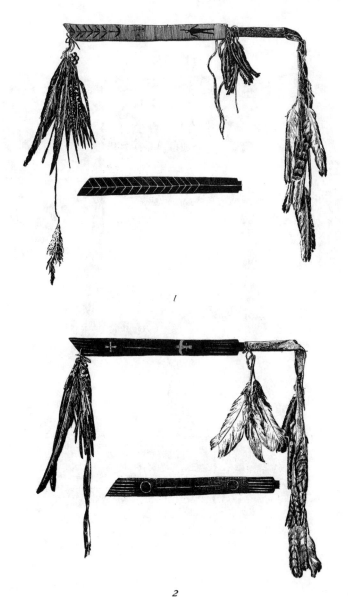

1

2

CEREMONIAL WHIPS.

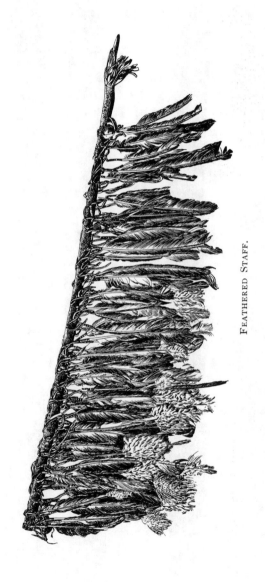

FEATHERED STAFF.

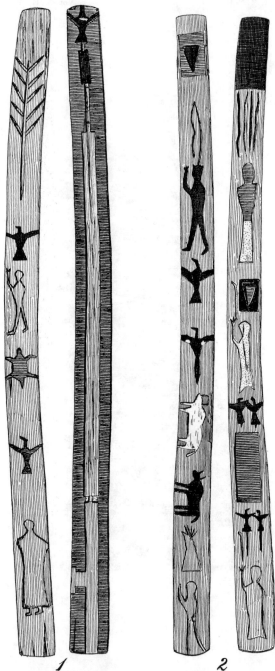

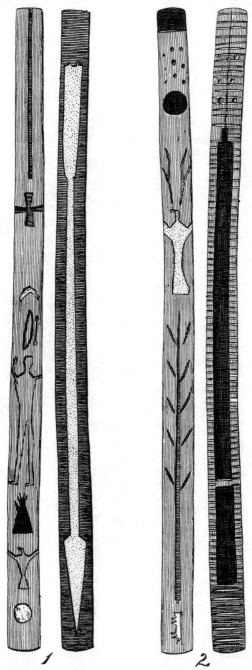

CARVED STICKS BELONGING TO THE SACRED-PIPE MODEL.

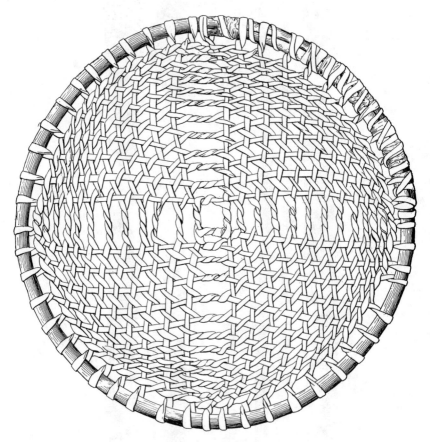

Netted Game-hoop.

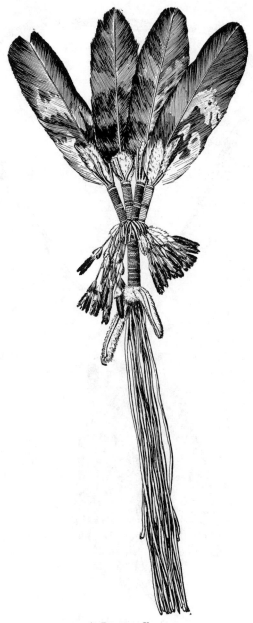

A PEYOTE FAN.

A Peyote Amulet.

Bracelet used as an Amulet.

HEAD-DRESS.

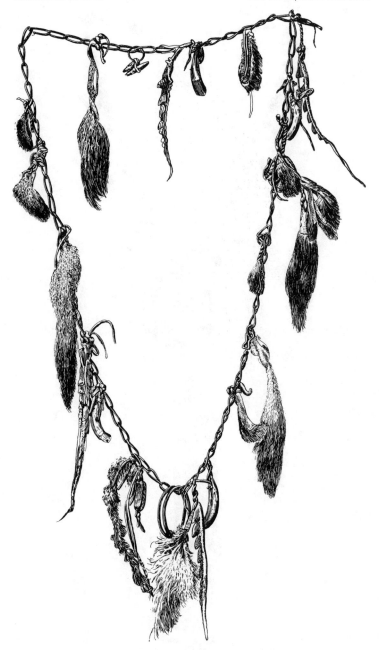

AMULETS AND MEDICINE.

WAR CHARM.

INDEX.

Age and sex denoted in symbolism, 58.

Age-societies, pairing of colors in regalia of, 417.

Alphabet used for rendering Arapaho, 2.

America and the Old World, numerical bases in, 413.

Amulets, 441–443, 452.

Animals in symbolic representation, restriction to the smaller, 54, 148.

Arapaho, characterization of the, 3, lack of information regarding, 4.

Armlet, ornamentation of, 51, 52; worn in second dance, 175, 178.

Arrow-head, symbolism of, 441.

Assiniboine, visit to, in 1901, 1.

Bääsa^{n}wūune'na^n, 5, 6.

Back and chest, cure for pains in the, 420.

Badger, supernatural power acquired through, 419.

Bag, contents of the sacred, 310; for food, 115, 119, 121; from a parfleche, 111; manner of making rawhide, 104; "owner" of the sacred, 311; varicolored, 120; with robe design, 120.

Bags, designs on rawhide, 104–131; of soft hide, 101–103; sacred, 30–35, 207, 209.

Ball, symbolism of colors on, 395; used by women, material and decoration of, 394.

Ball game, 394–396.

Basketry, use of, 393.

Baskets, dice-tossing, 391–393; material and use of, 25.

Bäyaa^{n}wu, the, average time between ceremonies of, 155; ceremonies constituting, 153; degrees of, 228; duration of ceremonies of, 155; eligibility to societies of, 153, 156; English equivalents for terms in ceremonies of, 154; functions of societies of, 157; honorary degrees in societies of, 155; myth relating to ceremonies of, 158; summary of characteristics of, 225; symbolism in ceremonies of, 226; system of, 227.

Bäyaa^{n}wu and sun-dance, difference between, 152, 226; similarity between, 169, 226.

Bear's foot, a, conventional representation of, 90.

Bed in Arapaho tent, position of the owner's, 12.

Bells representative of hail, 338, 342.

Belt, of owner-of-the-tent-poles, 219; of white-woman, 217; worn in second dance, symbolism of, 173; worn in women's dance, 215.

Belt-pouches, for women, 88–94; without flap, 91.

Berdaches, 19.

Berrying-bag, 132.

Biitaha^{n}wu, the, participation in dance-lodge ceremonies by, 289; ride around camp-circle by, 280, 281.

Black, in Arapaho decorative art, 149; limited use of, 416.

"Black war-bonnet," 246.

Bleeding, manner and season of, 438.

Blue, rocky mountains indicated by, 114.

Bone or seed game, scoring points in, 388; winning stakes in, 387.

Border-lines, purpose of, 122; time of making, 122.

Bow and arrows, making of, 24, 25.

Bowls, making of, 25.

Bracelet, peyote, 409, 410.

Brown in Arapaho decorative art, 149.

Buckskin, pictographic designs on, 311.

Buffalo, calling the, 437.

Buffalo-hunting, account of, 22.

Buffalo-robe, making of, 33–35.

Buffalo-skin, ceremonies with, 283.

Buffalo-skull, decoration of, 284; in dance, use of, 293.

Bull-roarer, 396.

Buzzer, use of, 396.

California, principal art of north-western, 147; realism in decorative art of northwestern, 147; reproductions rare in art of, 148.

Cane used in ghost-dance, 357.

Carving, rarity of three-dimensional, 430.

Cedar-Woman, ornamentation of tent by, 71–77.

Centipede, cure for bite of, 438.

Ceremonial objects, character of, 410–418; decoration of, 149, 150.

Ceremonies, kinds of, 151.

Ceremony preparatory for dance, 285.

Charm against injury by cloud, 431.

Cherry-bag, 125.

Cheyenne, rectangular form of ornament typical of the, 63.

Chiefs, choice of, 8.

Circle, connection of four with idea of the, 413; unusual in rawhide painting, 111.

Circlet, power of owl-feather, 193.

Cloth, "giving away" of, 283.

Clothing, sacrifice of children's worn-out, 300, 303.

Clouds, symbolization of, 149.

Coat, pictographic representation on, 268, 269.

Color-dualism, 416, 417.

Colors, ghost-dance symbolism of, 338; indicated by devices, 36; symbolism of, 149, 417, 418.

Colors and directions, connection of, 415.

Colors and states of mind, no connection between, 417.

Company, the kit-fox, 154, 181; the star, 154, 181.

Conjurer, feats of, 434; paraphernalia of, 425.

Cough, medicine for, 419.

Courtship, customs regarding, 13, 14.

Cradle, decoration of, 66–69; making of, 16.

Crazy-dancers, freaks of the, 192.

Crescent, an omen for good seen in the horizontal position of, 428.

Crow belts, 339–346; symbolism of, 342, 343.

Crow-dance, 320, 363–368; dress and painting of dancers in, 364; motions in, 364; use of forked sticks in, 358.

Crupper, design on, 135.

Cup-and-ball game, scoring points in, 397.

Cupping instrument, 439.

Cups, material for, 25.

Dance, directions given by Thunder for, 368; origin and signification of the Omaha, 368; carrying of spoons in, 367; with bows and arrows, 367.

Dance-lodge, "altar" for, 304; ceremonies connected with centre pole of, 289; completion of, 290; differences between the northern and southern Arapaho, 303; erection of, 286; order of species of trees used for screen behind "altar" of,

305; paraphernalia for, 287; position of people while painting poles of, 288; preparations for, 284; procession for painting poles of, 288; procession from rabbit-tent to, 287, 302.

Dancer of highest degree in second dance, 169.

Dancers, magpies personated by, 367; motions of, 291; painting of, 290, 294; repainting of, 296, 298, 299.

Dancers and pledgers, painting and dress of, 287.

Dances, Arapaho term for, 151; discontinuance of, 158; special, 366, 367.

"Dancing against the sun," 301.

Dancing, in the first dance, 183; in the fourth dance, 198; in the second dance, 165–168; in the third dance, 190; in the women's dance, 212.

"Dancing-in," 290, 302.

"Dancing-out," 300, 303.

Dead, the, customs regarding, 16, 17; property of, 317.

Decoration, characteristic tribal manner of thinking of, 146; classes of objects having fixed tribal, 147; infinite variation of, 147.

Design, sacredness of the biinäbi't, 120.

Designs, variability in all, 120.

Detail in ornamental decoration, diversity in, 98.

Diarrhœa in children, cause and cure of, 438.

Dice, 387–394; forms of, 388; material of, 387, 393; symbolic interpretations for markings on, 389.

Dice game, scoring of points in, 387, 393; sticks for, 393.

Disease, homœopathic principle for curing, 451.

Disputes as to deeds of honor in war, settlement of, 319.

Dream, painting of a, 433.

Dress, of boys, 28; of men, 28; of women, 28.

Drum, stretching skin for a, 400.

Drums used in the second dance, 165.

Eagle, catching the, 22.

Ear-piercing, 365; symbolization of, 19.

Earth, the, diving for, 360; growth of, 61; sex of, 313.

Elk-tail, double use for, 424.

Embroidery, materials for, 28; statements regarding, 29.

Entertainment practised at night, 318.

Face, the, painting of, in ceremonials, 28.

Fan, peyote, 405, 409.

Fans, use of, 22.

Fast, breaking of the three-days', 300.

Feather-bag, 129.

Feathers, attachment of, to thongs, 321–323; use of, as brushes and head-dresses, 407.

Fetish, great tribal of the Arapaho, 308; source of power of, 452.

Fetishism, basis of, 452, 453.

Field Columbian Museum, model at, 304.

Fifth dance, 154, 206.

Fifth degree of women's dance, 222.

Fire, making of, 24.

First dance, the, account of, 182–187; characteristic paint-design of, 183; manner of dancing in, 183; regalia of, 184–188; stick carried in lowest degree of, 186–188; sword of dancer in, 184, 185; symbolic reference to buffalo in, 188.

First knowledge of Arapaho, 3.

Fits, cure for, 426.

Fog, how to clear, 317.

Food, dance around kettle of, 366; given in remuneration for painting, 292.

Food-bag, design on, 125; lack of symmetry in decoration of, 123; representing a mole, 122.

Formula for securing old age, 315.

Fourth dance, account of, 196–206; degrees in, 197; duration of practices and restrictions during, 200; manner of dancing in, 198; painting in, 199; regalia of, 198, 201–206.

Fringe, on bag, 125; on rawhide objects, 119; on scarf, 201.

General description of Arapaho, 3.

"Ghost arrow," 437.

Ghost-dance, the, color symbolism in movement of, 417; dress for, 346, 347; headdresses for, 321–336; necklaces and belts for, 336–339; symbolism of scarf for, 338; whistles for, 351, 352.

Ghost, keeping off, 437, 447, 452.

Goose-water, drinking of, 300.

Grandfathers, 155, 160, 226.

Green and blue, Arapaho use of, 121.

Gros Ventres, the, age-companies among, 155; dialect of, 6; kinship between Arapaho and, 4; participants in ceremonies of, 156; tent-ornaments of, 63; terms of relationship and affinity among, 9, 10; visited in 1901, 1.

Guessing-game, 368–382; composition of, 371; head-dresses for, 369, 371, 379.

Guessing-game set, an elaborate, 375–378; different uses for, 369, 370; ornamentation of, 369, 370.

Haⁿanaxawúune'naⁿ, 5, 6.

Haa'ninin, 6.

Häçawaanaxu-root, giving of, 183, 193, 200; peculiar property of, 183, 193; use of, in women's dance, 212, 219, 220.

Hair, manner of dressing the, 27.

Hand mirrors, use of, in ceremonials, 356.

Haseihaⁿwu, meaning of, 152, 280.

Haxuxanaⁿ, accounts of, 19.

Head-dress, arrow, 342; bird, 329; cross, 327; double, 332; hoop, 330; of bird-skin, 333; of bow and arrows, 331; of feathers, 333, 340; of owner-of-the-tent-poles, 218; of white-woman, 216; red-stand, 214; representing a snake, 335; representing wheels, 329; simplest, 334; white-stand, 214; worn in fourth dance, 202; worn in second dance, 174, 178, 179; worn in women's dance, 214.

Head-dresses, collection of, 336; ornamentation of, 52–54.

Health, charm for retaining, 420.

Heart, medicine for pain in, 420.

Hemorrhages, cure for, 420.

Hiiteni, signification of, 40, 144, 149.

Hinanae'ina, 5, 6.

Hitoune'naⁿ, 5, 6.

Hoop game, 382–386; scoring of points in, 382.

Horse, precaution taken before breaking, 431, 432; remedy for kick of, 431.

Horses, given away, 296, 366; how first obtained, 24.

"Household medicines," 444.

Human being, symbolization of, 58.

Hypnotization, implement used for, 359.

Infant, on death of mother, disposal of, 16.

Inheritance, rules of, 11.

Insanity, 20.

Insects, cure for bite of, 422.

Intercourse between relations, restrictions regarding, 10, 11.

Intoxicants, 20.
Introductory, 1.
Invitation-sticks, use of, 381.
Itch, cure for, 422, 451.

Jesup, Mrs. Morris K., 1, 279.

Knife-cases, ornamentation on, 87, 88.
Knives, making of, 24.
Knots for keeping tally, 199, 201.
Kwakiutl, ceremonial organization of, 156.

Lance, carried in second dance, 175-181; symbolism of, 176.
Language, of the Arapaho, 3-5; of the Blackfoot, 4, 5; of the Cheyenne, 3-5.
Languages, the western Algonkin, 4.
Leg-bands worn in second dance, 175.
Leggings, designs on, 46-50.
Lightning, in painting, symbol for, 281, 298, 299.
Lodge, the, bringing of centre pole for, 286; position of participants in first dance in, 182; position of participants in second dance in, 162.
Lung-disease, cure for, 420.

Manliness, horse given as proof of, 319.
Marriage, restrictions regarding, 11; statements on, 12-14.
Meadow-lark, belief as to song of, 318.
Meat, manner of boiling, 25.
Medicine, instrument for grinding, 439.
Medicine-bag, contents of, 422, 424, 435, 444, 445; description of, 117-119.
Medicine-case, symbolic design on, 436.
Medicine-cases, description of, 132-135.

Medicine-man, various means employed by the, 452.
Mescal, effects of, 21.
Mescal-plant, for peyote ceremony, preparation of, 399.
Mexicans and Arapaho, use of numbers by, 413.
Moccasins, ornamentation on, 36-49.
Modern ceremonies, 319-410.
Mole, effect of touching a, 422.
Moon, sickness predicted by position of, 428.
Mooney, James, 3, 7.
Morning star, symbol of the, 149.
Mountains, blue used to denote rocky, 114.
Mourning, time of, 17.
Murderer, status of, 17.
Mussel-shell, uses for, 440.
Myth, of Arapaho, tribal, 309; of creation, pictographic designs in reference to, 311, 312; of Tangled-Hair, 22.

Name, changing of, 296, 365.
Navel, in decorative symbolism, 56; unvarying symbol for the, 144.
Navel-amulets, 54-58.
Navel-string, preservation of, 54.
Nä^{n}waçinähä'äna^n, 5-7.
Necklace of rabbit feet and feathers, 339.
Niäätä^n-root, use of, 32, 201.
North Pacific coast, duplication of pieces of art in, 148; realism in decorative art of, 146.
Number four, connection of circle with Indian conception of, 413; connection of colors with, 414; significance of, 412.
Numbers, Arapaho sacred, 411.

Oklahoma branch of the Arapaho visited in 1899, 1.
Old age, death by war preferred to,

23; formula for securing, 315.

Ornamentation, colors characteristic of Arapaho, 64; diversity and general similarity coexistent in, 98.

Osages, friendship with the Arapaho established by the 8.

Owner-of-the-tent-poles, 211–213, 218, 219; regalia of, 218–220.

Paint-bag, of dog-dancer, 200.

Painting, in dance, keeping tally of, 199, 201; of dancer's wife, 200.

Paint-pouches, typical forms of, 77–85.

Parfleche, description of, 104–114; opening of, 105; synchronous painting on four sides of, 122; use of, 104.

Pawnee, friendship with the Arapaho established by the, 8.

Penalty for sleeping during recital of a story, 318.

Peyote, effects of, 320, 403.

Peyote ceremony, the, the eagle-cry imitated by leader of, 403; eating peyote at, 402; erection and preparation of tent for, 399; last acts in, 404; lineage of, 410; making altar for, 401; passing of earth in, 402; path for thoughts of worshippers at, 401; place of director of, 401; place of fire-tender of, 401; praying at, 401, 403; songs at, 403; unsalted food for, 400; use of eagle wing-feather at, 401–403; use of sage at, 402; use of sharp instruments at, 400.

Peyote objects, probable source of, 410.

Peyote worship, 398–410; headdress for, 407–409; new form of, 405; objects most used in, 405.

Pictography and symbolism, differentiation of, 149.

Pillow, description of buffalo-skin, 65, 66.

Pipe, the, compliance secured by use of, 13, 159, 200, 201; form and material of, 21, keeper of sacred, 280, 283, 286–289, 291, 294, 298, 300, 308, 309; model of sacred, 359; prayer to model of sacred, 362; sacred, 308; sacredness of, 21; smoking of, 21, 160–162, 164, 198; tent of keeper of sacred, 281; truth-telling secured by passing and smoking of, 319.

Pipe-sticks, pictographic carving on, 360–362.

Pipe-stoker, 21.

Pole, centre, fastening of objects to, 289; felling and bringing of, 285; placing of white skin at foot of, 295; scouts sent out for, 282.

Porcupine-quills, pouches for, 77, 130.

Pottery, making of, 25.

Pouch, peyote, 406.

Pouches, for porcupine-quills, 77, 130; ornamentation and uses of soft skin, 77; symbolism in designs on, 93.

Power, representation of acquisition of supernatural, 134.

Practices, semi-ceremonial, 18.

Prayer, beings addressed in, 313; to model of sacred pipe, 362; used before eating, 314; used on changing name, 313.

Present, giving of, 18, 19; manner of making known wish for, 18.

Property, transportation of, 23, 24.

Quill-flattener, 29.

Quirt used in ghost-dance, 354.

Rabbit-tent, the, abandonment of, 302; erection of, 302, 303; position of, 281; singing and rites in, 282, 284, 302; taken down, 290.

"Rain-dance," 342.

Rattle, difference between medicine-man's and that of tribal ceremonies, 445; of medicine-man, 424, 426, 446–450.

Rattlesnake-bite, cure of, through agency of dream, 421; medicine for, 424, 437.

Rawhide, uses of, 25.

Realism in decorative art, of North Pacific coast, 146; of northwestern California, 147.

Red-stand, regalia of the, 220.

Regalia, case for, 195, 220, 225; indicative of rank, 226; making of, 160–162, 182, 189, 196, 212; of first dance, 184–188; of fourth dance, 198, 201–206; of high degree, reverence for, 219; of the owner-of-the-tent-poles, 218–220; of rank and file, 223; of red-stand, 220; of second dance, 171–181; of the calves, 222; of third dance, 188, 189, 193–196; of tribal age-ceremonies and modern ceremonies, difference in, 410; of white-fool, 189, 193–196; of white-stand, 221; of white-woman, 216–218; of women's dance, 212–224; presentation of, 164, 198; worn in second dance, symbolism of, 173, 176.

Relationship and affinity among the Arapaho, terms of, 9.

Rhomboid in decorative art, significations of, 413.

Sacred bag, 310.

Sacred numbers, 412.

Saddle as a substitute for stirrups, 59.

Sage, use of food-dipped, 296, 299.

Scarfs, symbolism of feathered, 338.

Second dance, account of, 158–181; armlet worn in, 175, 178; club used in, 159, 170; dancer of highest degree in, 169; dancing in, 165–168; degrees in, 159, 175, 178–180; drums used in, 165; head-dresses

worn in, 174, 178, 179; holders of degrees in, 159; incentive for, 158; lance carried in, 175–181; leg-bands worn in, 175, 178; license in, 166; making of regalia for, 160–162; obtaining singing-leaders for, 165; painting in, 169; position, in grandfather's tent, of participants in, 161; position of performers at, 161; presentation of regalia at, 164; regalia of, 171–181; symbolic reference to thunder in, 168; symbolism of regalia worn in, 173, 176.

Second lodge, characteristic paint-design of, 169.

Seven, a ceremonial number, 155, 202, 203; value of, as a number, 428.

Sewing, tools for, 28.

Sex, symbolization of, 58.

Shamanism, means for reception of, 453; not a profession, 419.

Shield-cover, 135.

Sioux, the, dance brought by the Omaha to, 368; introduction of Omaha dance by, 23.

Sitting-Bull, head-dresses made by, 326, 431.

Sixth dance, 207–209.

Skin, dressing of, 26; tools for dressing, 26.

Skin-scraper, 27; used for keeping record, 26.

Sky, sex of the, 313.

Sleeping during story-telling, penalty for, 318.

Smoke from fire in tent an index of disposition of occupants, 125.

Snow-shoes for hunting buffalo, 23.

Southern-berry water, effects of, 424.

Southwest, exact reproductions in pottery of the, rare, 148.

Speech, by a man at marriage of his daughter, 315; by father of a young man about to marry a Cheyenne woman, 315.

Spirit, form of the appearing and de-
    parting guardian, 419; represen-
    tation, on pictograph, of a, 323.
Spirits, disposition of, the reverse of
    that in life, 317; prevention of re-
    turn of, 317.
Spoons, material for, 25.
Spring, cause for drying up of, 317.
Stars, result of counting the, 317.
Stick, feathered, signal for starting
    dance, 357; forked, for taking meat
    from kettle, 358.
Stomach-ache, medicine for, 420.
Sun, deception practised by the, 301.
Sun-dance, the 279–308; Arapaho
    name for, 152, 280; breaking camp
    for, 300; buffalo-hunt at, 283;
    comparison of the northern and
    southern Arapaho, 301–308; de-
    scription of lodge for, 152; differ-
    ences between the northern and
    southern Arapaho, 305–308; dis-
    tinctive color-combination of, 416;
    duration of, 302; first day of dance
    of, 290–292, 302; first preliminary
    day of, 282, 301; individuality of
    painting in, 307; of 1900,
    279–301; opening day of, 280,
    301; second day of dance of,
    292–297, 302; second preliminary
    day of, 283–285, 301; self-torture
    in, 302; supplementary day of, 300,
    302; third day of dance of,
    297–300, 302; third preliminary
    day of, 285–290, 301; unmounted
    men in, indication for, 280.
Sun-dance and age-company cere-
    monies, correspondences between,
    303.
Sun-dance and age-fraternities, dif-
    ference in ceremonies of, 152.
Sun-shade of rawhide, 136.
Supernatural helper, representation
    of, 429.
Supernatural power, acquisition and
    transfer of, 418, 420, 421, 427, 428,
435, 436, 450, 451; belief as to
    source of, 454; fundamental con-
    ception of, 451; restrictions with
    giving of, 435; roots and plants
    employed by, 451.
Sweat-house, putting up of, 284.
Switch used in sweat-house, 316.
Sword of dancer in first dance, 184,
    185.
Symbol, various significations for
    each, 144.
Symbolism, by animals, restricted to
    the smaller, 54, 148; connection of
    Indian religious life and, 150; con-
    ventional system of decorative,
    146, 147; denotation of age and sex
    in, 58; equivalent of a circle in, 59,
    116; in designs on pouches, 93; in
    first dance, 188; individual interest
    in, 145; individuality in interpreta-
    tion of, 143, 147; no fundamental
    connection between shamanism
    and, 453; of arrow-head, 441; of
    belt in second dance, 173; of cane,
    358; of carving on pipe-sticks,
    360–362; of colors, 149, 417, 418;
    of counters for guessing-game,
    373; of decoration on hand mirror,
    357; of designs on pouches, 93; of
    dice ornamentation, 388, 389; of
    dress designs, 346–348; of drum
    and drum-stick designs, 350; of
    feathered stick, 357; of head-dress
    for guessing-game, 372, 380; of
    head-dress in fourth dance, 202; of
    lance in second dance, 176; of or-
    namentation on fan, 356; of or-
    namentation on hoop set,
    382–385; of ornamentation on
    quirt, 355; of regalia in second
    dance, 173, 176; of scarf, 338; of
    whistle designs, 352; positive and
    negative action of, 453; relative
    proportion of realistic and orna-
    mental, 58; religious thought con-
    nected with all Indian, 150; scope
    of, 148.

Symbols, comparison of embroidered and painted, 143; list of, with reference to plates, 138–143.

Taboos, 15, 16.
Tally for painting, kept by knots, 199, 201.
Tarantula, cure for bite of, 438.
Tceäk'çaⁿ, sign of friendship, 23.
Tcâoçoçihiit, 318.
Tcetcäätcei-root, hypnotic influence of, 190, 191.
Tent, conventional ornaments of, 59–64; for keeper of sacred pipe, 281, 309; ornamentation of, in accordance with dream, 348; position of entrance to Arapaho, 12; temper of occupants of, indicated by smoke from, 125.
Tent-ornament, ceremonies for attachment of, 70–77.
Territory of the Arapaho, 3.
Thanks, manner of expressing, 365.
"Thanks," word for, 318.
Third dance, account of, 188–196; building fire for, 190; dancing in, 190; license in, 190; regalia of, 188, 189, 193–196; weapons of, 189; white-fool of, 189, 193.
Thunder and lightning, ideas regarding, 317.
Thunderstorm, power of water caught in, 21.
Toad, regard for horned, 56.
Tobacco, origin of, 22.
Toilet-pouches, description of, 94–98.
Tools, for dressing skins, 26; for sewing, 28.
Top, name for game with, 397.
Tribal myth of the Arapaho, 309.
Tribal religious customs, 308–319.
Turtle, the protection promised by, 428.
Twins, mythical, 22.

Utes, bravery and strength of the, 8.

Vision on third day of fasting, 420, 421.

Waistcoat, beaded, 59.
Wand, attachments to, 353; ornamentation on, 353.
War, truthfulness in recounting deeds of, 23.
War-amulet, 423, 426, 440.
War-party, ride preparatory to the starting-out of a, 282.
Wheel, keeper of sacred, 310; sacred, 309.
Wheel game, 386, 387.
Whirlwind-Woman, 61, 361; designs first made by, 109, 110, 121.
Whistle, ornamentation of, 352.
White-fool, regalia of, 189, 193–196.
White-stand, regalia of, 221.
White-woman, 211–213; regalia of, 216–218; similarity between white-fool and, 225.
Wind-storm, cause of a violent, 301.
"Wolves," sending out of, 282.
Woman, as a factor in the development of design, 270; who dreamed of bears, 434, 451.
Women during menstruation, customs of, 15.
Women's dance, the, account of, 210–225; dancing in, 212; degrees in, 211; order of procession in, 213; points of resemblance to other dances in, 225; regalia of, 212–224; simulation of buffalo in, 213.
Work-bags, as receptacles for tools, 28; women's, 100.
Wyoming branch of Arapaho, visit to, in 1900, 1.

Yanahut, an Arapaho term for pledger of the sun-dance, 280.
Yellow in peyote worship, 405.
"Yes," word for, 318.